THE LAST
PARTNERSHIPS

THE LAST PARTNERSHIPS

*Inside the Great Wall Street
Money Dynasties*

Charles R. Geisst

McGraw-Hill

New York   Chicago   San Francisco   Lisbon
London   Madrid   Mexico City   Milan   New Delhi
San Juan   Seoul   Singapore   Sydney   Toronto

Library of Congress Cataloging-in-Publication Data

Geisst, Charles R.
    The last partnerships : inside the great Wall Street dynasties / Charles R. Geisst.
    New York : McGraw-Hill, 2001.
        p. cm.
    HG5129.N+
    0071369996
    Includes bibliographical references.
        1. Wall Street—History. 2. Securities industry—Mergers—New York (State)—
    New York—Case studies. 3. Stockbrokers—Mergers—New York (State)—New
    York—Case studies. 4. Partnership—Mergers—New York (State)—New York—
    Case studies. 5. Business failures—New York (State)—New York—Case studies.
    6. Securities industry—United States—History. 7. Stockbrokers—United States—
    History
    12318649

McGraw-Hill

A Division of The **McGraw·Hill** *Companies*

1 2 3 4 5 6 7 8 9 0   DOC/DOC   0 9 8 7 6 5 4 3 2 1

ISBN 0-07-136999-6

This book was set in New Caledonia by Tina Thompson.
Printed and bound by R. R. Donnelley & Sons Company

This book is printed on recycled, acid-free paper containing a
minimum of 50% recycled, de-inked fiber.

For Margaret & Meg

CONTENTS

ACKNOWLEDGMENTS

I would like to thank the following, all of whom helped contribute information not found in the usual sources: Victor Grey of the Rothschild Archive in London; Meg Ventrudo of the Museum of American Financial History in New York; Steve Wheeler, archivist at the New York Stock Exchange; and the staff of the Georgetown University Library special collections department.

Kelli Christiansen of McGraw-Hill was instrumental in helping keep the narrative on track and helped oversee the book process from beginning to end.

My wife, Margaret, deserves special thanks for her extraordinary patience while the book was being written.

TIMELINE

1818   John A. Brown & Co. founded
1832   Vermilye & Co. founded
1836   S. & M. Allen & Co. (founded 1808) fails
1836   Enoch Clark founds Clark Dodge & Co.
1837   August Belmont & Co. founded (dissolved in 1924)
1838   Drexel & Co. founded
1848   Lazard Freres founded (continues today)
1858   Lehman Brothers founded
1861   Jay Cooke leaves Clark Dodge & Co. to found Jay Cooke & Co.
1864   J. & W. Seligman founded
1864   George Peabody & Co. becomes J. S. Morgan & Co.
1867   Kuhn Loeb founded
1869   Goldman Sachs & Co. founded
1871   Drexel & Co. merges with J. S. Morgan & Co. to become Drexel, Morgan & Co.
1873   Jay Cooke & Co. fails
1873   Jay Cooke's son-in-law reestablishes firm as Charles D. Barney & Co.
1894   J. S. Morgan & Co. becomes J. P. Morgan & Co.
1903   E. F. Hutton founded
1905   Vermilye & Co. becomes William Read & Co.
1910   Salomon Brothers founded
1914   Merrill Lynch founded
1920   William Read & Co. becomes Dillon Read
1930   Brown Brothers merges with Harriman family interests to become Brown Brothers Harriman (continues today)

1934   Drexel, Morgan & Co. reverts to its original name, Drexel & Co.

1934   J. P. Morgan & Co. spins off Morgan Stanley (J. P. Morgan continues today)

1937   Charles D. Barney acquires Edward B. Smith & Co. to form Smith Barney & Co.

1966   Drexel & Co. acquires Harriman Ripley & Co. to become Drexel Harriman Ripley

1970   Drexel Harriman Ripley becomes Drexel Firestone

1971   Drexel Firestone merges with Burnham & Co. to become Drexel Burnham

1974   Kidder Peabody acquires Clark Dodge & Co.

1976   Drexel Burnham merges with William D. Witter and acquires the name of a major investor in Witter to become Drexel Burnham Lambert

1981   Salomon Brothers merges with Phibro to become Phibro-Salomon (becomes Salomon Brothers again in 1985)

1984   Shearson American Express acquires Lehman Brothers

1987   E. F. Hutton bought by Shearson

1990   Drexel Burnham Lambert files for bankruptcy

1994   Shearson American Express divests Lehman Brothers, which continues today as Lehman Brothers

1997   Smith Barney merges with Salomon Brothers to become Salomon Smith Barney, today a unit of Citigroup

1997   Bankers Trust & Co. acquires Alex. Brown & Co.

1997   Dillon Read acquired by Swiss Bank Corp.

1997   Morgan Stanley merges with Dean Witter to become Morgan Stanley Dean Witter

1997   Alex. Brown acquired by Bankers Trust. Continues today as unit of Deutsche Bank

1999   Goldman Sachs sells initial public offering

THE LAST
PARTNERSHIPS

INTRODUCTION

FOR MORE THAN 150 years, their names were synonymous with Wall Street. The most successful became the subjects of folklore, envy, and political vilification, and notorious symbols of wealth and power. No longer household names today, in the nineteenth century many had barroom songs and jingles written about them. Before there were sports stars and pop musicians dominating the news, they were among the first true celebrities in the country.

They were, of course, the famous names behind the great Wall Street partnerships. Some became extremely well known, while others preferred to remain behind the scenes and tend to business without attracting much attention. Their heyday was from the War of 1812 to the end of World War II, when most Wall Street securities firms were still organized as partnerships. A roll call sounds much like the social register of New York, where most made their livings. Without their business success, many of the country's cultural institutions would probably not have developed as significantly as they did. The Metropolitan Opera, Metropolitan Museum of Art, and many of the other significant cultural and educational institutions benefited from their partners' largesse over the years. The names on the buildings of many college campuses read like a Who's Who of banking, especially those names famous before World War II.

The rise of the famous Wall Street banking dynasties is a testimony to the rags-to-riches stories of the nineteenth century. A young immigrant came to the United States from Northern Europe and set up his own humble business, usually peddling sundries door-to-door around the South or Midwest. Within several years, he graduated to the dry goods business and was quickly opening stores in different states before gravitating to New York. In another few years, he and members of his family were in the banking business, financing bills of exchange and trading stocks and bonds. In twenty to thirty years, his firm was one of Wall Street's elite. Within a generation, family members were in the Social Register, members of New York's elite clubs, and contributors to the arts. They supplied capital to a country hungry for it and also supplied millions of dollars to nonprofit institutions equally hungry for the money necessary to grow.

This celebrity status often obscured the role of Wall Street firms in American society before the Second World War. The banking dynasties were not only the subject of much folklore, they were often its source. American banking grew up along with the United States in the nineteenth century, and its central figures became American heroes. The name "Jay" was a favorite to give a newborn son because of Jay Cooke's success at selling Union war bonds to finance the Civil War. So many people invested in them that Cooke became a household name and an overnight success as America's best-known banker. Without the generosity of the Seligmans, Mary Todd Lincoln would not have been able to live in a decent style in Germany, which was where she eventually she fled to after her husband's assassination. They provided her with a stipend when Congress was slow in granting pensions for presidential widows. And Clarence Dillon became so well known that one of his nicknames, the Wolf of Wall Street, became the title of a movie in the late 1920s. A French vineyard continues to bear his name.

Stories like this are not simply the plots of a Horatio Alger children's novel but are true of many of Wall Street's best-known investment banks. In fact, Alger himself was the tutor to Joseph Seligman's children after the Civil War and learned part of that partnership's growth firsthand from the patriarch of J. & W. Seligman & Co., one of New York's most respected banking houses in the nineteenth century. Alger's rags-to-riches stories owe much to his experiences as the Seligmans' tutor, listening to the family stories of how the brothers came to America and got their start. But the Seligman example was not an isolated one. He could easily have used Alexander Brown, founder of Brown Brothers Harriman, or Marcus Goldman, founder of

Goldman Sachs, or Henry Lehman, founder of Lehman Brothers, as his examples. The firms profiled in the first several chapters of this book all have remarkably similar beginnings. How could so many firms have had similar origins? The fact that they did illustrates some of the basics for success in banking in nineteenth-century America. The story became so well known that many other immigrants continued to follow the dream well into the twentieth century.

Occasionally, the Wall Street partners even proved inspirational. Thorstein Veblen, the turn-of-the-century economist who coined the phrase "conspicuous consumption" in his widely read *Theory of the Leisure Class* in 1899, used August Belmont Sr. and Jr. as his models since both were known to be lavish spenders. Not only did the Wall Street partners help create the modern economy, they also became its individual well-oiled engines of growth—consumers whose demand helped propel the country into the twentieth century. During the bull market of the 1990s, Wall Streeters were known to spend lavishly, and more than one popular magazine was published catering to their own peculiar form of conspicuous consumption. A century earlier one of their most avid readers undoubtedly would have been Belmont, whose wine bill before the Civil War was more than $20,000 annually. Despite his success, his estate still had to be sold upon the death of August Jr. to pay off debts.

More important, the Wall Street partnerships were an integral part of the development of the country. Brown Brothers financed the first transatlantic steamship service between the United States and Britain. When one of its flagships, the *Arctic*, sank, it became the greatest shipping disaster until the *Titanic* sixty years later. The Brown family also suffered heavily, losing several family members in the *Arctic* catastrophe. The partnerships helped finance every war the country became involved in. Without Jay Cooke, the state of the Union may have turned out much differently save for his expert salesmanship in the mass marketing of Civil War bonds, a new phenomenon in American finance. The Allies relied heavily on Wall Street's ability to raise funds during World War I. But the reparations imposed on Germany after the war, guided by J. P. Morgan & Co., were so severe that German economic and political instability resulted. The lessons were well remembered. During the Second

World War, Franklin D. Roosevelt and his treasury secretary kept the Street at arm's length when raising funds to fight the Axis.

The partnerships often were shrouded in intrigue. August Belmont, the immigrant banker who became the Rothschilds' agent in New York, was involved in several incidents over the years that cast a long shadow over his business practices, especially when taking deposits from foreign investors, several of whom never saw their money again. Many of the best-known, and foreign-born, New York bankers gathered secretly before the Federal Reserve was created by Congress to discuss the advantages and disadvantages of creating a new central bank. The origins of the Fed from those meetings at Jekyll Island, Georgia, have never been forgotten and are often raised by conspiracy theorists who believe that the Fed should be reformed, abolished, or purged of its "clandestine" elements. Wall Street notables have continued to play a major role in popular discussions of economic policy long after their actual importance has faded.

A history of the partnerships also helps clear the smoke from some of their reputations, which have become the subject of some intensely populist, and wrongheaded, accounts of their influence and place in history. Almost half of the partnerships discussed here were Jewish by origin. J. & W. Seligman, Goldman Sachs, Lehman Brothers, August Belmont, Kuhn Loeb, Lazard Freres, Salomon Brothers, and even Dillon Read all had Jewish origins and exercised the influence of their success the way the Yankee bankers of the same period did. Unfortunately, they have been the subjects of conspiracy theories over the years, ranging from that clandestine control of the Federal Reserve to being the invisible power behind many a political throne. A clear view of their history shows how many of the theories got started in the first place, especially in the case of Belmont, but their outright fantasy swamps the facts. In the nineteenth century, all bankers exercised authority that would be incongruous in the contemporary world, but the Jewish bankers did not exercise any unusual power. In fact, they exercised less than their well-connected Yankee banker counterparts such as Brown Brothers, J. P. Morgan, Kidder Peabody, and Clark Dodge.

The conspiracy theories do not stop with the Jewish banking houses, but extend to the best known of all the Yankee bankers, J. P. Morgan.

His role in American finance is unique, and the mere thought of the de facto power he exercised over the American banking system caused most of the securities and banking legislation of the 1930s to be passed. But the role and importance of Morgan is often misunderstood by serious students of history as well as by conspiracy buffs looking for a cabal under every stone. Morgan was not simply a major figure in American finance. He was *the* dominant figure for a generation, and his son Jack was the dominant figure after him. Without their bank, Washington would have suffered greatly during several key moments in American history, probably defaulting on its debt on at least one occasion. When Congress passed the Glass-Steagall Act in 1933, curtailing the power of investment bankers, it was Morgan whom Congress had in its sights. Few bankers could ever think of possessing such power even in the unregulated world of American banking in the nineteenth century. The history of his partnership is important on two levels: for the development of Wall Street in general and as a mirror for the weaknesses of the American banking system until the 1930s.

The very existence of the partnerships helps to underscore the peculiar nature of what is known as American capitalism. Since Alexander Brown began his firm in Baltimore before the War of 1812, the financing of all American wars and corporate endeavors traditionally has been the province of several dozen privately held firms. Over the years, they helped raise billions of dollars for a variety of causes. Without them, the Mexican War, Civil War, and the Allies' efforts in World War I might have failed. Since there was no formal government apparatus in operation to raise funds, many of the partnerships made enough money in the nineteenth-century conflicts to establish themselves in business. Their collaborative efforts in financing the war in 1915 became the basis for a government lawsuit charging antitrust collusion thirty years later. In all cases, the Wall Street firms were accused of profiting at the government's expense, which was only partially true.

The history of Wall Street partnerships also exhibits several serious shortcomings that have characterized the securities industry for years. Most of the partnerships, especially those dating from the nineteenth century, had no formal management structures, and many of their procedures for capturing business and keeping it were only ad hoc at best. The firms would be divided on a simple division of labor, with partners overseeing areas that they knew best. Business would develop following the success of the individual partners. When they died or left their firms, there often was no formal mechanism for keeping the business. Over the years, the most successful partnerships were those where a family kept control or was succeeded by employees who knew the family formula for success. Otherwise, the record of management success at many of the Street's best-known firms was not particularly strong.

But the recurring theme throughout the histories of the various partnerships is that of capital. When a securities firm underwrote a new issue of stock or bonds it would need to assume the risk of that undertaking until it was sold. The actual cash needed for the transaction was obtained from a bank, but the firm still needed equity capital on its books to obtain even a short-term loan. The capital was supplied by either the partners' funds or later by shareholders' equity in the firm. The smaller that base became, the more difficult it became over the years to underwrite larger and larger offerings of new issues. After the Second World War, new issues became larger and those firms that did not grow with their customers and the economy began to fall behind. Finally, even the traditional well-heeled firms felt the need to go public. The remarkable part of the history is how long some of the firms were actually able to hold out before succumbing to these modern pressures.

The partnerships remained the dominant form of business organization for more than a century while the United States developed into an economic superpower. They were able to last as long as the tenor of everyday economic life remained slow to moderately paced. When new underwriting deals became larger, requiring the partnerships to have larger amounts of capital on their books, many were not able to respond and folded shop or were acquired by larger firms. In the 1970s, many Wall Street firms began to go public, selling shares to raise the additional capital needed to expand. Many of the older partnerships refused to do so, finding the idea repugnant. Their fierce independence over the years made the idea unthinkable, but by the 1990s almost all had gone public. History had finally caught up with them.

The capital problem plagued Wall Street firms throughout their histories. As we will see, capital also provided an element of discontinuity to the development of Wall Street securities houses because it was transient. Representing partners' funds, it could be withdrawn by older members of the firms upon death or retirement, and when that occurred many firms found themselves in difficult straits. And the problem was not confined to the smaller houses. J. P. Morgan & Co. found itself short of capital in 1940 and was forced to go public, finally succumbing to the pressure of a capital-intensive world.

The relationship between Wall Street and Washington also comes to light through the partnerships. Almost since the beginning of the Industrial Revolution, Washington has relied on Wall Street. Less clear is Wall Street's reliance on Washington. While the former is an institutional relationship, the latter is more personal. The Seligmans relied heavily upon their relationship with Ulysses S. Grant, forged before the Civil War, to court business. Jay Cooke's personal relationship with treasury secretary Salmon Chase enabled him to win the mandate for selling the enormous Treasury bond issues during the war. Bankers from Kuhn Loeb and Lehman Brothers were instrumental in advising on the establishment of the Federal Reserve between 1908 and 1912. Conversely, dozens of investment bankers went to work for government agencies in both world wars. In the postwar years, several have served as treasury secretaries, including Douglas Dillon and Nicholas Brady of Dillon Read, William Simon of Salomon Brothers, and Robert Rubin of Goldman Sachs. Pete Peterson served as Secretary of Commerce before joining Lehman Brothers, while more recently Felix Rohatyn of Lazard Freres served as Ambassador to France. But the institutional relationship is of vital importance to Washington, since it is reliant upon Wall Street to finance a large portion of government borrowing.

The adulation surrounding Wall Street bankers did not survive the Crash of 1929 and the New Deal reforms of the 1930s. After the 1929 Crash, vaudeville comedian and erstwhile investor Eddie Cantor quipped that "3,795 women bought certain investment trust stocks because they had Goldman Sachs appeal." But there was little to swoon over once the smoke cleared from their investments. Much of the allure of the famous family names and their highly regarded reputations was seriously damaged by the Crash, and many never survived the turmoil of the 1930s. The excesses of the 1920s brought down August Belmont & Co. as well as Lee Higginson & Co., Boston's best-known investment bank in the nineteenth century and one of the most private. The Seligmans effectively gave up the investment banking business to concentrate on fund management. J. P. Morgan's vast empire effectively was fragmented by Congress without anyone ever mentioning his name publicly. Equally, Goldman Sachs and Kuhn Loeb were chastened by events in the early 1930s.

The partnerships emerging from the turmoil of the Depression and World War II again led Wall Street in the 1950s when the bull market began during the Eisenhower administration. But the pressures created by an expanding consumer society proved their business structures to be vastly out of date, and most eventually went public or were acquired by the new powerhouse on Wall Street—the wire house, or retail broker, which was moving into more traditional areas like mergers and acquisitions and investment banking. These securities firms were hardly from genteel stock and used marketing as a key to their success, something the older investment banks eschewed. Despite the changing nature of Wall Street and the dominance of these newer full-service financial firms, the long-established partnership names are still held in high esteem. The traditional investment banking dynasties still retain their aura in an age where mammoth financial institutions are adopting names that sound uncomfortably bland, even in the new financial environment where competition has won a victory over tradition.

1

THE YANKEE BANKING HOUSES: CLARK DODGE AND JAY COOKE

The SECURITIES BUSINESS had very humble beginnings in the early part of the nineteenth century. Some of the best-known names in investment banking began their careers as itinerant merchants, peddling all sorts of wares throughout the East and the South. Others sold commodities and traded on the frontier. Although many of the early American bankers aspired to be the American Rothschilds or Barings, few had the resources or the family connections to follow in the Europeans' footsteps. Baring's importance was probably best expressed by the Duke of Richelieu after the Napoleonic Wars when he stated that there were six great powers in Europe—Great Britain, France, Russia, Austria, Prussia, and Baring Brothers. The Americans, on the other hand, were content to seize any opportunity that presented itself and develop it into a profitable business. Between the War of 1812 and the Civil War, the opportunities were expanding constantly, but the early partnerships had to be industrious and farsighted as well. Without a clear view of the future, many would not survive the rapidly changing American business scene.

The years between those two wars proved to be a watershed in American history. The country was shifting from a mercantilist and agrarian-based economy to one that would soon be industrial on a scale never imagined. Shortly after the Constitution was signed, Alexander Hamilton, Secretary of the Treasury, recognized the need for switching from an agricultural economy to one that would help the new nation become more self-sufficient. The United States was not able to trade freely with many European countries because of barriers put in place by the Europeans, and the lack of two-way trade was retarding the country's potential. In *The Report on Manufactures* (1791), Hamilton wrote: "The embarrassments which have obstructed the progress of our external trade have led to serious reflections on the necessity of enlarging the sphere of our domestic commerce." The remedy would be to encourage manufacturing and thus make the country less reliant on trade with Europe.

But what Hamilton envisioned as manufacturing—producing ships, armaments, and other simple types of goods—could never have foreseen the development of the steam engine, railroads, and steamships, to name but a few early-nineteenth-century industrial innovations. What Hamilton originally had in mind was manufacturing goods that would aid American exports, which were still mostly agricultural. Eli Whitney, the inventor of the cotton gin, was the personification of Hamilton's ideas. While developing the cotton gin in the 1790s, he was able to help increase American cotton exports to Europe almost fifty times over. And when he ran into financial difficulties, he expanded into rifle manufacturing, helping to revolutionize the firearms industry in the process. Like Cornelius "Commodore" Vanderbilt, Whitney was able to recognize the constantly shifting winds of change and adapt to them rather than simply remain the supplier of only one good or service. But his career showed that obtaining adequate financing for his activities was difficult because the Americans were long on ingenuity but short of the capital necessary to bring their ideas to fruition. Unlike the Europeans, the Americans could not rely upon the long-standing banking houses to supply them with capital or a wealthy domestic investing public that would buy stocks and bonds. There was not enough private capital in the new country to satisfy investment needs. The government could not provide capital for the same reason: not enough money was available from the citizenry. The early American bankers would prove that capital would not come from the government but from foreign sources that were quick to finance any idea that could make them a buck. In the early years of the republic, the federal government was not a significant financial force, nullifying Hamilton's vision of a national community where government would make up any shortfall in private investment.

Before the early banking houses could provide capital to newly emerging industries, they would have to develop to a point where they could be trusted with other people's money. Ironically, the early Yankee bankers developed their reputations aiding the federal and state governments by raising funds, but the results often fell far short of the sort of public policy that Hamilton envisioned. America was hardly a wealthy country. When the federal government needed money, it sold bonds. Its other sources of capital were limited. Taxation was applied sporadically and income taxes did not exist. But one method of raising money proved extremely popular. Lotteries were widely used by the states and the federal government to raise funds. Recognizing this, two brothers from upstate New York quickly got into the business of selling lottery tickets. Soon they would be among the first homegrown merchant bankers of the pre–Civil War period.

Wheel of Fortune

Solomon and Moses Allen formed S. & M. Allen & Co. in Albany, New York, in 1808. The two came from a very humble and obscure background; their father was an itinerant preacher who roamed New York in search of converts. The War of 1812 proved to be a watershed for them, as it would for many other aspiring bankers of the time. The finances of the United States were strained as a result of the war, and selling lottery tickets became a good way of raising money. The populace quickly became enamored of purchasing tickets. Local governments and private institutions also participated in the craze. Union College in Schenectady, New York, in the Allens' backyard, sold lottery tickets in 1810 with a potential payout of $100,000. The Allen firm was well placed to participate in the boom and opened twenty offices along the East Coast, extending as far south as Alabama. But selling lottery tickets also had its drawbacks, because the potential for profit was very limited. For the firm to survive and profit, another activity was needed.

At the height of the Allens' fortunes selling lottery tickets, the New York Stock and Exchange Board was formally organized in Manhattan and the Allens, notably Solomon, recognized that selling financial assets was preferable to being lottery ticket merchants. They quickly began shifting their business to securities, and by the mid-1820s had withdrawn from their former enterprise entirely. Their branch office system proved to be an invaluable asset, since buyers of securities were found along the entire East Coast, not simply in New York. But the new marketplace carried pitfalls that made the lottery business tame by comparison.

S. & M. Allen & Co. became one of the first members of the newly organized stock market. The market moved indoors from its traditional al fresco Wall Street location and was growing in size and stature. But the Allens soon discovered that the market was fraught with risk. The public that invested in securities was more fickle than the one that bought lottery tickets and would often react negatively to bad economic news by withdrawing its money from the market. The Allens' wide distribution network had worked well for lottery tickets, but it was not that much of an advantage with securities. Different parts of the country presented different sorts of risks for investors, as they were soon to discover. The very sort of wide distribution that securities firms would clamor for in the twentieth century was no advantage in the nineteenth. Ironically, the Allen firm was too far ahead of its time. Structural problems in the national banking system affected even lottery agents.

One of Wall Street's major setbacks in the 1830s was caused by the failure of the second Bank of the United States in 1832. Andrew Jackson's opposition to the nationwide federally chartered bank and its president, Nicholas Biddle, eventually caused it to close its doors. When it did, the regionalism of American banking became even more pronounced. Foreign investors, notably the British, upon whom the Americans depended heavily for investments, became worried. The New York stock market slipped badly and an economic crisis developed that would later cause a massive series of bank failures up and down the eastern seaboard. The crisis quickly absorbed the stock market and the Allens began to suffer serious losses. By 1836, the firm was forced to close its doors, one of the first major casualties of the nationwide economic crisis. But the lessons learned by them were not completely lost on posterity, because one of their partners quickly set up his own firm to explore new lines of business, intent on not making the same mistakes. That year was to become a milestone in Wall Street history, but the reasons would take several decades to unravel.

The market crash that followed became known as the Panic of 1837. Many banks began to fail, and dozens of brokers failed as well. The most notable casualty was J. L. & S. Josephs, a Jewish banking and brokerage house that thrived because of its association with the Rothschilds. The Josephs were originally from Richmond and made their way north, founding their securities firm with $20,000 of capital in the early 1830s. They became wealthy very quickly, channeling the Rothschild funds into all sorts of enterprises. Business was so good that they began to erect a large granite headquarters at the corner of Wall and Hanover Streets, at the very southern tip of Manhattan. But then the roof fell in, literally.

The new building was a portent for the stock market. In March 1837, as it was nearing completion, the entire building collapsed under its own weight due to shoddy workmanship. Three days later, the market collapsed. The 1830s binge of speculation on borrowed money came to a screeching halt. The Josephs closed their doors after the Louisiana cotton industry collapsed in 1837, leaving them holding millions in worthless paper. Their house, once with capital of $5 million, was now totally bust. Of more than 600 banks and brokers in the country, half of them failed in the wake of the panic, leading to the worst economic crisis the country had yet seen. The Allens were not alone in their misery.

One of the Allens' distant relatives was Enoch Clark, who was a partner in S. & M. Allen until its collapse. Clark established his own firm immediately in Philadelphia with the aid of a brother-in-law, Edward Dodge. The new firm would suffer its own travails but was destined to become one of Wall Street's longest-standing partnerships. At the same time, the Rothschilds, dismayed over the dealings of the Josephs, dispatched a new representative to the United States from Germany. They were no longer willing to leave their agency business in purely American hands. The new envoy was Augustus Schonberg. When he reached New York, he changed his name to August Belmont in an effort to sound more appealing to his new American clients and business partners.

Clark and Dodge established their firm in Philadelphia with capital of $15,000 for the original purpose of "stock and exchange." Clark was born in 1802 and lived in Easthampton, Massachusetts, until his teens. He then joined the Philadelphia office of the Allens. Several years later, when he was legally able to represent them, he was sent to open a branch office in Providence, Rhode Island. Young men, barely out of their teens, were common in the banking and securities business at the time. While helping the Allens succeed, he began to speculate on his own in the Boston stock market, losing all of his savings in the process. When the Allens failed, he returned to Philadelphia to open the firm that would bear his name for the next hundred years. Clark learned early in life that providing solid business for others was more steady and profitable than speculation in the markets.

Also established in the 1820s were Prime, Ward & King in New York; Thayer & Co. in Boston, which later would become Kidder Peabody & Co.; and Alex Brown & Co. in Baltimore. In addition to trading the occasional stocks, bonds, commercial bills, and commodities, the early securities dealers like E. W. Clark Dodge began aiding merchants in their need for working capital and investing. One of the more lucrative aspects of their business was dealing in banknotes and trading gold bullion. Trading in banknotes, in particular, was a valuable service to clients because of the variety of paper money that existed in the United States. Recognizing the values of different sorts of notes was a specialty of the new firm, a skill that Clark had learned while working for the Allens. It was a talent that combined credit analysis, forgery detection, and common business sense. It was also very profitable. One of their young employees, Jay Cooke, wrote that "our office is continually crowded with customers and we do a tremendous business. We buy and sell at from ⅛ to ¼ commission and thus in doing $50,000 per day you will see it pays well."[1] Most private banks of good reputation combined money and note dealing with a gold-trading business. Banking houses of repute that had their notes used as currency needed to maintain a supply of gold that would back the notes, and gold trading became as important as trading in securities.

Business soon prospered, and Clark and Dodge began expanding into other cities in need of such skills, especially since the Bank of the United States was no longer a force in American finance. Within two years, they had branches in St. Louis; New Orleans; New York; Boston; Springfield, Illinois; and Burlington, Iowa. They were so successful in the Midwest that their own drafts issued by the branch became one of the major currencies in the region. After the Panic of 1837, investors and businessmen favored banknotes that were backed by specie (gold or silver). Clark and Dodge became major forces in finance in a remarkably short period of time by assuring the public that their notes were fully backed if necessary. As a result, they won their confidence quickly and demand for their services quickly increased. They opened the office on Wall Street in New York to be close to the center of the financial world. Continuing success required that their main office be relocated, and on August 11 they put a notice in the New York newspapers announcing that the Boston and Philadelphia houses had formed the New York firm that would be the standard bearer in the years to come. They shared a building with the Aetna Insurance Company on Wall Street before moving to their own building in 1845 with $50,000 in capital. The amount was not large, even by the standards of the day. The major New York commercial banks dominated the market, and about twenty-four of them accounted for capital of around $20 million. While that amount dwarfed the capital of private banks like Clark Dodge, the commercial banks were not as venturesome as their smaller counterparts. But the branch system proved to be one of the new firm's enduring qualities. In the years after the Panic, prosperity returned and business confidence again soared. The only cloud on the horizon was the American annexation of Texas. Fears were growing that a war with Mexico was imminent. When war did break out, Clark Dodge & Co. would be in the forefront of its financing. Financiers had made reputations before helping the United States raise capital during the 1790s and again during the War of 1812. The war with Mexico would help solidify the reputation of Clark Dodge as one of the country's premier private banking houses.

Despite the young firm's early peacetime success, it was the Mexican War that helped make its reputation. The war lasted less than two years but still required financing for the Treasury from the private sector. Corcoran & Riggs, a well-known Washington, D.C., banking house, provided the financing along with E. W. Clark Dodge & Co.

The government raised more than $60 million in the form of bonds offered to the public at 6 percent interest. The bulk of the financing was given to Corcoran & Riggs to sell, with Clark Dodge taking the remainder. Clark and Dodge made more money floating funds between their branches than they did by actually selling the bonds for a commission, and they were criticized in some quarters for taking advantage of a hard-pressed Treasury.

Clark and Dodge were generous employers. They regularly gave parties for their younger employees on weekends, took them to the theater and shows in Philadelphia, and threw lavish parties at the holidays. One of those young employees, Jay Cooke, remembered them fondly, saying that "they were generous and noble men and I am proud to recall that their affection and confidence were extended to me during all our business connection and during all their lives."[2]

Clark and Dodge were the original two partners in 1845 when Clark Dodge & Co. officially opened its new main office on Wall Street. Younger partners were admitted to the ranks of the smaller banks where the prospects for success, and advancement through the ranks, were greater. Clark Dodge admitted Thomas Huntington as a partner in 1848, and Joseph W. Clark and Luther Clark in 1849. Jay Cooke was also admitted in 1849.

Working for the Allens helped Enoch Clark realize that a branch network had its advantages, especially when handling and clearing funds. Floating funds between the branches earned the firm much-needed cash but was not a simple operation. Law required the Treasury to deposit the proceeds of the bonds at a specified sub-Treasury office at various locations around the country. The sub-Treasuries were created after the demise of the Bank of the United States so that not all of the Treasury's cash would be in one place, in keeping with Andrew Jackson's notion that its use might fall under the control of a small group of elite bankers. Clark's St. Louis office took the deposit and mailed it to its New York office, collecting interest on the amount while the slow mails handled the letter. Then the funds were delivered back to St. Louis, which did not have a sub-Treasury branch, so Clark Dodge issued a bond to the Treasury for the funds, backed by the full faith and credit of the firm, which the Treasury was more than willing to recognize.

When the transaction was finally complete, the firm had more than doubled the amount it had made from selling the original Treasury bonds themselves, having engaged in what would later be known as "floating" funds to its own advantage. All of which was perfectly legal because of the less-than-ideal state of the U.S. Treasury at the time. Jay Cooke, who played a prominent role in the operation, wrote in his memoirs that "our firm had a branch office in St. Louis and we proceeded to sell exchange on Philadelphia and New York at a handsome premium, say two and a half or three per cent . . . the mails were sometimes from ten to fifteen days in transit and in addition to the advantage of interest, we had a large profit in the premiums on exchange over and above the profit we made on the loan."[3] While this was not the ideal arrangement for the Treasury, it was certainly more advantageous than previous bond-selling efforts where the few private banking underwriters that could be found often took 10 percent for their efforts, sometimes leaving the Treasury short of the actual funds it needed.

Clark and Dodge realized that establishing good relations with the government was vital to their future business. This was a well-known business principle at the time, one long practiced by the Rothschilds in Europe. The famous German-Jewish banking house had established its reputation by forging strong alliances with various governments around Europe, and many of the young American banking houses aspired to do the same in the United States. But a major difference in the ways that the alliances were forged doomed many of the Americans to short-lived relationships with their government. The Rothschilds built their relationships on personal ties with European prime ministers and finance ministers as well as with royalty. The Americans were faced with administrations in Washington whose hold on power was much more tenuous. The clash between Andrew Jackson and Nicholas Biddle, the flamboyant president of the second Bank of the United States, illustrates the independence that government asserted from the private sector and bankers. Both Jackson and his successor, Martin Van Buren, refused several entreaties from Wall Street banks to rescind the "specie only" orders (pay in gold) so that the banks could settle their claims in paper money only, rather than rely on money backed by gold. Wall Street banks claimed that the original order from Jackson helped cause the Panic of 1837 after the charter of the second Bank of the United States was not renewed. Specie-only orders tended to deprive private businesses of the cash needed to operate, causing a cash and credit crunch in the process. All of this was a far cry from the close relationships that European heads of state had with their favorite banking houses. It also allowed the Europeans a greater degree of financial stability than the Americans experienced before the Civil War. Without a legitimate central bank, the Americans would not have a standard currency or a stable method of ensuring the value of paper money. When compared with the British, French, or Dutch, the American economy was very primitive indeed, relying on small private banking institutions to guide it in the absence of a central bank.

The other factor that separated firms like the Allens and Clark Dodge from the Europeans was their insularity. Both conducted domestic business where they could find it. They did not court European investors. The Europeans, mainly the British, Dutch, and some German Jews, were the main suppliers of capital to the United States. When they invested in America, they normally did so through one of their own or their agents. Barings of London had a substantial investment presence in the United States, as did the Rothschilds, but both lacked an American branch as such. The Rothschilds replaced Barings as the U.S. Treasury's main London representative in the early 1830s and funneled their investments through their own American agents, many of whom made a handsome living from them, as did the Josephs before their collapse.[4] But the Yankee firms did not have the necessary connections to court the European bankers, so they forged their own domestic business connections wherever they could. If the new American private banking houses wanted to emulate the Europeans by courting the Treasury successfully, they had to provide an invaluable service. Raising money during wartime was certainly one. So in addition to providing advice regarding the many types of banknotes in existence and buying and selling securities, Clark and Dodge got involved in Treasury financing. But other activities also vied for Clark and Dodge's attention. One of them was railway financing, the hot new technological innovation of the 1840s that would revolutionize travel and financing. Like any new enterprise, it was highly rewarding but also extremely risky because it was capital intensive and capital was something in short supply in America.

Clark Dodge helped float bonds for most of the early railroad companies, including the Rock Island Line, Pennsylvania, Northern Central, and the Philadelphia and Erie. Railway construction began to explode geometrically in the 1850s. In 1856, construction almost exceeded the total mileage in the country ten years earlier. Bonds and stocks of the railroads became investor favorites, and the securities houses rushed to underwrite as many of the early deals as possible. But clouds that spelled trouble for the country's banking system were again on the horizon. The payments system between banks in the East and the rest of the country was not functioning properly, and bankers were beginning to feel uncomfortable about the soundness of many banks. Enoch Clark, who was in retirement in Europe, wrote to Jay Cooke as early as 1854, anticipating the financial problems that were to come. "I see you are having rugged times at home. I am not disappointed and do not look for much relief at present. I hope you are acting on safe principle. Keep snug and do not try to do a large business."[5] Enoch Clark died in the summer of 1856, before troubles began. Just as the railway boom got under way, a new panic developed that was more serious than the one twenty years before. The Panic of 1857 caused havoc in the financial system and forced many Wall Street houses to close. Clark Dodge did not continue unscathed.

On the surface, the Panic of 1857 looked much like the one two decades earlier. Speculation in land, securities, and gold again was rampant. In August, the Ohio Life Insurance & Trust Co. failed, causing widespread havoc. The Ohio was also a bank, so many of its obligations caused merchants and other banks to fail as well. Its stock had been trading at as high as $100 per share and it paid a 10 percent dividend, so its failure was a double blow to both savers and investors. The market was again short of gold to back many obligations of the banks and had been counting on increased shipments from California to offset the shortage. Adding to the panic, a ship called the *Central America*, on its way east from California, sank with more than $2 million in gold on board. Most banks suspended specie payments as a result, and widespread bankruptcies followed.

The stock market crash of 1857 was as severe as any yet witnessed. Reports circulated of once-wealthy investors driving teams of horses up and down Broadway with For Sale signs on them in an attempt to raise cash. Most odd was the case of Samuel Thompson, who had taken a page from Enoch Clark's book and extended it by publishing a periodical called *The Bank Note Detector*. Readers could learn what banknotes were good credit bets as well as learn to detect counterfeits, a common problem. Suddenly, Thompson disappeared from view during the panic and was nowhere to be found. Finally, according to the *New York Herald*, a banker discovered him in a dim, dilapidated building a short distance from Wall Street, dressed in work clothes, in a loft making candles. He was suspected of using his publication to fraudulently obtain funds from his subscribers and then play the market, leading to his rapid downfall.

The public panicked. Merchants and ordinary citizens by the thousands began running from bank to bank in lower Manhattan, seeking one that would pay specie for their banknotes. It was becoming clear that there was more paper money in circulation than there was gold to support it, and that if banknotes could not be redeemed for specie it would soon be worthless. When the smoke cleared from the Crash of October 13, 1857, eighteen banks had failed, although the major commercial banks such as the Bank of New York had survived. But several, predominantly gold dealers, had succumbed. Paper money became the accepted norm when almost all banks with the exception of the Chemical Bank suspended payments in specie. The stock market fell substantially as a result and stayed in the doldrums for the next year.

The panic began to ebb by the summer of 1858 and the country slowly returned to normal. But the toll the panic took on Wall Street was high. E. W. Clark Dodge was forced to close its offices in New York, Boston, St. Louis, Burlington, and Springfield. The Philadelphia house was able to remain open. When specie payments began again, the firm reopened its doors as Clark Dodge & Co. in February 1858, dropping the E. W. from its official name. The new Clark

Dodge listed six partners in its new partnership agreement, published on February 18. One name was conspicuously absent, however: that of Cooke. Jay Cooke withdrew from the firm with which he had been associated for the past twenty years, for private reasons. His resignation was the greatest loss that Clark Dodge would register in the nineteenth century, despite its trials and tribulations in the market. Cooke was to remain in retirement for four years, until the outbreak of the Civil War. He later wrote, "I have often reflected that this preparation of rest and disentanglement from all business providentially fitted me to carry cheerfully . . . the most enormous financial burdens I verily believe were ever placed on the shoulders of any one man." He was correct. The financial burdens of the Civil War were fifty times those of the Mexican War and began by costing the Treasury more than $1 million per day. Clark Dodge and the new firm of Jay Cooke & Co. would play a central role in its financing.

Cooke founded his new firm with one partner, William E. C. Moorhead. Cooke held two-thirds of the partnership, Moorhead one-third. Over the years, the relationship was never easy and Moorhead and Cooke often found themselves at loggerheads over firm policy, especially during the Civil War. And Cooke always remained the decision maker of the two, giving the firm a strong but autocratic tone. That go-it-alone attitude would work well during the war but was less successful in the postwar years. His brothers Henry and Pitt also joined the firm, and while Cooke often valued their advice more than that of Moorhead, he clearly remained in charge of most of the decision making. H. C. Fahnestock joined the firm as a partner in the Washington office and became Cooke's most valued lieutenant over the years.[6] Another partner, Edward Dodge, was a member of the New York Stock Exchange and held the seat on the exchange for Jay Cooke & Co. after 1870.

Saving the Union

The life and career of Jay Cooke is perhaps the finest example of banking and patriotism—two words not usually uttered in the same sentence on Wall Street—that the nineteenth century produced. Patriotism came with a price, because the task of financing the Civil War was the most daunting of the nineteenth century. Cooke was born August 10, 1821, in Sandusky, Ohio, to Eleutheros Cooke and Martha Carswell. The original Cookes emigrated to America from Britain in 1638 and settled in Massachusetts. Cooke later recalled that his father named him Jay, after Chief Justice of the Supreme Court John Jay, for a very specific reason. Eleutheros believed that his long first name had cost him an election to the Ohio legislature because voters could not fit his name on the write-in ballot. Determined that the same fate should not befall his progeny, he gave them relatively short, and sometimes historical, first names. Jay's older brother was named Pitt and his younger brother Henry. Two other offspring died early— Eleutheros Jr. and Catherine. Originally, he proposed to call Henry "Fox" instead, after Charles James Fox, a popular British politician at the time. But his mother created such a fuss about a child being named after a British statesman that Eleutheros relented and settled on Henry, in keeping with the strong family tradition of fierce American independence. The family had a long record of military service in the Revolutionary War and the War of 1812. The Carswells had a similar history. Martha Carswell's father was a prisoner of the British in Canada during the War of 1812, so her fondness for the mother country was somewhat limited.[7] Eleutheros Cooke went on to become a member of the Ohio legislature and eventually the House of Representatives. He was a member of the House when Jackson effectively dissolved the second Bank of the United States.

Jay Cooke joined Clark and Dodge in 1839, being invited to join by a friend working for the firm. Within a year, he had already made his mark as a valued employee, being referred to as the "counterfeit clerk." Like Clark before him, he had become expert in detecting bogus banknotes, and his keen eye made him invaluable to Clark Dodge almost from the outset. He also took up a part-time journalism career. The editor of the *Daily Chronicle*, a Philadelphia newspaper, invited him to write a daily money market column for the paper, which he did gladly. He wrote mainly about the condition of the bond markets along the East Coast and on conditions in the exchange market. Although the enterprise gave Clark Dodge good exposure in the market, Cooke gave up the effort after a year because it was consuming too much of his time. The experience did, however, mark him as one of the first financiers to display a journalistic flair—a trait that many others would pursue part-time after the Civil War with greater fanfare.

During his early retirement from Clark Dodge after Enoch Clark died, Cooke busied himself with occasional railroad financing and looking after his own private affairs. He kept a desk at his old firm so that he would not be totally divorced from the banking business. The late 1850s proved to the last period of railroad expansion, because the Civil War would soon intervene, putting most projects on indefinite hold. When South Carolina seceded from the Union, Cooke rapidly decided to form his own firm and return to what he knew best— raising bond issues for government bodies. He founded Jay Cooke & Co. when he was only thirty-nine. Although Cooke worked for Clark Dodge and the firm became well known on Wall Street, Cooke remained a Philadelphia banker for his entire career.[8] His flair for financing and his strong patriotic bent made him a natural to raise money when it was becoming more and more difficult to find. The war scared away many of the traditional foreign investors, and Cooke realized that the funds would have to be raised mainly from domestic investors.

Opportunity came when Pennsylvania needed funds at the outset of the war. The job was not easy, for Cooke or anyone else. Pennsylvania had been one of a handful of states that defaulted on its debt in the municipal bond crisis that roiled the markets when the second Bank of the United States failed, causing the Panic of 1837. In the interim, its reputation had not improved. One British writer sarcastically wrote before the Civil War, "We all know the Americans can fight. Nobody doubts their courage. I see now in my mind's eye a whole army on the plains of Pennsylvania in battle array, immense corps of insolvent light infantry, regiments of heavy horse debtors, battalions of repudiators, brigades of bankrupts with *Vivre sans payer ou mourir* on their banners."[9] Clearly, money for the Union war effort would not be coming from Britain. Some British newspapers even suggested that the Confederacy had as much right to secede as the original thirteen colonies had years before. But Jay Cooke's genius for raising funds won the day. It also gave a new twist to the term "Yankee banker."

Pennsylvania commissioned him to raise a bond of $3 million, not an easy task for a state already in debt by more than $40 million. Pennsylvania needed the money to defend its southern border against attack. It named Drexel & Co., a well-established Philadelphia banking house, and Cooke as agents for the issue. (Drexel was to become a familiar name in investment banking over the next century and a quarter, especially when the young J. P. Morgan took an interest in the firm after the Civil War.) Being joint agents raised eyebrows in some quarters, because Cooke was new to the banking scene as an independent although his reputation at Clark Dodge preceded him. He organized a massive selling effort. The bond was oversubscribed and rated a great success. No stranger to advertising and a bit of self-promotion, Cooke then turned and sent the list of subscribers to all the major newspapers in the country. He even sent a list by post to Jefferson Davis in Richmond to show that the population of the North was fully behind the effort. Individuals and banks on the subscribers' list included all of the major banks in Pennsylvania, Drexel and Jay Cooke & Co. themselves, as well as F. A. Muhlenberg Jr., the son of the first Speaker of the House of Representatives. Cooke found that patriotism sold well in Pennsylvania. A precedent had been established for the next round of fund-raising for Washington.

Salmon Chase was Secretary of the Treasury in the Lincoln administration, charged with raising money for the war effort. Cooke traveled to Washington, hoping to become involved in the financing effort. His brother Henry, previously the editor of the *Ohio State Journal* in Columbus, offered to introduce him to Chase. Cooke seized the opportunity to meet the secretary. In 1861, he participated in a small part of a Treasury issue that was not going well and succeeded in selling it. The way was now paved for further participation, but it was certainly not automatic. Cooke took it upon himself to gather subscriptions for Treasury bonds and then hand them to Salmon Chase, who could not but take notice of the Philadelphia banker's dexterity in raising subscriptions so easily. But Cooke was sure to tell Chase at every opportunity that he was doing it at no commission for himself.

The same was not true of the rest of the Treasury bond offerings that Cooke helped sell to the public. Chase was duly impressed with

Cooke's ability to sell public debt and enlisted him to participate in future offerings, which grew larger and larger as the war dragged on. Chase offered Cooke a job in the Treasury as an undersecretary, but he refused it after some serious thought. Cooke clearly thought that the best way to serve his country was by selling as many bonds as possible, not by becoming a bureaucrat tied to Washington. He continued to gather subscriptions nevertheless. The Treasury's tenuous position and Cooke's rising importance were evident in the aftermath of the Battle of Bull Run. Sounds of the battle could easily be heard in Washington itself, but the city was stunned by the unexpected news that the Union army had been routed and was in disarray. Fearing that Confederates would overrun the city in the near future, Cooke became even more intent on raising as much money as the government needed to defeat the rebels. He opened an office in Washington and, upon hearing of the rout, began to make the rounds of the banks in Washington to line up even more potential subscriptions. His fortitude and determination began to show in what he considered his patriotic duty to defend the Union. Naturally, there was also a financial side. Some of this fund-raising would have to repay the tireless efforts of the fund-raisers themselves.

Cooke's role in the Civil War financings became a model for bankers of the future, who would use it to become even more successful in their own right. One was J. Pierpont Morgan, who would note the adulation that Cooke received because of his closeness with Salmon Chase and the indefatigable effort he put into selling bonds nationwide. In fact, Morgan would eventually try to capture the market for Treasury bonds from Cooke's houses after 1865.[10] But the road to Chase's heart—and the Treasury's pockets—was not easily traveled. Chase was a conservative, hard-money man who accepted change only when forced to do so. The Battle of Bull Run became the lightning rod for change in the Lincoln administration and for Cooke's own personal fortune. Chase packed off for New York to raise a new bond issue of $50 million, dubbed "the 5-20s" (an early callable bond issue). He asked Cooke to accompany him, to fortify him, when he asked the New York banks for such a large sum. Cooke did accompany him, and the money was raised after some initial arm-twisting. Among the participants were Clark Dodge; Fisk &

Hatch; Livermore, Clews & Co.; and Vermilye & Co., the predecessor of Dillon Read. Cooke and Chase had formed a bond that would make future financings much easier.

When Cooke sold the 5-20s to the public, he required payment in specie or by banknotes backed by collateral. But specie was in short demand. The Treasury subsequently suspended specie payments and issued greenbacks, one of the most controversial parts of the war financing. The green printed money bore no backing and was the brunt of fierce attacks by hard-money advocates for years to come. Salmon Chase himself was not in favor but clearly recognized that if some method was not devised to create money the war could well be lost. The U.S. Treasury was almost empty in 1862, so arguments against the issuance of greenbacks became academic. After their issue, credit conditions returned to normal and the public and businesses accepted the new money without any apparent hesitation. One useful side effect of the greenbacks was that they helped cut down on the old Clark Dodge habit of bankers negotiating a Treasury issue by knocking down government debt to a substantial discount before selling it, netting a handsome profit for the bankers, who then sold it for face value, but netting less proceeds for the government itself. Greenbacks became accepted and the shortage of money eased, so there was no longer any need to sell the new, large government bond issues at a discount. The new currency had an unanticipated, beneficial side effect. Cooke would still be able to profit handsomely from the new environment despite the lack of deep discounts. Even if the new bond issues were sold to the selling agent at only a 2 percent discount, a large issue would still compensate well. When Cooke was appointed sole agent for new Treasury issues shortly thereafter, all of that percentage—less associated selling costs—was his to keep.

Cooke also found himself enmeshed in Washington politics. During the early war years, he and his brother Henry helped organize the first streetcars to serve Washington. They organized the Washington & Georgetown Street Railroad Company and bought stock in it, as did the other major banking houses involved with the war financing. The company became very successful and was hailed as a success. But Salmon Chase objected that men of color who were serving in the Union army were not allowed to use the service, that it was confined to whites only. Chase wrote the directors of the company an impassioned plea to allow Negroes to use the service, but the board of directors refused. The Cooke banking house then promptly sold its stock in the company and returned to selling bonds, leaving the stickier issue of the streetcar and racial discrimination to others.

In 1862, the war was not going well for the Union, and Cooke felt the heat. Cooke's bank came under some scrutiny from the Treasury for being too slow in dispensing funds already raised, suggesting that a bit of floating was taking place again, as it had during the Mexican War financings. Cooke protested but managed to keep busy with other matters, mostly involving railroad financing, which he had been engaged in for some years before the war. Some of those railroad dealings became difficult because the government frequently monitored telegraph messages. Cooke's bank devised an elaborate cipher system so that it could transmit messages to its branches without fear of government snooping. It routinely substituted banking terms and other bankers' names for political and military ones, and what appeared to be standard banking transmissions were actually reports sent between his branches of military news to which the government censor might have objected.[11] Doing business with Washington did not mean that the government was going to call the tune on otherwise private matters.

The Napoleon of Finance

Jay Cooke had achieved some notoriety by 1862, but the events in the latter part of that year were to bring accolades and fortune. Despite sanguine predictions, the war showed no signs of abating, and the second battle of Bull Run again brought it tantalizingly close to Washington's door. More money was needed to bolster the troops, and Salmon Chase again would call Cooke to the Union's side to aid in the financing. Their brief falling-out over the disbursement of funds was only an interlude in Cooke's fund-raising attempts. Chase again needed him badly, and it was not long before a new bond issue was planned.

Critics of Cooke trace the planning of what became known as the 5-20 loan, or bond, to the beginning of his wealth. This was the largest bond issue in American history to date, and it would require all of his resources to be successful. The 5-20s were actually 6 percent bonds that matured in twenty years but could be redeemed after five years. Cooke was appointed sole agent for the issue, which had actually been selling poorly for some time. But when he entered the picture, the effort changed. All sorts of sales techniques were mobilized, from using his extensive network and employing traveling agents to having journalists write favorable articles about investing in government bonds.

The articles were very effective, appealing to the average citizen's patriotism and pocketbook. They also had an educational function, pointing out the virtues of "putting out money at interest" and emphasizing that the government needed help in the vast war enterprise that only solid citizens could satisfy. The technique worked. Subscriptions poured in from all over the country. Cooke had 1,500 agents in the field who sold bonds to anyone who could afford as little as $10. Unlike previous Treasury bonds, the denominations were made small so that the average citizen could subscribe. Journalists cranked out articles in a continuous stream, and the prose ranged from the technical to the floral. One from the *Philadelphia Inquirer* in April 1863 began by stating, "It would rejoice the heart of every patriot if he could witness in person the daily operations at the [Cooke] agency of the national loan in this city. The people are there to give aid and comfort to the government by investing their savings and their capital in the Five-Twenty bonds." Anyone attempting to sell securities after the Civil War had to take notice of the precedent that Cooke established with the 5-20s.

But not everyone considered Cooke the unselfish savior of the Union. He was being compensated for selling the 5-20s at about a 1 percent commission rate—less than in the past but still enough to make an enormous profit given the size of the total issue. The bonds were being sold at about $2 million per day in the beginning, totaling more than $500 million by the time the sale was complete, suggesting a commission of $3.5 million before costs were subtracted. Cooke himself claimed he made only $200,000 net, but the numbers were suspect. In 1863, the *New York World* took him to task in no uncertain language when it stated, "If, however, Jay Cooke and Company receive from the government one-half of one per centum on all the notes funded, we can readily see a powerful motive for that house to procure as large a sum to be converted into bonds as possible."[12] The newspaper did not do the math for its readers, but the numbers were indeed large. Eventually, one half of one percent of $500 million would have netted Cooke $2.5 million. Regardless of the costs, the public outcry could be expected to be shrill. But the *World* also noted that "our people seem to delight in being cheated. The serenity with which they swallow the false statements of the success of our arms . . . the repudiations and cunning contrivances of the Treasury Department leave little doubt that the luxury of being humbugged is only equaled by that of being imprisoned without law, wasted by war, and impoverished by taxes."

Similar attacks on Cooke came from the Senate, where his detractors claimed that he made millions at the Treasury's expense. Salmon Chase, a man of high conscience, was uncomfortable with some of the attacks, but after reassuring himself that Cooke was acting mostly in the national interest, he stepped in to defend his agent and the books were closed on the 5-20s. Cooke was a national hero and had amassed a small fortune as a result. Cynics would later say that the day the war ended he began a grandiose project to build the palatial home of his dreams, which would cost more than $1 million. But the financings were not yet finished and more bond issues were on the way.

The next Treasury financing that Cooke led were the 7-30s (7.30 percent interest maturing in three years). Chase had left the Treasury, and Cooke had to deal with a new secretary, William Pitt Fessenden. He quickly recognized Cooke's past service and enlisted him to sell the new bonds. But Fessenden was not a secretary of the caliber of Chase and the new bonds did not fare well under his supervision. Many of those not taken by Cooke remained unsold. Fessenden reported the problem to Cooke and asked for his guidance. Cooke's recollection of the conversation was revealing:

"What do you want for them?" Cooke asked without hesitation.

"I want par and your commission will be the accrued interest," the Secretary answered.

"I will take them myself," said the banker in his inimitable way. "I will take three millions at once, and you can give me an option on the rest of the ten millions. Which I will close after a visit to New York."[13]

After that encounter, Cooke quickly became Fessenden's man on the ground. The secretary replied by remarking, "I have heretofore thought you a protégé of Mr. Chase, but I now see that he was your protégé." Cooke became the sole agent for the 7-30s, and he displayed the same sort of enthusiasm that he had given the 5-20s. And the task was even greater. The new bond would eventually total more than $830 million, making it the largest financing instrument in American history to date.

The marketing of this enormous number of bonds proved to be the undoing of the Confederate cause. The bonds also became the indirect undoing of Jay Cooke himself. Dealing with such vast amounts of money, often committing for large amounts in very short periods of time, as he had done with Fessenden, gave Cooke the impression that business would always be successful and fast. Once the war ended, however, such huge sums no longer would be the norm and life would begin to return to normal. But at the time, the 7-30s and the 5-20s were so large when combined that Jay Cooke was able to say that he was the first financier to raise more than a billion dollars, a measure new to the finance lexicon.

While the war lasted, Cooke ruled the Washington roost. But the wolves were knocking at the door. Several gold panics developed during the war that severely tested the resolve of the Treasury. Critics attributed them to Jewish interests on Wall Street, usually a not-so-subtle reference to Jay Gould. But some were done simply because it was easy to speculate and make money without much legal consequence. In 1863, the young J. Pierpont Morgan "cornered" gold in the New York market, forcing its price up and the price of Treasury bonds down. The result was that selling the 5-20s and later the 7-30s became very difficult. The reasons for the corner were hard to determine. Speculating in gold was a favorite pastime on Wall Street, and many of the established firms had gold-dealing rooms in which they made prices for customers and other houses alike. But speculation at the time that Treasury war bonds were being sold sounded suspiciously like treasonous activity, designed to destabilize the financing while casting doubt over the value of gold and chasing away investors. At best, it sounded like an attempt to discredit Jay Cooke & Company. Cooke was aware of the developments and often made trips to New York when a strong selling effort was required. Potential buyers of bonds resided on Wall Street, as did potential enemies of his financial cause.

The heavy financings did not end with the surrender of Richmond or the assassination of Lincoln. The 7-30s, on which Cooke had to constantly renegotiate the commissions with the new Treasury secretary, Hugh McCulloch, Fessenden's successor, finally paid him ¾ of 1 percent, an amount he insisted was necessary to pay all of the associated costs. From that moment, the 7-30s became even more successful than their predecessors. With the success of the 7-30s, Cooke clearly had become the best-known financier in the country and enjoyed his status. Other ventures were beckoning once the war financings began to quiet down. The private sector again became the place to invest, and in post–Civil War America that primarily meant investing in railroads. The West was calling, and it would prove to be Cooke's downfall.

At the end of the war, Cooke's banking house remained much the same as it had been before he became involved with Salmon Chase. It sold securities, dealt in bills of exchange and gold, and also accepted deposits. The deposit business was to become the Achilles heel of the firm, as it would for so many other merchant bankers in the nineteenth century. Taking deposits and dealing in securities often made the depositors nervous. When customers decided to withdraw their funds, the bank could quickly become short of funds necessary to carry on business and would have to shut its doors. It was an age-old problem that was bound to repeat itself again and again.

"A Magnificent Undertaking"

At war's end, Cooke began planning a new, palatial home in Philadelphia called Ogontz (after an Indian chief), which eventually cost $1 million and gave his critics much ammunition as they derided his excesses. Throughout his life, Cooke would be known for throwing lavish dinner parties and treating his guests royally. One of his most famous guests after the Civil War would be Ulysses S. Grant, who stayed at Ogontz on numerous occasions. But he could not remain retired from the excitement that the Treasury financings had brought. He quickly became involved with a new railway project that would link the Midwest with the Pacific Northwest, appropriately called the Northern Pacific Railroad. The line was a resurrection of an older line that had not succeeded, and Cooke was determined to make the new project work. His partners were much less enthusiastic and gave the project only lip service. That was unfortunate, because one partner, William Moorhead, became involved in the negotiations for foreign investors and he clearly was not a wholehearted supporter of the railway plan.

For the first time, Cooke realized that he would need foreign investment support if his idea was to succeed. He dispatched Moorhead to London to talk with the Rothschilds. Their support of the project would give it instant credibility. Cooke wanted them to purchase a sizable number of bonds in the railroad, which was to be highly leveraged. The Rothschilds' presence in the United States was limited to August Belmont, who had started his own firm thirty years before and acted on behalf of their interests only when asked. But the legendary banking family was not impressed despite Moorhead's efforts. Entrepreneurs were scouring Europe at the time, seeking railroad financing from many other European and Middle Eastern countries, so the idea of a new American railroad was not exactly novel. In addition, London financiers with long memories remembered the municipal bond of the 1840s that cost European, and mainly British, investors millions in defaulted interest and principal repayments. The climate was not conducive for another railroad bond, even one supported by someone as famous as Cooke.

The Rothschilds entertained Cooke's proposal but eventually turned him down. Costs for building a railroad differed considerably in the United States, and Cooke's new line was estimated to be among the most expensive.[14] Experience already proved that the higher the cost, the more borrowing that was necessary, and the risk was also present of issuing excessive stock, commonly known as "stock watering." That was a blow, because it denied him capital when he sorely needed it and impressed upon him that he would have to finance the project himself, with domestic assistance only. Eventually, Cooke sold stock in the enterprise to a veritable Who's Who of political figures, both in Washington and in his native Ohio. He became quite messianic about the undertaking, which required new rail lines to be built from the Great Lakes to the Pacific Northwest around Puget Sound. He was quite enamored of the area, claiming it was the most beautiful in America. In a letter to a friend, he professed his love for it, wishing all to go to "the great Northwest, where there are no heart-burnings, Ku Klux or carpet baggers"—a not-so-subtle reference to the South, where Reconstruction was getting under way.

After intense lobbying in Washington, Cooke and his supporters managed to persuade Congress to pass a bill authorizing the Northern Pacific line through the Northwest. The legislation provided a land grant for the railroad to proceed through the territory, itself larger than several states together. However, the financial aid he hoped would accompany it was not forthcoming, and he had to adopt an alternative plan. The railroad was being built at great cost, and money was in short supply. Cooke decided to appeal again to the Europeans for money, and in 1870 he turned his attention to Germany, which was friendly to American railroads in general even if it was not as flush with cash as the Rothschild houses and their connections. Arrangements had been made to issue a bond in dollars for German investors when an unforeseen development occurred: The Franco-Prussian War began and fund-raising was put on hold. In the interim, building continued and the costs climbed even higher.

While Cooke was involved in the affairs of the Northern Pacific, another Treasury financing arose that he took time to arrange. The 5-20s now could be redeemed legally, and the Treasury asked Cooke to arrange a refinancing whereby those 6 percent bonds could be replaced by 5 percents. Many of the bonds were in Europe, having been sold to European investors by their original American owners. As a result, Cooke had to assemble a European banking group to arrange an exchange of bonds; an American group would assemble the American side. He did not have the full resources to arrange the whole deal, since the Northern Pacific enterprise took so much of his time. To arrange for the refinancing, other banks would need to be invited into the deal so that he alone could not dominate its terms and conditions. The term "syndicate" was born (derived from the French *syndicat*), a word used to describe the system whereby other bankers would subscribe to the deal and play an important role in designing it. The American newspapers quickly seized upon the term, poking fun at Cooke in the process. The New York *Tribune*, especially, had a field day with it, publishing the following poem:

> **Pray, what is a syndicate**
> **Intended to indicate?**
> **Is queried abroad and at home.**
> **Say, is it a corner, Where Jay Cook-e Horner**
> **Can pull out a very big plum?**[15]

Even with the entry of other banks into the bond deal, suspicions arose that Cooke had orchestrated the deal in his own interest or would again attempt to get terms that were advantageous to him. Then, in modern fashion, Cooke published the list of the banks participating in both the American and European sides of the deal, something that was unprecedented in financing. The American banks included, in addition to Jay Cooke & Co., Vermilye & Co., Henry Clews & Co., Clark Dodge, and the First National Bank of New York. Although both groups of banks on either side of the Atlantic arranged for only $25 million of the exchange, it was the first time that the list of deal makers was published in such a fashion. Much larger amounts soon followed. The syndicate would become a standard method for distributing securities issues that one bank alone could not adequately handle.

Cooke entered other arrangements to exchange Treasury bonds in 1872. One deal involved an alliance with the Rothschilds on the European side and Drexel, Morgan & Co. of Philadelphia on the domestic side. It was one of the few deals done with the Morgan firm, which Cooke fully recognized to be a keen rival for business. But while all of these deals were being done, the Northern Pacific remained foremost in Cooke's mind. The line was proceeding across the northern states, from Minnesota to Montana. The Franco-Prussian War had provided the first obstacle to financing it properly. Now a domestic crisis erupted that would prove to be the death knell for the ambitious project. Another panic, this one in 1873, would claim Cooke as its major victim.

The Panic of 1869 had severely shaken Wall Street and the country. The panic had its origins in a clandestine operation in the gold market orchestrated by Jay Gould and his cohorts. Ever since the early days of the Civil War, the relationship between gold and greenbacks had become the subject of interest among speculators and market manipulators. Shortages of gold quickly and adversely affected the price of securities. Shortages meant that the backing for many bonds, and the supply of money, was lacking, causing selling in the market. When greenbacks came on the scene, it also became quickly obvious that shortages of the new paper money could also affect the prices of securities. By locking up greenbacks temporarily, a squeeze could be created in the market that would rapidly deflate prices, enabling short sellers of securities to make a quick killing. This became the *modus operandi* of several well-known speculators, notably Jim Fisk and Gould, the latter portrayed by the press as the personification of the devil himself.

Gould was so unpopular, and feared, on Wall Street that plots were occasionally hatched to force down the value of his holdings. One had a broker named Sam Leopold, who bore an uncanny resemblance to Gould, offered $20,000 by Gould's broker enemies to impersonate the devil and have his face smeared with blood. He would roll around at the corner of Broad and Wall pretending to be hurt and then be rushed in an ambulance to a local hospital. While there, he was to be sequestered so that no one could contact him. It was hoped that the bad news would put selling pressure on his holdings and they would decline in value. The broker declined the offer because he feared the repercussions from other brokers if they discovered the scheme. The possibility of a reaction from Gould himself was also a powerful deterrent.

The "devil's plan" for the gold corner was extremely clever, but it was not unlike other corners organized in the nineteenth century, only grander in scale. Gould accumulated a large amount of gold, forcing its price up to a premium of 160 (gold was quoted in percentages of its par value). That caused many who were short, especially in the New York market, to cover their positions, helping to keep the price propped up. Rumor had it that President Grant was persuaded not to intervene by releasing gold from the government's coffers, helping to keep the price high. One of Gould's cohorts in the operation was Abel Corbin, Grant's son-in-law, and it was widely assumed that Gould used him to keep the President at bay. When Grant finally did intervene, Gould appeared to have had advance notice and was prepared for it. After gold was released, the price began to fall, but Gould had already sold his positions, netting a fat profit of more than $10 million and leaving the gold bears to count their losses. Cooke was reputedly among them, selling short the commodity so that the interest payments on the Treasury bonds he was selling would not become excessive. When the smoke cleared, Gould benefited while much of Wall Street was caught unawares. The failures that followed created the panic. Gould became one of the most vilified men in the country. Most important, the financial status of Cooke and Clark Dodge became compromised. This was a bad omen for Cooke, because the Northern Pacific was requiring more and more money constantly.

Gould's plan to corner the American gold market became part of nineteenth-century financial folklore. It was reported shortly after the fact in 1871 by Charles Francis Adams and his brother Henry in *Chapters of Erie and Other Essays*, a book devoted primarily to the shenanigans of Gould and Fisk, the operators of the notorious Erie Railroad in New York. Shortly thereafter, the Credit Mobilier investigation in Congress began and its revelations cast most members of Congress and railroad financiers under a long shadow of suspicion and doubt. It also made raising funds for the Northern Pacific even more difficult. Cooke had trouble paying his work crews in 1873, and if fresh money were not forthcoming, the entire enterprise would shortly be in doubt. As it turned out, the financial position of the two finance houses was even more precarious than had been suspected.

Later in 1873, the unthinkable finally occurred. The venerable house of Jay Cooke & Co. closed its doors—or was "forced to suspend," as the stock exchange put it. Almost incomprehensible was the fact that the New York house closed without the knowledge of Jay Cooke himself. Cooke admitted that he had no part in New York's action. That was difficult to believe since he had ruled the firm almost single-handedly since its inception. Then, like a thunderbolt, Clark Dodge & Co. also closed its doors. Crowds gathered in New York, Washington, and Philadelphia upon hearing the news and the origins of a panic began. The newspapers quickly lamented Cooke's failure. Most of them recognized his service to the country in eloquent terms, but the *Philadelphia Inquirer* laid the problem squarely on the shoulders of the Northern Pacific project. "Whoever says, as some did say yesterday, that the disaster was owing to gold or stock gambling, says that which is not true. The house suspended because its chief essayed to assist to a successful conclusion, the great Northern Pacific Railroad."[16] Post–Civil War political developments had finally created a hurdle too large to clear.

Several of Cooke's allies in past financings also failed, including Livermore, Clews & Co., and Fisk & Hatch. Cooke's branches suffered withdrawals and became illiquid very quickly. Bank runs occurred throughout the major banking centers. The Treasury issued more greenbacks to cover the problem, but it was far too late. The Panic of 1873 caught the country unawares, and it would be several years before it regained its financial feet. Two panics within four years was the most severe economic crisis the country had faced to date.

A Pact with the Devil

The demise of Jay Cooke & Co. in 1873 remains one of the most curious chapters in American financial history. The rift between Cooke and his partners was apparently wider than the old financier had thought. Bankruptcy proceedings against the firm and the individual partners began soon after the collapse, and it was discovered that some of the junior partners had escaped the debacle unscathed, apparently anticipating the fiasco by putting their own financial houses in order before the end came. The bankruptcy court liquidated the firm and the personal possessions of Cooke, who retired into a life of apparent obscurity. He moved into a relatively small cottage while his larger estates were seized.

Jay Cooke & Co. was reorganized, with Jay Cooke Jr. and his son-in-law, Charles D. Barney, as principals. The firm became Charles D. Barney & Co. The senior Cooke was out of the business and would not return to Philadelphia or Wall Street finance. But his business interests did not end with Jay Cooke & Co. He was introduced by a friend to a highly speculative investment in a silver mine in Utah. For the modest sum of $3,000 he bought controlling interest and traveled west to see his investment firsthand. To be profitable, the mine needed a railroad connection. Having had some experience with railway building, Cooke traveled to survey the situation. He also stopped to visit the manager of the Union Pacific Railroad in Utah. Explaining that he needed a rail line, the manager introduced him to none other

After Jay Cooke & Co. failed, the firm was taken over by Cooke's son-in-law, Charles D. Barney, who assumed his seat on the New York Stock Exchange. Barney's firm became one of Wall Street's mainstays over the years. In 1937, it merged with Edward B. Smith & Co. after that firm ran into financial difficulties and needed a partner with strong capital. Smith's firm was founded in 1892. Barney, born in 1844, lived to see many of Wall Street's most momentous changes. He retired from his firm in 1906 and busied himself with numerous corporate directorships and his family. When he was ninety-three, he learned of the death of his old crony, John D. Rockefeller, and told his physician, "Keep me alive longer than Mr. Rockefeller." He lived so long that he had been forgotten as one of Wall Street's elder statesmen. After his death in 1945 at age 101, his firm was cited in the famous "Wall Street Seventeen" case brought by the Justice Department. In 1993, the firm was bought by the Travelers Group and was combined with Salomon Brothers in 1997. Today, Salomon Smith Barney is the securities subsidiary of Citigroup.

than Jay Gould, who was visiting Utah at the same time and was in the office when Cooke visited. Gould, the president of the Union Pacific, and Cooke agreed on a deal to build the line. Despite Gould's reputation, Cooke proposed that they make the deal without signing a contract. Gould agreed, built the line, and took a stake in the venture. When the smoke cleared several years later, Cooke had netted $1 million for his small initial investment. He was probably the only person who would speak well of Jay Gould in the years that followed and perhaps the only person who would actually trust him with a verbal agreement. The pact made with the devil worked out well in the end.

The profit enabled Cooke to repurchase the palatial Ogontz, long since stripped of its ornaments and furnishings, and his second home in Ohio. In his later years, Cooke became an investor in various business ventures. The great irony was that the Northern Pacific was completed several years after the panic that ruined him and began paying a dividend to its shareholders. The company was taken over by Henry Villard, who would guide it for some years before being destroyed financially by J. P. Morgan. The Northern Pacific continued to be a familiar name in railroading and would become the object of an enormous stock market battle early in the twentieth century between Morgan and Harriman interests.

Jay Cooke died in 1905. His son and grandson, both of whom remained active in finance, kept the Cooke name alive but under the banner of Charles D. Barney. The famous name that helped finance the Union cause would never again be associated directly with a Wall Street firm.

Clark Dodge, the firm where Cooke got his start, remained in business under the same name until after World War II. Like many other established firms, it entered the investment management business in the 1920s and devoted considerable effort to advisory services. Over the years, its reputation and preeminence slipped, and it was remembered in later years more for its storied past than for its financial prowess among the post–World War II financial giants. Finally, it was acquired by Kidder Peabody in the mid-1970s and its operations were folded into the investment management side of Kidder. But if traced back to the Allens and Cooke, Clark Dodge can be called the first true dynasty that Wall Street witnessed. The three firms proved that when the vision of their founders was strictly adhered to, their success was notable. It was when they began to deviate from the well-established path that they faltered. The lesson would be remembered well by dozens of other firms vying for business in the years that followed.

2

"OUR CROWD":
THE SELIGMANS,
LEHMAN BROTHERS,
AND KUHN LOEB

ALTHOUGH CLARK DODGE was the only one of several banking houses tracing its origins from the Allens to survive, it was not the most successful of its era. The Allen and Cooke houses failed to keep themselves through successful family dynasties that were able to maintain an ironclad grip on their family businesses. The Clarks and Dodges were more successful, but none of the families or the houses they built was to become a major force in finance after the founding fathers of their firms were replaced by younger generations. That distinction was left to another group of onetime peddlers who would dominate American finance for several generations.

Unlike Jay Cooke, the Jewish banking firms that began to organize around the time of the Civil War opted to avoid the limelight whenever possible. This clearly could be traced to the fact that Jews formed a tiny minority of the population. But there was also a European connection: Most of the early aspiring Jewish bankers used the Rothschilds as their exemplars, and the baronial European family was the very model of discretion. They did not advertise their services, as Cooke and Clark Dodge were wont to do on more than one occasion, because the Rothschilds would not think of doing so. What that family might do became the frame of reference for the young American bankers of mostly German origin, keen to emulate their famous role model whenever possible.

The German-Jewish firms added a dimension to American finance that was sorely missing in the nineteenth century. The traditional suppliers of capital from abroad had been the British and, to a lesser extent, the Dutch. When either country pulled its capital out of the country, as the British did during the War of 1812, the consequences for the United States were clear. Without that imported capital, new investments dried up and economic development was put on hold until it returned. But the British also displayed solidarity with the Confederacy during the Civil War, sharply illustrating the fact that the country was at the mercy of foreign capital again. The Jewish firms developed ties with German financiers, sympathetic to the anti-slavery cause, and that connection served the United States well, reducing the need to rely on the British.

Most of the banking firms that set up shop in the nineteenth century were successful in a short period of time. The Seligmans were perhaps the best example. Their habit of opening offices around the country was the key to their success. Jay Cooke and Clark Dodge used their branches to float funds by assisting the Treasury in its financing operations and to trade gold. The Jewish houses used their branches to facilitate merchant and commodities trade. The Allens had originally used their branches to sell lottery tickets. Those branches helped supply what the United States otherwise lacked, a financial infrastructure that could trade bills of exchange between different parts of the country and with international customers. Private bankers offered what the government itself could not supply because of the constant battles before the Civil War over the Bank of the United States. After watching Jay Cooke succeed, another immigrant quickly recognized the opportunity as well.

Joseph Seligman was an immigrant from Germany who would use his connections with his motherland well. Born on November 22, 1819, the oldest of eleven children, he left his Bavarian home after attending the University of Erlangen. The Seligman clan lived in Baiersdorf, Bavaria, on a street named Judengasse, literally "Jews Street." The Rothschilds themselves, who hailed from Frankfurt, originally lived on a street of a similar name, an illustration of the fact that Jews were confined to specific areas within their hometowns. The Seligmans were intent upon escaping that environment. Armed with the knowledge of several languages, Joseph departed Germany at age seventeen and booked passage to America. After a month-long Atlantic crossing, he joined a family member in Pennsylvania in 1837, the year of the panic. He went to work for Asa Packer, whose company built canal boats. Later, Packer founded the Lehigh Valley Railroad and endowed Lehigh University. But in 1837, canals were the innovative form of transportation and the young Seligman was hired at the booming firm for $400 per year. Packer would not be able to keep his erudite young assistant, however. Within a short time, he saved half his salary, bought some sundries, and set out to sell them as an itinerant peddler. Within a year, Seligman had saved enough money to repay his mother the $100 she had loaned him to make the journey and to send for two of his brothers. The Seligman dynasty already was in its infancy, although its origins were very inauspicious.

After his brothers William and James joined him, Joseph opened a general merchandise store in Lancaster, Pennsylvania. The "house" of Seligman was officially born. Shortly thereafter, they moved their base of operations to Selma, Alabama, because they had discovered that the South had greater potential for profit. They remained in Alabama until 1846, when the brothers opened a Manhattan store on William Street. Other members of the family continued to arrive, and the men were immediately given jobs in the growing partnership. Another store was opened, this one in Watertown, New York, run by another brother, Jesse. A frequent customer of the store was a young army lieutenant, Ulysses S. Grant, who immediately struck up a friendship with the merchant that was to last for years and be of great value to the Seligmans when Grant was elected president.

In the years before the Civil War, a store in San Francisco was added. The Seligmans were still in the dry goods business, but that was about to change. The stores in New York and San Francisco were contracted to supply the army with uniforms and decorations. Government finances were shaky at the outset of the war, and the army was soon in arrears to the Seligmans and other suppliers, placing them in a precarious financial condition. Joseph Seligman wrote to his business agent in Washington, demanding money that was owed: "Under the severe pressure of this burden we authorized you to make an arrangement for the payment of 400,000 of this sum in Treasury

7.30 Bonds . . . If I am unable to realize this sum very promptly I see no alternative but the suspension of our house which will drag down twenty other houses, and throw 400 operatives out of employ."[1] The agent saw to it that the bill was paid. More important, the dry goods merchants discovered the virtues of the famous 7-30s and took an immediate liking to Treasury obligations. They were even more impressed by the activities of Jay Cooke & Co.

Joseph Seligman volunteered his company's services to the government to sell bonds in Europe, but at first was rejected by Salmon Chase. Then, with the support of John Cisco, an assistant treasurer of the United States and rival of Jay Cooke, they finally won the day and were allowed to take subscriptions for the 7-30s. The commission was even smaller than that which Cooke received, only 0.20 of 1 percent, but it put the Seligmans on a new track that would change their business and introduce them to securities selling. Their idea was to use former connections to sell the bonds in Germany, known for its sympathies for the Northern rather than the Southern cause. Joseph departed for Europe to sell the bonds and soon was selling Cooke's 5-20s as well. In the past, the brothers had been fairly adventurous when opening new markets and stores for their goods, but the securities business was still somewhat new to them and the sums certainly were staggering when compared with the dry goods business. Unlike Cooke, the Seligmans would not commit to selling specific amounts of bonds and as a result had to remain content to be a part of Cooke's army of selling agents. They did succeed in placing more than $100 million worth of bonds, however, and gained the notice of the Treasury as a result.

Success convinced Joseph to become a banker. The Civil War was proving to be a crucible for Wall Street in ways that could not have been anticipated. Prudently, the older dry goods business was kept while the new banking house was being organized. J. & W. Seligman & Co. was established on May 1, 1864, and opened offices on Exchange Place in New York. James Seligman became a bond member of the New York Stock Exchange when it admitted separate members to its government bond department in 1869. Later, the house also joined the NYSE as a stock-trading member but never had a partner represent it on the floor. Unlike the Allens a generation before, the brothers realized that precipitously shifting from one business to the other was a mistake; they maintained their old offices as they slowly withdrew from the merchant business.

The Seligmans' interests were helped in the latter stages of the war by their close connections to Hugh McCulloch, Lincoln's last secretary of the treasury. Like their role models, the Rothschilds, they quickly recognized the importance of political ties that could advance their commercial interests. In America, Jay Cooke was the best example of that to date; the Seligmans recognized the benefits that his association with the often querulous Salmon Chase had produced over the years. But their advance into finance and Wall Street was slow. They contented themselves initially with trade finance, discounting bills of exchange, and gold dealing, and their house in San Francisco was particularly useful in that respect. They did not plunge into securities dealing immediately. With the two panics yet looming on the horizon, the choice proved to be a sound one. Instead, they worked closely on their relationships and moved slowly into the securities business.

Immediately after the war, new offices were opened in New Orleans and Paris. Relations with the Treasury were maintained despite some quarrels with officials about the partnership acting as a depository for the government. Business was good, especially in the South, where financing for the cotton business was in strong demand. But it was the election of Ulysses S. Grant as president that helped the Seligmans rise to prominence in a field becoming crowded with merchant bankers. In addition to the Yankee houses, several Jewish houses were also active. Goldman Sachs, Lazard Freres, and the House of Lehman all recognized the same opportunities as the Seligmans and were actively competing for business. Because of the vast size of the country, commodities prices varied considerably and businessmen with a talent for buying and selling in wholesale amounts quickly prospered. Solid business acumen and connections in high places would be vital for continued success. President Grant would provide the connection, although it would prove to be of dubious value owing to his administration's reputation for graft.

After her husband's assassination, the brothers took an active interest in the welfare of Mary Todd Lincoln. Mrs. Lincoln had developed a dubious reputation because of erratic behavior. At the time, presidential widows were not granted pensions by the government, so Mrs. Lincoln attempted to auction her personal belongings to raise money for herself and her son. She offended many by advertising an auction of her personal belongings in the New York newspapers. Her plight did not go unnoticed by the Seligmans. They actively petitioned President Grant on her behalf for a pension. At first Congress would not grant the pension. Despite the fact that Mrs. Lincoln was something of a profligate spender, the brothers paid her fare to Germany and paid some of her expenses while she lived there. Their generosity was widely noted. Mrs. Lincoln effectively was out of the public view and the government was spared the embarrassment of watching her live in poverty, although ironically her husband had left an estate of about $100,000. Congress eventually created a pension of $3,000 for the former first lady. The Seligmans' generosity was always assumed to have stemmed from their patriotism and love of their new country. It also provided invaluable public relations value for the new banking firm.

Immediately after the war, Joseph scored another major public relations coup when he invited Ulysses S. Grant and Confederate general P. G. Beauregard to dinner at his home. Seligman proved to be a gracious host, and by all accounts the two generals thoroughly enjoyed themselves, although Grant apparently drank too much. Diplomacy and tact proved to be valuable assets to the fledgling bank and would be well used in the future. This would prove particularly valuable when the house entered the securities markets, where political and business contacts were vital to success.

The Seligmans began to underwrite new securities in the late 1860s. Their first issue was for the New York Mutual Gas Light Company, one of the first companies to provide gas lighting for New York City. The fees on these early corporate bonds were certainly higher than those on Treasury issues, and revenues to the New York house began to increase substantially. The Seligmans also dabbled in railroad issues, but Joseph did not fully appreciate the business and as a result the firm's participation was limited. The increased underwriting profits helped them become even more active politically and they wholeheartedly supported Grant for reelection. The profits also provided a cushion against the unforeseen. The Panic of 1873 had no serious effect on their finances, and they survived the crisis intact. At the height of the panic, Joseph wrote to the London house, saying, "We have quite a panic in Wall Street and numerous failures, and the end is not yet. Jay Cooke & Co. suspended yesterday afternoon . . . Let us thank God that we have made no losses."[2]

Being able to survive the panic put the Seligmans in good stead. They would soon participate in the refinancing of Treasury bonds in which Jay Cooke and the Rothschilds participated on both sides of the Atlantic. Their relationship with the Grant administration and the Treasury proved somewhat tenuous, however. Eventually, they agreed to participate with the Rothschilds in the distribution of the new Treasury 5 percent bonds. At first, the London branch of the Rothschild house did not want the Seligmans included. They were still considered parvenus by the established bankers. But Joseph persisted and eventually won a part of the deal. Said Joseph: "Our connection with Rothschild will do us an immense deal of good both here and abroad and maybe lead to more transactions . . . Morgan [J. P. of Drexel, Morgan] is very bitter in his jealous expression about our getting the loan."[3] Many of Morgan's financial enemies, later to become colleagues in corporate bond syndicates, would learn that the powerful banker was intent on keeping them in second place. In a bond deal issued in 1877, Morgan clearly attempted to exclude the Rothschilds. That slight prompted Nathaniel Rothschild to remark that he "refused to join any American syndicate and be at their mercy or command, and would only take it up if we were given the lead to work it our own way with a group of friends around us."[4] But at the time, the Seligmans' influence with Grant was seen as indispensable. One of J. P. Morgan's partners remarked, concerning the relationship between Grant and Joseph Seligman, that, as long as he "fills the Presidential Chair the Seligmans will have the inside track in any of the operations of the Treasury and anybody wishing or intending to have any share of or a part in any syndicate for the funding of the public debt . . . will have to accept the situation and work with S."[5] The friendship proved to be one of the most enduring between a politician and a banker in the nineteenth century before the rise of J. P. Morgan.

Grant's friendship with the Seligmans both aided and hindered the family's reputation, especially since several of the Seligman brothers were also friendly with Jay Gould and his family. When Gould was jailed in 1868 for his activities at the Erie Railroad, the Seligmans posted his bail. When the gold corner occurred in 1869, the price hit 160 (of par) before the Treasury intervened, forcing its price down again. The first sell order came from Joseph Seligman after the peak

Jay Gould's reputation followed his heirs as well. During the closing stages of World War II, one of the war's stranger twists involved a member of the family. The former Florence Lacaze, the wife of Frank Jay Gould, Jay's youngest son, made a startling admission. She revealed that she had paid a large ransom to a bank in Monte Carlo in 1945 to prevent the Nazis from abducting her husband. The Germans interviewed Gould at his home on the Riviera but "never molested him." Apparently, they considered him French rather than American because he had lived in France for more than thirty years. Treasury Secretary Henry Morgenthau announced in Washington that an unnamed American and his wife were under investigation by French authorities for suspected collaboration with the Nazis because the bank to which the ransom was paid was Nazi controlled. Morgenthau later acknowledged that he was referring to the Goulds, stating, "I want to make it clear that the facts as to what they did are in the hands of the French government." The American army was sweeping through France at the time and the French were reasserting control over the country. Mrs. Gould not only admitted paying the ransom to keep her husband from being deported to a concentration camp but also arranged to have the French forces kidnap him after the ransom. She wanted to make sure that the Nazis did not get their hands on him after the deal. "After this money was paid I was not even then sure that I could trust these people, so I planned to have my own husband kidnapped," she said.

Shortly thereafter, she also admitted that she had donated two rare French tapestries from the family collection to the Metropolitan Museum of Art in New York to keep them out of the hands of Hermann Göring. Jay Gould's wealth proved to be something of an albatross for his heirs.

had been hit, and the price began to tumble afterward. Although assured that Washington had not ordered a release of gold, Gould decided upon hearing the news that he would sell his holdings before the price collapsed. He later noted that "I can only say that it is one of those conclusions that a man sometimes arrives at intuitively, that are correct in themselves, and yet if you undertake to give the evidences by which they are reached you could not tell how it was done."[6] Gould may have been telling only half the truth. Shortly before the sell order was given, Joseph visited Grant at his summer home in Long Branch, New Jersey. Grant asked for, and was given, a report by Joseph on the activities in the gold market. Joseph correctly deduced that Grant was about to act by supplying gold and told his son-in-law Abel Corbin, Gould's henchman, to get out of the market. The assumption afterward was that either Corbin or Seligman, or both, tipped Gould before the intervention came.[7] But those who saw a Jewish conspiracy at every corner assumed that the Seligmans had tipped Gould, allowing him to sell at a fat profit before the price collapsed.

While Joseph suspected the Rothschilds of being jealous of his increasing financial strength in the United States, anti-Semitism raised its head. It began to be evident even though Jews were a very small percentage of the population. Before Joseph died, he and his family decided to take a vacation at Saratoga Springs, New York, a familiar spot for them to relax, but they were denied admission to their once favorite hotel because they were Jewish. The slight was highly publicized, and most of the major banking houses, including Morgan, August Belmont, and the First National Bank of New York, came to their defense. There was even some social unrest in Saratoga Springs itself because of the slight. Oddly, the furor did not die down quickly, and many hotels in the Adirondacks began to openly dissuade Jews from registering.

After being in the country for forty years, Joseph could point with a great deal of pride to the position he had achieved in American society. But the affair at the hotel burdened him in his later years. When he died in April 1880 at age sixty-one, he was quickly and widely eulogized as one of the country's leading bankers and philanthropists. The general feeling, at least in the United States, was that the banking house he built had earned him the unofficial title "American Rothschild." One of his children's tutors, Horatio Alger, witnessed

After the Civil War, a young aspiring writer recently graduated from Harvard went to work for the Seligman family in New York as tutor to their children. He was able to witness firsthand the work ethic that made Joseph Seligman famous and wealthy. The Seligmans liked to perpetuate the up-the-hard-way stories after they had made their fortunes, especially in the face of competition they encountered from J. P. Morgan, who everyone knew had inherited his family's banking business. When the tutor—Horatio Alger—finally turned to writing children's novels, he had the perfect model for his own rags-to-riches stories. His *Ragged Dick* and scores of other stories about boys who worked their way to fame and fortune made him one of the best-known writers of the century.

Joseph's rise to fame and power firsthand and based some of his rags-to-riches stories on the elder Seligman's own life story. His rise was to become a legend in American banking circles and amply illustrated how success could be achieved in nineteenth-century America. What could not have been foreseen, however, is that the House of Seligman had already reached the pinnacle of its power under Joseph and would face increasingly stiff competition from other Jewish-American banking houses as the turn of the century approached. The Lehmans, Goldman Sachs, and Lazard Freres were already in similar lines of business and were diversifying about the same time as the Seligmans were. "Our Crowd" was becoming very crowded indeed.

Rise of the Lehmans

Unlike the Seligmans and Jay Cooke, the House of Lehman got its start south of the Mason-Dixon line and remained there for a long time. The similarities with the Seligmans were otherwise striking. Henry Lehman, the founder of the firm that would bear his name into the twenty-first century, was born in Germany in 1821. He emigrated to Alabama, where he set up a general-merchandise store in Montgomery in 1845. Like the Seligmans, Lehman began by trading general merchandise as well as cotton. After establishing himself, he sent for two of his brothers, Emanuel and Mayer.

Henry Lehman never lived to see his firm past the Civil War. He died of yellow fever when he was thirty-three, and his two brothers succeeded him at the firm. The Lehmans prospered and were slave owners before the Civil War.[8] Emanuel set up an office in New York City in 1858, recognizing that most of the cotton trade, especially international trade with Europe, was negotiated there. After the Civil War began, the blockade placed on trade with the South severely affected the Lehman brothers' business. But their success in helping the South avoid the blockade helped their reputation with the Confederate government considerably. Mayer developed many close contacts with the government in Richmond and became a trusted trade adviser despite his status as a new citizen. At the same time that the Seligmans were courting their friendship with Ulysses S. Grant, the governor of Alabama asked Mayer Lehman to travel north on a relief mission on behalf of the state. Armed with a letter from Jefferson Davis, Mayer hoped to persuade General Grant to allow him to conduct a relief mission for Southern prisoners of war. The governor of Alabama wrote a separate letter describing him as "a businessman of established character and one of the best Southern Patriots."[9] Mayer traveled north, but he was never able to gain an audience with Grant and his mission failed. His reputation and diplomatic skills were not yet as well developed as those of Joseph Seligman, but the firm's reputation would begin to expand during the years of Reconstruction.

After the war, Emanuel Lehman reinvigorated the firm's business in New York City following a three-year hiatus. The cotton business in the South resumed on a strong note, and the firm prospered. For the next fifteen years, the firm remained involved primarily in commodity-based trading. Then in 1880, Meyer Lehman, Henry's oldest son, joined the firm as a junior partner. Sigmund Lehman, the oldest son of Mayer, joined about the same time after graduating from Cornell. The second generation of Lehmans began to prosper in its own right and provided an element of continuity that would be vital to the firm's success in future years.

Lehman Brothers remained primarily a commodities-trading firm until the turn of the century. The firm was a founding member of many of the futures exchanges in New York, including the New York Cotton Exchange and the Coffee Exchange, and it joined the New

York Stock Exchange in 1887. When the firm was not trading or financing commodities, it engaged in many merchant banking activities in the cotton industry as well as mining and real estate ventures in the South. Like many of the merchant banking firms of the period, it also engaged in numerous railroad ventures. Banking also attracted the Lehmans' attention, and the firm helped establish many banks in and around New York. Probably the best known of these was the Trust Co. of America, founded in 1899.

As the second generation of Lehmans asserted their influence over the firm, the commodities business became less and less important and offices in the South were slowly closed. As the Industrial Revolution advanced, investments in railroads continued, but new industries were appearing constantly, especially in communications, manufacturing, and fuels. These new businesses presented opportunities to underwrite new securities and take equity positions as well. The rates of growth were greater than those in the traditional commodities business, and the young generation recognized the potential immediately.

The young Lehmans also took advantage of their family's increasing wealth and importance by marrying into other wealthy Jewish families in New York. In some cases, they married cousins, and these matches ensured that the firm would stay under family control for years to come. They also formed strategic friendships with their counterparts at other Jewish-American houses. Philip Lehman in particular was closely associated with Henry Goldman, the son of the founder of Goldman Sachs. The House of Lehman and Goldman Sachs united in many investment banking deals in the years before World War I; perhaps the best known was an initial stock offering for Sears, Roebuck & Co. The two houses shared about sixty investment banking clients, which they split when they went their separate ways, Goldman getting the lion's share. The two houses agreed not to actively compete with each other for business. The alliance was crucial to Lehman's initial success in investment banking and to the firm's development afterward as well.

Through the years, family control of the firm was absolute. No outsider was admitted to a partnership until 1924. Over the years, ten Lehmans were full partners in the firm, the best known of whom was Herbert Lehman, who became a partner in 1908 and retired in 1928 to enter public service. He eventually was elected governor of New York and U.S. Senator. In his later years, he was best remembered for a confrontation with Senator Joseph McCarthy at Senate hearings investigating purported Communist influence in the U.S. government in which he successfully called McCarthy's bluff over a document alleged to contain "treasonous" material. In 1953, McCarthy challenged Lehman, supposedly over his office's use of the franking privilege, into a wider discussion of his opinions on certain laws and his suitability for public office. The fight was best remembered for Lehman's steadfast refusal to be intimidated by McCarthy or to yield the Senate floor to him so that McCarthy could use the opportunity to bait him. The former investment banker's eye for detail and distaste of innuendo and hyperbole showed themselves. That particular battle was easily won by Lehman.

After 1900, Lehman Brothers turned its attention to investment banking. In the nineteenth century, the term had not been widely used or understood. Banking, as Jay Cooke & Co. and Clark Dodge and other investment firms practiced it, was actually a combination of commercial banking, securities dealing, and venture capital. This banking was actually the same sort of service provided by European firms such as the Rothschilds and Barings. Philip Lehman, the son of Emanuel, led the Lehman entry into investment banking. One of the first deals in which the firm became involved under his leadership was for the Electric Vehicle Company in 1897. Along with John Jacob Astor and P. Widener, Lehman helped establish this company that would develop the new manufacturing technology for the automobile. They also became involved in the establishment of several rubber companies that made tires for the new horseless carriages, especially the Rubber Tire Wheel Company and the Consolidated Rubber Tire Company.

At the turn of the century, syndicates were being used on a regular basis to underwrite new securities issues. The technique had evolved substantially since the days of Jay Cooke and now was the established method of bringing new securities to market. Lehman was included in many of the important syndicates, which also included Kidder Peabody & Co., Clark Dodge, J. P. Morgan, Goldman Sachs, and Kuhn Loeb. The House of Lehman was able to achieve this lofty status rather quickly, in view of its history as a commodities trading house. The high esteem in which it was held was due to its solid reputation in the commodities markets. Reputation and staying power character- ized the formation of syndicates in the prewar years and continued to do so into the 1920s. Unfortunately, to the outside world, these rela- tionships smacked of monopoly. At congressional hearings investigat- ing the money trust in 1912, the major investment bankers were interviewed concerning the way in which these syndicates were formed. George Baker of the First National Bank of New York testi- fied that when it came to inviting other banks into a syndicate, his bank dealt with "our friends rather than people we do not know." Jacob Schiff of Kuhn Loeb added a degree of functionality to the answer: "We make alliances for the occasion," he said. "We have no standing alliances."[10] Jewish firms had to scamper for business more than their gentile brethren did when it came to the underwriting business and therefore often would not enter into syndicates with one another.

The Lehmans' sterling reputation did not mean that they were conservative, however. Philip Lehman recognized many trends in American business in their early stages—some that other investment bankers failed or refused to recognize. The firm underwrote new issues for the Underwood Corp., the Studebaker Corp., and F. W. Woolworth Corp. All were new companies in new industries, and many traditional investment firms such as J. P. Morgan were reluctant to underwrite them. Morgan's neglect of the incipient auto industry before World War I was a major mistake that cost the bank millions in lost revenue. Lehman Brothers, on the other hand, gained a repu- tation for being both farsighted and savvy. Woolworth was the best example of the new trend in chain store expansion. The Lehmans rec- ognized the potential in having stores throughout the country; it was the same principle that they had practiced on a much smaller scale in their own business a generation before.

The Seligmans' history in the last years of the nineteenth century was remarkably similar to that of the Lehmans. Their friendship with President Grant continued after he left the White House, especially when he fell upon hard times. In 1884, a Wall Street firm in which the former president was a partner went bankrupt, costing Grant almost $250,000. The active partner in the firm, Ferdinand Ward, had embezzled more than $2 million from the firm, causing it to close. The affair severely affected Wall Street, and the market dropped considerably on the news. In the last year of his life, Grant was financially ruined and his family reputation put under a severe cloud. Jesse Seligman offered Grant financial assistance, but Grant refused. As he had often done during his presidency, Grant tended to trust the people around him, especially when it came to financial matters, but Ward was a charlatan and his shenanigans left the president a broken man and certainly hastened his death.

Both good luck and bad luck followed the firm in the post–Civil War years. In 1880, the Paris office asked New York to join a venture with a French company, headed by Ferdinand Marie deLesseps, to build the Panama Canal. The House of Seligman quickly agreed and joined a syndicate together with Drexel, Morgan & Co. and Winslow Lanier & Co. in an attempt to raise more than $100 million. Unfortunately, the venture was abandoned in 1889, incomplete and far above budget. The project was resurrected more than a decade later, during the administration of Theodore Roosevelt, with a different group of banks. Another twelve years was needed to complete the canal, which opened for sea traffic just as World War I was beginning. When it was completed, Panama had declared independence from Colombia and the canal became an entirely American affair. The Seligmans' participation waned over the years, but a sign of the times was about to affect the family again.

Anti-Semitism again raised its head in Jesse Seligman's later years. His son, Theodore Seligman, was denied membership in the Union League Club in New York. Membership should have been automatic since Jesse had been vice president of the club for years. The family eschewed any contact with the prestigious club in the following years. Like Joseph before him, Theodore took the slight very badly and it visibly disturbed him until his death in 1894.

Despite the growing anti-Semitism, the investment banking business proceeded as many new companies were coming to market. The firm underwrote the Buffalo Gas Company and participated with J. P. Morgan in the organization of the United States Steel Corp., the successor to the Carnegie Steel Company, which Morgan had purchased from Andrew Carnegie in 1900 for a record $500 million. Over the years, the Seligmans worked closely with the other Jewish firms as well as J. P. Morgan and August Belmont. During the first decade of the twentieth century, they had reached the top echelon of New York investment banks, a small club that was dubbed the "money trust" by members of Congress investigating the concentration of financial power in the United States. In an era of trusts, suspicion abounded that there was a money trust that dominated American banking without which it would be impossible to raise loans, bonds, or new stock issues. In reality, the trust was more akin to an oligopoly—what today we would call a "shared monopoly." About ten New York private banks overwhelmingly controlled the money made available for capital investment, and the Seligmans were certainly among them. In banking circles, it was an honor to be included and an obvious source of pride. It meant that a bank had reached the pinnacle of its profession.

Jacob Schiff and Kuhn Loeb

While the Seligmans and the Lehmans were establishing their family dynasties, yet another banking house was being formed. The path to New York for what would become Kuhn Loeb & Co. would be somewhat different from that of the Seligmans and the Lehmans. Abraham Kuhn and Solomon Loeb did not found their firm in New York until they had already amassed a small fortune in the textile and clothing business in Cincinnati. When they did finally open a New York bank, it was only at the prompting of Loeb's second wife, who could not bear Cincinnati and would think of living nowhere except New York.

Solomon Loeb had emigrated to the United States from Worms in the Rhineland in 1849. His mother chose Cincinnati as his destination because distant relatives lived in the city. Abraham Kuhn was already settled there and owned a factory that manufactured trousers. The two soon joined forces and opened a dry goods store on Nassau Street in New York to gain a much-needed outlet on the East Coast. Loeb became the New York partner, while Kuhn remained in Cincinnati to run the manufacturing operation. Before long they had married each other's sister and the family dynasty had begun. But fate appears to have interceded when Loeb's wife died in childbirth with the couple's second child. Characteristic of someone from a small, tight-knit clan of German Jews, Loeb returned to Germany to seek another wife. His second wife, Betty, whom he married after courting only briefly, accompanied him back to Cincinnati. She soon grew to detest the city and its two major industries, textiles and pork. A few years later, the partners were already thinking of retiring. Betty Loeb then realized that her husband had about $500,000 in assets, all accumulated in the previous twenty years. When she realized he was that rich, she insisted they move to New York. He obliged, and Loeb's assets became the start-up capital for Kuhn Loeb & Co., founded in 1867. Two partners were added—Abraham Wolff and Louis Hersheimer.

Shortly thereafter, Abraham Kuhn decided to retire and move back to Germany. The banking business was not to his liking, and he longed for his motherland. Again, fate came into play when Abraham met a young banker named Jacob Schiff. Impressed with the young man's banking skills, Kuhn suggested that Schiff write to Loeb in New York asking for job. Loeb offered one and Schiff embarked for New York, arriving in 1873 at the age of twenty-six. The firm he was joining was only six years old at the time and in desperate need of a strong guiding hand. Under Schiff's leadership, Kuhn Loeb would grow to become a rival of Lehman Brothers and the House of Seligman by the turn of the century. Schiff himself would become the second-best-known banker in New York after J. P. Morgan. The path to glory was mostly through railroad financing. Contrary to popular opinion, Kuhn Loeb was never the Rothschilds' agent in New York and had only a limited amount of business with the legendary European banking house.[11] Its fortune was made in New York purely as an American banking house.

Schiff's journey to Kuhn Loeb was as circuitous as Kuhn's own career. Unlike the Seligmans or the Lehmans, Schiff was born in 1847 into a wealthy, well-connected Frankfurt family of bankers, brokers, and scholars. They shared a house on the Judengasse with the Rothschild family. Jacob was a slight teenager, only about 5 feet 2 inches tall. His father, a stockbroker on the Frankfurt Stock Exchange, commandeered his son to work with him when the boy was sixteen. But young Jacob had other ideas. He escaped his family's clutches and ran off to New York. With newly made connections, he planned to open his own brokerage firm. Unfortunately for him and his potential partners, he was not of legal age. He returned to Germany and took a job working for a commercial bank where he quickly became bored, dreaming of one day returning to America. It was then that he met the retired Abraham Kuhn at Loeb's suggestion. If any of the German émigrés could lay title to the term "American Rothschild," it was Schiff, for it was he who was their social and intellectual equal. And the enormity of the projects in which he was engaged required a sharp intellect.

The major project for Kuhn Loeb in the years before the turn of the century was financing for the Union Pacific Railroad. The sorry history of the railroad since the Civil War, especially during the years of Jay Gould's leadership, had brought the railroad to its knees. Like most railroads of its era, the Union Pacific required grants of millions of acres of land and a large government subsidy for track building. More than $60 million of funds was made available, and of that amount, the public paid only $500,000. The federal government provided the balance by borrowing bonds, which were sold to the public. Schiff recognized the opportunity to both serve the government and earn investment banking fees in the process, much as Cooke and the Seligmans had before him.

After the panic of 1893 was resolved, and William McKinley was elected president, the country went through a period of prosperity. The first great merger boom occurred and hundreds of companies consolidated to form corporate America. In addition to U.S. Steel, other notable companies were formed, such as General Electric, American Telephone and Telegraph, and Westinghouse Electric and Manufacturing Co., to name but a few. The modern investment banking business emerged and bankers were earning fees from underwriting securities and taking equity positions in the new companies. As a result, the Kuhn Loeb partnership expanded. Between 1897 and 1903, the firm admitted some of its best-known partners, including Felix Warburg, Otto Kahn, Mortimer Schiff, and Paul Warburg. All were related to either Solomon Loeb or Abraham Loeb directly or by marriage.[12] This ensured continuity at the firm under Jacob Schiff. Deal making suited Schiff's personality perfectly. Since his teens he had displayed an aversion to dull, everyday work, and restructuring the railroads was the sort of task he reveled in. Ever since the Interstate Commerce Commission was formed in 1887, the major investment bankers in New York had competed furiously to dominate the railroad industry. J. P. Morgan made a vain attempt at consolidating the railroads immediately after the ICC was formed. Kuhn Loeb's dexterity in arranging financing was the major factor behind its success in the late nineteenth and early twentieth centuries. Major deals for the Pennsylvania Railroad, Southern Pacific Co., Royal Dutch Petroleum, and Shell Transport and Trading continued to ensure Kuhn Loeb's good reputation well into the twentieth century. These bond issues were sold both in the United States and abroad, helping the firm achieve an international reputation. Despite the firm's successes in the marketplace, however, the partners were not entirely devoid of the larger perspective of international banking.

Schiff also became an adviser to Theodore Roosevelt. Both men were concerned about the weakness of the banking system in the absence of a central bank. They worried especially about the inelasticity of money, meaning that the supply of money was not particularly sensitive to market conditions. This became very important during panics, especially the one in 1907, because the amount of money in circulation could hasten a bank's failure. At that time, J. P. Morgan arranged standby lines of funds to instill into the system along with funds provided by the Treasury. But arrangements like those were becoming more and more difficult as time wore on, because Progressive critics maintained that Wall Street manufactured many of the panics so that it could make money on the bailouts it helped provide. But Schiff also realized that proposals for a new central bank were radical and had to proceed diplomatically, especially since there was still a strong anti-Semitic undercurrent in the country and Kuhn Loeb and the other Jewish-American bankers did not want to openly advocate the import of foreign ideas into American banking.

Paul Warburg, Jacob Schiff's brother-in-law, had only recently immigrated to the United States from Germany and spoke English with a clipped British accent. As one of a handful of Jewish-American bankers in favor of creating a central bank in the years prior to World War I, he was invited to a clandestine meeting organized by Senator Nelson Aldrich of Rhode Island at Jekyll Island, off the Georgia coast, in 1910 to discuss the potential organization of a new central bank. At the time, he was not yet an American citizen; he would be naturalized in 1911. Warburg actively supported the creation of the Federal

Reserve System and subsequently accepted a seat on its board when nominated by Woodrow Wilson in 1914. While still an active partner in the firm, Jacob Schiff often told him to keep his remarks to himself regarding the issue because Schiff was opposed to the idea for political rather than economic reasons. Warburg had recently written a paper concerning his ideas for a central bank and sent a copy to James Stillman, chairman of the National City Bank of New York. Shortly thereafter, he was confronted in his office by Stillman, who asked, "Don't you think the City Bank has done pretty well . . . why not leave things alone?" Warburg's answer was based on his understanding of past panics. He replied, "Your bank is so big and so powerful that when the next panic comes, you will wish your responsibilities were smaller."[13] His remarks proved prescient for National City, although the Crash of 1929 was still almost two decades away. National City would become one of its most visible victims, losing both its chief executive and its lucrative investment banking subsidiary.

Like Stillman and National City, most of the New York private banking firms opposed the idea of the new central bank simply because they were making too much money without one. When the U.S. Treasury required assistance in raising bonds for either war or reserves, the private bankers were more than willing to step in and assist—for a price. A new central bank meant that they would ultimately have to surrender some of their authority in the money and capital markets. This was a particularly American banking fear, since the Europeans had far more experience with central banks and did not necessarily fear their power. The Americans remembered the chaos created when the second Bank of the United States failed during Andrew Jackson's administration and wished to avoid a repeat of that particular fiasco. But Schiff's advocacy of more efficient banking did not mean that he openly supported all of the money trust's activities.

Being a member of the highest echelons of banking did not compromise Schiff's principles. In 1915, J. P. Morgan helped arrange the largest single financing to date, a massive bond issue called "the Anglo-French loan of 1915." The proceeds were to be used to help finance war efforts against Germany. All of the major banking houses were invited to participate, including Kuhn Loeb. But Jacob Schiff objected. He wanted assurances that proceeds would not be passed to

Russia, which had a record of anti-Semitism. Naturally, such assurances could not be given, and Kuhn Loeb did not participate in the issue as an underwriter. Its partners, however, privately subscribed for large amounts on an individual basis.

Years of anti-Semitism had not been forgotten. Rarely had principle intervened in investment banking deals the way it did in this particular instance. But the media did not see it as a matter of principle. One newspaper made it headline news by trumpeting "Kuhn Loeb, German Bankers, Refuse to Aid Allies." More repercussions followed. The Germans assailed Kuhn Loeb, emphasizing the partners' purchasing of the bonds individually. In an attempt to salvage the firm's image, Schiff then advocated the underwriting of a Belgian bond even though his partners feared that the proceeds might well fall into the hands of the Germans.[14]

The period between the Civil War and World War I was both profitable and hazardous for investment banking firms. Those houses that survived the panics of 1869, 1873, 1884, 1893, 1903, and 1907—not to mention the closing of the New York Stock Exchange for several months at the outset of World War I—found themselves well positioned to take advantage of the boom that followed the war. The economy and the marketplace were becoming larger constantly, and the partnerships needed to expand to provide both necessary capital and extra manpower. Despite the Clayton Act of 1914, many investment banks placed their partners in directorships of as many companies as possible. J. P. Morgan & Co. proved to be the most powerful, with the partners holding hundreds of directorships of various companies. But "Our Crowd" was not far behind. While having fewer partners than Morgan, the Seligmans, Lehmans, Kuhns, Loebs, and Schiffs were all strategically placed on the boards of public companies to take advantage of as much business as possible. Despite congressional probing, the "money trust" was alive and well and survived the trust-busting years of Roosevelt, Taft, and Wilson.

The New Era

After the dismal days of the First World War, the 1920s became what many commentators called the New Era. Consumers had more money to spend, and industry developed new goods and services to help them spend it. Radios, automobiles, and new housing all expanded at record rates. The short yet severe recession of 1920–21 only delayed the greatest boom in American history. Most of the investment banking firms participated and reaped the benefits of the great boom by engaging in their traditional activities as well as dipping their toes in retail brokerage. Others were not convinced that selling stocks to the public was a business they wanted to engage in.

Of the three major Jewish-American banking houses, the Seligmans were middle-of-the-road in their approach to new business. Before the war, they became involved in financing General Motors along with Lee Higginson & Co. and Kuhn Loeb after GM's founder, William C. Durant, lost control of the company for the first time. He would lose control a second time, permanently, as the 1920s began. The Seligmans also continued their traditional advisory business by becoming financial advisers to Nicaragua with Brown Brothers & Co., an old, established New York banking firm. But the 1920s brought new challenges and the firm began to change its traditional nature to take advantage. As the 1920s began, several of their partners and longtime employees retired and the need for new blood became evident. Albert Strauss, a partner, remained in his post at the Federal Reserve Board, and only one senior partner remained at the beginning of the busiest decade in years. New partners were needed quickly, and a decision was made to use the firm's legal advisers, Cravath and Henderson, to recruit new faces.

The new partners helped bring about a gradual transformation of the Seligman House. Since its inception, J. & W. Seligman had been primarily an underwriter of bonds and occasionally preferred stocks. But the New Era was not characterized by conservative investing. A small revolution on Wall Street brought many new investors to the market—investors who previously had kept their savings in banks. The new prosperity brought many of these new investors into securities investments for the first time. The Seligman firm recognized the trend and began to underwrite more and more common stocks. In 1924, it underwrote its first common stock issue of the postwar period for Briggs Manufacturing Co. Underwritings followed for Dodge Brothers, Cunard Steamship Company, United Artists Theaters, and

Schubert Theater Corp. A retail sales department was opened in 1927 by a salesman brought in from another retail-oriented firm, and the company opened offices in Albany, Chicago, Philadelphia, Pittsburgh, San Francisco, and Washington D.C., in addition to New York.[15]

By the late 1920s, J. & W. Seligman had ten active partners, with Henry Seligman the most senior among them. Frederick Strauss was also a senior partner, and in many ways the captain of the ship. He numbered many industrialists and statesmen among his colleagues and friends. One day a new receptionist at the office announced to him that "there is some nut out here who claims he's John D. Rockefeller and wants to see you. What shall I do with him?" The founder of Standard Oil was shown into Strauss's office.

In the years immediately preceding the Crash of 1929, corporate underwritings continued at a brisk pace. Perhaps the best-known deal the partnership underwrote was for the Minneapolis-Honeywell Regulator Company, later known as Honeywell Inc., the future electronics and computer company. Then in 1925, another partner, Francis Randolph, made a proposal that would have a profound long-term effect on the House of Seligman. He proposed that the company sponsor an investment company, today known as a mutual fund. Several years later, the issue was raised again. In the interim, several hundred funds had been established on Wall Street and the trend appeared to be growing. The funds were not necessarily pitched at the very small investor but at those with sizable assets and little experience with investing.

The new investment fund was an immediate hit. It was named the Tri-Continental Corporation, since it invested on three continents, not solely in the United States. The Seligmans hired full-time staff and analysts to oversee it, not just market it to investors. The first fund sold out very quickly, and the second was launched shortly thereafter. Unfortunately, the second was launched on August 15, 1929, two months before the fateful market drop in October. In the summer, however, the market was still very strong and euphoria prevailed. Ironically, the first investment for the new fund was an order for U.S. Steel, a stock that plummeted sharply when the market turned down. It was also the same stock that J. P. Morgan would try to prop up by asking Richard Whitney, president of the NYSE, to place an order to buy as the Crash was occurring.

The Crash provided a wrenching experience for the traditionally small but influential Jewish-American partnerships. The Dow Jones Industrial Average's 10 percent collapse, the largest to date, signaled a change in the market structure in the United States and would usher in a new political era as well. In this respect, it was much more than just an old-fashioned panic. It had all of the hallmarks of a radical change in American society. The clubby atmosphere of the partnerships would continue for another generation, but their smug attitude toward investors and even the stock market would begin to change irrevocably. By 1929, the Seligmans were certainly one of the firms with the most patrician attitude. The day the market crashed, October 28, Jefferson Seligman visited the floor of the NYSE for the first time. He was the partner of the firm to whom the seat on the exchange was assigned, but he had never been on the floor before. In fact, no partner of the firm ever visited the floor in the firm's history, although the seat had been purchased in its early years. *Fortune* magazine commented that he was there "to see what a market crash was like." While the market was collapsing in bedlam around him, Seligman watched bemusedly, dressed in a frock coat and striped trousers with a bright flower in his lapel—his usual business attire.[16] While one of the New York afternoon papers commented that his presence had a calming effect on the market, it was stretching the point. Visits from senior bankers were not going to stop the rout any more than buy signals from J. P. Morgan were. The day the market dropped, society and Wall Street attitudes quickly changed with it. In a sense, the days of the partnerships were already numbered, although the cycle would not be complete for another fifty years.

Although the Seligmans were hurt by the Crash, the severity of the impact was not as great as it might have been. The partners decided to adopt a long-term strategy, in the hope that the market would rebound. They trimmed their staff and then rehired many of those employees shortly thereafter. But the market for shares of investment companies took a severe beating during the latter months of 1929 and into 1930. The travails of the investment trusts marketed by Goldman Sachs were the best-known, but not the only, examples of funds that behaved very poorly as the market dropped.

The postwar years brought prosperity to Lehman Brothers as well, but the firm adopted a more aggressive game plan than did the Seligmans. The corporate underwritings that began about 1906 proceeded full steam after the war, but the manpower problem was similar. At war's end, Lehman had only five partners, including Philip, Herbert, and Arthur. The first nonfamily member, John M. Hancock, was admitted in 1924. Another nonfamily member, Paul Mazur, joined shortly after and would become known for his writings on the retailing industry, a neat fit with the firm's underwriting history.

Philip Lehman kept the firm on an even keel by continuing to finance the same sort of firms that the unofficial alliance with Goldman Sachs had produced before the war. Retailers were brought to market along with underwritings for automobile manufacturers and food companies. While the Seligmans preferred bond underwritings, Lehman underwrote both common and preferred stocks primarily. In fact, it did not establish a bond department until 1922. The boom years of the 1920s were not totally devoid of new bond offerings; in fact, much of the underwriting business was devoted to them rather than stocks. But the hefty fees were to be found in common stock issues, and that is where the Lehmans shined. The increased profits finally led them to occupy their own building at One William Street, replete with its own entertainment and dining facilities, said to be the most lavish on Wall Street.

Kuhn Loeb suffered the worst in the postwar years when it lost its guiding light. Jacob Schiff died in 1920 at age seventy-three. His death was a major event in New York, reported on the front page of all the major newspapers. The day of the funeral, the streets were lined with poor Jews from the Lower East Side who were not allowed into the services, and Governor Al Smith and the mayor of New York attended. At his death, Schiff left an estate of $35 million, less than half that of J. P. Morgan, who had died eight years before.[17] His death left the firm with only four partners. Like the Seligmans', the firm's underwriting track record was impressive, but was mostly for bonds rather than common stocks. Kuhn Loeb did not tally the number of underwritings done in a year and compare itself to others; it would total them for a decade or twenty years. This was part of the firm's emphasis on its long track record with its corporate clients. The best-known partner after Schiff's death, Otto Kahn, summarized the partnership's long-term approach to investment banking when he said, "It has long been our policy and our effort to get our clients, not by chasing after them, not by praising our own wares, but by an attempt to establish a reputation."[18] In this respect his philosophy was not unlike that of the Seligmans, but both firms were in fact emulating J. P. Morgan. In front of a congressional committee investigating banking in 1912, Morgan claimed that no man could get a nickel from him for a loan if he did not trust his character. Chasing business was beneath many investment bankers, or so they would have the world believe, but they all actively and aggressively courted business at every opportunity.

Like other financiers, Otto Kahn of Kuhn Loeb was worried about the inflated stock market in the late 1920s. Bernard Baruch, Joseph P. Kennedy, and Charles Merrill would all correctly anticipate the market crash and adopt defensive positions so that their funds and firms would survive. Economist and statistician Roger Babson had also been proclaiming that the end was near, and apparently Kahn agreed, but not publicly. Former partner Paul Warburg, previously a member of the Federal Reserve Board and roommate of Kahn in London during their younger days, constantly warned him about the danger inherent in the market, and Kahn took the advice seriously. Kuhn Loeb maintained very conservative positions during the late 1920s, and they saved the firm serious losses when the Crash occurred. But Kahn's public utterances about the condition of the market were more of the standard Wall Street line. As late as 1928, he stated that the market "curve is upward and will continue so for many years." Concerning Babson, he said that he was "as wrong as any other man who deals solely in statistics . . . there is nothing in the underlying conditions in the business world at this time to indicate anything but a continuance of prosperity."[19] The lack of candor about the market was natural for someone who made a living from it, but it would prove somewhat lukewarm when congressional hearings were called to investigate the Crash.

Despite their straitlaced business philosophy, both Lehman Brothers and Kuhn Loeb managed to have fun with their corporate clients. Both were active underwriters of motion picture studios, and their partners were involved with the studios on a personal level as well. Kahn of Kuhn Loeb was one who had become smitten with Hollywood. Despite his strong work ethic and the fact that he had once

Otto Kahn of Kuhn Loeb was a benefactor of the Metropolitan Opera in New York. He served as its president for years and attempted to introduce reforms that were considered too radical for the times. In 1929, he helped produce a German opera, *Jonny Spielt Auf,* which departed from classical opera. It was mostly jazz and included an onstage car crash. Opera patrons were outraged, especially since it called for saxophones in the orchestra, which were not traditional orchestra instruments. In the late 1920s, Kahn also made plans to build a new opera house in midtown Manhattan that would reflect the times by being more democratic in its architecture and interior layout. The number of boxes for the wealthy would be reduced so that more orchestra seating could be made available. This, too, raised the ire of other existing patrons, including J. P. Morgan Jr. The outcry was so fierce that Kahn eventually abandoned his plans.

Kahn also supported the early cinema and actors. Along with Clarence Dillon, he became something of a legend for being mentioned in a film. Dillon even had one named after him, *The Wolf of Wall Street.* In her first talking picture, *My Man* (1928), Fanny Brice sang a song addressed to Kahn:

> **Is something the matter with Otto Kahn**
> **Or is something the matter with me?**
> **I wrote a note and told him what a star I would make.**
> **He sent it back and marked it "Opened by mistake."**

Kahn remained a fan of Brice throughout her career. And the song helped his celebrity considerably.

considered running for Parliament before coming to the United States, Kahn enjoyed the worldly pleasures of the motion picture industry. In 1928, he made a speech in front of Paramount executives in which he stated that the industry "has opened up dull, narrow lives with romance and beauty, novelty and stimulation." Hollywood was just as happy to attract serious financiers, because it gave it an aura of respectability. Kahn ventured west to Hollywood, accompanied by Ivy Lee, the acknowledged founder of the public relations industry and adviser to John D. Rockefeller. He wanted to visit and see first-hand the industry that he had adopted as his own. He became friends with noted actors of the period, including Charlie Chaplin, and soon discovered how exciting the business could be when he agreed to finance several actresses so that they could study in Europe. The Hearst newspapers quickly picked up the story, although Kahn vigorously denied it. However, it was somewhat difficult for him to completely disavow the story because, before he began his trip, he cabled a Paramount executive asking him to arrange a reception with plenty of members of the opposite sex present, "though it is not necessary to have it 100 percent blonde, inasmuch as fortunately tastes vary."[20] Thus began a Wall Street flirtation with Paramount and Hollywood that would last for decades.

Kahn was also a major benefactor of the Metropolitan Opera, becoming a major shareholder in the opera company shortly after its founding around the turn of the century. His involvement with it lasted for more than thirty years, and he poured several million dollars into the company, ensuring its rise to prominence as one of the world's renowned companies. He also owned one of the first serious movie houses in the country devoted to serious, artistic films rather than popular, Hollywood-style productions. Like many members of Our Crowd, his involvement with the arts helped New York achieve a status on a level with London and Paris. The contribution was significant because several generations before, Jay Gould and Jim Fisk had endowed the arts, in a manner of speaking, with an opera house adjacent to the offices of the Erie Railroad. Fisk kept close relationships with some of the "actresses" on the company's payroll until a male friend of one of them shot him dead, touching off a major New York scandal. Now the arts were becoming respectable in New York and were a source of pride rather than simply a vulgar showcase for rich financiers' dreams.

Passing of the Old Guard

Although the three partnerships survived the Crash of 1929, events over the next four years would change their business philosophies and futures substantially. Late in 1932, Herbert Hoover launched an investigation into stock market practices that eventually led to a drastic overhaul of the securities industry. The investigators floundered at first, but in 1933, while Franklin Roosevelt was awaiting inauguration, they picked up substantial momentum and began interviewing both stock market officials and investment bankers concerning the Crash.

These became known as the Pecora hearings, named after their chief counsel, Ferdinand Pecora. Dozens of witnesses were called to testify, including J. P. Morgan and other senior investment bankers of the period. The focus of the hearings was similar to that of the hearings a generation before. The top New York investment bankers dominated Wall Street and charged what appeared to be noncompetitive fees to their underwriting clients. Pecora was a feisty New York lawyer in the Progressive mode who favored competitive bidding by investment bankers for new issues of securities rather than negotiated fees, which were the norm. His hearings, which proved sensational, occurred at the same time that the new Roosevelt administration had to deal with the banking crisis during the darkest days of the Depression. As a result, they provided strong impetus for Congress to pass both the Securities Act of 1933 and Banking Act of 1933, the latter known as the Glass-Steagall Act.

Pecora had little difficulty demonstrating that the investment bankers acted with impunity, serving their own interests before those of clients. One of his main areas of contention was the investment trusts that had grown so popular in the 1920s. After the Crash many of them dropped significantly in value, some becoming almost worthless. The Goldman Sachs funds, which performed poorly, were singled out by Pecora as marketing gimmicks that had little value in a bear market. The Seligmans' funds did not come under criticism, but the activities of Kuhn Loeb did, much to the distresses of its partners, who were not accustomed to criticism from the outside.

Pecora was particularly interested in the organization and financing of the Pennroad Corp., a holding company that was organized in 1929 just months before the Crash. The purpose of the company was to allow the Pennsylvania Railroad to acquire properties that could be used for expansion. In reality, it was a vehicle used for fending off the Alleghany Corporation, a holding company organized by J. P. Morgan to encroach on other railroads' properties. The company's stock, most of which was provided by the existing shareholders of the Pennsylvania, was entrusted to the railroad's directors and locked up for ten years so that the actual shareholders had no vote in Pennroad's affairs. Pecora seized upon the lack of accountability of the Pennsylvania to the shareholders and the fact that the new shares also were distributed to friends and preferential customers of Kuhn Loeb. It was pointed out that Kuhn Loeb designed the company and was largely responsible for the financing scheme. The firm's profits for the undertaking were more than $1 million, and by selling stock options it made almost $3 million more, which it retained for itself. All of this came at a time when the country was mired in depression; investment banking profits looked especially obscene in the wake of widespread unemployment and economic ruin.

Otto Kahn testified that in the four years that had passed since the Pennroad Corporation was formed he had had a change of heart about its organization. Realizing that the shareholders were placed at a disadvantage, he stated that many of details of the organization were "inventions of the devil." Perhaps he had a double-entendre in mind, although Jay Gould, the master of railroad financing, had been dead for forty years. And Kahn had other problems with Pecora. The interrogator pointed out that Kahn had paid no income taxes between 1930 and 1932 and had been involved in what he thought were underhanded stock dealings with his daughter so that he could claim losses. Kahn pointed out in his clipped British accent that he had no knowledge of such things, that they were always left to his accountant. He did try to square things with the committee by denouncing short selling, singled out by Herbert Hoover and Pecora as one of the market's most self-destructive devices. "The raiding of the stock market, the violent marking up and down of other people's possessions, is in my opinion a social evil," he declared to Pecora when the committee's attention had turned toward market practices.[21] While politically correct at the time, the comment showed the distance that the private bankers tried to maintain between themselves and the rough and tumble of the market.

Ultimately, both Kahn and Kuhn Loeb escaped the full wrath of Pecora, although it was becoming painfully obvious to the old guard of investment bankers that their practices were no longer sacrosanct and that they were now coming under the public eye in ways not imagined twenty years before.

The Pecora hearings also enabled Kahn to describe Kuhn Loeb's approach to banking. By the late 1920s, it was clear that the old-line investment banks were on different tracks. The Seligmans had gone the way of investment trusts, Lehman was underwriting small and medium-size companies, and Kuhn Loeb maintained its traditional business of advising larger corporations in what would become known as relationship banking. Kahn described the approach when asked how his firm conducted its business. He responded, "It has long been our policy and our effort to get clients, not by chasing after them, not by praising our own wares, but by an attempt to establish a reputation which would make our clients feel that if they have a problem of a financial nature, Dr. Kuhn Loeb & Co. is a pretty good doctor to go to."[22] This was essentially the same concept propounded by J. P. Morgan at the committee hearings, and it was similar to the testimony given by Pierpont Morgan at the Pujo Committee hearings twenty years before. White-glove investment banking meant that the firm's reputation would enable it to remain above the common fray of having to hustle for business. Morgan and Kuhn Loeb were the best practitioners of the method, although Kidder Peabody and Dillon Read also liked to think that business came to them because of their reputation. Relationship banking would survive for another forty years before succumbing to competitive pressures. In the 1930s it was an indirect admission that a money trust still existed that valued relationships above competitive pricing for securities issues. But as described by Kahn, it seemed an enviable position to be in at the time.

But it was not the Pecora hearings that proved most drastic to the old-line partnerships. Congress passed the Securities Act of 1933 and then, a month later, the Glass-Steagall Act. The Securities Act was particularly vexatious to investment bankers, because it required companies that wanted to sell securities to register them with a government agency (a year later, the authority was transferred to the newly created Securities and Exchange Commission) and provide full financial disclosure. No investment banker was in favor of the law, and many started to organize against it. But when Glass-Steagall was passed, their anger turned to rage because of its major provision. Within twelve months, banks had to decide which part of the banking business they wanted to remain in. They could be either investment banks or commercial banks, but not both. A provision in the law limited the amount of revenue that a commercial bank could earn from securities dealings to 10 percent or less. Congress had effectively created a divorce between the two sides of banking. The only remaining question was which direction the banks would choose.

The question was relatively simple to answer for Lehman and Kuhn Loeb. Both were essentially investment banks that also accepted deposits, so when the time came for a decision, deposit taking was shed in favor of the securities business. The firms quickly recognized that they could survive without taking deposits. The idea was to separate deposits from the risks of the markets, but the theory and the actual results were quite different. Most of the banks that underwrote securities in a meaningful way survived the Crash of 1929 and their depositors did not suffer any significant losses. But this legislation was a convenient way of getting the investment bankers out of the business of controlling credit. The law was actually a radical departure from the past. After 1934, the notion of a private banker became almost defunct. Banks now took deposits and made loans, and securities firms underwrote and distributed securities. The twain would not meet again until the last year of the century. But it was the beginning of a significant change for the fortunes of the partnerships, which now found themselves regulated for the first time.

The Seligmans also changed, but in a different manner. The change to investment management through Tri-Continental convinced the partners that fund management was their future, not investment banking. They spun off the securities business to the newly formed Union Securities Corp., and the House of Seligman became fund managers exclusively. Francis Randolph, the president of Tri-Continental, put it succinctly when he said that "suddenly the federal government had thrown a great big rock into the channel, diverting it radically. At first, the tendency was to curse the rock, but before long we realized that as investment men our job was not to belabor the diversion but to figure out where the stream was going."[23] From that moment, the House of Seligman was no longer a factor on the "sell side" of Wall Street. They were now to become major players on the "buy side." Union Securities continued in the investment banking business until 1956, when it was merged with Eastman Dillon & Co. to form Eastman Dillon, Union Securities & Co.

The only traditional private bankers to opt for commercial banking were J. P. Morgan and Brown Brothers Harriman. Morgan spun off Morgan Stanley & Co., a new investment bank, headed by his son and former employees of the bank. Drexel & Co., a longtime Morgan affiliate, was also spun off as a separate investment bank. Morgan apparently believed that the Glass-Steagall Act and the Roosevelt administration would be short-lived and that the two sides of banking would be reunited when the country came to its senses. Unfortunately for the Morgan partnership, both assumptions proved incorrect. It was the most serious miscalculation Morgan had made since his father and former partners had refused to take the automobile industry seriously. The Roosevelt revolution on Wall Street proved to be the most influential factor affecting the organization of the securities firms since the Panic of 1837. Within a few years, it became painfully obvious to Wall Street that it was the most influential of the century.

Changing Tides

The 1930s and 1940s were quiet decades for Wall Street in general. The Depression did not bring much opportunity for fat profits, and the war years that followed were similarly quiet. During the war, most financing occurred for the U.S. Treasury, which needed to raise enormous amounts to finance the war effort on both fronts. Wall Street firms certainly helped in the effort, but the margins of profit on commissions were negligible and most firms that helped the Treasury did so purely out of patriotism. Politicians in Washington remembered well the stories about Jay Cooke and the financing of the Civil War, and many had personally experienced the financing arranged by the investment bankers that brought so much criticism during the First World War. The war against Germany and Japan would be devoid of criticism when compared to those previous conflicts.

Once the war was over, prosperity returned—and with it the fortunes of the Wall Street partnerships. But a new phenomenon appeared that actually bore the seeds of the partnerships' destruction, although it would take another generation to run its course. The small investor appeared on the scene in the 1950s in numbers that made the 1920s look serene by comparison. Rising wages and pent-up demand for all sorts of consumer goods—and securities—brought the retailers into the spotlight. Sears Roebuck, Marshall Field, and Paramount Pictures all proved enormously popular, as did the products of General Motors, General Electric, and RCA. But the banks that had brought many of the retailers to market years earlier were not so lucky, because the concept of retailing was not well developed on Wall Street. And the firms that did specialize in selling stocks to the public were still frowned upon by the old-line investment bankers. Wall Street was going to have to learn to play catch-up with American society as a whole.

Some of the smaller Our Crowd firms that entered the investment banking fray late were more attuned to the change than were the old-line firms. Loeb, Rhoades & Co. was founded in 1931 at a time when prospects for Wall Street were not particularly healthy. Carl Loeb, who had retired as president of the American Metal Company, founded the company. His son, John, who married a daughter of Arthur Lehman, ran the new firm, which absorbed an older firm, Rhoades & Co., shortly after its own founding and developed into a medium-size firm that had a large retail operation. Throughout its short history, John Loeb, who ruled the partnership in a manner akin to that of Jacob Schiff or J. P. Morgan, dominated Loeb Rhoades. His paternal attitude and generosity for favorite causes were legendary, but he clearly belonged to the previous generation. He opposed several reforms that were beginning to take shape on Wall Street, notably a move toward negotiated commissions by NYSE member firms. He also opposed investment banks selling stock in themselves and going public, something that Donaldson, Lufkin & Jenrette and Merrill Lynch accomplished much later, in the early 1970s. His firm was clearly doing business more characteristic of a 1920s firm than one of the late 1960s and early 1970s. But the investment banking and brokerage business was good for Loeb, who proudly displayed a portrait of himself painted by Salvador Dali in his Westchester home.[24] Although the firm was an underwriter for many companies, brokerage was an important part of its revenues, a fact based on the simple principle that selling what one underwrote was an important part of the service provided to corporate clients.

If the firm had survived as an independent, its stature undoubtedly would have been greater. It could easily have been compared to the Seligman firm or Kuhn Loeb, since its clientele, both retail and institutional, was from the wealthy ranks. Under Loeb's guidance, it achieved a remarkable degree of success until its fortunes turned down in the early 1970s. Loeb himself was named an "honorary WASP" by *Time* magazine, a title that would have made the Seligmans of previous generations envious. But the firm's undoing also was attributable to the bull market of the 1960s and all of the investors it attracted. In the late 1960s, the sheer volume of orders experienced by many of the brokerage firms led to a serious breakdown in backroom activities, the place where customer orders were processed. The problem became so bad that the stock exchanges and member firms proclaimed a holiday during the workweek to attempt a cleanup. It was not entirely successful. Many firms actually succumbed to the pressures of lost or unrecorded customer orders and finally were forced to close their doors or seek merger partners with healthier firms. Loeb, Rhoades was hit with the same problem because its management did not pay attention to such mundane matters, and it lost money. As a result, in 1977 it sought a merger with another medium-size member firm, Hornblower, Weeks, Noyes & Trask. After the merger, the situation worsened when it was discovered that Hornblower's back room was in even worse condition.

The situation lasted until 1979, when the firm was bought by Shearson Hayden Stone and became Shearson Loeb Rhoades. The deal was executed by Sanford Weill, who years before had begun his career as a runner at Bear, Stearns after graduating from Cornell. Like many Wall Streeters, he had a difficult time finding his first job before landing one that enabled him to learn the ways of the Street. The merger was a major coup for Shearson but something of a setback for Loeb, Rhoades, which had always considered itself the embodiment of the traditional, somewhat supercilious investment banking tradition begun in the previous century. It was an example of what would become a long line of mergers that would leave few traditional firms still perched at the top of the Wall Street tree.

The great irony for many prestigious firms was that although their prowess in the market was never doubted, their capital was limited. Some of the activities they engaged in, like advising on mergers and acquisitions, required market savvy and strong corporate relationships, but little actual capital had to be deployed. Kuhn Loeb and Lehman were very adept at advising on mergers; it was a natural extension of their vast contacts in the corporate world at a time when American industry was consolidating at a record pace. But in areas where capital was required, such as underwriting and trading, partnerships were proving to be a liability. The firms had to have enough capital on their books to satisfy their bankers and commit to deals that were becoming larger and larger all the time. New stock and bond deals were setting records every year for amounts raised in the 1960s and 1970s. As revenues increased, so did the urge to cash in on the good fortune. Traditionally, partnerships had allowed the individual partners to cash out when they retired or occasionally to tap the partnership pool for money. Lehman put a stop to the practice after the war and required partners to leave their money with the firm until retirement, and then take it only on a periodic basis. Clearly, the partnership format was rapidly becoming obsolete in a world where deals were becoming bigger all the time. Permanent capital was needed.

In the postwar years, Kuhn Loeb began to experience the winds of change more quickly than did some of the larger names. Still one of Wall Street's most prestigious firms, its focus was somewhat narrow when compared to that of its larger brethren. The firm never sold securities directly to the public, preferring to distribute its underwritings to selling agents instead—those houses on Wall Street that could not or did not underwrite new securities. The top brackets for most corporate underwriting deals were still clubbish, with Morgan Stanley, Kuhn Loeb, Lehman Brothers, and Kidder Peabody among the firms that used others as selling group members to distribute securities. As in the days of Jay Cooke, fees for this group were smaller than those for the underwriters, although it was recognized that crumbs from the table were better than no crumbs at all. But a revolution stirring at the middle of the Wall Street pecking order was beginning to work its way slowly to the top. Investment banks with extensive sales forces were commanding more and more respect and were being invited into deals because of their ability to sell to the public. Those firms that could not make that claim found themselves increasingly isolated in a changing world and soon needed to seek merger partners.

Finally, in 1977, the inevitable occurred when Kuhn Loeb lost its independence and merged with Lehman Brothers. The firm was running very low on capital and was in danger of having to scale back its operations in order to survive. Pete Peterson, the president of Lehman, masterminded the deal. Shearson under Sanford Weill also had been in hot pursuit of Kuhn Loeb after it absorbed Loeb, Rhoades, but the Kuhn Loeb partners felt more comfortable being absorbed by another Our Crowd firm than by the brasher Weill and his Shearson firm, which was more of a retail house than Lehman. But Weill was not yet out of the picture: Lehman itself was the next target on his acquisitions list.

Lehman Brothers was ruled for more than forty years by Robert "Bobbie" Lehman. The son of Philip Lehman, Bobbie was responsible for the shape of Lehman Brothers in the twentieth century. He directed the company to form the Lehman Corp. in 1928, just before the Crash. Like the Seligmans, the Lehmans directed their fund management business to the newly formed company. The Lehman Corp., although separate from Lehman Brothers itself, relied on its parent company for its actual fund management. Under Bobbie, Lehman Brothers was run like a fiefdom. The partners all had individual specialties and often would go in their own separate directions. The only unifying element in the firm was the desire for profit. Administratively, Bobbie ran the firm and doled out the annual bonuses. One partner remarked that Bobbie ran things much like a Mafia don and that his specialty was keeping people at each other's throats. Being an old-line Our Crowd firm, Lehman was able to get away with that management philosophy until the years following World War II. But beginning in the 1960s, loose management and a lack of business detail began to take their toll. Lehman was censured in the early 1970s for its sloppy backroom operations—the same sort of problems that affected Kuhn Loeb and drove dozens of other firms out of business. When Bobbie died in 1969, the firm entered a dark period. None of the remaining partners commanded the respect that he had, and a power struggle began.

Frederick L. Ehrman, who had joined the firm during the Second World War, took up the chairmanship. He tried in vain to establish internal guidelines and discipline at the firm, but to no avail. After four years of unrest, Ehrman was ousted in a palace coup by George Ball, formerly an undersecretary of state in the Kennedy administration and ambassador to the United Nations. But Ball did not become chairman of the firm. The job was left to Peter G. "Pete" Peterson, a former secretary of commerce, who had joined the firm only a few months before the coup.

Peterson was born to Greek immigrant parents who settled in Nebraska after arriving in the country earlier in the century. Young Peterson vividly remembered the Ku Klux Klan parading outside the café his parents had opened, protesting the fact that they were foreigners.[25] Nebraska did not hold the young Peterson for long, and he enrolled at MIT and then Northwestern and the University of Chicago to study business. After working at Bell & Howell, he joined the Nixon administration in 1970 as Assistant to the President for International Economic Affairs. Subsequently, he was appointed Secretary of Commerce after falling out on more than one occasion with Treasury Secretary John Connally. Then Ehrman called him and recruited him to work for Lehman Brothers. Within two months, Ehrman had been ousted and Peterson, with no investment banking experience, had succeeded him. Many of the senior members of Lehman Brothers were not happy with his appointment, but he acquitted himself well. As Felix Rohatyn of Lazard Freres put it, "He took over the firm and in a short time he did an absolutely brilliant job."[26] But even the management skills Peterson had honed at Bell & Howell as its chief executive were to be severely tested at the unstructured investment bank. And the firm would not maintain its independence for long despite his good efforts.

Lehman displayed a problem common at old-line investment banks that were attempting to come to grips with the new financial environment: It began trading in securities relatively late in its life. A commercial paper department was established, and by the late 1970s it was a significant contributor to the partnership's bottom line. Lewis Glucksman, a trader who was the exact opposite of the average Lehman partner and longtime foe of Peterson, headed the department. He possessed a fiery personality and was extremely blunt, the sort of characteristics the Lehman partners attempted to avoid displaying publicly. But his department made profits out of all proportion to its strength in personnel and representation on Lehman's partnership committee. The result was envy and more internecine squabbling among the partners and staff. The trader/investment banker cultural clash was on full display at Lehman and was hurting the firm's ability to plan for the long term.

During the years of Peterson's guidance, it became apparent that Lehman would not be able to survive on its own. Peterson was succeeded as CEO by Glucksman after the trader, serving as cochairman, forced him into early retirement in 1983. Glucksman further angered the investment banking partners by skewing bonuses and compensation in favor of the traders, causing much discontent and some defections. Rumors abounded that Lehman would merge with A. G. Becker, S. G. Warburg, and Prudential (all investment banks) or ConAgra, the agricultural products company. Extensive talks were in fact held with ConAgra, but in the end the Lehman partners realized that a merger would not be a good fit. Finally, in 1984 talks were held with Shearson American Express. The large investment bank/wire house was the product of a 1981 merger, engineered by Sanford Weill, between Shearson Loeb, Rhoades and the American Express Co. Lehman's product lines complemented Shearson's weaknesses, and after extensive discussions a merger was announced. The new company, called Shearson Lehman American Express, immediately became the second-largest securities house on Wall Street. Buying Lehman cost Shearson more than $350 million. The Lehman partners split 90 percent of the purchase price between them. On average they took home between $4 million and $10 million each. The high purchase price was a strong motivating force in the partners' decision. The sale became Glucksman's legacy, since it was negotiated after Peterson's departure. The internecine warfare threatened the firm's very existence and literally put its nameplate up for sale.

The Lehman partnership finally succumbed to economic pressures and an inability to cope with the changing markets, which had become more transaction-oriented and less dependent on personal relationships with clients. In the late 1970s, the firm actually began the junk bond market by helping companies with less than investment-grade credit ratings, such as the LTV Corp., Fuqua Industries, and the Zapata Corp., come to market with new bonds. Shortly thereafter, it relinquished the business by default to Drexel Burnham, which would go on to become a major Wall Street underwriter based on the junk business. The Lehman partners did not consider underwriting junk bonds to be a valid source of business, although Glucksman supported the practice. Clearly, the partners thought junk bonds to be of no consequence and wanted nothing to do with them. That lack of enthusiasm would cost the firm hundreds of millions in lost underwriting fees and leave the door wide open to Drexel, a firm desperately in need of a new product line at the time. A Lehman employee summed up the decision by saying, "All the establishment firms were slow coming into this business because they wanted to protect their franchise with the blue-chip companies. Drexel had no franchise to protect."[27]

In its reincarnation, Lehman was the jewel in the crown of a new financial superstore that was beginning to dominate the financial landscape in the 1980s—firms that offered as many investment banking and brokerage services under one roof as the law would allow. The new fit with Shearson American Express was not fated to be a success, however. Again, cultural problems with the new wire house continued to plague the parent company, and ten years later, in 1994, American Express itself began to restructure after suffering financial losses. A year earlier, it had begun to dismantle the superstore by selling the retail brokerage operations to Smith Barney. Then it spun off Lehman Brothers, which emerged again in its original name, only this time as a public corporation rather than a partnership.

The new Lehman continued to do business in many of the same areas that it had for decades. Advising on mergers and acquisitions and serving the retail industry continued to be prominent in the firm's activities. Wall Street musical chairs helped bring Lehman into the twenty-first century, but not without a great deal of strife and accommodation.

3

WHITE SHOES AND RACEHORSES: BROWN BROTHERS HARRIMAN AND AUGUST BELMONT

J. P. MORGAN IS the best-known nineteenth-century banker, but prior to 1890 he was not the most respected in New York City. That distinction belonged to two other bankers who made their way to the United States in the early part of the century. Over the next 100 years, these immigrants and their successors variously would become bankers, a diplomat, chairman of the Democratic National Committee, and benefactors to numerous worthy causes that vaulted them to a social position equal to that of the Astors and the Vanderbilts. Their children would carry on the family tradition in their own right. And, unlike many of the notable financiers of the century, both banking houses generally were able to escape the barbs of the muckrakers who made Wall Street personalities the targets of their frequent attacks, especially after the Civil War.

August Schonburg, better known as August Belmont, was sent to New York by the Rothschilds in 1837 to become their agent. Alexander Brown was a young linen merchant who emigrated from Northern Ireland at the end of the eighteenth century and set up a textile business in Baltimore. Both men achieved wealth and a degree of fame quickly, then branched out into other endeavors. Brown Brothers became one of Wall Street's premier private banking houses, and despite merging with Harriman interests during the Depression, remains so today, one of the few true partnerships to survive. The Belmonts, the leading agents for Rothschild interests in the United

States, also would be remembered for their contribution to the New York social scene and, much later, for some mysterious dealings with Russian money before the overthrow of the czar. Their banking house survived for almost 100 years before succumbing to the pressures of doing business in the twentieth century.

Both houses gave Wall Street a strong, desperately needed psychological boost after the Civil War. The shenanigans of Jay Gould and the misfortunes of the Grant family only added to Wall Street's image of a constant battleground between those who ran up the price of stocks and those who bet on a company's misfortunes by selling stock short. The successful Wall Street trader was capable of making a fortune but was still considered something of a parvenu socially. Belmont understood this, and in a brief period he would accumulate a small fortune and then quickly enter New York society in a way that made other Jewish immigrants envious. The Browns became the most successful banking family in New York to survive the trials and tribulations of three centuries, although they never engaged in traditional Wall Street investment banking business. They remained the quintessential private bank long after the New Deal legislation of the 1930s destroyed most of the other private banking firms. Ironically, although Brown and Belmont became two of Wall Street's best-known names, neither was a traditional Wall Street "house" in the true sense of the word, since neither ever became a powerhouse in stocks.

From Linen to Investments

The Brown firm established a typical early-nineteenth-century pattern that was later followed by the Lehmans, Seligmans, Kuhns, and Loebs. Alexander Brown was born in 1764 in Ireland's Ballymena, County Antrim, and was an auctioneer in Belfast's linen market before emigrating. In 1800, after following his brother Stewart to the United States, he opened a textile business in Baltimore. Within five years, Brown had expanded his interests to include trading in tobacco and other agricultural commodities as well as foreign exchange. His sons helped the firm expand, establishing branches in Philadelphia and, later, New York. The original Brown bank was founded in Philadelphia in 1818 and was called John A. Brown & Co., named after one of Alexander's sons. Brown Brothers & Co. eventually followed in New York, founded by James, another son, to deal primarily in trade with the British house the family had founded in Liverpool. Brown Brothers' various offices slowly consolidated into the New York office over the years. The original Baltimore house, Alex. Brown & Co., a regional investment bank and stockbroker, remained independent, maintaining its own securities business, while the other Brown houses amalgamated. Using his sons to great commercial advantage, Alexander Brown saw his original firm grow to become one of the leading international trading houses within twenty-five years of its opening in Baltimore. In 1810, the firm had $120,000 in capital. Within twenty years, it had increased its assets to more than $3 million, considerably more than the worth of some of the other Yankee banking houses of the period.

At the time of Alexander Brown's death in 1834, the firm was already one of the preeminent American international banking firms.[1] Despite the fact that Alexander preferred to do business in Baltimore and never stray far from home, his presence in his adopted city became the model for bankers who followed. Although a merchant by profession, he kept a copy of Adam Smith's *Wealth of Nations* in his office, becoming one of the first businessmen known to dabble in economics when time permitted. He worked diligently at marketing Maryland state bonds in the English market and provided strong moral support in Baltimore in times of financial crisis. In 1834, a month before his death, the Bank of Maryland collapsed, causing a panic in the state. The bank failed in the wake of the demise of the second Bank of the United States after Andrew Jackson refused to extend its charter. Some of its officers were found to have embezzled money and invested the bank's cash in an ill-advised manner. Brown stepped into the breach to support the business community. "No merchant in Baltimore who could show that he was solvent would be allowed to fail," he declared.[2] The crisis abated shortly thereafter, and Brown was considered the savior of the city. When news of his death came, all of the ships in Baltimore harbor lowered their flags to half-mast to honor him. Brown became the model for other prominent bankers, notably J. P. Morgan, who would practice his own form of civic diplomacy later in the century.

83

Crisis struck again several years later. The Panic of 1837 proved to be a crucible in Wall Street's development, and the fate of Brown Brothers hung in the balance. It was not speculation that threatened the firm's existence but the rapid deterioration of business conditions that accompanied it. During the slowdown that followed, trade fell significantly and much of the agency business that the Browns did with merchants both in the United States and Britain began to suffer. When the panic struck, Joseph Shipley quickly began to assume control of the operations of the Liverpool house. Shipley, a Quaker banker from Delaware, had been made a partner in the Liverpool house several years before. The volume of business conducted by Brown diminished quickly, and Shipley feared for the Liverpool house's survival. Shipley wrote, "We do not suffer from any speculation of our own. As we enter into none, we are suffering from the imprudence and misfortunes of others to whom we have given credit."[3] The Liverpool branch needed a temporary injection of liquidity. Without it, the whole firm on both sides of the Atlantic was in danger of collapsing.

Shipley wrote to the Bank of England requesting temporary assistance. Since the Bank of the United States was no longer in a position to help banking houses in need of temporary funds, Brown ironically was forced to request assistance from the Old Lady of Threadneedle Street, the nickname of the English central bank. After deliberation, the governors of the bank decided to make advances that would cover the Liverpool house's obligations temporarily. Another Anglo-American banking house, Peabody & Co., arranged to guarantee the advance. The affair was concluded successfully, although it underlined the fragile position of American banks that found themselves in financial difficulties without a lender of last resort to back them up.

In the aftermath of the panic, Brown's New York office was in search of new premises. Ironically, the building at the corner of Wall and Hanover Streets, which had been built for J. L. & S. Joseph & Co. prior to the panic, was available. After the new construction collapsed just before the panic, the Josephs sold the building back to its developer, who then rebuilt it before it was purchased by the Browns late in 1841. Apparently, the Browns were not superstitious, and they eagerly made the premises their new home. Two of the original Brown sons, John and George, sold their shares in the firm to William and James following the panic. James ultimately became the head of American operations.

While many other bankers were involved with securities, the various Brown houses occupied themselves with trade and shipping instead. Alexander Brown & Co. of Baltimore invested heavily in ships that carried trade between the East Coast and Britain. The other Brown houses also were involved to varying degrees. The combination of shipping, banking, and the commodities trade continued to produce decent profits for the Browns. When the Panic of 1857 occurred, their financial strength demonstrated itself amply. Some of the American partners wrote to Joseph Shipley, warning him of the deteriorating conditions in New York. Although already several years into retirement, Shipley was prepared to request assistance from the Bank of England, as he had done twenty years before. The panic caused serious economic problems in Britain as well as the United States. On October 14, 1857, the New York banks suspended specie payments. Crowds gathered outside the offices of many banks on Wall Street, including Brown Brothers, and there were threats of street violence as the panic spread. But Brown Brothers remained intact and never required assistance from either banks in United States or the Bank of England. In fact, Brown Shipley & Co., the new name for the Liverpool operation that also opened a London office, made an advance to George Peabody & Co. in Britain so that the firm could remain in business, reciprocating their loan to Brown Brothers in the Panic of 1837. The Bank of England advanced over a million dollars to ensure that Peabody survived, and Baring Brothers also contributed. The managing partner of Peabody at the time was Junius Spencer Morgan, the first in a line of legendary bankers who would become New York's best-known banking family. Favors of that nature were not forgotten in the world of private banking. The Browns survived the Panic of 1857 with only minimal losses and were well positioned to continue business as usual in its aftermath.

Another well-known banker got his start as a result of the Panic of 1857. After the Civil War, Henry Clews and his firm, Henry Clews &

Co., became synonymous with Wall Street. Much of the firm's fame came from its founder, who had been in the dry goods business prior to seeking a career on the Street. He bought a seat on the NYSE for $100 and opened a firm called Livermore & Clews, later to be named solely after him. Like most of the other brokers of his day, Clews originally was a banker and broker, although as time went on brokerage became his firm's preoccupation. His firm lasted until the 1930s, when new banking and securities laws began to take their effect on firms with only marginal capital despite a long-standing tradition. Clews is best remembered for his comments on the history of Wall Street and other sundry matters. He was one of the Street's most vocal exponents of capitalism in its unabashed form and took every opportunity to lecture on his economic and social views.

The Civil War caused serious tensions among the various Brown houses. The New York office strongly supported the Union, while the British and Southern offices leaned toward the Confederacy. At the time, the Browns had offices in Savannah, Mobile, and New Orleans as well as Baltimore. The war caused serious disruptions in the cotton and commodities trade and strained many old business relationships. The firm responded to the hostilities by closing the Southern offices until the war was over. Despite the fact that the wealthy could pay for a stand-in to fight for them during the war, several members of the Brown family enlisted and fought for the Union. The various offices quickly withdrew from the banking side of the business during the war so that their ability to collect debts from distressed customers would be kept at a minimum. They contented themselves with trade in foreign exchange and doing agency business, neither of which would open them to political attack. And unlike so many of their purely American counterparts, they did not participate in the selling of Treasury bonds during the war. In fact, an investment the firm made in U.S. Treasury bonds was liquidated early so that the firm would not be seen to be financially siding with the Lincoln administration. For the most part, they were able to avoid the attacks that were leveled against members of other Anglo-American banking houses, especially those suspected of Confederate sympathies, such as Junius Morgan at Peabody. But in the constant quest for new and profitable business, they did occasionally stub their collective toes.

Speak of the Devil

Brown Brothers discovered that prudence and a reputation for integrity were not necessarily shields against attack, especially in the postwar years. Like many other banking houses of the period, they became involved with the railroads in the latter half of the century, although shipping remained the firm's great preoccupation. The company that managed the liner *Arctic* was partially owned by Brown Brothers. It held the American franchise for mail delivery on the North Atlantic route and was subsidized by the U.S. government. Cunard Lines, which received a stipend from the British government, ran the British side of the business. Brown Brothers later became involved with the Pacific Mail Steamship Company as well, the company that held the franchise on mail delivery with California and China. Both relationships brought the firm under close scrutiny, more so than any other business relationship in its history. The Pacific Mail, which would remain in the news for years, eventually came under heavy criticism because of its future principal owner, Jay Gould.

The Browns' relationship with the two shipping companies was reported in a crusading newspaper called *The Revolution,* owned by Susan B. Anthony and edited by Elizabeth Cady Stanton and Parker Pillsbury. In an 1868 edition, the paper ran an article charging Brown Brothers with looting and wrecking both companies. The tone was decidedly political. The paper claimed that Brown's mismanagement of the firm virtually handed the North Atlantic route to Cunard. "If Messrs. Brown Bros. and Co. had been bribed by the Cunard Line or Europe to sweep American steamships from the Atlantic, they could not have done it more effectively than they did, by their policy and management of the Collins line. Why?" This remark particularly vexed James, who had lost his son, daughter-in-law, and grandchild in the *Arctic* tragedy years before, when one of the line's ships sank with a heavy loss of life. American influence on the seas had been lost because of the Browns' mismanagement, according to the paper, and would not be regained easily. The same criticism was leveled against Brown's ownership of the Pacific Mail Steamship line. After examining the financial statements of the line, the paper concluded that "Pacific Mail, like the Collins line, is on the verge of dissolution at the hands of the same doc-

The Brown family was dealt a severe blow personally by North Atlantic shipping in 1854. In September, a transatlantic steamship liner, the *Arctic*, sank off Newfoundland. It was the greatest shipping disaster in American history prior to the sinking of the *Titanic* in 1912. James Brown lost six members of his immediate family in the tragedy, including a son, William B. Brown, who recently had become a partner in Brown Brothers. James was so grief-ridden that he was not expected to survive. The sinking, caused by an iceberg, was scandalous because almost half of the officers and crew survived whereas only about 15 percent of the passengers did. No women or children survived at all. The affair was later remembered by the phrase "women and children last." Like the *Titanic* tragedy sixty years later, the sinking was a severe blow to New York society and Wall Street.

tors, the eminent bankers Messrs. Brown Brothers & Co."[4] Essentially, this was a direct way of accusing the firm of looting the cash of the two companies, leaving them rudderless. Given Brown Brothers' reputation, the accusation was left indirect. Although the tone of the article was suspect, it had the facts right, especially the reports of Pacific Steamship's poor financial condition. The Browns divested themselves of it in 1870 and it was taken over by Jay Gould in 1873.

But the story was a bit more complicated than the record from the newspaper suggested. A subsidy provided by the government, almost $400,000 per year, was the real target of the shareholders, according to one crusading journalist some years later who claimed that the Browns owned the works that provided boilers and iron for the line and that was the real source of their interest along with the subsidy. They were challenged on the fact, and the issue wound its way through the courts. After the Browns divested, the subsidy was increased, and that attracted new entrepreneurs to the company, among them Russell Sage, who became president of Pacific Steamship during Gould's tenure. While transportation was the ostensible reason Gould and Sage wanted the company, the real reason suggested was that the subsidy made the enterprise profitable to them. Without it, it probably would have floundered.[5]

James Brown also had the distinction of being credited with placing the sell order for gold during the Gould-Fisk corner in 1869. As one commentator of the period put it, "Many of the bears, terrified at last, were now pouring into the office of Smith, Gould, Martin & Co. of which Jay Gould is a partner, and were settling up their contracts to the amount of millions. But the heavy foreign bankers still stood firm under the standard of Brown Brothers, Duncan, Sherman & Co., Seligman and others."[6] When the price of gold rose as Gould anticipated, Brown put in an order to sell $1 million at a premium of 162 (of par, or 100). That and similar orders broke the back of the gold corner and restored gold to a more logical price. Rep. James A. Garfield, chairman of the House Committee on Banking and Currency, wrote in a report in 1870 that "the situation of all those whose legitimate business required the purchase of gold was exceedingly critical, and the boldest of them, under the lead of Brown, joined the great crowd of speculative bears in desperate efforts to break down the conspiracy and put down the price by heavy sales."[7] Brown's reputation was enhanced as one of Wall Street's upstanding bankers, anxious to return the Street to a place where corners were not easily tolerated. Some of the sharp image surrounding private bankers also was softened by the Browns' generosity to Union Theological Seminary in New York, to which they gave freely of both their time and money over the years.

After 1870, the Browns indulged themselves in railroad financing, as did most Wall Street bankers. Since the 1850s, the New York office had underwritten the odd railroad bond, often to the objection of the English offices, which wanted most of the firms' resources devoted to Anglo-American trade and shipping. The Illinois Central was one of the first such bonds in which they made an investment. Then, in 1887, the Browns were summoned to the offices of J. P. Morgan in New York for what was to become one of the noteworthy meetings of major New York bankers concerned about the plight of the railroads. It also became a veritable feast for the muckrakers who smelled collusion at every turn on Wall Street.

Railroads in the period following the Civil War expanded quickly and soon crossed the continent. But their finances were often in dire shape, and many of them were operating in the red or with little or no net worth. To make matters worse, Congress created the Interstate Commerce Commission in 1887 to deal with the rates railroads charged their customers. The idea of a federal commission with regulatory powers alarmed many railroad owners and bankers who were not accustomed to serious government interference in their affairs. J. P. Morgan called several secret meetings at his New York home to discuss the problem and put forth his own remedy for redressing it—namely, a cartel of railroad owners and financiers that would set rates nationwide, ostensibly giving the ICC no reason to intervene. However, in a climate of strong antimonopoly feelings, just the suggestion of such an altruistic group stirred the critics of both Wall Street and the railroads.

Those invited to the meetings read like a Who's Who of American railroads and finance. Jay Gould of the Missouri Pacific and the presidents of the Pennsylvania, Chicago, Milwaukee & St. Paul, Chicago St. Paul & Kansas City, and Union Pacific represented the railroads. Bankers included representatives from Drexel, Morgan & Co., Kidder, Peabody & Co., and Brown Brothers. Although the Browns' interest in railroads was not as keen as that of Kidder or Drexel Morgan, they were still included because of their influence in New York banking circles. Morgan held several meetings to deal with the topic but could not get the various groups to agree on anything of substance. At the last one, in December 1890, he was so exuberant that he actually provided a newsworthy quote for a newspaperman, something normally out of character for him. "Think of it," he exclaimed, "all the competing traffic of the roads west of Chicago and St. Louis placed in the control of about 30 men." The comment did not go unnoticed. Quickly, the *New York Herald* ran the headline "Railroad Kings Form a Gigantic Trust."[8] The group never agreed on a plan of action, so the newspaper was premature in calling it a trust, but the point was made nevertheless. Financiers were in league with the railroad barons, and Brown Brothers was one of them.

Being allied with the group that would later be dubbed the "money trust" in the early twentieth century was a dubious honor for Brown Brothers. The firm had never been heavily involved in investment banking—that is, with the underwriting of securities. The family contributed many, but not all, of its partners over the course of the century and most of them were very conservative in their approach to the family business, preferring to avoid securities wherever possible. They did build up a small investment management business over the years, but did not consider it significant. At the turn of the century, the firm was still dominated by family members, who held half of the partnership seats and preferred to concentrate on its traditional businesses. But times were changing, and the firm was pushed into the twentieth century by forces beyond its control.

A Railroad Legacy

Railroads would play a significant role in Brown Brothers' future—but in a way no one imagined at the turn of the century. Long after they became a major force in American trade financing, a little-known entrepreneur from New York began his career by buying and selling small railroads in much the same way as the great railroad barons had before him. Eventually, he was to become the greatest of them all and begin his own family dynasty, which would include financiers, politicians, diplomats, and socialites. But in 1880, the name E. H. Harriman was still obscure as the railroads expanded westward.

Critics would maintain that the Brown Brothers would have to be dragged into the twentieth century, although the partners themselves would counter that they were simply pursuing the businesses they knew best. Four years before he sold Carnegie Steel to J. P. Morgan for almost $500 million, it was rumored that Andrew Carnegie wanted to speak with John Crosby Brown, the managing partner of Brown Brothers, about a large transaction. Brown showed no interest in any transaction with Carnegie that would involve selling new stock or borrowing bonds, feeling that the amounts of money already borrowed by Carnegie were too large for him to digest and that a new transaction was not feasible. As a result, Carnegie approached Morgan instead and the largest merger in American history was consummated in 1901 when Morgan formed U.S. Steel, using Carnegie's company as its foundation.

The firm remained relatively conservative until 1909, the year John Crosby Brown died. Brown Brothers began to feel pressure from the twentieth-century economy in the years preceding World War I. The number of international trade transactions continued to climb, and international trade itself became more and more complex. Although the Browns always had adequate capital, the partners' funds were becoming somewhat limited in the new, higher-powered financial environment. As a result, Brown Brothers admitted five new partners, none of whom was a family member. But as a way of attracting fresh capital from the new partners, the method was somewhat limited. Some of the younger family members already had begun talking about seeking potential merger partners, perhaps jokingly. By the time the next great financial boom came after the war, the search would begin in earnest, ending with the merger with the Harrimans in 1930.

Harriman railroad interests had increased geometrically since the early 1880s when Edward Henry Harriman bought and sold his first railroad, the Sodus Bay & Southern Railroad, a small line that served downstate New York. His prior background was very similar to that of many railroad barons. Born on Long Island in 1848, Harriman bought a seat on the New York Stock Exchange in 1870. His original partner in the firm he established was James Livingston, scion of one of New York's oldest families. Harriman soon bought out Livingston and struck out on his own. After some success dealing in stocks for notables such as Jay Gould and the Vanderbilts, he married Mary Averell, whose father ran a small railroad outside New York City and helped him make his purchase of the Sodus line. Shortly thereafter, he and some Wall Street cronies purchased another small upstate line, the Lake Ontario Southern, and completely renovated it so that it was again efficient and safe. The line was then sold to the Pennsylvania Railroad, and Harriman now had enough money to continue his ventures. He purchased enough bonds in the Illinois Central to bring him to the attention of Stuyvesant Fish, one of the line's senior investors. By the late 1880s he was considered the major figure in railroads in the country, and more than one political cartoonist of the day portrayed him as occasionally giving instructions to Jay Gould on big deals they were involved in. His reputation as a railroad baron had been well established.

Toward the end of the century, even bigger and more notable deals were made. After Gould's negligent reign at the Union Pacific, Harriman rebuilt the transcontinental link so that it regained the superior place in east–west transportation that it was intended to occupy after the Civil War. Then he began to clash with the top financiers on Wall Street and usually won the battles. The battle for control of the Union Pacific was one notable example. In 1895, J. P. Morgan rejected the idea of reorganizing the Union Pacific, which had been tottering on the brink for years. The Treasury was demanding its money from loans made during the post–Civil War period, and a major battle was developing concerning who would win the right to put the railroad back on its feet. Harriman crossed swords with Jacob Schiff of Kuhn Loeb, who had designs of his own on the reorganization. But Harriman proved that he could raise the necessary capital to rebuild the line at a rate cheaper than Schiff could provide. Kuhn Loeb eventually capitulated and reorganized the railroad according to the Harriman plan. Harriman himself was named chairman of the board and later president of the railroad.

In 1901, competing interests flared anew when the Northern Pacific Railroad again raised its head. Since the days of Jay Cooke, the railroad had had a troubled history under various managements before a war for its control developed. Harriman began to buy stock in the line to compete with its major shareholder James J. Hill, a Morgan customer. Using Kuhn Loeb to help him finance his venture, he successfully bought a large block of its stock before it came to the attention of Morgan and Hill. The buying set off a frenzy on Wall Street and the two forces bought more stock than actually existed, forcing prices to rise astronomically to more than $1,000 per share, a gain of more than $900 in one week alone. Then the collapse came, as the short sellers ran for cover and finally had to settle to cover themselves at a loss at a negotiated price. The *New York Times* ran the story, giving it much drama when it said that "the greatest general panic that Wall Street has ever known came upon the stock market yesterday, with the result that before it was checked many fortunes, the accumulation in some cases of years, had been completely swept away."[9] The panic, in reality, was a short one and the market soon regained its footing, but the battle underlined the importance of railroads and finance in the economy—and the importance of personalities in helping move market prices.

The battle for control resulted in the formation of a holding company, called the Northern Securities Company, that was controlled by both warring factions. This was the sort of organization Morgan had had in mind years before when the ICC was formed, and the antimonopolists quickly seized upon the newly formed company, using it as a rallying point. The United States subsequently filed suit in court claiming that the holding company was a monopoly of railroad interests, and the Supreme Court agreed, striking down the company as an illegal combination designed to restrain trade. Undaunted, Harriman went on to build railroads nevertheless and had elaborate plans to develop a railroad empire outside the United States, stretching from Siberia to Manchuria. But the grand plans were interrupted by his death in 1909. The American railroad baron did not live to see his international plans come to fruition. Fortunately, his sons had become able financiers in their own right and would see that the family tradition was carried on.

Moving Toward Merger

Harriman's name, like those of so many nineteenth-century financiers, lived on because he was able to pass his legacy to his offspring. While he made his reputation in the nineteenth century, the family name in banking was not established until the twentieth. His oldest son, William Averell Harriman, founded W. A. Harriman & Co. in 1919, and in the 1920s he and his younger brother, E. Roland Harriman, founded Harriman Brothers & Co. Both were investment banking houses, actively engaging in the sorts of deals the senior Harriman had put together during his lifetime.

The 1920s boom brought many new companies to market, and the trend underlined the need for a merger partner for the Browns. More capital would be needed if the firm was to compete effectively in the new environment. In the years prior to the Crash, all of the major New York banks added underwriting to their sphere of activities, usually through securities affiliates. Stock underwriting was not as popular as bond underwriting for the banks, and many, including Brown Brothers, accumulated a large number of bonds on their books that were unsold at the time of the Crash. Once economic activity began to diminish, the bonds were difficult to sell and severe strains were placed upon the partners' capital. Brown Brothers had accumulated a large amount of South American bonds, and they proved especially difficult to sell.[10] The partners realized that they had a problem on their hands. Years before, Baring Brothers in London had suffered a collapse because of South American bonds and had required a bailout. Realizing that the Crash was just not another market "break," in 1920s parlance, the Browns saw that a merger with the Harrimans began to make more and more sense.

The Browns and the Harrimans had been friendly for decades, and members of the families had been at Yale together as undergraduates. The announcement of the merger was made jointly by Brown Brothers managing partner Thatcher Brown and E. Roland Harriman. The marriage brought together the Browns' long tradition of conservative banking and a fresh infusion of capital from Harriman. Ironically, it was announced in the *New York Times* on the same day (December 12, 1930) that the failure of the Bank of United States in New York was announced, the largest commercial bank failure in American history. The bank collapsed under suspicions of fraud and graft, taking $300 million worth of customer deposits with it. Without a merger, the fate of the two houses could have been quite different, because many bankers and brokers were suffering the effects of the Crash. One of the partners from Harriman Brothers joining the new bank was Prescott Bush, father of future U.S. president George H. W. Bush.

Clearly, access to the Harriman fortune through the sons was the prime motivating force behind the merger. The Harrimans were a growing but yet not major force on Wall Street when the merger was announced. But the combined firms instantly became a Wall Street powerhouse, ranking alongside Kuhn Loeb and J. P. Morgan as investment banks with considerable influence. When Congress passed the Glass-Steagall Act during Franklin D. Roosevelt's first one hundred days, however, the powerhouse status proved to be ephemeral. Investment and commercial banking were separated by the act, and banks had one year to choose which side of the business they wanted to engage in. Brown Brothers chose commercial banking, not so much a radical choice as a natural return to the company's nineteenth-century roots.

The securities business was separated from the bank as required by the law, and some partners of the firm joined the new firm, Brown, Harriman & Co., the purposely created securities affiliate. Members of the National City Bank's securities affiliate, National City Company, also joined in the venture. The name was later changed to Harriman, Ripley & Co. in 1938 after merging with a smaller broker, Joseph P. Ripley & Co., when it became apparent that the Glass-Steagall Act and the Roosevelt administration were not flashes in the pan and that the financial reforms were permanent. Brown Brothers Harriman once again became a commercial bank and remained a partnership. It was allowed to keep its seat on the NYSE because it conducted only agency business through it, acting as a broker for its clients rather than as a principal. It was the only bank allowed to do so. The other private banks all chose investment banking, so the new law forced them out of the commercial banking business while the commercial banks divested their securities affiliates. The Wall Street revolution was complete, and Brown Brothers again looked much like it had in the nineteenth century, this time with a fresh infusion of capital.

History always played a significant role on Wall Street at crucial moments in its development. When the Glass-Steagall Act was passed, this was particularly true. Congress looked carefully at the record of private bankers and securities firms when determining the thrust and impact of new laws, especially ones as radical as the banking legislation and two pieces of securities regulation that would be passed in 1933 and 1934. The bankers' track records often determined whether they would be treated harshly or lightly at critical moments. Brown Bothers' reputation plus its unobtrusive approach to financing put them fairly low on Congress's list of bankers who needed to be constrained. J. P. Morgan topped that list, and the legislation, especially Glass-Steagall, affected his bank the most of any on Wall Street. In a sense, Glass-Steagall was also an effective piece of antitrust legislation, although it was never billed as such at the time.[11] The money trust that had irritated Progressives earlier in the century was effectively broken, although Brown Brothers did not figure prominently in the deliberations because of its record.

After the Second World War, Brown Brothers Harriman continued in the commercial banking business and also provided investment management services for its clients. As part of the latter service, it also provided "buy side" research on equities in much the same way that the Seligmans had after their departure from private banking. Through the years, it remained a private bank. Its behavior in the markets has always been dictated by the fact that it chose to remain private, accepting the limitations that a relatively small capital base dictates. As a result, it has remained one of Wall Street's more conservative institutions. In 2000, it announced that it would cease providing the brokerage services to its clients that it began providing in the 1980s and 1990s, recognizing that other, larger, full-service investment banks provided better services. It was the sort of announcement that Alexander or James Brown easily would have understood more than a century before.

The Flamboyant Banker

Whereas the Browns preferred to remain in the background and practice conservative financing, other nineteenth-century bankers were more flamboyant and craved public attention. The best-known socialite banker in the nineteenth century was August Belmont, an example of a young man who rose from obscurity in a very short period of time. But Belmont was no Horatio Alger–type character. His sudden rise to prominence was almost totally based on good connections and deft maneuvering in the correct political and social circles.

August Belmont's name was the francophone version of his native German, literally meaning "beautiful mountain" in both languages. The name was changed to the French as a political expedient when his native German town was under occupation by Napoleon's troops while Belmont was a child. Belmont was born in 1813 in the small Rhenish village of Alzey. His parents were descended from Spanish Jews who had escaped Spain during the Inquisition three centuries before. And he was fortunate to possess valuable family connections. While he was still in his teens, his parents convinced friends in Frankfurt, the Rothschilds, to hire him as an apprentice in their banking house. By 1828, the family's banking reputation was already well established and the job was a plum for the teenager. After several years, he gained positions of increasing importance, and in 1832 he was named a secretary to one of the partners. He began to travel, especially to Italy and the Vatican, and added Italian to his language arsenal, which already included French and English. This particular job opened the world to him and would prove crucial to his professional development.

In 1837, civil wars on the Iberian peninsula required the Rothschilds to send a man to Havana to look after their interests in Cuba, and they picked Belmont for the assignment. To reach Cuba, he first had to sail to New York and then catch a connection to Havana. It was a connection never to be made. Arriving in New York at the time of the 1837 crisis, Belmont was fascinated by the United States and the consternation caused by the panic. He postponed his trip to Havana and began searching New York for the means to set up shop for himself. He quickly decided to open his own banking/brokerage firm, which he called August Belmont & Co. From the very beginning, he was quick to point out that he was the Rothschilds' man in New York, a connection worth its weight in gold in a country starved for investment capital. Unlike Jacob Schiff some years later, he did not return home.

The connection with his now former employers did not conflict, because the banking family had never opened a New York branch. The Rothschilds' influence was found mainly in Europe, where they had opened a series of branches over the years. Their primary strength lay in their ability to personally arrange financings with kings and finance ministers, and they had had little serious competition for their services since branching out from Germany earlier in the century. But there was no New York connection, because the family would have entrusted the opening of a new branch only to a family member. In fact, Belmont was not even sent to take over the Havana office but only to gather facts and report back to Frankfurt. James Rothschild, the reigning partner, considered exploiting the possibilities that the panic had created in New York but evidently regarded this sort of job far in excess of Belmont's capabilities.[12] That judgment backfired. Before anyone had time to take stock of the situation, Belmont had set off on his own. The upstart was now in business for himself. He established the banking family in New York de facto before any of the partners could object. Not having an American presence, there was little the Rothschilds could do to protest. Before long, Belmont's assumption was accepted by all parties.

Over the years, the Rothschild connection served Belmont well. He began by sorting out the mess left by the failure of J. L. & S. Joseph and then moved into the traditional sort of merchant banking business—dealing in foreign exchange, deposits, and commercial bills of exchange. Success was almost instantaneous. Since the Rothschilds were the major source of foreign capital for the United States along with Barings of London, customers realized that dealing with Belmont was in their own best interests and his business immediately prospered. Belmont, however, continued to give the Rothschilds fits. In 1841, he fought a duel over a lady's honor and was wounded in the leg, which gave him a permanent limp that would hobble him throughout his life. When the banking family learned of the affair, they were horrified and contemplated taking the agency business that he had developed away from him. He was able to assure them that he was supported by the "best elements" in New York society and eventually succeeded in mollifying them.[13] After the affair, he settled down and became part and parcel of New York society. The social legend was beginning to build alongside the banking legend, but the limp was never quite forgotten.

Like many of his contemporaries, Belmont fully exploited the Mexican War to his own purposes. Along with Clark Dodge, he became a major underwriter of the Mexican war bonds issued by the Treasury. But unlike his Yankee banking compatriots, he found himself oddly divided because of the Rothschild interests. Belmont committed a substantial amount of his firm's funds to underwriting a $15 million payment through the issue of U.S. Treasury bills to indemnify Mexico for territory ceded to the United States. The Rothschilds thought that this sort of activity exceeded his authority to act on their behalf and eventually sent a young member of the family to New York to sort things out. But the emissary was impressed by Belmont's role in American finance and the success he had achieved in such a short time. He wrote to London, describing Belmont's role as "a position which is at once semi-dependent and semi-independent, simultaneously that of an agent and a correspondent." On top of Belmont's strengths, no members of the family seemed willing to relocate to

New York, so August Belmont & Company's future was assured.[14] However, the tension between New York and the European interests would continue far into the future.

Belmont channeled Rothschild investment funds into many domestic projects. Bonds of state and city governments were favorites. The money was welcomed—by the states especially—but political and racial overtones were never far from the surface. Belmont learned this firsthand when several states defaulted on their obligations in the first municipal bond default after the Panic of 1837. Without the second Bank of the United States to provide them with necessary funds, the states found themselves short of liquidity and reneged on their interest payments. Not paying interest was quickly translated into a patriotic duty. The governor of Mississippi declared that his state would default on its interest so that the Rothschilds could not make "serfs of our children." Paying interest to foreigners apparently was different from paying it to domestic investors and carried an emotional message. In times of financial crisis, Belmont and his heir, August Jr., would hear more of the same because of the Rothschild connection.

Outside diversions soon competed for Belmont's time. Before the Mexican War, he accepted an offer from Austria-Hungary to become its consul general in New York. The appointment allowed his company to become even more prominent than before, adding an international aura to the cachet of Rothschild influence. He severed the relationship in 1850 to devote all his attention to American politics, an avocation that was providing greater and greater attraction as time went by. And the diversions of social life in New York also vied for his time. Society and politics interested him more than banking, which he saw as the natural way to make the money necessary to indulge his tastes. At the same time that he accepted the job from Austria-Hungary, he supported James K. Polk in the presidential election of 1844 and became actively involved in Democratic Party politics. He became a U.S. citizen the same year.

Outside activities did not deter Belmont from banking, although he clearly made some poor judgments along the way. When the Mexican War was ending, the Treasury gave him the right to be its transfer agent so that he could pass U.S. funds to the government of Mexico.

He decided to clear the transaction without taking a fee, a strategy that Jay Cooke would later use in the early Civil War financings. But the strategy backfired slightly when the United States later decided to float another bond. Belmont bid for it, assuming that he had won all of the deal and would make a hefty commission for his trouble. He did not realize that the Treasury had granted Clark Dodge a similar number of bonds to sell and netted only half of what he had anticipated earning. Trying to win Treasury business by performing some transactions gratis was becoming a well-known ploy among banking circles and did not necessarily spell success. Too many bankers employed the strategy for it to be profitable for everyone.

In 1849, Belmont married the daughter of Commodore Matthew Perry, a hero of the Mexican War and scion of one of the country's older families. Although he was a Jew, religion apparently was not much of an issue, and they were married in the Episcopal Church of the Ascension in New York. At the time, a New York newspaper estimated his annual income to be $100,000, a tidy sum for someone who had entered the country only twelve years before. He joined the Union League, New York's most prestigious club, and comfortably settled into the New York social scene. The event underlined the remarkable transformation of an immigrant who only a decade before had been considered neither clever nor old enough by the Rothschilds even to open a New York office for them. It also marked an even more remarkable transformation: Belmont had grown from being a mere Jewish immigrant banker to an accepted member of New York society, a group that was not known for welcoming newcomers or outsiders. Within a few years, his ethnic status would never again be mentioned socially, although it was probably not completely forgotten. It was quite a remarkable series of events considering the personal history of the other major Jewish families, most of whom married within their clans rather than seek spouses from American gentile society. Belmont succeeded in capitalizing on his brashness, while other immigrant bankers relied more on business acumen and family relations to build their businesses.

Of all the bankers who became overnight success stories before the Civil War, Belmont displayed perhaps the least business acumen. He continued to rely on the Rothschild connection to make money, and while it served him well, it did mean that he had to toe the company line to an extent to keep the relationship alive and well. While engaging in financing for the railroads and other new companies coming to market and continuing to do trade deals, his firm missed a major opportunity with the Civil War financings that made Jay Cooke famous. But the Civil War also gave him the opportunity to display loyalty to his new country and dissuade the Rothschilds from doing business with the Confederacy.

At the beginning of the war, the Confederate Congress authorized the issuance of a $50 million loan to finance its war effort. Belmont stridently opposed the underwriting of any such bonds, comparing them to the worthless bonds issued in France during the Revolution—a clever ploy, since it was just those sorts of issues that the Rothschilds shied away from. The family already had subscribed to Union bonds, and rather than play both sides of the fence, it declined an offer to underwrite, leaving the job to other sympathetic banks.[15] The way was then clear to help Salmon Chase raise money for the Northern war effort.

At first, Belmont sounded very much like Jay Cooke when he counseled Chase about raising money for the Treasury. "Before the war can be brought to a satisfactory termination, we shall require from 50 to 60 millions of dollars," he told Chase authoritatively when he first visited Washington to discuss the war effort. His idea of marketing bonds was also familiar: "A national subscription ought to be opened in all our large cities; amounts as low as one hundred dollars, or even fifty dollars, should be accepted, and bonds for those fractions issued." But he felt that not all of the estimated amount could be raised domestically. "It is impossible to say how the capitalists of England and the Continent may be affected toward an American loan. There is evidently a belief in the European cabinets that by withholding all aid from us, they may force us into a settlement of some kind with the Southern states."[16] The only way to discover European intentions was to visit the various governments, something that Belmont volunteered to do.

Any opportunity to play a major role in helping Washington was soon lost. Belmont traveled to Europe to help Washington sound out the possibility of selling bonds there to help the Union effort. His mission was unofficial but sanctioned by Chase, who recognized the banker's extensive European connections. If the market was not favorable for a bond, it was better to know before launching one rather than have it fail for lack of subscriptions. He visited London, Paris, and Frankfurt, and after lengthy conversations with senior bankers and statesmen, concluded that support was very thin and that an issue would not be successful. As a result, the Rotshchilds did not participate in the earlier war financings in a meaningful way. The lack of European support opened the door for Jay Cooke, who was able to fill the void with his own form of aggressive marketing of bonds to all strata of the public, from the institutional investor to the workingman. Only after the Rothschilds and Belmont saw the success of Cooke firsthand did they decide to participate in what became the first true syndication of a bond issue with the Treasury refinancing after the war.

While bankers like Cooke, Clark Dodge, and the Seligmans were putting their efforts into the war, Belmont already had wandered off into other areas of interest. Representing the Rothschilds carried a social responsibility, and he was determined to meet it fully. Living well was his hallmark, and he quickly became known in social circles as someone of substance who loved to give dinner parties and live life fully and as expensively as possible. His wine bill often topped $20,000 per year, and he introduced many matters of social etiquette and practice into New York society. Often, his socializing was done with a bit of arrogance along with his usual flamboyance. He employed his father-in-law, Commodore Perry, as his wine steward and often sent him to fetch a bottle in front of guests. Few would have imagined they would be served claret by one of the country's better-known war heroes.

While Joseph Seligman was the model for Horatio Alger's rags-to-riches stories, Belmont was more the model for Thorstein Veblen's "conspicuous consumption" of the Gilded Age. Spending money gave one social status in nineteenth-century New York, and Belmont was one of the idea's best exponents. Belmont set the standard for New York society by throwing lavish dinner parties for as many as 200 people at a sitting and giving fancy dress balls. At one ball, he dressed in a full suit of gold-plated armor said to have cost $10,000. He also was fond of dressing as Napoleon, who was always a Wall Street favorite; more than one trader had been labeled the "young Napoleon of finance" over the years. But he spent the most money on his residence, a lavish mansion on Fifth Avenue that became the standard in New York society. Rumor had it that the Astors had snubbed him several times before by not inviting him to their own lavish parties at their home in Greenwich Village. Belmont, in turn, built the Fifth Avenue mansion to show that he was not a man to be snubbed. While not universally accepted by all of the proper New York social cliques, he was still a man to be reckoned with.

Belmont often spent more time working on political projects than he did on banking. One of his pet projects before the Civil War was working with the Democratic National Committee. Having voted Democratic in every election since his naturalization, he was convinced to work for the party by his wife's uncle, former congressman John Slidell of Louisiana. His political career began in 1851 when he agreed to manage James Buchanan's presidential campaign in New York. When Buchanan lost the party's nomination to Franklin Pierce, Belmont threw his support wholeheartedly behind the chosen candidate. Then he discovered that his newly adopted country, and especially the New York opposition, quickly raised the Rothschild scepter when needed. The *New York Times,* in particular, assailed Belmont for employing "Jew gold" from abroad to support Pierce. Later, the paper stated that "the Rothschilds and the Emperor of Austria were both of them rather anxious for the election of Pierce and the consequent establishment of such a policy as would permit them to monopolize" a potential Pierce administration. And he was not allowed to forget his other foreign ties—namely, the job as Austrian consul in New York. The *New York Tribune* labeled that a "dual allegiance."[17] Belmont discovered that the road to riches and influence was not always as smooth as he anticipated.

It was remarkable that Belmont was able to turn his attention to politics so quickly, having been in the country only fourteen years before beginning to dabble in the fortunes of the Democratic Party. This apparent dalliance made excellent business sense because it sought to forge political ties in much the same way that the Rothschilds had done in Europe over the decades. Friendly politicians were always better allies than hostile ones, and Belmont sought to practice the American version of gaining political favor as quickly as possible. And his sortie into politics proved successful. Pierce defeated Winfield Scott in the 1852 election, and Belmont emerged with a reputation as a good organizer with the right connections. He also received something more tangible from Pierce: He was offered the ambassadorship to the Netherlands, a job that he readily accepted. His remarkable rise continued unabated. He now had the distinction of holding two diplomatic jobs for two different governments within the span of ten years.

While serving as ambassador to The Hague in the 1850s, Belmont saw his business in New York begin to suffer. There were several cases of embezzlement and mismanagement at the office. In one case, $14,000 disappeared from the firm and Belmont's chief cashier offered a reward for the culprit. It was later revealed that the cashier himself had stolen the money; the cashier offered to repay all of it if he could keep his job. Belmont took a different view, however, and had him jailed for embezzlement. Shortly thereafter, a fire destroyed the warehouse where Belmont kept his possessions in storage while he and his wife lived at The Hague. By the time his tenure was finished, he realized that it was time to return home before the business and his personal life were in ruins.

Pierce was succeeded by James Buchanan, and Belmont's star continued to rise in the Democratic Party. In 1860, when the party chose Stephen A. Douglas to oppose Lincoln, Belmont was named a member of the Democratic National Committee and then, quickly afterward, its chairman. While the post was not as important as it later became, his ascendancy was still noteworthy. His money was also a crucial factor, as it soon became apparent that the party delegations from the various states all expected him to fund their activities. On more than one occasion, Belmont personally wrote checks so that local parties could meet their obligations to the national committee. He quickly became irritated with having to do so, however, recognizing that they needed him for his money more than for his organizational skills. His tenure at the Democratic National Committee lasted until 1872, when he decided to step down. The party's decline during the Civil War years blemished his chairmanship, although he was able to make the job a full-time commitment rather than the part-time post for political amateurs that it had once been. It is generally agreed that Belmont helped make the job a high-profile one.

Politics was not Belmont's passion, however. One of his favorite pastimes was horse racing. He loved horses and began to accumulate them and build stables as soon as he was able after arriving in the country. That love was passed to his son, August Jr., who succeeded him at the family firm. August Belmont Jr. was born in 1853 in New York City and graduated from Harvard in 1874. Throughout his life, he liked to be called a sportsman as well as a financier, and he was a sprinter at Harvard. Realizing that runners needed better traction on the cinders, he helped bring the spiked track shoe to the United States, where other runners quickly adopted it. When August Sr. died in 1890, he assumed leadership of the family bank and continued his father's tradition of representing the Rothschilds.

Like his father, August Jr. is remembered more for his pastimes than his financial prowess. His love of horses led him to develop the racetrack in New York that became known as Belmont Park, a lifelong passion. He helped with the finance and construction of the New York City subway system, which opened in 1904. And he also was instrumental in developing the Cape Cod Canal, completed in 1914. The canal was designed to allow ships to save time on the Boston–to–New York run by traversing Cape Cod. The family owned a stake in the canal, which the U.S. government used extensively during World War I. Although he was less political than his father, August Jr.'s extensive contacts made involvement in public projects easy. But when the firm engaged in financings that were controversial, the press made no distinction between August Sr. and Jr. A Belmont was a Belmont, and the muckraking press treated the son much as it had previously treated the father when it came to the Rothschild connections.

In the later stages of his political career, August Sr. became embroiled in the 1876 presidential election, won by Rutherford B. Hayes over his Democratic rival Samuel J. Tilden. Although he was confident of his party's victory, his background and connections again became issues in the campaign itself. Newspaper articles began to circulate that the Rothschilds contributed $2 million to ensure Tilden's victory so that they could control the U.S. government when he won. Speaking to a local party gathering, Belmont Sr. addressed the issue whimsically, although he was far from whimsical about the newspaper attacks. "It was my custom to read the Republican papers," he said.

"I have read that after the election it is the intention of Mr. Rothschild and myself to buy up the whole United States. Mr. Rothschild has not written to me yet on the subject . . . but I know that Uncle Sam will not sell out."[18] The remarks were greeted with laughter, but the point was made. While the matter was amusing at the time, a rumor was established that lingered long into the future: a Jewish conspiracy among international bankers planned to overthrow the government and/or seize control of venerable American institutions, and Belmont and the Rothschilds were at the heart of it. Another rumor was revived about the same time, with more damaging implications.

After the Civil War, an Irish revolutionary group called the Irish Revolutionary Brotherhood deposited $25,000 with Belmont in New York. The deposit was one that would haunt him for years. When

---

Adding to Irish anger was the fact that August Belmont owned a popular racehorse called Fenian in the 1860s, at the same time that he was doing business with the revolutionary movement. The connection between the disputed funds and the name of the horse was not lost upon the Irish community in New York. Thomas Meehan, the editor of the *Irish-American*, a New York newspaper, wrote to Belmont asking about the connection between the funds and the horse at the time of the original lawsuit. Belmont wrote him a short note stating that "the connection of my horse with the Fenian fund is not quite concisely stated and if you will kindly call here any time this morning I will give you the exact facts as they are. I can do this much better orally than by letter, and not being well enough to go out this morning must ask you to favor me with your visit."* No record exists of the conversation, but the second lawsuit against Belmont suggests that the Irish community was not mollified by Belmont's explanation to Meehan. The horse's performance was certainly better than the Irish luck at getting their money back. It won the race named after its owner, the Belmont Stakes, in 1869— at the time, the most popular horse race in the country.

* August Belmont to Thomas Meehan, October 21 note, no year. *Thomas Meehan Papers*, drawer 1 file 1, Georgetown University Special Collections.

Belmont attempted to transport the money across the Atlantic to Dublin at the group's request, the British government seized it. The Fenians, as they also were called, sued Belmont to recover the funds but lost in court. That did not stop the rumors from circulating that Belmont still had the money and refused to relinquish it. But the Fenians' credibility was suspect. In 1866, a large swindle was uncovered in New York in which they had sold worthless IOUs to Irish immigrants, many of whom had low-paying jobs and thought they were helping to fight for Irish nationhood with their contributions. Some of the lost money from the IOUs was probably the proceeds from the swindle that Belmont was unwittingly trying to send to Ireland when it was intercepted.

The Irish issue raised its head almost twenty years later when Belmont sued the publisher of the *Irish Nation* for continuing to spread the Fenian funds rumor long after he thought it had been settled. The motive was, of course, political. His son Perry was rumored as a Democratic candidate for the governorship of New York, and the opposition had set out to smear the Belmont name. When the case went to trial, the full extent of the anti-Belmont feelings that surfaced at elections again popped up. Realizing that Belmont had an old image problem, the newspaper's attorney went quickly on the offensive. The lawyer sparred with Belmont before attacking his credibility. "Where were you born?" the lawyer asked. The judge himself objected to the relevancy of the question when the lawyer retorted that "we are in a position to show that this man's name is not Belmont, or at least that he has used another name."[19] Upon hearing that, Belmont became enraged and the courtroom broke into pandemonium. Belmont protested but never answered the question directly. The name Schonberg was never mentioned, nor did he admit to being born with the name. Technically, it was Belmont, only in a different language. After the stormy proceedings, the result of the case was more to Belmont's liking: the publisher was found guilty and sentenced to sixty days in prison for maligning Belmont. He had struck a sensitive chord. In more proper, discreet social circles Belmont's background was never mentioned. In political circles, the opposition never let anyone forget it.

August Sr.'s funeral was a testament to the central role he had played in finance and politics during his lifetime. The funeral was held at the same church at which he had been married years before. Among the pallbearers were J. P. Morgan and former president Grover Cleveland.[20] Over the years, Belmont maintained a close connection with Morgan. The marriage of August Jr.'s son to a Morgan produced an heir, Morgan Belmont, who would eventually wind up the bank's affairs in the 1920s after the death of his father. The two banks participated in many financings together and were involved in some of the more controversial operations for the U.S. Treasury in the last quarter of the century. One occurred during August Sr.'s later years, and the other after his death. But from the reactions of the press it was clear that the Belmonts represented the Rothschilds and that was all that mattered.

In the later 1870s, Treasury financing again became an issue, as it had been during and immediately after the Civil War. Without tough Treasury secretaries like Salmon Chase in office, Treasury financings again fell under a cloud of suspicion. Jay Cooke had since departed to concentrate on his railroad ventures, and the Treasury was left with its usual list of top Wall Street banks from which to seek financing. As in the past, that proved to be an expensive list. In 1877, the United States needed to borrow more than $250 million, and Treasury Secretary John Sherman used a banking syndicate headed by J. P. Morgan that included his bank at the time, Drexel, Morgan & Co., along with J. & W. Seligman and August Belmont. The bonds were sold successfully but the commissions were expensive. The rate was far in excess of the normal charge for selling bonds. The syndicate charged up to 4 percent for its services and earned even more money charging what became known as "double interest." This involved a variation of the old game that bankers used to play with Treasury securities before the Civil War. In addition to the usual interest paid on bonds, bankers exacted a rate charged for the currency that was issued to support them. Congress eventually investigated the total commission structure on the large issue two years later, but the bankers pocketed their profits nevertheless. In addition to Belmont's participation, critics started openly mentioning Rothschild participation, although they made their purchases through Belmont in the usual manner. The *London World* was more sanguine, at least on behalf of the Rothschilds, implying that it was their American agents who bore closer scrutiny. The newspaper noted that "we may reasonably doubt whether the Rothschilds would act in a dishonorable manner; there is no room for doubt on that point in reference to certain of their critics."[21] By using the Jewish banking houses in the syndicate, Morgan was purposely arousing indignation over foreign influences, although the desire to place the bonds abroad was probably a more clear reason, since Drexel Morgan was acting for J. S. Morgan of London, his father's firm.

The bond issue of 1877 raised some hackles in the populist press, but nothing like the intervention on behalf of the Treasury in 1893 during the gold reserve crisis did. The United States began to run dangerously low on its gold reserves following the crisis in Europe in 1890 that saw the first failure of the venerable British bank Baring Brothers. At the same time, the United States adopted silver as a reserve along with gold, and the prospect worried investors who felt that it was nothing more than a caving in to political pressure from the western states. Without gold in reserve, the markets began to suffer badly as foreign investors, vital to the economy, began to withdraw their support. Silver was not an acceptable substitute for them. Dozens of railroads went into bankruptcy and thousands of businesses failed nationwide. The currency in circulation was only partially backed by gold, and that prospect frightened many foreign investors. August Jr. believed that the panic was caused mainly by poor credit conditions and a general fear of debasing the currency by backing it with silver rather than with gold exclusively. Normally reticent in public, August Jr. actually went on record about the panic when questioned by a reporter from the *New York Times*. Asked whether he had any doubts that the Sherman Silver Act would be repealed, he answered unequivocally, "None whatever. I believe the pressure upon Congress will be so great from all parts of the country . . . that the repeal will be effected very promptly."[22] He went on to describe how merchants and businessmen should act to stave off illiquidity or bankruptcy until conditions improved.

The Treasury under the Cleveland administration asked Morgan for assistance, and along with Belmont he provided it by issuing a Treasury bond that was sold to foreign investors. That helped bring gold back into the country, and the crisis soon subsided without the United States having to face the ignominy of defaulting on its other debt. But the intervention came at a price: Morgan and Belmont were accused of profiting from the Treasury's travails.

Critics of the syndicate said the bankers made profits of between 5 and 10 percent on the transaction—too large for an operation designed to restore the gold reserves. The press was especially critical of Belmont and Morgan for selling to foreign interests, but there was no other way to reverse the flow of gold without importing it. But that did not stop the papers. The *New York World,* run by Joseph Pulitzer, pulled no punches when it described the syndicate as a group of "bloodsucking Jews and aliens." And Henry Adams wrote that the "Jews of Lombard Street threaten to withdraw their capital if there was even a danger of free coinage of silver."[23] He was referring to the Rothschilds on London's most famous financial street. And Morgan was included in this group, because J. S. Morgan was a British firm and J. P. Morgan at Drexel was clearly acting on its behalf. The affair again underlined the importance of foreign capital to the United States. Without it, the country would have been short of investment capital and August Belmont probably would have been out of a job.

One Last Intrigue

August Belmont & Co.'s fortunes began to change after the First World War. The firm's reliance on the Rothschilds remained as great as ever, although the country's reliance on foreign investors began to diminish. Many of the Rothschilds' best clients in Europe were now rebuilding and were in no position to send capital abroad. The family's influence in international finance began to ebb as a result. For the first time in its history, the United States became an exporter of capital and its reliance on foreign investors subsided as the number of domestic investors increased dramatically. The general prosperity of the 1920s attracted millions of new investors to the market. Although the numbers were not as great as they would be later in the century, this vast new source of investment funds was actively courted by Wall Street, especially by brokers such as Charles Merrill. At the same time, the phenomenon diminished the importance of Belmont and the other Jewish banking houses that relied on foreign investment. They either adapted to the new trend or disappeared. Belmont did not adapt.

After the death of August Jr. in 1924, the family firm was dissolved. Its business had diminished after the war to the point where it was effectively defunct by the time the official liquidation began. Its seat on the NYSE lapsed with his death and the firm's affairs were wound up. At the time of August's death, the Belmonts were not a wealthy family. The Cape Cod Canal holding was one of their major assets. The job of winding the firm down was left to Morgan Belmont, who succeeded to the chairmanship after the death of his older brother, August III, in 1919. The family share in the Cape Cod Canal was sold to the government. The family estate on Long Island eventually was purchased by William Randolph Hearst as a gift for his wife. Morgan offered to sell the firm's name to August IV, the son of August III who also had graduated from Harvard. But the youngest family member to bear the name declined and struck out on his own on Wall Street, seeking a job with another firm as a clerk. But one bit of intrigue still managed to follow the firm into the first Roosevelt administration.

Another lawsuit claiming malfeasance of funds was filed against the firm. Prior to 1918, the Petrograd Metal Works in Russia had deposited a small sum of money with August Belmont & Co. How the money came to be deposited with Belmont and its exact date are a mystery.[24] After the fall of the czar, the new Soviet government was not recognized by the United States until Franklin Roosevelt became president. In 1933, under the Roosevelt-Litvinoff agreement, all former Russian funds due from Americans were assigned to the United States by the Soviet government to settle previous debts. A lower court upheld the Belmont heirs' refusal to return it and the case ultimately went to the Supreme Court. The court reversed the lower-court decision and ordered the Belmonts to repay the money. At the time, the amount was $25,438.[25] But similar cases were in the pipeline, because the Soviets had more than $8 million on deposit in the country that would revert to the United States once the suit was settled successfully.

The Belmont banking dynasty ended with the end of the Rothschilds' influence, much as it had arisen on the family's name 100 years before. But its importance, especially during the life of August Sr., cannot be overestimated. During the nineteenth century, the American economy depended on foreign capital, and Belmont was the conduit for a large portion of it. Without him, the money would surely have found another agent, but no one perhaps as colorful and willing to be American at any price.

4

CRASHED AND ABSORBED: KIDDER PEABODY AND DILLON READ

THE HEADS OF ALL OF THE Jewish banking houses on Wall Street in the nineteenth century wanted to be affiliated with the Rothschilds. August Belmont was the only one who succeeded, and his success was assured although his firm did not survive the 1920s. Among the Yankee banking houses, the only direct tie with a foreign firm that would spell success was a link with the venerable British bank Baring Brothers. In many respects, that link was even more difficult to achieve because, while the Rothschild power was begrudgingly admired, Baring was closely allied with the British crown—a source of much controversy during times of financial crisis. But one Yankee bank managed to forge the link, and it paid off handsomely over the years. The other forged an even more significant link, but it came too late.

Kidder Peabody and Dillon Read were two major banking houses of the nineteenth century referred to as Yankee bankers. Their businesses were not substantially different from those of the other Yankee bankers in the nineteenth century—with one exception: Kidder developed a relationship with Baring Brothers of London early in its history that would serve it well over the years. Doing international business in the nineteenth century meant allying closely with a British bank, since the British were the largest investors in the United States, providing a major source of capital both before and after the Civil War. As August Belmont proved, once the United States became self-sufficient in terms of capital the importance of that link began to fade.

By the 1920s, American investment banking had begun to change substantially and the British played little role in domestic developments. Banks affiliated with them also underwent major internal changes as a result and had to adapt quickly to survive.

Most of the private banks that emerged before the Civil War became legendary names on Wall Street, where their longevity and reputations were prized. Kidder Peabody and Dillon Read were no exceptions. Kidder developed an early reputation for conservative investment banking that initially appealed to the powerful Baring and earned it a solid if not spectacular reputation on the Street. Dillon Read did the same and, like the powerful Jewish-American banking houses, contributed some of its partners to Washington politics, further enhancing the firm's reputation. After years of relatively conservative investment banking, it was ironic that both firms' futures were severely affected in the 1990s by rogue traders whose shenanigans proved fatal for Kidder and caused Dillon Read to find new allegiances.

The early years of Kidder Peabody were similar in many respects to those of Brown Brothers or Clark Dodge. The firm was founded in Boston by Henry Kidder, Francis Peabody, and Oliver Peabody in 1865. The Peabodys were not related to George Peabody, who had started the successful London bank that bore his name. The three partners took over the firm previously known as Thayer & Co., a well-respected Boston private bank founded by John Eliot Thayer in 1824. In the thirty years that Thayer & Co. existed before its founder's death, it had become a fixture in Boston finance along with Lee, Higginson & Co., perhaps Boston's best-known private investment bank in the nineteenth and early twentieth centuries. Thayer had helped establish the Boston Stock Exchange as a genuine national market in 1834. Previously, the exchange existed in a smaller, more limited capacity, serving mostly New England. But Thayer & Co. was extremely limited in its organization. The two original partners were Thayer and his brother Nathaniel. After Nathaniel was admitted to the partnership and the firm changed its name to J. E. Thayer & Brother, he began to lead it into railroad financing. Henry Kidder was made a partner in 1858. Other alliances with banks and insurance companies led the firm to become more of an investment bank and less of a broker, a trait that helped it survive the Panic of 1857.

Nathaniel did not have any offspring who could carry on the family tradition, and after his retirement during the Civil War, two of his former clerks, Oliver and Francis Peabody, took over the reins of the firm with Kidder and reorganized it as Kidder, Peabody & Co. The firm they inherited was in a strong position because of its extensive business connections both in New England and around the country. Having served Thayer for more than twenty years meant that they also were intimately familiar with the business, not simply outsiders taking over from an original partner of a successful firm. The essential link for success and succession was forged much in the same way that Clark Dodge had ensured its own survival around the same time. But if Kidder Peabody was to survive the expansion years of the post–Civil War era, when the demands for capital became larger and larger, it would have to forge links with other banks.

In the 1860s, Kidder Peabody's business was very similar to that of Clark Dodge or Brown Brothers. It engaged in loan making, securities dealing, letters of credit, and foreign exchange. It was not particularly active in the Treasury bond business during the Civil War, but the success of Jay Cooke did not go unnoticed by the firm's partners. By the early 1870s, Kidder was actively involved with the refunding of the war issues. Participation in the refundings, along with the international exposure given by the letter-of-credit business, prompted Kidder to begin doing business with Baring Brothers in London. Within a decade, the firm was appointed Baring's sole American agent, a highly coveted designation that ensured a continual stream of business for years to come. In 1885, Thomas Baring, until then working for the British bank in Liverpool, became a partner in the New York office, taking a full 20 percent of the profits. His presence aided Kidder immeasurably, for one of his first tasks was to help establish better relationships with Drexel and Brown Brothers. His nephew, working for Kidder, wrote that "one of his chief contributions was establishing a better relationship between Kidder Peabody and such rivals . . . they used to snarl at each other, but now the partners of both houses have all been in here, and we have dined with them and what not . . . Belmont also—a dog Jew—has been very civil and appeals to Uncle Tom's stomach—which is more than one can say for any of the others."[1]

In a short period of time, Thayer's original firm had achieved the same status as that of August Belmont in New York. Like Belmont, Kidder Peabody was able to remain in the forefront of domestic finance because of its Baring connections. Yet the partners' personal styles could not have been more different from that of Belmont. None of the three original partners was a socialite or ventured into the public eye very often. Other than the occasional political connection, Kidder partners remained very private. Henry Kidder quietly ruled the firm as managing partner until his death in 1886.

Thayer became involved in railroad financings quite early in his career, and Kidder continued the tradition. The partners became the prime bankers to the Atchison, Topeka and Santa Fe Railroad after the Civil War and remained so for years. One of the stock-trading posts at the Boston Stock Exchange was nicknamed the Atchison Post, and the exchange traded the bulk of the company's stock rather than the NYSE as a result of Kidder's Boston headquarters. Baring also was persuaded to invest heavily in the railroad and became a major shareholder, along with Kidder. The railroad later became known simply as the Santa Fe, and Kidder was recognized as its major banker, holding several board seats. As the partnership expanded, the bank's partners were added to the railroad's board of directors until they came to dominate the executive committee. Control of the Santa Fe was the major preoccupation of Kidder during the late nineteenth century, and the fees derived from it contributed to the bank's major-league standing in the investment community. It also added to the firm's reputation as a bank capable of reorganizing companies in financial trouble, since the railroad was not in good financial shape prior to Kidder's involvement.

The bank's investment in the railroad also protected it from Jay Gould, who had expressed an interest in it. Unfortunately, its fate would probably not have changed. During the Panic of 1893, scores of railroads were forced into bankruptcy, and the Santa Fe was one of them. But Kidder's reputation was already made. When J. P. Morgan called his famous meeting of railroad barons and bankers after the Interstate Commerce Commission was formed, Kidder and Brown Brothers were the only two bankers present besides Morgan himself. Many others, including Kuhn Loeb and Clark Dodge, also engaged in railroad financing, but only the successful Yankee bankers merited an invitation from Morgan.

Kidder's conservative business practices helped it easily survive the economic upheavals of the nineteenth century. The Panic of 1873 had little effect, although the Panic of 1893 hit somewhat closer to home, affecting more than 25 percent of the nation's railroads adversely. Despite the Santa Fe bankruptcy, Kidder survived intact. And in the political arena, the conservativeness displayed itself when issues close to the firm surfaced. Like most banks, Kidder opposed the Sherman Silver Act because the partners believed that silver was deterring capital from flowing into the country from abroad. Francis Peabody wrote to President Benjamin Harrison that the Treasury's support for silver "impresses me as an unnecessary evil to us all."[2] He urged repeal of the act, which came shortly thereafter during the administration of Grover Cleveland.

After Morgan and Belmont accomplished the support operation to shore up Treasury reserves, the economy rebounded and a boom began that benefited Kidder especially. Like many other investment bankers of the day, the house helped finance the explosive boom in mergers that occurred during the Republican administration of William McKinley. The merger boom, already simmering, was given a strong boost by a Supreme Court ruling in the case of the *United States v. E.C. Knight Co.*, in which the Court struck down the government's attempt to prosecute the company under the Sherman Antitrust Act. A phenomenal number of mergers ensued in almost every industry in the country, and the trend was halted only somewhat by the Court's opposite ruling in the Northern Securities case against Morgan and the railroad barons. In the five-year period between the two cases, investment bankers helped construct hundreds of new, larger companies, and Kidder Peabody fully benefited from the trend. Mergers and acquisitions became one of the specialized skills that it would practice for decades to come.

During the later 1890s, Kidder became a major banker and financial consultant to numerous companies, the better known being the American Sugar Refining Company, P. Lorillard & Co., and American Telephone & Telegraph. American Sugar was built by Charles Havenmeyer, who began gobbling up smaller companies until the trust controlled well over 90 percent of sugar production in the country. It also came under severe criticism for having a watered capital structure. One notable critic was V. I. Lenin, who wrote, "Havenmeyer founded the Sugar Trust by amalgamating fifteen smaller firms whose total capital amounted to $6.5 million. Suitably watered, as the Americans say, the capital of the trust was declared to be $50 million."[3] In other words, the new whole was larger than the sum of its parts, and Kidder Peabody added its expertise in achieving the new capital structure of the company. The fees it reaped were substantial, and Kidder helped the United States into the first great merger boom in its history.

Of all the companies that Kidder Peabody helped finance, none was more important to the firm's history than AT&T. At the turn of the century, the smaller telephone companies were experiencing financial difficulties because of the intense capital nature of the business. An opportunity existed to finance the smaller phone companies, many of which operated under license from Edison, and consolidate them into a larger, nationwide entity. First involvement with AT&T came in 1899 when Kidder helped finance a bond issue for the company. The Boston location proved helpful, because for much of the nineteenth century the Boston Stock Exchange had been a major home for trading industrial stocks and bonds while the NYSE traded mostly shares of financial companies and the railroads. While the shift to New York had been slowly developing over the years, Kidder built up substantial expertise in industrial companies and AT&T recognized the firm as a leader in industrial financing.

Using the Baring connection, Kidder became the major Boston banker to AT&T. J. P. Morgan, and to a lesser extent Kuhn Loeb, were the company's principal bankers on Wall Street; that relationship would last until 1907, when Morgan assumed the role. Robert Winsor, realizing the shortcomings of doing new financings in Boston, asked Morgan and Kuhn Loeb to play more of a major role in financing AT&T on Wall Street. Although Kidder had had a New York office since 1868, it was still considered a regional firm until the twentieth century. Kidder was being used as a regional investment banker at a time when nationwide distribution of securities for companies needing fresh capital was still fairly rare. Many of the bonds were sold outside the United States, and the Baring connection proved invaluable since foreign investors displayed a voracious appetite for quality American companies whose balance sheets accurately reflected the companies' financial positions.

For most of the nineteenth century, Kidder Peabody remained a small partnership. It never had more than a dozen partners and did not admit its fourth partner until 1872, when George Magoun was admitted, followed by Thomas Baring of the London Barings in 1886. The conservative policies established by the original partners therefore continued well into the latter part of the nineteenth century. Reorganization followed in 1891, after Baring Brothers in London failed because of poorly performing South American securities. Barings found itself crushed under the weight of unsold South American bonds and its capital was severely depleted. The venerable house was saved by intervention by the Bank of England and subsequently reorganized. The Boston office kept the Kidder Peabody name, while the New York branch renamed itself Baring, Magoun & Co. Kidder Peabody's capital was around $5 million in 1891, not a substantial amount of money when compared with that of some of the other major firms on Wall Street.[4] It was not the firm's balance sheet capital that was of primary concern on Wall Street, but its access to the overseas investment capital provided by Baring. Kidder had become the Yankee, Christian equivalent of August Belmont & Co., and while the fact was not discussed openly it was still of primary importance on Wall Street because dislike of foreigners and anti-Semitism were never far from the surface.

Being a small partnership, Kidder Peabody kept most of the arrangements among the partners on an informal basis. The role the partners played in the firm as well as the amount of money they made annually was never written down; rather, it was a matter of informal record only. During the nineteenth and early twentieth centuries, that sort of arrangement worked well, but by the 1920s, as Wall Street was becoming larger, the informal relationships began to strain under the volume of new business and the need to expand. Like most old-line firms, Kidder did not practice what today is known as risk management. It relied on a conservative philosophy of extending business relationships to see it through good times and bad. As long as the relationships with Baring and, later, J. P. Morgan worked well enough, there was little cause for concern. But when the Baring connection proved shaky, as in 1890–91, the firm had to reorganize legally to avoid problems. Under those circumstances, the firm relied to a great extent on the goodwill of J. P. Morgan in the United States for its new business. Besides the AT&T deal, Morgan invited Kidder in 1901 into the organization of U.S. Steel, which became a great source of profit for the firm. After Morgan officially reorganized AT&T in 1907, even more deals followed for the telephone company, catapulting Kidder into the first rank of Wall Street underwriters and investment bankers.

Business was so good before World War I that Kidder found itself atop the Wall Street league tables. Along with Morgan, Kuhn Loeb, and Lee Higginson, it became a member of the "money trust," the name given to the bankers who helped finance the giant trusts of the day. The group got its name from the Progressives who saw the bankers operating in the same way as the giant industrial companies of the day. All members of the putative trust were Morgan allies, and their partners were close colleagues of J. P. Morgan, who valued their conservative banking practices and steady management practices. Kidder was a prime example of both. The last surviving original partner, Francis Peabody, died in 1905, and the firm passed into younger hands, with Frank Webster and Robert Winsor running the firm. Webster was the older, having started with the firm during the Civil War, whereas Winsor joined the firm in the 1890s after graduating from Harvard. While the partnership was making great strides in investment banking, traditional deposit taking was occupying less and less of the partners' time. However, in 1907 the firm accepted a $10 million deposit from the Italian government as a result of a Baring recommendation. Many foreign companies and governments were placing funds on deposit outside Europe, as the Petrograd Metalworks did with Belmont. Unfortunately, the Italian deposit would prove to be a bane for Kidder Peabody some years later and cause major distress for the partnership just before the Glass-Steagall Act was passed in 1933.

Before the First World War, a congressional committee headed by Rep. Arsenee Pujo of Louisiana began hearings into what had become known as the "money trust," the concentration of banks in New York that was reputed to control the reins of credit in the United States. In its final report, the committee wrote: "It is a fair deduction from the testimony that the most active agents in forwarding and bringing about the concentration of control of money and credit through [investment banking] processes above described have been and are: J. P. Morgan & Co., First National Bank of New York, National City Bank of New York, Lee Higginson & Co., Kidder, Peabody & Co., and Kuhn Loeb & Co."[5] According to the Pujo Committee, these six institutions effectively controlled the path to market for American corporations and actively cooperated, if not colluded, to ensure that capital was raised on their terms at their prices. The group was notable both for those firms included as well as those omitted. First National and National City were the two largest New York commercial banks and were included simply for their sheer financial muscle. First National was headed by George Baker, the second most powerful banker in New York after J. P. Morgan; National City was headed by James Stillman; and Kuhn Loeb was headed by Jacob Schiff—all extremely well known in their own right. Kidder and Lee Higginson were somewhat different.

Lee Higginson was founded in 1848 by John Lee and George Higginson, both from Boston. The small firm was originally a stockbroker and dealt in commodities, as did many firms of the period. The original partners carried on diligently, but the firm did not begin to grow larger until the next generation of their respective families entered after the Civil War. One notable connection was made in 1853 when the firm opened an account with Baring Brothers and began doing a substantial business with it in foreign exchange and notes receivable. But a link with Barings was not easy, nor was it earned quickly. In 1848, Lee Higginson offered to be Baring's Boston agent for the sale of securities and foreign exchange, but the offer was declined. The London bank felt that the Boston bank's capital was too small. Even when the connection was made in 1853, the Boston bank's capital was only $250,000, too small for the firm to act effectively as agent for the legendary London bank.[6] But the original relationship developed between them established a long-standing connection with the British bank that would contribute considerably to the firm's future success, although it was never on the order of Baring's relationship with Kidder.

The most notable partner of the firm was Henry Lee Higginson, who joined after graduating from Harvard and serving in the Union

Army. Henry, like many of his generation, was not keen about having to work for a living. His father and brother both worked for the firm, but he claimed that "I was taken in at the beginning of 1868 as a matter of charity, to keep me out of the poorhouse; I had been in the War, had been planting cotton at the South, and lost all I had, and more too."[7] His friend and college classmate Henry Adams recalled that he was, "after a difficult struggle, forced into State Street." Fortunes began to change after he joined the firm. He was about $15,000 in debt when he joined, but quickly made enough money to pay his creditors. The partners sent him to the Boston Stock Exchange, where he worked as a broker on the floor, trading in shares of local companies and the regional railroads. Shortly thereafter, he traveled to London to raise much-needed cash from the Barings and indulge himself in the arts. The money was useful in fending off the effects of the Panic of 1873, and the firm survived intact. By 1881, only thirteen years after joining Lee Higginson, Henry had helped found the Boston Symphony Orchestra and had begun devoting most of his time and attention to the arts. In many ways, his career resembled that of August Belmont, who also began his extracurricular activities relatively early in his professional life.

Like August Belmont & Co., Lee Higginson & Co. would survive until the late 1920s before a major scandal forced it to retrench. But at the time of the Pujo hearings, it was a major Boston private banking house with close ties to Baring Brothers. The official money trust, while certainly representing the powerful New York banks, did not include all of them by any means. Notable for their absence were the Seligmans, Brown Brothers, and Goldman Sachs. What the money trust did have in common were ties to Morgan and access to foreign investors. Henry Lee Higginson was a personal friend of J. P. Morgan; without that and his Baring alliance, it is doubtful that Lee Higginson would have been included in the group.

Morgan deals helped Lee Higginson to prosper in the late nineteenth and early twentieth centuries. In its early days, it invested in mining stocks and did quite well, accumulating enough capital to contribute to the business. When it acted as underwriter, it had Morgan to thank. Early deals included the formation of General Electric and American Bell Telephone, the predecessor of AT&T. Before the First

World War, it joined with August Belmont & Co. to help underwrite the New York City subway and the Holland Tunnel under the Hudson River. In both cases, the friendship between its senior partner, Gardiner Lane, and August Belmont Jr. paved the way for the firm's participation. The firm eventually incorporated in 1924, but its fortunes took a downward turn when it became allied with Swedish financier Ivar Kreuger in the 1920s. Kreuger's mysterious death in 1932 and the collapse of his highly leveraged international empire was an embarrassing episode the firm never overcame. Although it continued in business until the 1960s, the firm never recaptured its once eminent place on Wall Street and State Street.

Despite all of the successes the private bankers had in achieving fame and fortune in the nineteenth century, it was clear that J. P. Morgan was the dominant figure in New York banking. The money trust was to a large extent actually a group of banks organized by Morgan that controlled access to long-term capital. This was not done by sheer financial muscle alone. The private investment banks in the money trust—Kidder Peabody, Lee Higginson, and Kuhn Loeb—did not have much capital between them when compared to the large money-center banks, but their influence was still strong. Kidder's capital was less than $7 million before the First World War. The partners sat on the boards of many companies, often with Morgan partners and commercial bank officers. The interlocking directorships meant that raising capital was done in very small circles by men who knew each other very well and were suspected of handing out investment banking deals with generous fees to their colleagues regardless of the amounts paid. They were enriching themselves and their friends at the expense of depositors and companies who had no say in the deployment of their money. As Louis Brandeis said in his famous book published after the Pujo hearings, the bankers made a fortune using other people's money.

The bankers recognized the issue but refused to acknowledge it as a serious problem. Responding to a question from Samuel Untermyer, chief counsel to the Pujo Committee, George Baker made it clear that the concentration of power at the top was not a problem as long as the proper sort of men exercised control. Untermyer asked him if the concentration of financial power had gone far enough, in his opinion.

Baker responded that, "in good hands, I do not see that it would do any harm. If it got into bad hands, it would be very bad . . . but I do not believe it could get into bad hands."[8] The reason for the optimism was simple. Morgan and Baker would see that it did not get into bad hands. They controlled the concentration of top investment bankers and admitted to their group only those who toed the unofficial Morgan line. The requisites for belonging to the money trust were fairly simple: bankers had to be discreet, have serious influence in the market for new bond and stock issues, and have access to foreign investors who were needed to purchase the new issues. Although one or two Jewish firms could have been included in the group, Morgan used them only as he thought appropriate. In his later years, Morgan even began to distrust some of his older friends in the business who aligned themselves with his business enemies, like John D. Rockefeller of Standard Oil. First National Bank was Rockefeller's main banker. Around 1904, Morgan contemplated a merger with Baring Brothers, thinking himself isolated in New York banking circles. One of the Baring partners recalled that Morgan "inveighed bitterly against the growing power of the Jews and of the Rockefeller crowd, and said more than once that our firm and his were the only two composed of white men in New York."[9]

Morgan's famous dislike of the nouveau riche was something of an indirect compliment to those bankers who made their mark on American finance in the nineteenth century. Fortunately for Kidder Peabody, its Boston location and Baring connection made it acceptable. Like other congressional investigations and court cases that were to follow, the hearings helped Kidder's public relations image considerably. The hearings displayed the full extent of the bank's corporate influence. After 1905, the bank's five Boston partners held nine directorships in New England banks and a dozen directorships in nonfinancial companies, underwrote the securities of more than one hundred corporations of all sorts worth more than $1 billion, and had dozens of financial relationships with other companies. The congressional report concluded that Kidder, along with the other members of the money trust, represented a "handful of self-constituted trustees of the national prosperity."[10]

The years immediately preceding the World War proved to be a watershed for American business and finance. In addition to the Pujo hearings, there was the Supreme Court's breakup of Standard Oil and American Tobacco. The Federal Reserve was created by Congress. On Wall Street, the hearings forced the investment banking community to form a trade organization for the first time. The Investment Bankers Association was formed in 1912 to organize a disparate group of 200 investment banks into a single group so that it could contend with criticisms and formulate coherent objectives for the future. As the previously loose regulatory and professional framework under which the Wall Street firms operated became more formalized, the influence of the larger Wall Street houses became slightly diminished, although no one would argue that J. P. Morgan remained at the very top of the hierarchy. But the effects of the war and the new prosperity in the 1920s would also signal monumental changes for Kidder Peabody as the importance of the Baring connection began to fade.

The New Era

Despite the revelations of the Pujo hearings, the investment bankers again appeared in their usual concentrations to help finance the war effort. The Treasury had great success selling the various Liberty Loans directly to the public, usually employing the investment bankers to solicit the public by mail. The investment bankers busied themselves with the occasional domestic bond as well as those for foreign countries. The money trust was again in full stride, and few disputed its ability to raise funds during wartime.

AT&T raised a huge bond issue during the war, and Kidder Peabody naturally participated along with the usual Morgan syndicate. The Winchester Repeating Arms Company also raised money, using Kidder as its investment banker, and the house participated in the loans to the Allies and Russia that Jacob Schiff at Kuhn Loeb objected to. The issuing activity was not out of the ordinary, in view of the war. The firm remained the same size throughout the war years, and like the other firms of the period did not add any new partners or expand greatly in size. By the time the 1920s began, it needed to expand to keep pace with the new consumer-driven society. But the need to expand was not adopted wholeheartedly. Kidder was on the verge of the New Era without a clear commitment to a specific direction.

Unlike many Wall Street firms in the 1920s, Kidder was still headed by a relatively old (in Wall Street terms) investment banker more attuned to the prewar years than the 1920s. Robert Winsor still headed the firm as the 1920s dawned, and he was sixty-one years old. His affection for State Street in Boston was apparent, and he traveled to New York only once a week to visit Kidder's New York office located in the NYSE building. And he did not trust equities or the stock market. As a result, Kidder continued to underwrite mainly bonds. Issues of AT&T bonds still dominated the firm's profit margins. The neglect of equities cost the firm some clients, since many investors were turning their attention toward stocks in the first great move toward investment by the general public in American history. One notable exception to the rule was AT&T stock, which Kidder actively promoted at the behest of the company's president. Most telling about the AT&T stock issue was that Charles Francis Adams wrote a letter to the president of the telephone company, Harry B. Thayer, that he thought Winsor's firm had done a remarkable job of promoting the issue.[11] The juxtaposition of old Boston names was not unusual, but whether the sort of business Winsor insisted on promoting would see Kidder through the hard times ahead was another matter.

Throughout the 1920s Kidder Peabody continued to practice business as usual, with a mix not unlike that practiced at the end of the nineteenth century. Underwriting continued apace, but the emphasis on bonds rather than stocks knocked down the potential margins for profit. Kidder did, however, add retail sales to its mix in an attempt to reach the small investors who were making their presence felt in greater and greater numbers. One of the more unusual services the firm offered was a code book, distributed to its better customers, that they could use to keep in touch with the offices at home when traveling internationally. In a 1923 edition, published jointly with Baring, Kidder offered a wide array of code words customers could use when cabling either one of the two firms' offices. Ironically, the cable code word for Kidder in New York was MULCTED, while for Baring it was MULATTO.

Retail sales became an integral, although not particularly large, part of Kidder's operations. The company opened retail sales offices in Massachusetts and in New York City. It even opened its own in-house sales school to train the brokers in effective selling techniques. But the product range was somewhat limited. Most of the sales force pushed AT&T common stock only, and did not encourage margin accounts from customers. That limited scope helped save the firm from the worst ravages of the Crash of 1929. Ironically, it was the traditional private banking business that caused serious difficulties.

The stock market crash troubled Kidder Peabody, but the firm survived intact. But events in 1930 caused it to fail, creating a low point in the firm's history. The informal structure of the company came to haunt it when many of its senior partners decided to retire, taking their capital with them as they did. The new partners who had been admitted over the years were never required to bring new money with them, so the firm was suffering withdrawals of capital at the same time as the Crash. In financial circles, the situation became well-known and depositors began to withdraw their funds, creating a situation not unlike that which befell Jay Cooke seventy years before. The final blow occurred when the Italian government withdrew the balance of its deposit, causing the firm to seek outside assistance in order to survive. Kidder Peabody became the best-known victim of the financial crisis of 1929 on Wall Street. The only question was who would pick up the pieces so the firm could begin again.

In a move reminiscent of previous Wall Street panics, Kidder was bailed out by J. P. Morgan. In times of financial distress, it was natural for larger, solvent firms to extend assistance to the smaller, and 1930 proved to be no exception. The original tab for the bailout was $15 million. Kidder approached Morgan, who agreed to help out an old banking friend. The negotiations lasted months. Morgan organized a bailout group consisting of New York and Boston banks and several private investors, one of whom was Mortimer Schiff of Kuhn Loeb. The group provided $10 million, while Kidder was required to raise another $5 million on its own, which it did without much difficulty. Just when all appeared well, however, the bank's fortunes quickly sank again. The $15 million was not enough, and a further transfusion was needed to avoid catastrophe. Someone from the outside was needed to bring in both cash and fresh expertise.

The new talent came in the form of Chandler Hovey, Albert Gordon, and Edwin Webster. Although separated by twenty years in age, the three all had some connection, either direct or familial, to Kidder in the past. Webster's father, the founder of Stone & Webster, an engineering firm, had worked for Kidder in the nineteenth century before setting out on his own. Hovey, from an old Boston family, was Webster's brother-in-law, whereas Gordon was his classmate at Harvard. The three reorganized Kidder Peabody, keeping the firm name intact since its name and connections were considered its greatest assets. No one from the old firm was taken as a partner, and the new firm started in March 1931 with around $5 million in capital. Most of the capital was provided by Webster's father; Hovey and Gordon contributed about $500,000 between them.[12] The firm, with seats on the NYSE and the Boston Stock Exchange, was back in business, but its capital was only the size of Clark Dodge's a century before.

Ironically, Kidder reorganized before the Glass-Steagall Act would have required it two years later. At the time, it was no longer a full-service private corporate bank but an investment banking partnership, dedicated to the securities business alone. In 1931, it absorbed a smaller house, Kissell, Kinnicutt & Co. of New York, and merged its operations with its own, taking in a few of the firm's partners as well. Unfortunately, the reorganization came during the worst part of the Depression. Kidder would be able to keep its head above water but certainly did not report outstanding financial results for the balance of the 1930s. But better days were coming, and Kidder waited for them along with the rest of Wall Street.

Starting Anew

The new Kidder Peabody survived the ordeal of the 1930s but still had a serious problem. Capital was becoming an issue on Wall Street in the postwar years, and firms like Kidder were always short of it. That situation was tolerable as long as underwriters had someone to sell their new issues to, whether they were retail or institutional customers. The old Kidder used Baring as an outlet for many of its underwritings, but when that connection began to fade the firm was left on its own to find investors. The new Kidder did not have the same luxury and quickly was thrown into the frying pan of Wall Street at a time when investment bankers were hardly popular. In addition, the new firm had to play by a new set of rules, because after 1935 the newly formed Securities and Exchange Commission was beginning to consolidate its power and exercise influence on the Street.

Combining these factors seemed to be a serious deterrent to the success of the new partnership. But Kidder plodded along and survived the 1930s intact. With business at low ebb, developing methods of survival was not easy. The Securities Act, passed in 1933, required companies needing to issue new securities to register them with the SEC after it was established in 1934. The new law badly irritated many on Wall Street, and many investment banks found ways to circumvent it by bringing new issues—especially bond issues—to market privately. These were known as private placements, and if they were properly constructed, they avoided the rigors of the new law. But new-issue activity was also at low ebb, and private placements were not going to make the investment banks rich. New ways were needed to generate profits in a dismal market.

Adding insult to injury, the Securities Exchange Act, passed by Congress in 1934, created the SEC itself and laid down a stringent set of rules by which the stock exchanges would have to operate. New rules were put in place that governed stock trading from the time an order was taken from a customer to the actual trade on the exchange floor. Rules governing short selling, wash sales, and many other practices that had often been abused in the past strictly governed brokers' behavior, with the SEC as the overseer of the secondary market. Floor traders also were skeptical of the new rules yet had little choice but to follow them. Amid all of the confusion, Kidder somehow managed to develop new techniques that would carry it through the 1930s, proving that it had the ingenuity if not vast of amounts of capital to help it survive.

Of the three new partners, it was Gordon who was most responsible for helping the new partnership weather the storm of the 1930s. He developed new strategies for the new Kidder on different sides of the business. The new firm could not lay claim to any of its predecessor's investment banking clients, not even AT&T. George Whitney, partner at J. P. Morgan, told Gordon that Kidder's participation in future AT&T syndicates would depend entirely on merit, not the firm's previous ties. As a result, Gordon decided to find new investment banking clients. Chasing the largest corporations was fruitless because of their previous ties, but smaller companies often were overlooked by Wall Street. Taking a page out of Lehman Brothers' book, he sought out companies that did not yet have established investment banking ties. The only way to entice them to use Kidder was to become expert in new securities pricing. Gordon developed a reputation on Wall Street as one of corporate finance's most expert pricing specialists, striking a balance between what a company should pay for its securities and what investors were willing to pay on the other side.[13]

The other side of the business he developed was selling and buying large amounts of stock away from the exchange floor. This was known as block trading. Customers could cross their large orders with Kidder rather than pass them through the floor brokers, paying less commission and obtaining a better price in the process. This was particularly important inasmuch as the exchanges were very wary of doing business in large sizes in the 1930s because of the general economic climate. After the stock indices had recovered slightly from the post-1929 fiasco, another recession sent the averages tumbling again in 1937. Using an investment banker to find another customer and do the deal quietly proved to be a great service to those customers who were actively trading in the 1930s despite the overall state of the economy.

Wall Street did not revive until the 1950s. The war years were dominated by massive Treasury financings, and corporate securities activities were put on hold. But once the Korean War ended, the market was again poised for a rally. Capital investment increased and consumers went on a buying spree not seen in thirty years. It was a period of great expansion, especially for the medium-size companies that Gordon had begun focusing on twenty years before. As a result, Kidder again rose to the top tier of investment banking as Gordon became its guiding light throughout the expansive 1950s and 1960s. In addition to its usual activities, Kidder became expert in underwriting new issues for utilities companies and municipal bonds, and packaging and distributing mutual funds.

However, throughout the expansion, capital remained a problem since bond and stock deals were becoming larger all the time. The capital problem again was leading to reorganization.

Finally, in 1964, Kidder reluctantly decided to incorporate. Potential liabilities were becoming too large for the firm to continue as a traditional partnership. The firm's forty partners became shareholders in the new company and Gordon remained as head of the firm. But the incorporation was not the same as going public. Kidder was still a closely held partnership in the true sense of the word, but it incorporated to protect its principals from unlimited liabilities from some unforeseen event. Some of the travails of Wall Street in the late 1960s and early 1970s proved the decision to be a sound one, even though Kidder emerged from the backroom paper jams of the period unscathed. While still not highly capitalized, it managed to avert the general Wall Street crisis of the period and make an acquisition of its own in 1974, when it purchased Clark Dodge & Co. Two of the Street's oldest firms finally wed, but by the 1970s Clark Dodge was coveted mostly for its customer base and twenty-odd branches rather than its position atop Wall Street's league table of powerful firms.

Kidder Peabody managed to reestablish itself as a major Wall Street investment bank in the postwar years under the guidance of Gordon and, later, Ralph DeNunzio. DeNunzio joined the firm after graduating from Princeton in 1953 and worked for it until he was elevated to the executive committee in 1969. He was also chairman of the New York Stock Exchange at a particularly turbulent time in its history. Not all of the period was positive, because the firm became involved with financier Robert Vesco, who was intricately involved with members of the Nixon administration charged with influence peddling. But by the early 1980s, Kidder was again a premier investment bank in terms of influence if not of capital.

Handwriting on the Wall

After competing successfully on Wall Street for more than fifty years, Kidder Peabody again began to feel a capital pinch in 1986. By the end of 1985, Kidder was falling short of capital requirements of both the SEC and the NYSE because it had a large portion of its existing capital tied up in municipal bond inventories from which it could not easily extricate itself. DeNunzio realized that the firm needed a massive transfusion of cash from outside sources. On the last day of 1985, the firm realized that it was short of cash and turned to a time-proven method of raising it: it arranged to borrow cash from a syndicate of banks and investors. While that had been successful in 1930, it proved to be a very short-term palliative in 1986. New areas of interest, like derivatives trading, and the old stalwarts, like underwriting corporate securities, were extremely capital intensive and Kidder could not raise enough to keep abreast of the growing financial marketplace. The borrowing facility proved to be only a drop in the bucket for Kidder, and many established executives at the firm began to feel uncomfortable about its future.

In the spring of 1985, the writing was on the wall and Kidder sold 80 percent of the firm, closely held among the partners, to General Electric. Technically, the stake was sold to the finance subsidiary of GE. The sale increased its capital to $350 million. At the time of the sale, DeNunzio held 7 percent of the firm's stock and Gordon still held 6 percent. Another $150 million of capital was added to the balance sheet, bringing Kidder into line with other top-tier investment banking firms. At the same time, Morgan Stanley went public—an option Kidder resisted as being inadequate. The number of private partnerships was dwindling quickly in the rapidly moving financial environment of the 1980s.

Shortly after the purchase, GE announced a major shake-up in Kidder's management designed to ensure that the parent company maintained control of the investment bank. DeNunzio was replaced as chief executive by Silas Cathcart, a GE director. DeNunzio remained as chairman, but it was clear that GE wanted to control the operation closely. Investment banking was a new endeavor for the old-line electrical company, which had diversified itself substantially over the years. GE, one of the original Dow component stocks, was formed by J. P. Morgan, who bought a controlling interest from Thomas Edison in the nineteenth century. By the 1980s, it was a vast, diversified company with interests in financial services as well as manufacturing and broadcasting.

Kidder Peabody enjoyed another decade of prosperity before the roof crashed in. The new financial environment, to which it adapted successfully, finally took its toll on one of the country's oldest continuously operated investment banks. Ironically, the demise of Kidder occurred in the same short period of time that also claimed its long-time ally, Baring Brothers. And perhaps the greatest irony was that it succumbed to underhanded tactics in the Treasury bond market by a rogue trader who later claimed that the firm knew what he was doing from the first moment and condoned it as long as it made money.

Kidder was purchased from GE by Paine Webber in 1995, ending the Kidder name after more than a century in the market. Paine Webber paid $670 million to GE. The acquisition increased its capital by around 14 percent to over $4 billion, still not the top of the league among securities firms but substantially larger than it had been before. GE and its chairman, Jack Welch, became tired of dealing with the investment banking culture that naturally surrounded Kidder, but it was a scandal in the Treasury market that finally caused the sale of the firm. Several years before, Kidder had hired Joseph Jett as a bond trader in its Treasury bond department. He was assigned to trading zero coupon Treasury bonds, securities that did not carry large profit margins with them when traded unless interest rates changed substantially. For a few years Jett was relatively quiet—before making an enormous splash in 1992 and 1993. His department showed enormous profits and he was awarded a bonus in 1993 of $9 million. Clearly, he had become the darling of Kidder. But the profits soon evaporated when it was discovered that they were not real—they were achieved only by manipulating Kidder's internal accounting system. Jett was subsequently fired and sued for restitution, and the case lingered in the courts for several years. But the damage to Kidder was terminal.

Further, GE had not been fully able to integrate the investment banking firm into its corporate culture and discovered that it was spending an undue amount of time on the firm given its small impact on its overall bottom line. Welch then took the opportunity to sell Kidder, without much fanfare. Adding to the lack of profits, the Jett affair ran counter to the corporate chain of command and responsibility at GE and left Welch furious. "Having this reprehensible scheme, which violated everything we believe in and stand for, break our more than decade-long string of 'no surprises' has all of us damn mad," he fumed when questioned about the Jett affair.[14] GE, which eventually paid a total of $600 million for Kidder, sold it for about 12 percent more than it had paid ten years before. One of Wall Street's oldest and most estimable firms disappeared through the cracks of a corporate culture unsympathetic to investment banking culture and a new financial environment it never fully adapted to.

The Rise of Dillon Read

There were dozens of banks with brokerage operations on Wall Street after the Civil War. Most were small operations run by several men supported by up to a dozen clerks. The panics usually reduced their ranks greatly, since their customers did not provide enough support in times of financial crisis. Those firms that did survive were led by strong individuals who followed a conservative business philosophy, as in the case of Brown Brothers and the Seligmans. The same proved true of another small Yankee firm founded before the Civil War that was content to pursue its business quietly until a strong-willed individual joined it and gave it direction.

Vermilye & Co. was an old firm, tracing its origins to 1832. Officially, it began as Carpenter & Vermilye, with George Carpenter and Washington Vermilye as the two original partners. Of the two, Vermilye was the more influential and had access to more family wealth. The young firm originally dealt in stocks, lottery tickets, and commercial trade bills—in short, anything that would yield a profit. But it was only one of dozens of similar firms on the Street scraping out a living. It did manage to survive the Panics of 1837 and 1857 intact but remained a small, undistinguished, family-run firm until the Civil War. Then a stroke of good luck changed its fortunes considerably. Wall Street became preoccupied with the huge Treasury financings, and Jay Cooke required some help selling the bonds.

Washington Vermilye was a strong supporter of the Union, and his firm plunged into the financings with Cooke without hesitation. Since foreign support for the Treasury bonds was not strong, Cooke needed domestic help distributing them, and he turned to the small firm through a personal contact. Vermilye & Co. was not serious competition for Cooke, but it was helpful in selling the bonds nevertheless. As a result of Cooke's success, Vermilye became one of Wall Street's better-known names, although its business was still very conservative. It also became involved in gold dealing after the Civil War, a business fraught with danger as long as Jay Gould was active. But because of its conservative nature, it never suffered serious losses. Vermilye remained agent for many transactions but never acted as principal, removing the risk of serious losses that befell so many other dealers of the period.[15]

Vermilye also participated in the Treasury refinancings organized by Cooke after the war. By the early 1870s it was known as a conservative government bond house that eschewed risk even when it might have meant greater profit for the firm. It remained as such until the death of Washington Vermilye in 1876. His brother William, also a partner, died soon thereafter and the firm was left without a family member to succeed. Management of the firm fell to William Mackay, who began to include more adventurous activities in its business plan. Banking was included, and the firm began to participate in railroad financings, something Vermilye assiduously avoided. Business was strong enough to admit new partners in the 1880s, and one, William A. Read, was admitted in 1886. Having already worked for the firm for several years, Read understood both the strengths and weaknesses of Vermilye's business. Bonds were its strength, whereas conservativeness was something of a drawback. As a result, be began to devise strategies and techniques to advance the firm's reputation, having it trade on its brains rather than its modest financial brawn. Despite its growing reputation, its capital was far behind that of many competing firms.

Internecine fighting among the partners finally led to the firm's dissolution in 1905. Unable to agree on the distribution of the profits of the partnership, the warring factions led by Read and Mackay went their separate ways. Read opened William Read & Co., while Mackay opened Mackay & Co. with his own allies. The name Vermilye was officially dead on Wall Street after having achieved notable successes in bond underwriting, especially since the mid-1890s. Vermilye had been able to fight its way into major underwriting syndicates and even win deals in its own right under Read's leadership. Now two firms would be competing for old customers. Clearly, Read had the edge. His new firm continued to win mandates from borrowers and reaped underwriting fees, mostly for bond issues. Read was not enamored of equities in general, and when the partner who held a seat on the NYSE died, he did not even bother to purchase a new one. William

Read & Co. was a bond house that traded on its brains and timing, not on the stock market. That served him well during the First World War, especially since the NYSE was closed for several months after the outbreak of hostilities in Europe.

Continuity spelled success for Read, and his firm developed a reputation as one of the best in the bond business, but he was still not in the league of the Wall Street leaders. He slowly added new staff, insisting on keeping expenses down. One new staff mamber was William Phillips, a New Englander hired after graduating from Harvard. Serendipity struck one day in 1913 when Phillips encountered an old college friend visiting New York, Clarence Dillon. Dillon had been working somewhat unhappily in Milwaukee, and Phillips suggested that he come to the firm, where he would introduce him to Read. Dillon did not initially show much interest, but he agreed to go because he was bored with Milwaukee. Read subsequently offered him a job in his Chicago office, which Dillon accepted. A long relationship had begun that would help vault Read's firm into one of the most respected on Wall Street.

Dillon was destined to work on Wall Street, if his name and family background were any indication. His name originally was Clarence Lapowski, son of Samuel Lapowski, a Polish Jew who emigrated to the United States with his brothers in 1868. The brothers moved to San Antonio, where they set up a dry goods business. Samuel married the daughter of a Swedish immigrant, and Clarence was born in 1882. The family business quickly prospered, and new stores were opened in other Texas cities. But Lapowski was still a Jew living in the South and never forgot the problems that his heritage could cause his son. So in 1901 he arranged to have Clarence legally adopt his grandmother's maiden name. Clarence officially became Clarence Lapowski Dillon, the name that he used when enrolling at Harvard.

Clarence Dillon would leave a legacy at Dillon Read & Co. that matched those of his contemporaries J. P. Morgan, Otto Kahn, and Philip Lehman. Dillon worked at William Read & Co. for several years before making his mark with one notable deal after another. He was lucky to have gone to work for Read at all, since a freak accident almost cost him dearly when he was still working in Milwaukee. In 1907, while courting his future wife, Dillon was waiting for a train to return to Milwaukee after a brief vacation. As he stood at the station platform, a large St. Bernard ran in front of the train and was struck by the engine's cowcatcher. The dog was thrown across the platform and struck Dillon and his future mother-in-law with full force, fracturing his skull and breaking her hip. Both recovered, although Dillon was unconscious for a week after the incident. He took the compensatory award from the railroad and used it to travel in Europe with his wife, whom he had married upon recovering consciousness.

After working for Read in Chicago for a year as a bond salesman, Dillon moved to New York. His early specialty was bond distribution and management, and he completely overhauled Read's sales force, making it more efficient and profitable. He also established a compensation program based on the volume of sales—an innovation on Wall Street at the time.[16] This complemented the corporate finance innovations also instituted by Read and made the firm a more complete investment bank. But bond sales would not hold Dillon's attention for much longer. Big deals were in his future, and the speed with which he was able to gravitate toward them was remarkable given that he had entered investment banking only in 1913. Six years later, he would be an intimate of Bernard Baruch and a worthy adversary of Jack Morgan.

Big Deals

Dillon scored his first coup after World War I. A venerable American company, the Goodyear Tire & Rubber Co., had fallen on hard times during the recession of 1920 and desperately needed financial assistance. The estimated price tag for rescuing Goodyear was about $90 million, a substantial sum. Even Goodyear's investment bankers, Goldman Sachs, backed away, assuming that the company probably would have to declare bankruptcy. The recession of 1920 had made even bullish investors slightly gun-shy about the prospects for companies with poor financial results. Then Dillon entered the picture, having been recommended by the company's lawyers.

After carefully surveying the situation, Dillon proposed a financing package to save Goodyear that sparked controversy for years after. The package included what would later be known as high-yield bonds, debentures (unsecured bonds, an innovation usually attributed to William Read), and preferred stock. For his part, Dillon also took a special class of stock that would reward him when the bailout was finally successful. In addition, Goodyear entered into a contract with a consulting firm that would provide management talent for the company for an annual fee in excess of $250,000 plus additional sweeteners. Getting the refinancing package past the board was not easy, but in the end Dillon prevailed, the money was raised, and the company survived.

Then the lawsuits began. Shareholders sued the company over the terms of the bailout and Dillon's compensation. Matters were made worse when it was discovered that Dillon had an interest in the management company used by Goodyear as stipulated by the conditions of the bailout.[17] The case was finally settled several years later. Dillon made a handsome profit even after paying millions in lawyers' fees. His reputation soared as a result of the deal, and he became known as one of Wall Street's most acute minds—and something of a rogue as well. One contemporary described the deal as "unprecedented, considering its magnitude, to the extent that it was consummated without the assistance or consultation of J. P. Morgan & Co. or any of their principal associates."[18] Just how sharp he was would be demonstrated in the next major deal he was involved in—the one that he is most remembered for.

During the war, the young Dillon had scored a notable professional coup by serving as one of Bernard Baruch's assistants at the War Industries Board, the panel established by Woodrow Wilson to ensure that war materials for the Allies were supplied in an efficient and timely manner. After the war, Dillon accompanied Baruch to the Versailles Peace Conference to witness the terms and conditions of the peace firsthand. Upon returning to Wall Street, he began finding deals like the Goodyear one that helped establish his reputation as a new Wall Street wizard. In 1920, the firm's name was officially changed to Dillon Read & Co. to reflect the new leadership Dillon was providing. Rumor had it that Dillon imposed the name on the firm itself, threatening the other partners if they did not agree. Dillon's personality was said to have become even more volatile since the head injury he sustained from being struck by the flying St. Bernard.

Rather than assemble the partners to discuss a name change, he simply imposed it and then challenged them to object. No one did, and the firm's name was officially changed without further ado.

Dillon's best-known deal was yet to come. John and Horace Dodge were brothers and the principals behind the development of Dodge Brothers, the third-largest automobile manufacturer in the country. They had made their reputation by producing a strong, reliable product that won them many return customers over the years. As a result, they were much photographed and often made the news for both their business savvy and private doings away from the office. In 1920, they both traveled to New York to attend the automobile industry's annual show. While in New York the brothers, well-known for their hell-raising antics, ordered some bootleg liquor to be sent to their hotel room and spent the night on a drinking binge. But quality control during Prohibition was not tight, and both men were stricken with alcohol poisoning. John died shortly thereafter, and Horace lingered for almost a year before succumbing. Their families were left with a booming and complex company in which they did not show much interest. To continue successfully, Dodge Brothers needed a new owner.

The proposed sale was offered to a New York broker, who approached Bernard Baruch about possible buyers. Baruch recommended his former assistant as a possible financier, and Dillon was quietly asked to find possible buyers. The potential deal was not exclusively Dillon's, however. Other investment bankers, including Jack Morgan, also were keen to win the mandate and could make a good case to the Dodge estate because of their contacts with other large companies, notably Morgan's relationship with General Motors. But the broker, A. Charles Schwartz, signed a deal with Dillon giving him a finder's fee based on the price of the deal if Dillon succeeded. Dillon was involved from that moment, although he was still far from being the clear winner of the mandate.

When Morgan learned of Dillon's involvement in the potential deal, he sent representatives to warn the young upstart that he was treading on sacred ground. Essentially, he was told to step aside so that Morgan could present the deal to his friends at General Motors, who were looking at Dodge as a potential merger candidate. What transpired next gave an excellent indication of how quickly finance was changing in the postwar era. Dillon countered by suggesting that the interested parties submit competitive bids for the company and stand by the decision of the Dodge estate. Morgan agreed, not realizing that he was walking into a trap he probably did not fully understand.

Jack Morgan could have been forgiven if he thought the deal was his. Since his father J. P. had bought out Andrew Carnegie in 1901 to form U.S. Steel Corp., the Morgans were the kings of the merger and buyout business on Wall Street and had no particular reason to fear Dillon despite his reputation as an upstart. Morgan soon learned how wrong he was. He bid $155 million for the company, $65 million of which was in cash, the rest in securities. Dillon bid $146 million, all of which was cash with no securities or strings attached. His bid was clearly more attractive than Morgan's by a considerable amount because it was all cash. The estate quickly accepted Dillon's bid in 1925, recognizing a good offer when it saw one.

Wall Street was agog over Dillon's offer, which appeared to be far too high, especially in the face of Morgan's proposal. The calculation used was innovative, but appeared to be appropriate. Rather than use the book value of the company's assets as the basis of his offer, Dillon had instead calculated the value of its future earnings. He discounted the cash stream the company was expected to generate and based its purchase price on its present value.[19] His figures naturally differed from those of Morgan and probably gave a more accurate reflection of the company's present worth. Morgan had no choice but to capitulate, recognizing that he had been beat at his own game by a brighter competitor. The deal even outstripped Morgan's purchase of Carnegie Steel in 1901, then the largest takeover to date. The $480 million price tag of that deal was paid in bonds and common stock, not cash. This was what made Dillon's offer so remarkable. Since his college days, he had been known as "The Baron." Now he picked up a new nickname: "Wolf of Wall Street." The name became so popular that it was used as the title of a 1929 B movie starring George Bancroft. It was also the name of a novel that became a hit, although the wolf in the story is a floor trader on the NYSE, not an investment banker. "Is there a market price for love?" asked the promotional material for the film. If there is, "the titan of the ticker bids a fortune for it," ran the reply. Clearly, this was not a direct reference to Dillon.

Dillon formed a huge syndicate of more than 350 banks to sell the securities necessary to complete the deal. Again, as in the Goodyear transaction, he withheld some securities for his own use, giving him control of the company. The difference between this deal and others preceding it would not escape him in the years to come. He was not only financier to the deal, but now he was in control of Dodge as well. Clearly, he was a wizard at finance. The only question still unanswered was whether he was a corporate executive as well. Buying a company proved to be quite different from actually running one, especially one as capital intensive as manufacturing automobiles. Dillon soon realized his forte was doing deals, not manufacturing cars.

Dillon Read also participated in the investment craze of the period: investment trusts. True to their name, the vehicles were not mutual funds in the contemporary sense of the word but trusts where investors put their money, hoping that the fund manager would invest wisely. All of the major Wall Street houses operated trusts in some form during the period. Dillon Read's lack of a retail customer base suggests that its funds were not vehicles for the small investor. Investment trusts were constructed by the fund's managers, who usually used the money to make a highly leveraged purchase of a business that they would then control. Investors usually purchased shares in nonvoting stock while the managers retained ownership of the voting stock, effectively giving them control of the business for a small upfront investment. This was a highly popular form of investment in the 1920s and was used by all sorts of industrialists who used (in Louis Brandeis's words) other people's money to fund their own investment plans. Naturally, if the trust lost money everyone would lose, but the managers could stand to do quite well if the fund appreciated. The technique was used by the best-known houses on the Street, including Morgan, Goldman Sachs, and J. & W. Seligman.

Dillon Read began packaging and selling investment trusts in 1924. Clarence Dillon's rising reputation made the trusts an easy sell. The Dillon Read vehicles would allow the investor to capitalize on Clarence Dillon's brains and acumen, according to the company's sales pitch. The firm launched close-end investment trusts, one in 1924 and the other in 1928. The first, and the better known, was called the United States and Foreign Securities Trust (U.S. & F.S.).

Because of Dillon's reputation, it became very popular and sold out quickly. The same happened to the second, the United States and International Securities Trust (U.S. & I.S.). Between the two, more than $90 million was raised and Dillon Read was able to collect fees for packaging the trusts as well as maintaining management control over them. The subsequent performance of trusts in general after 1929 earned Clarence Dillon a place of "honor" at the Pecora hearings in 1933. The SEC later concluded in a 1937 report that "the creation of the U.S. & I.S. gave Dillon Read, through its initial investment of $5,100,000, control over combined assets as of October 31, 1928 in excess of $100 million. In short, the subsidiary provided a means to accelerate gains to the sponsor's original investment in the parent corporation. Hence, the game of $1 in the assets of the subsidiary resulted in 80 percent gain to the parent of which 60 cents accrued to the sponsor's investment."[20] There was nothing illegal about this, but it would prove to be disastrous for the public relations image of Wall Street. Investment banks appeared to be usurping control of the trust and its investments from investors who apparently were not shareholders at all, only passive sources of money.

Dodging the Bullet

Dillon's success did not extend to his management of the Dodge operation. After purchasing the company, he installed his own management team at Dodge to beef up the company's product lines and increase sales. But the effort turned out to be a disaster and Dillon quickly recognized that Dodge was turning into a white elephant. The much-heralded purchase of the century was quickly to turn into the sale of the century if a buyer could be found.

During the 1920s, consumers began buying automobiles in record numbers. The success of Henry Ford inspired many other manufacturers to enter the marketplace. By 1923, more than 13 million cars were registered in the United States, and dozens of manufacturers were offering full model lines to the public. Most were destined to fail, but the market was fully competitive—and saturated—by the middle of the decade. Cars of all sizes and shapes were available, but it was still the most reliable ones that captured the largest segment of the market. Until Dillon took over, the Dodge line was in that category. But changes in the cars' design took a toll on its popularity and its market share began to fall.

Under the new management, Dodges became unreliable and expensive when prices were raised too rapidly to recover costs of design changes to suit the buying public. Dillon began looking for a buyer, but he could only look up, not down. Smaller manufacturers could not afford the third-largest manufacturer, and General Motors and Ford would probably not pay Dillon what he needed to make a decent return on his investment, especially during a period of excess capacity. His options were clearly limited. One potential buyer was William Crapo Durant, the founder of General Motors, who at the time was president of Durant Motors. Durant had a flamboyant but checkered career in the early years of the automobile industry. After cobbling together GM, he lost control of the company twice to Morgan interests. In the 1920s, while ostensibly at the head of his own car company, he was actively speculating on the NYSE with enormous sums of money, most of which he would lose in 1929. Durant had a reputation as a speculator and something of a hustler. The partners at J. P. Morgan instinctively distrusted him, and Clarence Dillon felt much the same way. Fortunately for the principals involved, Durant did not become a contender for Dodge. A serious buyer was needed.

The obvious choice was Chrysler, the fifth-largest manufacturer in the country, headed by Walter Chrysler. Chrysler had just introduced a new model, the Chrysler Six, and it had proved to be a hit with the public and the press. Anticipating heavy demand for the car, Chrysler needed additional plant space to increase production. Dillon's company could provide him with it, but Chrysler realized that the price was going to be high and balked when originally approached about purchasing the company. After long, torturous negotiations, Dillon and Chrysler finally came to terms on the deal. Chrysler paid $170 million in stock for Dodge. To close the deal, Dillon had to engage in some sophisticated arbitrage so that he would have enough stock to deliver to Chrysler. At the eleventh hour, he was successful in finally obtaining the shares he did not personally own. In the end, Dillon Read earned about $40 million from the purchase.[21] The arbitrage transaction also added to the firm's already stellar reputation in the marketplace. Once again, Dillon emerged unscathed, and wealthier, from a transaction that many others would not have considered possible.

In addition to the domestic business developed in the 1920s, Dillon Read made some significant international deals. Many were with German companies attempting to rebuild after World War I. Dillon's connections from his days working with Baruch helped tremendously, and the firm began doing one deal after another. In the early 1920s, Dillon hired a young attorney named Ferdinand Eberstadt, a Princeton graduate whose parents had been German-Jewish immigrants. The new partner's main duties were to facilitate deals in Germany and

---

Walter Chrysler bought his first car in 1905. He took it home, took it apart piece by piece, and put it back together again, repeating the process dozens of times. He soon realized that he could produce a better car for less money and decided to go into the automobile business. Twenty years later, when he purchased Dodge from Clarence Dillon, the automobile industry was already producing too many models, suffering from overcapacity. Using Woolworth as his model, he decided to build the largest building in the world as a way of advertising his name and product. Although he succeeded, he was not aware that secret plans were being made to build the Empire State Building, which would eclipse his own as the tallest building.

After the Dodge deal was concluded, A. Charles Schwartz, the broker who had put Dillon in touch with the Dodge estate, threw a lavish party to celebrate his own earnings from the deal, which amounted to several million dollars. Ferdinand Eberstadt was one of the guests, representing Dillon Read. Dinner was served by footmen dressed in livery and consisted of numerous courses, each more exotic than the last. The evening was judged to be a great success until a Chinese cook, swinging a meat cleaver, chased one of the footmen through the dining room, causing a fair degree of alarm among the guests. The commotion did not seem to bother Eberstadt, who had a flair for haute living himself and had built a lavish home on Long Island to celebrate his own success at his new firm.

Europe and to use his numerous connections in the Jewish-American banking community. His first cousin was Otto Kahn of Kuhn Loeb, at the time perhaps the second most influential banker in New York. Eberstadt did not work for Dillon for very long, however. In 1931, he resigned to open his own investment banking firm in New York.

In the 1920s, Dillon Read added a retail sales force to its institutional business, as did many other traditional investment banks. But after the Crash, the sales force was disbanded. Then, quite unexpectedly, Dillon withdrew from the firm, handing over its day-to-day management to two of his partners, James Forrestal and William Phillips. He retained his majority interest in the partnership but obviously felt that it was time to pursue other interests, notably those that would give him a social position equal to his Wall Street reputation. He took time to travel, purchase a vineyard in France, collect art and other memorabilia, and spend time with his family. This was remarkable, since he was only forty-eight years old at the time.

Dillon was not alone in withdrawing from Wall Street during a tumultuous period in its history. Charles Merrill at Merrill Lynch did the same and Jack Morgan also stood at a distance from the Street in the early 1930s. After the Crash, criticism of Wall Street investment bankers abounded. Not many senior partners at the old firms displayed much leadership during the early years of the Depression. Many were content to adopt the line that the economic slowdown was only temporary and that the Street would right itself as it had in the past. There was much more grousing about the passing of the Securities Act in 1933 and the creation of the SEC a year later than there was constructive language about what needed to be done with the economy. But this was in line with Wall Street mentality. As in the Dodge deal, investment bankers proved to be very good deal makers but not quite as adept in following through when it came to managing their own companies. During the Depression, Wall Streeters did not contribute much to the public policy debate on how to set the economy right.

Dillon was certainly one of this group. As one of the Street's senior people in 1933, he had little constructive to say about public affairs. And like Morgan and Charles Mitchell of National City Bank, he was not accustomed to the public attention the Pecora hearings thrust

Jay Cooke,
around 1875

Enoch Clark
of Clark Dodge & Co.

August Belmont

James Brown
of Brown Brothers

Joseph Seligman

Alexander Brown

Abraham Kuhn

Solomon Loeb

Otto Kahn
of Kuhn Loeb

Edward H. Harriman

Jacob Schiff
of Kuhn Loeb

Henry Lee Higginson, around 1905

Anthony Drexel

J. P. Morgan

Bankers on the march during World War I. From left, Jacob Schiff, W: Frew, George F. Baker, Jr., and J.P. (Jack) Morgan.

Henry S. Morgan in 1934

upon him. Although he testified at the hearings at some length, along with other members of the firm, his testimony never brought about the fireworks that some expected. Dillon Read partners were well coached at the hearings, having hired Ivy Lee, John D. Rockefeller's onetime public relations adviser, as a consultant. Talking about past deals in a negative sense was not something deal makers relished. Whether Dillon saw the writing on the wall and anticipated greater government intervention in the markets is not known, but his partner Paul Nitze recalled that after the Crash, Dillon confided that he thought Wall Street would no longer be able to control its own destiny because critical decisions would be coming from Washington.[22]

The specter of Ferdinand Pecora himself may have helped convey the same image. The son of Italian immigrants, Pecora had worked his way through law school at night, and was the antithesis of the bankers sitting before him. Rather short and tussled looking when compared to the immaculately groomed bankers, Pecora was the embodiment of what the previous generation of old American families, like the Adamses of Boston, found most repugnant about the newer generation of American immigrants. He was openly ambitious and did not possess a distinguished East Coast lineage. Relationship banking meant little to him; he was more concerned about what he considered violations of the public trust by bankers who seemed to deal for themselves first, regardless of the consequences.

After Dillon withdrew from the day-to-day operations of the firm, new members began to enter. One new member was August Belmont IV. Belmont had decided not to revive the family name through the wobbling August Belmont & Co. in the 1930s and went to work for a smaller firm on the Street, Bonbright & Co. He became an authority in financing public utilities companies. After the Public Utility Holding Co. Act was passed in 1935, severely regulating utilities and investment bankers' relations with them, he became involved with their financings and finally was offered a job at Dillon Read after World War II by the firm's new chairman, Douglas Dillon, son of Clarence. Financing utilities companies had been a Dillon Read staple for some years, and Belmont's expertise fitted the firm well. One of Dillon Read's best-known clients since the 1920s was the North American Company, headed by Harrison Williams. North American was a giant utilities holding company that was formed in the heyday of utilities mergers in the 1920s, along with the behemoths created by Samuel Insull in Chicago and J. P. Morgan in New York. Dillon Read completed many underwritings for it and reaped healthy profits, but the new law passed by Congress put investment bankers at arm's length from these companies. Many new financings for them now had to be done through the process of competitive bidding, where the underwriter made its best offer to the company through a sealed bid. The lowest fees charged won the mandate for the securities issue. This technique was at odds with the way Wall Street did its traditional business, and any firm that continued to make a living financing utilities companies would have to adapt to it. Experts in this sort of financing helped Dillon Read throughout its history, and Belmont entered the firm at a propitious time. A famous name had joined an equally famous one, and the firm was poised to help companies finance themselves in the new economic expansion that was building after the war.

Dillon and Belmont were not strangers. They were classmates at Harvard and represented the new generation of investment bankers that would step into the limelight after the legends retired. Born in 1909, Douglas Dillon was always meant to enter the family firm, for his father knew well the need for continuity in the small, limited-purpose Wall Street firm that Dillon Read was despite its strong corporate connections. There were doubts about his interest in investment banking from his early years with the firm, and he never proved to be the strong executive that his father was. But Clarence remained behind the scenes pulling most of the strings, and Douglas entered the firm clearly to become its chief executive, acting in loco parentis. The reasons for Clarence's premature retirement have never been clear, but he maintained an active interest in the firm over the years from an office only a stone's throw from Dillon Read.

Dillon Read became entrapped in the same predicament in which the other small but influential Wall Street firms found themselves in the 1950s and 1960s. Its capital was not increasing as fast as the demand for new securities in the postwar environment, and it was left behind by the larger, full-service firms that were emerging, like Merrill Lynch and Shearson Loeb Rhoades. Unlike Salomon Brothers and Goldman Sachs, Dillon Read did not have enough of a major niche in the marketplace to ensure its survival and the firm began to slip from its once preeminent position among Wall Street's elite. Although the firm incorporated in 1945, as Kidder Peabody had done, new capital was not attracted. Remaining on the wholesale side of the market, the firm began to slide during the bull market of the late 1950s and early 1960s, and Dillon Read's last major gasp as a significant Wall Street powerhouse came during the 1940s when the utilities underwritings helped it earn fees in an otherwise quiet marketplace. During the 1940s, it ranked between third and fifth place in the underwriting league tables. By the early 1950s, it had slipped into the mid-teens along with Kuhn Loeb and Harriman Ripley, being replaced by firms like Halsey Stuart and Merrill Lynch. During the same time, Kidder Peabody, because of its more aggressive stance at acquiring new business from medium-size companies, continued to hold its place in the top ten. The real question was whether Dillon Read would be able to find a niche for itself in the rapidly changing marketplace or was destined eventually to disappear like Clark Dodge or August Belmont & Co.

The Justice Department under Attorney General Tom Clark filed suit against seventeen Wall Street firms in 1947, charging them with violations of the antitrust laws. Dillon Read was listed as one of the defendant firms. The suit contended that the investment banks had been conspiring since 1915 to rig underwriting fees and syndicates in their own favor to ward off potential competition. The government said that the Anglo-French war loan arranged by Morgan and others in 1915 was the beginning of the conspiracy and that it had lasted until the present day. After several years of testimony, Judge Harold Medina finally threw the suit out of court, stating that the government had not made its case. Wall Street was finally vindicated after years of pursuit by congressional committees and lawsuits and would begin the postwar period without a cloud hovering over it. It was the last time many firms, including Dillon Read, would be included in such an august group of Wall Street leaders, since the Street was soon to be headed for much upheaval and change.

Dillon Read prospered under Douglas Dillon but did not take the necessary steps to become a Wall Street powerhouse. Dillon himself was in and out of the investment banking business over the course of a career that mixed business with public service. He then bought a seat on the NYSE and traded for several years as a floor broker before rejoining the firm before the outbreak of World War II. He was put in charge of overseeing U.S. & F.S. and did a few notable investment banking deals after the war broke out in Europe. Then James Forrestal became a Navy undersecretary in 1940 and took Dillon and Belmont to Washington with him; there Dillon got his first taste of government service. Within a year, he saw active service as a naval aviator in the Pacific and returned home a decorated war hero. He remained with the firm until 1953, when he again saw government service—this time at a slightly different level when he was named Ambassador to France by Dwight Eisenhower.

Dillon's government service, along with that of Forrestal, created much goodwill for Dillon Read over the years. But he did not stop with the ambassadorship. Dillon also served as Undersecretary of State for Economic Affairs, Undersecretary of State, and finally Secretary of the Treasury under John F. Kennedy. The last was the most visible job and made Dillon something of a legend on Wall Street, but for reasons very different from those contributing to his father's mystique. He also was instrumental in setting up the Organization for Economic Cooperation and Development (OECD), headquartered in Paris, and the Inter-American Development Bank, located in Washington, D.C. For the first time in decades, Wall Street was sending representatives to Washington because of their financial expertise and policymaking skills. During the Depression, Wall Streeters had given embarrassing testimony at the Pecora hearings. Now that the Wall Street Seventeen trial was over and the economy was showing signs of strength, being an investment banker was no longer equated with being dishonest.

Dillon and Forrestal were not the only two Dillon Read partners who would serve various Republican and Democratic administrations. Three other partners served in high office: Paul Nitze, Peter Flanagan, and William Draper. A fourth, perhaps the best known of all, would follow in the 1980s. While this was marvelous for Dillon Read's image, its impact on its continuing business was minimal. Dillon Read was falling behind the times on Wall Street and would soon be in trouble.

Douglas Dillon left the firm again when Kennedy appointed him Treasury Secretary, and the duo of Frederic Brandi and August Belmont took over the reins. They represented the new and the old of Wall Street. Brandi was a German immigrant who had begun working for Dillon Read in the late 1920s, having studied accounting in his homeland. Over the years he worked his way through a succession of jobs until he was elevated to partner status. Like Belmont, during his tenure he witnessed most of the major changes that affected the partnership in the mid–twentieth century. But like the other partners, he was well versed in the distinctly old-world ways of the firm. Dillon Read practiced the English form of banking, which dispensed with many formalities and rested on the slogan "My Word Is My Bond." Unfortunately, that style of banking was already an anachronism on Wall Street; connections and social graces were giving way to analytical finance based on competition among investment bankers, where the best price for a new issue won the deal. Despite the tenor of the 1960s, Dillon Read forgot the legacy of William Read himself, who had won clients and kept them with his bond market ingenuity and inventiveness. Dillon Read did not employ analysts in the postwar era, when almost all of its major competitors already had full staffs of equities and bond market analysts, as well as economists and statisticians. When Brandi and Belmont reached retirement age, the firm was faced with a difficult problem. Who would succeed them? And would this successor be able to restore the firm's lackluster image?

Looking for a Parent

When Clarence Dillon was an active member of Dillon Read he was considered the firm's most valuable asset. Throughout the later 1930s and the war years, he still ruled the roost as the firm's majority stockholder but from a respectful distance from his Wall Street office. But as the years wore on, his overbearing presence began to take its toll on the firm. As long as Brandi and Belmont were in charge, their style did not clash with his own and the firm remained in the same mold as the one he had created in the 1920s. Dillon Read was a traditional nineteenth-century investment bank, providing financial advice to a group of captive clients and avoiding transactions of any type. The firm did not trade, make markets, or sell securities to customers. In short, it did not get its hands dirty. The only exception was a municipal bond trading desk established in the late 1960s. But Wall Street was becoming more of a working-class place where the newer, more competitive firms realized that servicing a client's needs meant providing any service needed, not just the ones the investment bank deigned to provide.

This new business approach was clearly at loggerheads with Dillon's entire career. During the late 1960s, new "concept" companies were coming to market in new industries such as pollution control, telecommunications, and leisure. Dillon Read would have nothing to do with them and continued on its familiar, well-worn path with clients established in the past.[23] Clearly, the firm was ignoring new developments in the economy at its own peril. And when it was time to choose a new head of the firm, for all practical purposes it looked as if the old guard philosophy was about to prevail again.

In 1971, the firm finally settled on Nicholas Brady as its new chief executive. Brady appeared to be in the same mold as his predecessors. Educated at private prep schools, Yale, and the Harvard Business School, he was the epitome of an East Coast Brahmin—just the sort of young associate Dillon Read liked to attract. Within a short period of time, however, Brady had become the major source of revenue for the firm, putting his family connections to good use. In many ways, he was just the sort of investment banker that Clarence Dillon approved of. At the age of fifty-one, he assumed the controls at Dillon Read, but he realized that the firm was in trouble because of its lack of aggressiveness in new areas of business. With this in mind, he convinced Douglas Dillon, who had been away from the executive committee for a number of years, to return to the firm. Dillon did so willingly, but with one proviso: that Clarence Dillon relinquish all control over the firm. The elder statesmen agreed, and the firm found itself without Clarence's direct influence for the first time in more than fifty years. The only question that remained centered around the firm's ability to survive in the face of its late start and its long-standing conservative legacy.

Clarence Dillon finally died in 1979. His old firm now had a new complexion, but it still harbored many of the old attitudes that he had vested it with years before. Like his predecessors, Brady was able to bring the firm new accounts as well as goodwill in the form of publicity. Enough new corporate accounts were added that the firm continued to prosper, although in a diminishing role on Wall Street. Some new areas were introduced, like bond trading in corporate issues and agency issues, in addition to municipals. Yet Brady's lasting legacy is found outside the firm. He is remembered for two memorable events that bear his name. The first was as a member of the presidential commission that studied the causes of the stock market collapse of 1987 and made recommendations in its aftermath. The group was known as the Brady Commission.[24] One of its more memorable recommendations was the institution of a "circuit breaker" that would come into play if the stock averages fell by a specific percentage on a trading day—that is, it would provide an orderly market by halting trading if the market turned sharply down. This measure was quickly instituted by the NYSE.

Brady became even better known away from Wall Street for the unusual bonds named after him during the later stages of the international debt crisis in the late 1980s. After the Brady Commission concluded, Brady was named Secretary of the Treasury by President Reagan, the second Dillon Read CEO so honored. During the early days of his tenure, a scheme was devised to swap Third World debt held by commercial banks into bonds. Wall Street firms, especially

---

In 1979, the paterfamilias of Dillon Read died. Clarence Dillon passed away at the age of ninety-six. He had lived for so long that even Wall Street insiders had long since forgotten him. Most recognized the name Dillon and associated it with Douglas, assuming that Clarence was long gone if they knew who he was at all. But Clarence left one legacy that survives to this day. In the 1930s, after withdrawing from the firm, he purchased a winery in France, the Château Haut-Brion near Bordeaux. He paid more than 2 million francs for it in 1935 simply because he liked the wine it produced. Then he had the winery and the accompanying chateau restored to their original glory. The winery remains in the Dillon family, and its various labels fall under the Domaine Clarence Dillon.

J. P. Morgan & Co., worked on the specifics, but they were dubbed "Brady Bonds" in honor of the secretary. They were collateralized with U.S. Treasury bonds so that their potential investors would not be frightened away. Bonds of this type became standard issue in helping many developing countries restructure their debt in the late 1980s and early 1990s.

In the 1980s, Brady clearly wanted to find a buyer for Dillon Read. The firm was too conservative to operate successfully in the new financial environment, and its capital was simply too small to compete in a transaction-oriented world. As he put it, "It became obvious at the time the situation had changed dramatically on Wall Street and you needed substantially more capital if you were going to function there."[25] The answer was an unlikely outside investor—the Bechtel Group, the giant, privately held construction company located in San Francisco. After fruitless discussions with several larger investment banks, Dillon and Brady decided to sell the family holdings in the firm to the company for approximately $25 million, an amount that gave Bechtel controlling interest. The price tag was low when compared to Kidder Peabody's original selling price and gave an indication of how far Dillon Read had sunk from its glory days when it was a major underwriter and serious competitor on the Street. The deal did not accurately reflect Dillon Read's value, however, since it was done at book value rather than the firm's market price. Nevertheless, the investment gave Dillon Read some badly needed capital and an opportunity to plan for the future.

Another major sign of change within the organization was the naming of a new head in 1981. John Birkelund became president and CEO, charged with expanding the firm's advisory and investment banking business. He was recruited after having been a cofounder of a Rothschild subsidiary in London involved with raising venture capital for new business, a specialty that Dillon Read wanted to pursue. Shortly thereafter, Brady took a leave of absence to make another trip to Washington to fill the vacant seat of Senator Harrison Williams of New Jersey, who had been forced from office after a scandal. The firm was clearly on the rebound. Under Birkelund, it was now successfully engaging in trading, venture capital, merchant banking, and mergers and acquisitions on a small but profitable level. But the departure of Brady also removed some of the old-boy ties that the firm had had with Bechtel, and the construction company now reassessed its strategy. Subsequently, Bechtel sold its controlling interest back to the partners and Dillon Read essentially returned to a partnership.

Soon after Brady left to join the Reagan administration, Dillon Read was sold to Travelers Insurance Company for $158 million. Despite the catch-up efforts made under Dillon and Brady in the early 1980s, the firm was still slipping in the Wall Street league tables and its capital was not increasing sufficiently to allow it to participate with the new breed of financial powerhouses on the Street. Travelers sold the firm back to the management group five years later for a $37 million loss. Travelers had sustained losses after the 1987 market decline and junk bond crisis of the early 1990s and could not afford to replenish the firm with capital.

The saga became more complicated when Baring Brothers stepped in and bought a 40 percent interest in the beleaguered firm as Travelers stepped away. Befitting its traditional conservativeness, Dillon Read maintained a majority interest and reserved the right to buy back the Baring stake in the future. As it turned out, the U.K. bank did not have the management structure or the capital that Dillon Read required in order to prosper, and Dillon Read's option proved to be invaluable for the firm's reputation. Even the venerable British bank could not provide a stable home for William Read's firm. Within a short time, Baring was itself victimized by a rogue trader. A young, inexperienced trader in its Singapore office lost more than $1 billion speculating with the firm's capital in the derivatives markets in 1994 and 1995. Operating with almost no supervision, he assumed positions that cost the bank dearly. After the Bank of England refused to bail out the institution, it was acquired by ING, a Dutch insurance company, and continued in business as ING Barings. Shortly afterward, Dillon Read's management bought back most of Baring's share for $117 million.

Dillon Read was again independent, but not for long. The merger trend of the 1990s was caused in part by banks merging with other financial service institutions, and a small but revitalized firm like Dillon Read was an attractive partner for a larger institution that could merge it successfully with its own corporate culture. Finally, the firm was purchased by the Swiss Bank Corp. for $600 million, a considerably larger sum than had been the case in the past. As a result, Dillon Read merged with S. G. Warburg & Co. of London, the investment banking arm of Swiss Bank Corp., and the two became known as Warburg Dillon Read. At the time, Dillon Read had fifty-two partners who controlled 75 percent of the firm, and they profited handsomely from the buyout. ING Barings could not compete with the Swiss bank under the circumstances and dropped out of the bidding, saying that its decision to withdraw "has been taken as a result of the two parties not reaching agreement on an organizational structure under which Dillon Read could become integrated with ING's corporate and investment banking business."[26]

Finally, after more than a century and a half as a successful partnership and several brushes with unsuccessful suitors, Dillon Read was integrated into SBC Warburg and became part of a large international investment banking operation. The conservative firm established by the Vermilyes ended its independence in much the same fashion: doing what it did best but failing to keep pace with the changing times on Wall Street. Like Kidder Peabody, it suffered from events beyond its control in the later stages of its history.

Clarence Dillon probably would have still raised a glass of Château Haut-Brion to Dillon Read's ultimate fate, for it managed to stay true to its original conservative nature through thick and thin.

5

CORNER OF BROAD AND WALL: J. P. MORGAN AND MORGAN STANLEY

ONE OF THE truisms of nineteenth-century banking was that investment capital needed to be imported from Europe. The firms that were the most successful all had a British connection or links to other Continental banking affiliates that ensured a flow of investor funds into the United States. The most successful banking operation of the nineteenth century—that of J. P. Morgan & Co.—began in Britain and gravitated toward the United States, bringing with it access to cash and connections sorely needed to help develop the growing American economic infrastructure.

The story of the Morgans' rise to financial power is less flamboyant than that of August Belmont and is more calculated and opportunistic. After Junius Spencer Morgan inherited the banking operation of Peabody in London, his son John Pierpont Morgan developed a parallel career in the United States. Within twenty years, he was the most widely respected, and feared, banker in the country. How such a remarkable accession to power was accomplished in such a short time makes the rise of the Seligmans or Goldman Sachs seem somewhat mundane by comparison. Needless to say, Pierpont had a head start on his eventual competition and did not exactly have to begin from scratch, but the actual power he was able to attain, and pass to his son Jack, was still breathtaking. Like all of his counterparts, Pierpont Morgan was opportunistic and detail-oriented to a fault, but it was his political instincts that differentiated him from the rest. The same political instincts would eventually fail his son Jack and his partners later in the twentieth century.

The rise of the House of Morgan was quite different from that of the other prominent banking houses in the nineteenth century. The founder of the dynasty, Junius Spencer Morgan, was neither an immigrant nor penniless when he began his career. Born in Massachusetts in 1813 to Joseph Morgan and Sarah Spencer Morgan, Junius spent most of his early life in and around Connecticut and western Massachusetts. Joseph Morgan was a businessman with varied interests. He owned a tavern, coffeehouse, and hotel, and was one of the founders of the Aetna Insurance Company in Hartford. Junius did not attend college but was apprenticed to a Boston businessman when he was sixteen. After a short stint in Boston, Joseph bought him a partnership in a New York private bank that became known as Morgan Ketchum & Co. But Junius was not destined to become a banker early in his life. A year and a half later, he left the firm to return to Hartford to enter the dry goods business with a local firm. Shortly thereafter, he married Juliet Pierpont and settled down to become a leader in the city's business community. It appeared that his fate was to become a fixture in the local business community and live out his days involved in New England affairs.

Junius remained in Hartford for the next fifteen years, becoming a prominent figure in local business. His firm, Howe, Mather & Co., was one of Hartford's most prosperous, and Morgan earned a very comfortable living. During the Panic of 1837, the crucible for so many Wall Street firms, he was sent to the South to maintain relations with merchants with whom his firm did business and to ensure that all money owed to Howe, Mather was paid in timely fashion. He also began to expand his own activities in Hartford, being invited to serve as a director of the Hartford Fire Insurance Co. and the New Haven and Hartford Railroad Company. In both cases, he owed the opportunities to his father, who was a major shareholder in each.[1] Very early in Junius's career, a precedent was established that would characterize the business philosophy of the Morgans for years to come. Old relationships would be remembered in business, and family members would be expected to carry the gauntlet of the business into the future. Unlike some of the Jewish-American banking houses, however, there were not that many family members in the Morgan dynasty, so the son always carried the gauntlet.

Joseph Morgan passed on all that he knew about business practices to Junius. While living in Hartford, Junius and his wife had five children, the first of whom was born just before the Panic of 1837. That son, John Pierpont Morgan, would be the child to whom Junius would pass his business knowledge and connections. Joseph died in the summer of 1847, leaving a large estate valued at more than $1 million, most of which was inherited by his wife and son. Junius continued to be extremely successful in business, and the firm for which he worked in Hartford officially changed its name to Mather Morgan & Co. But still hungry for more success, Junius kept his eyes open for a business with international connections as well. In 1850, Morgan branched out by going into partnership with James M. Beebe, a Boston dry goods merchant. Part of the partnership's business was importing goods from Europe, and Junius began to travel to London frequently on business. On one of the trips he met George Peabody, the expatriate American whose banking house was one of the most prominent in London. Peabody began business as a merchant but soon discovered that banking was more profitable. He became so successful that, despite being an American, he was held up to English schoolboys as one of the country's most successful businessmen, worth imitating. A biographer wrote that he developed banking almost as a sideline to buying and selling goods but soon discovered that "he became a banker as well as a great merchant, and ultimately much more of a banker than a merchant."[2] Never married, Peabody had no heirs and was actively looking for an American partner with whom he could share his business. After extensive meetings in London, Peabody offered Morgan a partnership in his bank. The partnership agreement was to take effect in 1854, allowing Morgan time to settle affairs in Boston and find a place to live in London. That partnership agreement officially began the history of the House of Morgan.

Morgan's deal with Peabody was advantageous, for it allowed him a share of potential profits that was far in excess of his own contribution to the firm's capital. The mid-1850s proved difficult for business in general because of war in Europe, the Sepoy Mutiny in India, and the Panic of 1857 in the United States. All would test the abilities of international traders like Peabody & Co. to the fullest. Panic in the American securities markets would affect Peabody the most, since the firm's primary business was dealing in the securities of American railroads and municipalities. Peabody conducted most of the usual merchant banking business—dealing in commodities, financing trade transactions, letters of credit, and foreign exchange—but it was most exposed to the securities markets because it served as an outlet for American securities to British investors. Its American agent in New York, Duncan Sherman & Co., was exposed to the same sorts of risks. The American house offered a clerkship to Junius's oldest son, Pierpont, just as the Panic of 1857 began, and the younger Morgan witnessed the financial crisis firsthand from his vantage point in New York.

The crisis put the capital of Peabody & Co. under enormous pressure, and it was quickly realized that the house needed a temporary transfusion of cash if it was to survive. Peabody and Morgan calculated that they needed a loan of £800,000. Some of their less-than-friendly competition in London could not be counted on to extend facilities, so Peabody sought aid from the Bank of England. The "Old Lady" agreed to help if the actual cash would be provided by other British banks. A rescue group was quickly arranged, and the bank was saved. The young Pierpont Morgan eventually saw the list of contributors and noticed Brown, Shipley & Co. on it—but for a subscription that he considered too small, given that Peabody had helped bail it out of difficulties during the Panic of 1837. He wrote to Junius that "this shows how little gratitude there is in some men as well as their littleness. After Mr. Peabody's exertions on their behalf in '37, it certainly seems outrageous that they show the spirit they have in this case."[3] Apparently, Morgan and Peabody expected greater help than they received from Brown. And it was quite apparent that the young Pierpont already was commenting on the firm's affairs while only an apprentice at Duncan Sherman, which itself almost sank during the troubles.

By 1859, Junius Morgan had assumed full control of the firm from Peabody. Pierpont had struck out on his own in New York after serving his apprenticeship at Duncan Sherman. The younger Morgan became familiar with his father's and Peabody's business by serving as secretary to Peabody for short periods of time and later by handling their business at the New York firm. Fluent in French and German, Pierpont had studied for a term at the University of Göttingen before traveling to New York. By the time he was twenty-one, he had started his own New York firm, J. Pierpont Morgan & Co., and was handling business for Peabody & Co. in New York, carefully passed to him by his father. But it was not long before controversy began to follow him, something the elder Morgan would find abhorrent.

Much criticism of Morgan arose because of business dealings occurring before and during the first years of the Civil War. George Peabody became something of a philanthropist in his later years, giving much money to American colleges in particular. This prompted Socialist writer and muckraker Gustavus Myers to comment that "evidently, it was the sight of the large benefactions which Peabody was then giving that prompted the remarks upon the origin of his fortune."[4] After the war began, Peabody & Co. was named as one of the United States' financial agents in London. Representing the Union was something of a conflict of interest for Peabody, because much of its business was with Southern states, especially in the commodities financing business. Several newspapers noticed that the fortunes of the firm began to increase substantially after the war began, giving rise to conflict-of-interest and profiteering charges.

The criticisms were little more than thinly veiled accusations of treason. Peabody allegedly dumped Treasury securities sold at large discounts in Europe to finance the war, helping to depress the market and make future sales highly unlikely—a problem that Jay Cooke faced when he assumed command of the bond issues. Adding insult to injury, Peabody also floated funds in his own favor against the Treasury, letting its disbursements to Europeans go into arrears while he collected interest on the cash. This was the same sort of complaint leveled against Clark Dodge during the Mexican War. The Springfield *Republican* commented that Peabody "participated to the full in the common English distrust of our cause and our success, and talked and acted for the South rather than for the nation . . . [and] contributed so much to flooding our money markets with the evidences of our debt in Europe, and breaking down their prices and weakening financial confidence in our nationality than George Peabody & Co., and none made more money, by the operation."[5]

One of Peabody's more profitable adventures—and one that drew no criticism—was its financing of Cyrus Field's Atlantic cable beginning in 1854. The transatlantic cable made telegraph between North

America and London possible, although early technical problems made the initial investment look precarious. The firm invested its own money in the adventure. Private capital was not particularly attracted to it because of the technical difficulties that surrounded laying cable from New York to Newfoundland to Ireland and then finally to London.

Some of the young Pierpont Morgan's ventures also came under criticism. Whereas Junius was the model of conservative banking, Pierpont, at least in his early years, appeared to be more willing to take on speculative ventures that would cast shadows over the family reputation. The first such adventure also involved accusations of war profiteering during the Civil War. Pierpont provided financing for a businessman, Simon Stevens, to purchase rifles so that they could be resold to General John C. Fremont. The rifles were considered surplus because they were out of date and needed retooling. Stevens paid $11.50 apiece for them from an arms dealer named Arthur Eastman, who originally paid $3.50 for them from the Army itself. Stevens then offered them to Fremont for $22 apiece. The circuitous path earned Morgan a few thousand dollars, but the entire affair became the subject of a government investigation into the procurement of Army ordnance. Morgan was subjected to charges of profiteering, although he only provided the finance for the operation and did not act as one of the principals in the transaction. The carbine affair ended tamely, although the muckrakers used it as fodder for years to come.

Another charge of profiteering at the government's expense came during the gold operations in the early days of the war. Pierpont's firm became involved in purchasing gold for clients, which opened him to charges of cornering the precious metal in the same way that Jay Gould would do later in the decade. During the war, Pierpont was acting as agent for several firms that purchased gold in the market to use as remittances for trade with firms in London. In one notable deal, Morgan purchased gold for Ketchum, Son & Co. so that the metal could be shipped to England. Ketchum was Morris Ketchum, with whom Junius had once been a partner briefly in Morgan Ketchum, and the son was Edward, with whom Pierpont also had business connections. He purchased the gold, forcing up the price, and then sold some that he had purchased for his own account, netting a profit of more than $100,000. The *New York Times* commented on the deal but concluded that no real damage was done to the stock market and attributed the affair to "a young house in Exchange Place, respectably connected on the other side" of the Atlantic.[6] That understated the importance of the operation. The gold trading was done at the gold room, a trading room located around the corner from the NYSE. Trading in the metal took precedence there above anything else. When the Union was victorious on the battlefield, the traders sang "John Brown's Body" in unison; when the South scored a victory, they switched to "Dixie." The lack of conscience displayed by the speculators infuriated many, including Abraham Lincoln, who asked a colleague, "What do you think of those fellows in Wall Street who are gambling in gold at such a time as this? For my part I wish every one of them had his devilish head shot off."[7]

Speculating in gold during the Civil War had more serious implications for the Union. The bonds being sold by Jay Cooke and others to finance the war relied on gold as their backing. If the value of the currency fluctuated, which it did during such operations, and was then exported to Britain, which had officially declared its neutrality in the conflict, then it could be reasonably assumed that the war financing was being undermined indirectly. When word of the operation was made public, Morgan did no more speculative deals. The operation followed the successful selling of the 6 percent bonds, known as the 5-20s, by Jay Cooke in the spring of the same year, 1863. The friendship with the Ketchums was put under further strain when Edward Ketchum was arrested shortly thereafter, having stolen $3 million in securities from his father's bank and forged over $1 million in gold certificates, some in Pierpont's name. The Morgans were horrified by the incident, and Edward was sentenced to a term in Sing Sing.[8]

The following year Junius's partnership arrangement with Peabody officially came to an end. The seventy-year-old Peabody decided to retire from the firm, taking his name with him, so the bank was renamed J. S. Morgan & Co. The firm was known as one of the most influential in London specializing in trade and securities with the United States, yet when Morgan struck out alone he employed only several clerks and had capital of only about £350,000. That was approximately £200,000 less than Brown Brothers' capital and was the subject of much discussion in London.[9] This helped underscore the peculiarity of nineteenth-century banking. Many trade transactions between countries were guaranteed or financed by small banks with sparse capital, which traded on the strength of their word and private assurances that the deals they participated in would be successful. Morgan was certainly in this category, although it was clear that it was wartime again and small capital bases were vulnerable. Junius needed a stronger link with the United States than Duncan Sherman could provide, and he continued to pass business to his son. Pierpont was quickly developing a reputation as a solid banker with extremely solid connections—tools necessary for success in international as well as domestic financing deals. Gustavus Myers recognized this when he wrote that Morgan was unlike many of the American bankers who had come up the hard way: "Morgan was not one of those magnates coming wholly under the classification of being a self-made man." He did not fit the nineteenth-century mold, but his success certainly became the model for all bankers, regardless of their beginnings.

Forging Links

While the family firms were flourishing on both sides of the Atlantic, Junius Morgan decided to forge another link with an American banking house. He chose Drexel & Co. of Philadelphia, a well-known house since it had helped finance Mexican War bonds along with Clark Dodge & Co. J. S. Morgan & Co. had successfully floated bonds for several foreign governments, including Chile and France, but its core business was still with the United States. When Anthony Drexel paid a courtesy call on Junius in London, the older Morgan broached the subject with him in much the same way Peabody had done with him years before.

Junius and Anthony Drexel, the senior partner of Drexel & Co., agreed to a link that would include Pierpont as a partner in the firm in 1871. It would name its Wall Street operation Drexel, Morgan & Co. The new firm would become one of the country's most prominent private banks. It provided the London bank with a stronger American ally, adding the link that J. S. Morgan & Co. had been seeking for some time. Although the two houses were separate, for all practical purposes the House of Morgan was thought of as having two sides, the London parent in J. S. Morgan & Co. and the American side in Drexel, Morgan & Co. Their business was quite similar to that of the Rothschilds and August Belmont, separate institutions thought of as one for practical purposes.

The newly forged alliance was not strong enough to assume that business would come to it automatically. The alliance also recognized that it had serious competition for business in the United States. When the Treasury decided to refinance the 6 percent war bonds with new 5 percent bonds, all of the country's major private banks entered into discussions to manage the deal. When Jay Cooke won the deal, Junius Morgan was clearly irritated by his success. Morgan saw Cooke as an outsider encroaching on his business, although Cooke was the senior of the two and had been in American banking since his days with Clark Dodge before the Mexican War. Morgan refused to join any Cooke-led syndicate. He wrote to Drexel, "I hesitate about joining because I can see that Jay Cooke & Co. have in view something entirely beyond the mere profit. They, if successful, will hope to make a reputation and put themselves in a more commanding position here."[10] Rarely did bankers make known so directly their feelings about others. While Morgan, like the Rothschilds and Barings, objected to the terms of the refinancing, an equal if not overriding consideration was the desire not to make Jay Cooke look too successful in the effort. At this stage, it became clear that Junius would tolerate little opposition to his self-assumed role as banker to the Treasury. That would translate into little sympathy for Cooke just a few years later.

The major victim of the Panic of 1873 was Jay Cooke & Co. The plunge that Cooke took into the Northern Pacific Railroad proved unsuccessful, and his house suspended operations, ending his brief but spectacular career as America's first truly national bond distributor. Since the United States did not have a central bank at the time, no governmental institution could come to the aid of failing banks, even one as prominent as Jay Cooke & Co. The Morgans, on the contrary, did quite well in 1873 and reported a healthy financial condition on both sides of the Atlantic and no serious repercussions from the panic. Although they did extend some short-term assistance to small brokers with whom they did business, there was certainly no attempt to extend a rescuing hand to Cooke. Cooke's banking operation fell quickly, especially after the New York operation technically failed without bothering to tell Cooke himself until it was too late. Although controversy swirled around Morgan's role in the failure, it would not be the first time that a major rival hit the financial skids at a propitious moment in the developing story of the House of Morgan.

Although still in the shadow of his father, Pierpont was developing traits that would come to characterize him in later life. His manner was already imperious, and he assumed the general aura of someone who was larger than the industry that was making him famous. But the imperious behavior provided a benefit nevertheless. Business for Drexel Morgan was increasing in two areas—loans to governments and railroad financings. In addition to helping finance later Treasury refundings, J. S. Morgan & Co. participated in a bevy of loans to European and Latin American governments. This brought both Morgans into contact with numerous government officials who were impressed with the air of authority displayed by Pierpont. And in railroad financing, the assumed air was an even more invaluable asset. The railroad barons of the day were the strongest personalities imaginable, and only someone of their own nature could deal with them effectively. This was especially true in Pierpont's first major railroad financing coup.

Pierpont made his name in railroads when he helped William Henry Vanderbilt sell his large stake in the New York Central Railroad, founded by his father, Cornelius "Commodore" Vanderbilt. Billy was his father's heir and had inherited the operation after the Commodore's death. Much criticism had followed him even after his notorious father died, and he had decided to sell his holdings. New York legislators were becoming much more strict toward railroads, especially those owned by one family, and Vanderbilt decided that it was time to divest. But the amount of stock he held was too large to simply sell on the market, so he arranged with Pierpont to sell it in an orderly fashion to private subscribers.

Pierpont contracted with Vanderbilt to buy 150,000 shares at $120 per share, with an option for an additional 100,000 if the initial sale proved successful. The shares were offered to the public in January

1880 at $131. Unfortunately, they came under heavy selling pressure on the NYSE and the price fell. But Morgan apparently was not disturbed. "We did not expect a quick turn when we commenced," he told Junius a couple of months later, "and we have no reason to be disappointed at the results so far." The assessment proved correct. Both houses made about $12 per share on their allocations, netting J. S. Morgan more than $500,000.[11] Vanderbilt made almost $20 million on the first part of the sale.

In the Morgan saga, money was not the only ingredient that proved alluring. As a result of the reorganization of the railroad, the number of seats on the board of directors was increased and Pierpont was given one as a condition of the sale. Two other seats were given to close allies of Jay Gould, who had to be placated so that the deal could proceed. Gould and Commodore Vanderbilt had been locked in mortal combat over control of the Erie Railroad, and any reorganization of the New York Central would have to pass Gould's approval to keep him from interfering in the deal by pursuing his own interests. When the reorganization was completed it was hailed as a major boon for the future of railways in the country, but internecine warfare between railroad barons broke out again shortly afterward. Pierpont had his seat on the board, however, beginning what critics would contend was a stage in his career endowed with other people's money. He had effectively dealt himself into the game by helping underwrite Vanderbilt's shares. Once in, he would prove difficult to dislodge, and the lesson would be carried over into other industries as well.

Morgan was the best-known private banker to negotiate his way onto corporate boards of directors, but certainly not the only one. Most other private investment bankers also served on boards of client companies, but Morgan was the most visible and later would be able to forge an empire out of such relationships. Since competition among bankers was virtually unknown during the latter nineteenth century, the board seat was recognition that the banker served as the company's main investment banker. Once established, the link was difficult, if not impossible, to break. Competition among investment bankers for a client's account was virtually unheard of until the post–World War II years, when Wall Street underwent a major transformation in the way it did business. The full extent of Morgan's influence would not be fully revealed until the Pujo Committee hearings a year before his death. In the thirty years that followed, the Morgan partners assumed a staggering array of seats on most of the country's major corporate boards.

Striking Out Alone

Railroad financing became the most significant part of Morgan's domestic business in the 1880s. Many of the major railroads were in an organizational mess at the time and needed financing. The New York Central deal made Morgan the most famous railroad financier, and his services were in much demand. While Junius was alive, the relationship between the New York and London houses was much like that between the Rothschilds and Belmont. Deals that originated in New York often used London to place securities with overseas investors, and the London connection became invaluable for Drexel Morgan since investors rightly assumed that the vast reservoir of foreign funds was at the disposal of the elder Morgan, who by the 1880s ranked high on the totem pole of international bankers.

The Northern Pacific Railroad became another of Pierpont's major coups of the 1880s and proved to be the first of his two victories over Henry Villard. The railroad had recovered from the days of Jay Cooke's initial investment, but by 1880 it needed a capital transfusion in order to survive. After years of delays and periodic financings, the line was still not finished, and its management approached Drexel Morgan about a bond issue that would allow completion of the line between Lake Superior and Puget Sound. If the money could guarantee completion of the line, the entire Pacific Northwest would be transformed quickly. Morgan agreed to raise a $40 million bond issue along with August Belmont & Co., but he soon encountered stiff opposition from a local entrepreneur in the area.

Born Heinrich Hilgard in Germany, Villard anglicized his name before arriving in the United States in 1853. He moved to Colorado, seeking his fame and fortune in the West. Originally, he bought a steamship company, and by an adroit watering of its stock, he raised enough funds to branch out into other endeavors. By 1880, he was the most prominent businessman in the entire region, but the Northern

Pacific posed a threat to his interests by opening the area to other investment. Villard decided to buy the company rather than compete with it, and he proceeded to mount some spectacular raids on its stock on the stock exchange. Emerging victorious, he was the sole owner of the railroad and appeared to have maintained his grip on the region. But he was undone by his own success and by the enemies he had made in the process.

Villard became the president of the railroad. Other financings were subsequently arranged at his behest. Junius Morgan joined the board of the railroad in 1883 in what was becoming a standard move for bankers closely involved in large bond financings and stock financings. Naturally, Villard began to influence the banking groups that provided financing for the railroad, providing competition for Morgan. Apparently, this new turn of events did not sit well with Drexel, Morgan & Co. Shortly thereafter, the stock of the Northern Pacific came under attack on the NYSE by Charles Woerishoffer, a professional short seller, or "plunger," in the mold of Jay Gould and Commodore Vanderbilt. He and Villard became enemies because he was part of the original group that helped corner the stock for Villard but was later denounced as having been less effective than others. He took to the raid on Northern Pacific with a vengeance, betting most of his fortune and reputation on the outcome. When the stock collapsed, Villard was ruined. He had to sell many of his personal possessions, and he suffered a nervous breakdown in the process. Woerishoffer added to his reputation considerably, although it was generally acknowledged that he was in the employ of Morgan forces and was determined to drive Villard out of the Northern Pacific. Although Morgan engineered the operation, Villard was charged with executing it. Morgan then persuaded Villard to resign and liquidated many of his holdings for him, expressing his sorrow for what had befallen the railroad's president. The two would do battle again some years later in another project close to both their hearts, but the outcome, unfortunately for Villard, would be much the same.

During the 1880s, Pierpont's activities brought him squarely into the developing world of monopoly concentrations. Many of the country's industries were consolidating at a rapid rate, and financing was needed to achieve the mergers and takeovers that dotted the industrial landscape. This meant opportunity for many of the bankers who helped firms merge: They were often able to negotiate board seats on many of the new, enlarged companies. But Morgan took the trend one step further for a banker by becoming part of it himself, both as a financier and as a principal player in the saga. His first step would be an attempt to consolidate the railroads and the warring railroad barons, who had not become any friendlier since the New York Central deal with William H. Vanderbilt.

Pierpont Morgan's attempt to bring the warring railroad barons into an alliance in 1889 was an outgrowth of his successful financing for the Pacific Northern and the New York Central. Although he had witnessed the sort of conflict that the railroad barons engaged in when he helped finance the Albany & Susquehanna Railroad against a takeover by Jay Gould and Jim Fisk in 1869, he also recognized the structural problems that the fiercely independent railroads faced. As a result, he was more than willing to try to unite them before the Interstate Commerce Commission, created by Congress in 1887 specifically to deal with the railroad problem, could make its presence felt on railroad rates and organization. Certain that price competition would lead to the ruin of the railroads, Morgan proposed setting up a rate structure that would reduce their internecine warfare while ensuring them a steady stream of revenue. The problem with the idea was that it smacked of collusion from the start and would clearly have led the railroads into a cartel. Although the idea failed shortly thereafter, Morgan realized that the idea had merit in a different industry. Too many critics of the railroads were constantly at war with the carriers to make any serious headway with them. The idea needed to be applied somewhere else.

The first successful large company forged by Morgan was the General Electric Company in 1892. It was the culmination of a long association between Morgan and Thomas Edison. Edison's first power-generating plant on Pearl Street in lower Manhattan was funded primarily by Morgan, and the two developed a working relationship over the years. But it was not until Henry Villard reappeared on the scene after spending time in Europe in the wake of the Northern Pacific deal that Morgan jumped into action and formed GE. Villard returned to the United States bent upon forging a monopoly in the new electric power generation business and eyed Edison's company as the perfect place on which to build his empire. Edison Electric was initially bought out by a combination of Villard and Morgan forces. Edison was distanced from the business he founded, and Villard became president of the new company. Villard quickly became acquisitions-minded and proposed that his company buy the larger Thompson-Houston Electric Co., one of the largest in the country. His mistake was approaching Morgan for financing. Morgan instead arranged with Thompson-Houston to take over Edison Electric. Once the deal was sealed, the new General Electric was the largest supplier of electric power in the country. Morgan then forced Villard out of the company, scoring his second coup over the German-born financier in a decade.

Pierpont already was considered the country's top banker when Junius died in 1890. While on a prolonged holiday in Italy, a carriage in which he was riding had an accident when the horse bolted. The elder Morgan suffered severe head injuries, and he died several days later. He was buried in Hartford. The funeral attracted hundreds of bankers and politicians, and he was hailed as the American equivalent of the Medicis and the Rothschilds. Pierpont now was fully in charge of both firms and was immediately elevated to an even higher pedestal than he had occupied before. His position as the country's greatest living banker was firmly entrenched. The London house had capital of some $10 million, which represented more than 80 percent of Junius's estate. Estimates at the time put the figure much higher.[12] But the capital alone did not adequately explain the Morgan influence. The house had advised many of Europe's prime ministers and kings and provided finances for many Latin American companies. Deals by Pierpont had brought him into contact with most American industrialists. Taken together, these successes made Morgan the equal of the Rothschilds and the Barings, both of whose influence was slowly starting to wane in Europe. The United States was a rising world power, and Morgan was its high-profile banker—a position he would exploit effectively over the next twenty years. Ironically, in 1890, at the time of his father's death, Pierpont appeared to be on the verge of retirement. His fame until that time was mostly in banking circles, and he seemed to be tiring of the game. His reputation was solid, but his role as financial savior of the great democracy of the West had not yet been made.

Saving the Country, Part 1

Morgan needed to add partners to his New York and Philadelphia operations in the 1870s and 1880s in response to the growing business being acquired by the Morgan and Drexel firms. Among them were J. Hood Wright, Egisto Fabbri, Charles Godfrey, James W. Paul, George C. Thomas, and Edward Stotesbury. They were followed some years later by George Bowdoin and Charles Coster. Coster came in for high praise on Wall Street as being the genius behind most of Morgan's reorganization plans until 1900, when he died. John Moody called him "Morgan's right arm . . . a notable example of a man who worked himself to death."[13] Offers of a partnership in the New York and Philadelphia operations were few and far between; Morgan and Tony Drexel were known to be very discriminating when choosing future colleagues. And partners were not chosen for their ability to bring personal wealth with them. Almost all partners admitted in the latter part of the nineteenth century were experienced bankers who at one time in their careers had been merchants. Despite the fact that being associated with Morgan was the highest position a banker on Wall Street could hope for, the bank had a reputation as a difficult place to work, with long hours and little support staff.

Nevertheless, the prestige of the position and the high income accompanying it convinced most that it was worth the work. Once admitted, they were expected to leave a portion of their annual earnings with the firm.[14] This was a key element in Morgan's continued success. The Morgan family connection provided only the chief executive of their operations. The partners were chosen for their abilities and future prospects. As a result, the Morgan banks did not have to seek merger partners or temporary infusions of cash. And dynastic marriages did not play a part in their game plan, although one marriage to a Belmont did occur in the 1890s.

During the period of the panic in the early 1890s, the Morgan banks underwent a reorganization that ultimately produced what would be the premier name in American banking for the next century. J. P. Morgan & Co. was founded in late 1894 when Pierpont announced changes after Anthony Drexel's death in 1893. The firm kept its Philadelphia and New York houses intact, although the Drexels themselves were no longer active in the firm. The old partners retained their positions and Pierpont was the senior partner at each house, including London. Otherwise, London remained a separate entity. The new bank had capital of $7.1 million, with Morgan personally responsible for $4.6 million. The figure was not particularly high, considering the central role that Morgan played in American finance. But Pierpont was now at the helm of the country's most influential bank, and his influence in the face of that relatively small capital base was soon to be tested.

Almost at the same time that J. P. Morgan & Co. was officially formed, Pierpont faced the first crisis that would cast him as the one of the most powerful men in the country. His influence was beginning to take on larger-than-life connotations. Since the demise of the second Bank of the United States, the country had been without a central bank. Most bankers had grown accustomed to the fact, even if they were not completely comfortable with it. Anytime a bank required a transfusion of funds, its only recourse was to approach other banks for a bailout. That made friendly relations with other bankers essential but also put the stronger banks in an enviable position. Other bankers could not afford to upset the powerful bankers and usually toed the official line when Morgan made his wishes known. What became upsetting to many was that Washington also found itself in the same position since the country was still dependent to a large extent on the import of foreign capital. Anyone having access to those funds was in the driver's seat with the U.S. Treasury.

After the Panic of 1893–94, the dependence of the United States on foreign investors became painfully obvious. While the debate at home continued about using silver to support the dollar in addition to gold, foreign investors began to lose confidence in their investments. Gold was viewed as the only acceptable standard, and they began to sell their holdings of stocks and bonds. The gold reserve began to diminish as a result, falling to $50 million, one half of the reserve considered acceptable. Then it began to slip even more, and drastic action was needed so that the Treasury did not become bankrupt.

A major obstacle to remedying the situation was congressional reluctance to authorize a bond issue designed to attract gold. A couple of small issues had served only to harden congressional authorization, because domestic investors were not paying for the bonds they did purchase with actual gold but only swapping one issue for another, collecting interest on the bonds without actually relinquishing gold. President Grover Cleveland desperately needed a solution to the problem before his government ran out of money, and it became obvious that foreign investors would somehow have to be courted if the Treasury was to avoid a default on its obligations.

Pierpont's first major foray into gold, during the Civil War, had been met with criticism, but his solution the second time around was adroit. Cleveland had called some prominent bankers to Washington for consultation, including Morgan and August Belmont, who maintained excellent relationships with members of the administration. Morgan offered an ingenious technical solution to the problem. Given that Congress would not sanction a new borrowing to shore up the reserves, he proposed that the borrowing be disguised to look like a purchase of gold coins using Treasury bonds, a tactic that had been used by Salmon Chase during the Civil War. Most important, the law did not require official sanction by Congress and could be accomplished by the men gathered in the room with little outside assistance.

The deal was quickly arranged. A syndicate led by Morgan and Belmont sold the government gold coins worth $65 million in return for 30-year bonds paying 4 percent interest. Shortly thereafter, the bonds were offered to the public at a large markup of 8 percent and they sold out quickly.[15] The European sale was conducted by J. S. Morgan & Co. and the Rothschilds. The deal saved the Treasury the embarrassment of a default and put the credit of the United States on a sounder footing. It satisfied all sides because it was done quietly and effectively without involving Congress, and it pleased the Cleveland administration because the gold was coming from abroad rather than from domestic sources. The importance of gold over silver was also underlined: almost no one except those in the western states favored silver as backing for the dollar. The Sherman Silver Act, which designated silver as official backing for the dollar along with gold, was repealed in 1893. But all was not well on the political front, because the deal set off howls of protest from silver advocates and the muckraking press.

Critics of the deal pointed to the two favorite bogeys periodically accused of skulduggery against the United States—Jews and the

British. It was an indirect way of referring to the Rothschilds. Charles Francis Adams ranted against the deal because it undermined the silver advocates, and Joseph Pulitzer's newspaper, the New York *World*, was even more explicit, referring to the syndicate as a group of "bloodsucking Jews and aliens"—particularly harsh because Pulitzer himself was Jewish.[16] If anyone needed a reminder that the United States sorely needed a central bank, this incident provided it. Private bankers with strong British connections were still the lenders of last resort, now even for the Treasury itself. Worse still, the syndicate made money on the deal while serving a vital national function.

Morgan's new role as unofficial central bank was temporarily obscured by the most notable deal in American business. Having acquired experience as a consolidator of business, Morgan turned his attention to the steel industry. Toward the end of the century, the political climate for business in general and mergers specifically was extremely conducive to large deals. With William McKinley in the White House, American business went on a consolidation binge never seen before, despite the fact that the Sherman Antitrust Act had been passed in 1890. The trend was given an immeasurable boost by a Supreme Court decision that was a blow to early antitrusters. In *United States v. E.C. Knight* (1895), the court ruled that the Sherman Act did not apply to cases where competition within states was suspected of suffering. Many of the mergers were interstate mergers, but it was clear the case hinted that antitrust enforcement might not be as strong as was thought when the Sherman Act was passed. And McKinley was known for his sympathies toward big business. The *Economist* of London wrote, "Mr. McKinley, as everyone knows, was mainly elected by the Trusts . . . during his presidency the power and wealth of the Trusts have grown to such gigantic proportions that it is now said that they control about 90 percent of the industrial capacity of the United States."[17] A giant deal would be relatively easy to forge during his administration. Several years later under Theodore Roosevelt, the situation would change dramatically.

Morgan's coup involved buying Carnegie Steel from Andrew Carnegie and cobbling it together with smaller companies to form the United States Steel Corporation in 1901. Carnegie and the Morgans had a long history that dated back to the post–Civil War period.

Junius Morgan had helped Carnegie raise money in London for his early steel-making adventures. The value of the Carnegie purchase—$400 million—easily made it the largest in history. The purchase price also made Carnegie the wealthiest man in the world. The price tag was paid for in stock and bonds, not cash. Carnegie later remarked to Morgan that he could probably have commanded more for the company, at least another $100 million. Morgan simply stated that he was probably correct in assuming that. Originally, Carnegie thought he had bested Morgan in the deal, but the future would prove U.S. Steel to be enormously profitable and representative of the American economy at its best. Ironically, Carnegie began to speak out openly against the consolidation trend occurring in American business, but only after he closed the deal. Knowing of the American love-hate relationship with tycoons and their money, the wily Scot industrialist thought it best to hedge his bets, coming down momentarily on the side of the Populists and Progressives who were firmly opposed to the giant industrial combinations being formed by Morgan and others.

Despite his hallowed reputation, Pierpont did not have things entirely his own way. The vexatious Northern Pacific Railroad was one example. The fight for control of the railroad was the last great railroad battle. After the competing forces of Morgan and Hill on one side and Harriman on the other combined in a merger, the holding company controlled a vast amount of railroad track west of the Mississippi River. After Theodore Roosevelt became president, he filed suit against the railroad for violations of the Sherman Antitrust Act. Roosevelt described the situation by stating that "a small group of financiers desiring to profit by the governmental impotence to which we had been reduced by the Knight decision, had arranged to take control of practically the entire railway system of the country."[18] After hearing the case, the Supreme Court agreed, citing the holding company and its far-flung interests as inimical to the United States—and ruling it an illegal combination. Not everyone agreed. The *New York Times* argued that the monopoly was good for business in those states affected. "The States and cities which lie 'at the mercy' of the railroads brought into one system by the Northern Securities merger, are growing rich and prosperous," it argued in an editorial.[19] But the die was cast. The trust-busters in Roosevelt's administration had won the battle, but the war would continue as Morgan continued to assemble industrial combinations with far-reaching interests.

Saving the Country, Part 2

Although the Treasury operation in 1895 was probably Pierpont Morgan's most controversial, fuel was added to his critics' fire as a result of actions ostensibly taken to save the stock exchange in the early years of the twentieth century. When combined with Morgan's continuous consolidations in industry, these actions served as the single most important catalyst to establishing the Federal Reserve. Morgan's capital in 1895 was $7 million, 7 percent of the Treasury's reserves. How was it possible that the New York bank was constantly bailing out important American institutions? Conspiracy theorists were given ample ammunition in their quest to prove that a cabal of New York bankers led by Morgan was running the country.

In the first decade of the twentieth century, stock market panics were as common as they were in the nineteenth. The first market collapse occurred after the Northern Pacific "corner," in which the combined Morgan and Harriman forces bought more Northern Pacific stock than actually existed in a successful attempt to force out of the market the short sellers who had been speculating in the stock. Once the smoke cleared on the disaster that befell the short sellers, the market resumed its momentum. A syndicate headed by Frederick Tappen of the Gallatin National Bank in New York pledged $15 million to help stabilize the market and confidence was restored. The next time a panic occurred, it was Morgan who would step into the breach and, unwittingly, the firing line as well.

In 1907, a well-known New York City institution, the Knickerbocker Trust Co., closed its doors after a run by depositors. The bank's president, Charles T. Barney, was discovered to have been speculating in a Western copper venture, and the news rattled his depositors, who made massive withdrawals. A director stated publicly that "there is no chance that the Knickerbocker Trust Company will reopen in its old form." Shock waves reverberated throughout the city. Confidence in banks fell quickly and a stock market panic immediately followed. Barney shot himself shortly after the announcement. Several of his large depositors also committed suicide. The entire affair, although lamentable, was not unlike many other panics of the nineteenth century.

The most powerful banker in the country could not be persuaded to come to the Knickerbocker's aid, however. After hinting that he might help, Morgan declined several opportunities to assist the bank, claiming that he was not responsible for its previous bad management. But he did aid the banking industry in general, especially the trust banks. What would soon be dubbed the "money trust" put together a rescue package of $25 million, most of which was provided by the Roosevelt administration. The money was deposited into the large banks in New York City so that the necessary liquidity would be on hand should any other banks fail. Morgan, Jacob Schiff of Kuhn Loeb, George Baker of the First National Bank, and James Stillman of the National City Bank persuaded Roosevelt that aid was needed to ensure the integrity of the banking system and, indirectly, the stock market. The operation was successful, and the banking crisis ebbed. But then the stock market began to wobble badly because of intense speculation. More assistance was needed.

The Panic of 1907 prompted the president of the NYSE to ask Morgan to provide assistance so that the exchange could keep its doors open for business. The bankers responded quickly with another $25 million, and the exchange was saved from speculation and a severe lack of confidence. Morgan was quickly hailed as the savior of the financial system in many quarters, but his detractors were equally vocal in claiming that the entire affair was a fiasco manufactured by the bankers to cast themselves in a good light and make money from it in the process. In the years that immediately followed, the critics would have their way when the Federal Reserve was founded. No one felt comfortable having a private banker and his cohorts provide lender-of-last-resort facilities to the banks because of the lack of a central bank. There was no institution in place that could provide a bridge between the Treasury and the banks and markets except the powerful private bankers. But it was the charges of collusion that would resonate long after the panic was over. If they were true,

The Panic of 1907 is remembered mainly for Morgan's assistance to the market. However, other Wall Street notables aided investors in other, less publicized ways. Hetty Green, the "Witch of Wall Street," recalled several incidents surrounding the panic. Green was Wall Street's first notable woman investor. A debutante and wife of a well-known Wall Street operator, she reportedly amassed a fortune of $100 million by emulating the robber barons of the time, participating in corners and short-selling operations. But she was hardly accepted socially. She recalled that after the market dropped, the Vanderbilts applied to her for a loan. They supposedly brought her a box full of the family jewels as collateral. Claiming she knew nothing about diamonds and other jewels, she rejected the collateral and denied the loan. When the Vanderbilts read about her statement regarding the loan in the newspapers, they were quick to deny it and made sure that the denials were published in the press. No one is certain whether the story was true, because Green's memory was beginning to fail her when she recalled the story in her seventies.

After her husband's death, Green became increasingly eccentric and lived in a rented flat in Hoboken, New Jersey. She believed that her husband had been poisoned and afterward slept with a gun tied to the foot of her bed, rigged to fire if anyone opened the bedroom door while she slept.

---

then the country was indeed being held ransom by Wall Street bankers.

One of the most vocal critics of Morgan and his allies was Senator Robert LaFollette of Wisconsin, the fiery Progressive critic of the American financial system. He claimed that the entire affair was manufactured when Morgan at first pledged assistance to the Knickerbocker and then withheld it. By doing so, he caused a run on another trust bank, the Trust Company of New York, which ignited the panic and other runs. The run on the Trust Co. had a different ending, however. The major bankers met with Treasury Secretary George Cortelyou in Manhattan to patch together a bailout package. After intensive meetings, the chairman of the New York Clearing House Committee emerged and said, "I think it is now safe to say that no other financial institution of the least importance will have to undergo the experiences of the Knickerbocker Trust Company. I feel optimistic for the first time since these troubles began."[20] By then the system was ripe for assistance, and the bankers convinced Cortelyou that they could provide stability if he provided the money. The proposed assistance did not come without strings attached, however. When the bankers later traveled to Washington to meet with the secretary, part of the deal involved Morgan's purchase of a large block of stock of the Tennessee Coal, Iron & Railroad Co. The stock was held by Moore & Schley, a well-known Wall Street securities firm that was in danger of failing without outside assistance. Morgan proposed buying the stock from it, thereby saving it from failure. The trip to Washington was necessary because of the antitrust implications of the transaction. Tennessee Coal would provide U.S. Steel with a valuable amount of resources, but Morgan feared antitrust retaliation from the administration. Morgan's representatives convinced Cortelyou that the transaction was not particularly significant but that it would help stabilize the markets. Roosevelt, who was not present at the meeting, later wrote, "I felt it no duty of mine to interpose any objections." He soon changed his mind.

Morgan's quid pro quo worked well enough at the time, but the incident provided fuel for the muckrakers and critics of Wall Street for a generation to come. Providing central banking services was one thing, but making a profit by further consolidating the steel monopoly was another. The purchase price of the securities firm's block of Tennessee Coal was $45 million. Estimates for its market value ranged as high as $1 billion.[21] The purchase was certainly a good deal, but the impact of the deal began to turn on Morgan quickly. Roosevelt subsequently ordered an antitrust investigation of U.S. Steel that lasted for years. A separate congressional investigation turned up other evidence that was not complimentary to Morgan. In the investigation, Judge Elbert Gary, president of U.S. Steel, was questioned at some length about the transaction. The questioning finally came down to the question of why, if the transaction was as unbeneficial to Morgan as Gary maintained, "did you not have any partners in misery?" The bailout of Tennessee Coal was solely a Morgan operation. Gary replied with the standard "Morgan Saves the Country" answer: "Mr.

Morgan is the one man who, on such occasions, will rise to the occasion and put his own money into the other banks or on the stock exchange or anywhere to prevent the panic or prevent trouble, and give the use of his name and his credit to help people who are in financial distress."[22] The second big trust bank to fail during the panic, the Trust Company of New York, was also a major shareholder in Tennessee Coal, and its stake would have to be sold if it was to survive. The final report of the committee concluded that George Perkins, a Morgan partner, concocted the run on the trust bank so that its holdings would have to be sold. Those findings agreed with remarks made by LaFollette. Later, in 1911, the Justice Department filed suit against U.S. Steel, charging it with violations of the Sherman Act. The outcome would not be clear for almost a decade.

Saving the country from its structural deficiencies made for good and bad press for Morgan, but consolidation was still his métier. Already having created General Electric and U.S. Steel, he turned his attention to communications. The telephone industry was an example of a revolutionary new business founded by an inventor who was a better technician than a businessman. Alexander Graham Bell's company was founded in 1884 to provide long-distance telephone service. The other, smaller Bell companies had been licensed by the inventor because he was short of capital to develop them. Beginning in 1907, Morgan, along with George Baker of the First National Bank of New York, began acquiring an interest in the company. They replaced Kidder Peabody as the company's main banker, although Kidder would remain in the syndicates for AT&T securities issues for years after. One of the bankers' most important changes was to install Theodore Vail as a board member and president. Vail was a relentlessly energetic executive who doubled AT&T's capacity over the next five years, seizing upon AT&T's virtual monopoly in the industry to give it an even stronger base of operations.

Morgan became the principal banker to AT&T when Robert Winsor, head partner at Kidder Peabody, realized that his Boston-based firm could not provide all the capital the company needed for its expansion plans. Then he sought out Morgan and Kuhn Loeb to help with financings in New York, realizing that he probably would lose the designation as the company's lead banker. The relationship established between Morgan and AT&T was to become one of the longest in investment banking history in the twentieth century. After the establishment of Morgan Stanley, J. P. Morgan & Co.'s successor in investment banking in 1934, AT&T became one of the prime clients for the new firm until the breakup of the telephone monopoly in 1984. While not one of Morgan's major achievements, AT&T proved to be its longest-standing major client.

The success of J. P. Morgan & Co. meant a continuous search for new partners. In 1910, Morgan made his most astute choice of a new partner when he asked Thomas Lamont to join the firm. The son of a Methodist minister, Lamont had graduated from Harvard in 1892 and gone to work as a newspaperman in New York. He was lured away from the news and eventually went to work for the Bankers Trust Co., a new trust bank organized in New York in 1903 by the major New York City banks as competition for the other trust banks that they thought were luring away their customers. As secretary and treasurer of the new bank, he was able to gain invaluable experience and see the competition that the banks were providing the private banks first-hand. After several years' experience, he moved to the First National Bank of New York, headed by George F. Baker. He was appointed to the Northern Pacific Railroad's board of directors shortly thereafter and appeared well on his way to success at the bank. Then, in 1910, J. P. Morgan invited him to become a partner at his bank. If he accepted, he would become Morgan's youngest partner at age forty. The partnership had opened because George Perkins, who had been roundly criticized for maneuvering the Tennessee Coal deal, had resigned to pursue other interests. Lamont would become the most valuable asset within the Morgan organization over the coming decades, rising to become chief executive officer of the bank under Jack, Pierpont's son and successor.

Pierpont's last years were filled with highly charged drama, the sort to which the Morgans were unaccustomed in their years of banking. Not all of it was unexpected. Several significant political developments were brewing that appeared to challenge the House of Morgan's hold on American banking. After the Panic of 1907, informal discussions began on the establishment of a new central bank; they were held at a private enclave on Jekyll Island, Georgia, known for its millionaire clientele. Momentum was growing for a central bank, and without including bankers in the discussions there would be little chance of success.

The Jekyll Island talks produced a varied debate over the form and function of a central bank, but the events that produced the most debate on Wall Street were the congressional hearings on the "money trust" that began in 1912. Instigated by Rep. Charles Lindbergh of Minnesota, the hearings were known as the Pujo hearings after Rep. Arsenee Pujo of Louisiana. After numerous legislative hearings into alleged antitrust violations at both the state and federal level, Congress finally leveled its sights at the financiers behind most of the large industrial combines. Lindbergh called them the "money trust," and the name became synonymous with Morgan, George Baker of National City Bank, James Stillman of the First National Bank, Jacob Schiff of Kuhn Loeb, Henry Lee Higginson of Lee Higginson, and Frank Webster and Robert Winsor of Kidder Peabody. Ordinarily, the name would have been claimed proudly by the bankers, but in an age strongly influenced by Progressive ideas, the notion of a cartel allocating credit throughout the country was politically volatile. Neither Lindbergh nor Pujo would play the starring role for the inquisitors, however. That was left to the counsel for the committee, Samuel Untermyer of New York.

The committee questioned many of the major bankers from New York and Chicago. Most were unaccustomed to the political limelight, not to mention the political hot seat. They represented private banks and were not comfortable being questioned publicly about their business dealings and relationships. When Morgan's turn to be questioned came, the gallery at the House of Representatives was packed. Pujo fired many questions at Morgan quickly and the banker responded to most equally quickly, although his answers were far from elaborate. The dapper Untermyer, resplendent with a mustache and a flower in his lapel, questioned the seventy-five-year-old Morgan about all sorts of business combinations in which he was actively involved, from insurance companies to the railroads to the banks themselves. In most cases, the picture that began to emerge was of a man who obviously wielded enormous power but refused to recognize it. Morgan played the game with Pujo as close to the vest as his gold watch chain would allow.

When questioned about the existence of a money trust, Morgan denied that one actually existed. Untermyer approached the topic by citing his control of U.S. Steel:

> Q. Suppose you owned all of the banks and trust companies, or controlled them, and somebody wanted to start up in the steel business—you understand, against the United States Steel Corporation. You would be under a duty, would you not, to the United States Steel Corporation to see that it was not subjected to ruinous competition?
> A. No, Sir. It has nothing to do with it.
> Q. You would welcome competition?
> A. I would welcome competition.
> Q. The more of it the better?
> A. Yes.
> Q. Your idea is that when a man has got a vast power, such as you have, you admit you have, do you not?
> A. I do not think I have.
> Q. You do not feel it at all?
> A. No, I do not feel it at all.[23]

Exchanges of that nature provided Untermyer with little new information that he could use against the money trust. It was not the testimonies that proved revealing, but the statistics and facts brought before the committee and read into the proceedings. The money trust was not a figment of someone's imagination but a small group of bankers who wielded inordinate power over the creation of money and credit.

Farther along in his testimony, Morgan made an assertion that left many bankers and economists incredulous. When Untermyer asked about the creation of credit, he began by asking:

> Q. Is not the credit based upon the money?
> A. No, Sir.
> Q. It has no relation?
> A. No, Sir, none whatever.
> Q. So that the banks of New York City would have the same credit, and if you owned them you would have the same control of credit as if you had the money, would you not?
> A. I know lots of men, business men too, who can borrow any amount, whose credit is unquestioned.

Q. Is that not so because it is believed that they have the money [in] back of them?

A. No, Sir. It is because people believe in the man.[24]

That money did not create credit and vice versa was a quaint nineteenth-century banking idea that put the individual's reputation above the concept of creditworthiness. Morgan's denial of a link between the two may not have been entirely credible, but it did underscore the link between nineteenth- and twentieth-century notions of banking. Morgan further testified, "A man I do not trust could not get money from me on all the bonds in Christendom." If he did not trust a man's character, he would not grant him a loan. That remark became the talk of the hearings but did not hold much sway otherwise. The Federal Reserve was about to come into creation in a clear attempt to control the supply of money and credit.

The Pujo hearings were Pierpont Morgan's first and last public appearance. He died several months later while traveling in Italy. The hearings seemed to have had an adverse effect on him. The cause of his death is not known, but the ailments he had at the time were probably the real cause. Pierpont had become increasingly corpulent over the years and refused to diet or exercise. When his son Jack took up playing squash regularly, he remarked, "Rather he than I."[25] He died in his sleep in Rome, and the body was sent back to the United States for burial. Memorial services were held in London, Rome, and Paris as well as in New York. The Pope sent his personal condolences upon hearing of Morgan's death. On the day of his funeral, the NYSE closed for business as a display of respect. The power that Morgan denied having was on full display only after his death. When his will was read, he was found to be worth about $68 million, excluding works of art that he had been accumulating for years. The amount prompted Andrew Carnegie to remark that Pierpont was "not very rich." More important, his mantle at the bank was passed to his son Jack, who would carry on the family tradition for another thirty years.

Although the Pujo hearings and Morgan's death were coincidental, Thomas Lamont was convinced that the hearings contributed directly to his death. He wrote later that Morgan was being made "the subject of innuendoes, charges, and the like by a lawyer [Untermyer] acting like a district attorney, whose object never seemed to be to gain the truth but to try to trump up some justification for a thesis all of his own which, flying in the face of clear testimony . . . he embodied in a report, every word of which he wrote himself."[26] The Pujo Committee concluded that a money trust did exist but that it was an informal group rather than a group of conspirators bent upon controlling the financial system. However, it mattered little in practical terms. The most powerful banker was dead and the Federal Reserve had been founded to attempt to come to grips with the nation's money supply and credit problems.

Carrying On the Tradition

Jack Morgan was the natural heir to the empire. Born in 1867, Jack was educated at Harvard and graduated in 1889. Unlike his domineering father, Jack was more gentle and reflective than Pierpont, who thought his son a bit too soft for the rigors of business. After leaving college, he spent six months traveling in Europe before returning to enter the banking business in Boston as the local agent of J. S. Morgan & Co. Within a year, he married and moved to New York to work directly with his father. Like everyone else, Jack was somewhat intimidated by his father, who was given to bouts of rage and manic depression. But he took quickly to the family business despite working in Pierpont's shadow. He became a partner in all the Morgan banks in 1892 at the age of twenty-five and was sent by Pierpont to London to learn the international side of the operation. From that time, he became privy to all of his father's dealings. He was clearly the heir apparent, and like his father before him, had been handed the family business after a short apprenticeship. While the Morgans had only one son each, they made it clear that they would have to continue the family tradition. Jack was more of a soft character than his father, however. It is doubtful that he would have called his enormous personal yacht the *Corsair*, as Pierpont dubbed the personal sailing vessel on which much private and sensitive business was conducted. As far as the business community was concerned, he was a Morgan nevertheless, and soon after his father's death he dropped the "Jr." from his name.

In the years leading up to the First World War, the critics of the money trust were stronger than ever before. Books published by Louis Brandeis, Ida Tarbell, and others all criticized the bankers for their powerful financial and corporate connections. The Pujo hearings revealed the extent of interlocking directorships among the bankers at the top New York banks. The directors of Morgan, First National, and National City held more than 340 directorships in more than 100 corporations that controlled assets of more than $22 billion.[27] And that did not include the other members of the money trust, only the three largest lenders in New York City. Clearly, the financial structure of the country was controlled by an oligopoly. Whether it acted in a conspiratorial manner was not as important as bringing it to heel. But the Pujo hearings produced no meaningful securities or banking legislation. They did produce a new antitrust law in the form of the Clayton Act, which was passed in 1914 in an attempt to control interlocking directorships, among other things. Ironically, the clamoring of the muckrakers (and Brandeis in particular) led to a major defeat in the Supreme Court as the 1920s began.

The war years provided something of a respite from the outcry caused by the critics of the banking cartel. In 1911, the monopolies created by American Tobacco and Standard Oil were ordered broken up, then the Federal Reserve was founded, the Clayton Act was passed, the muckrakers continued publishing their attacks, and Woodrow Wilson, elected in 1912, vowed to pursue the antitrust policies of his predecessors. The most notable Morgan success during the war was the packaging of the $500 million bond for the English and French, dubbed the "Anglo-French war loan." One bit of Morgan business was left outstanding—the antitrust suit filed against U.S. Steel during Theodore Roosevelt's administration. It was still winding its way through the courts, and its eventual verdict would be critical to Morgan's empire.

The Supreme Court finally ruled on U.S. Steel in 1920. The government claimed that the company had been a monopoly since its founding almost twenty years before when Pierpont Morgan bought Carnegie Steel. But the decision did not favor the argument. Two of the justices appointed since the original suit, James McReynolds and Louis Brandeis, had to recuse themselves from the decision because

At the beginning of World War I, the British ambassador to the United States called Jack Morgan requesting an urgent meeting. Even before the details of the amount of support Britain would need in the war were known, the ambassador wanted an answer to one question: Would Morgan support the British with all of his resources? It seemed a reasonable request at the time, since his father was once the best-known banker in Britain, especially after the House of Baring failed in 1890. Morgan's answer was simply "I will."

Morgan committed to the effort without signing any agreement. The British accepted him at his word and his bank went about financing war imports for the United Kingdom. It also arranged the massive Anglo-French loan of 1915. The entire affair added considerably to Jack's reputation. Journalist Clinton Gilbert wrote that "because he lacks the transcendent ability and virility of his father many people had become accustomed to think of the present head of the house as something of a financial nonentity—living on the family name—and that J. P. Morgan & Co. had abdicated from the position it once held." When this episode was revealed years later during the Pecora hearings, such opinions were quickly and finally dispelled.

of previous conflicts of interest. McReynolds had been an attorney general who had filed many suits on behalf of the Justice Department, and Brandeis had been ranting about Morgan-run enterprises for fifteen years. As a result, the decision favored U.S. Steel. The court ruled 4–3 that the company had not achieved the sort of monopoly the government claimed and that its influence was waning rather than increasing. In the language of the day, the company was judged a "good trust" rather than a bad one, meaning that its benefits far outweighed its alleged antitrust violations. U.S. Steel and Morgan were exonerated of monopoly charges. Brandeis was extremely unhappy when he learned of the decision. He lamented that the decision allowed "capitalists to combine in a single corporation 50 percent of the steel industry of the United States, dominating the trade through its vast resources."[28] Morgan celebrated, while Brandeis and other reformers would have to wait for a better day and another decision.

The Decade of the Deal

The 1920s brought a return to the political spotlight for J. P. Morgan & Co. A new group of partners assumed control of many of the bank's operations and were making their presence felt. George Whitney joined the firm as a partner and would become chief operating officer in the 1930s. Thomas Lamont was instrumental in writing many of the financial and economic clauses into German war reparations after the war. Edward Stettinius, formerly the president of the Diamond Match Co., joined during the war to head the bank's export department. Russell Leffingwell, a corporate lawyer and former Assistant Secretary of the Treasury, also joined in 1923 as an expert in international finance. The firm was relying more on its partners, both individually and as a group, and less on its namesake. For a short but fruitful period many Wall Streeters, especially some of the Morgan partners, were engaged in serious diplomacy as they participated in the debate over how much Germany should reimburse the Allies for damages. Lamont became familiar with the premier of France and the prime minister of Britain, as well as a score of other officials. The conservative financial expertise picked up at J. P. Morgan & Co. translated into financial advice given to many foreign governments. But this time it was not over bond issues or gold operations. For a short period at the beginning of the decade, Wall Street figures were able to bask in the sunshine of postwar policy making and financial advice. Unfortunately, the honeymoon would not last for long, and once it faded, it would take decades to reappear.

During the 1920s, Morgan again began consolidating industries on a level to rival the formation of U.S. Steel. The Steel decision was a blow to antitrusters and a boon to those who wanted to consolidate industry even further. With the economy in a boom after the recession of 1921, money was freely available to fund many of these new consolidations. And characteristic of Morgan, they were in an area where the competition from other banks would be limited. While the

Lehmans and the other newer firms were establishing a reputation in retailing, Morgan took on the most capital-intensive industry in the country—electric utilities companies. By the end of the decade, the House of Morgan would be the dominant force in providing electricity in the United States.

Becoming involved in utilities was a natural outcome for the bank, which had been responsible for the founding of the General Electric Company decades before. The 1920s became known as the decade that witnessed the birth of the giant utilities companies. World War I had demonstrated the increased need for electricity, and many entrepreneurs became involved in forming holding companies that aggressively purchased smaller utility companies. Then they formed giant electrical producers that spanned state and regional lines. One of the largest was Middle West Utilities, founded in Chicago by Samuel Insull, the onetime protégé of Thomas Edison in New York. In the South, the Southern Company was founded by James B. Duke about the same time that his American Tobacco Company was sued by the Justice Department. Morgan's interest at the time was confined mostly to the Northeast, where Consolidated Edison, Public Service of New Jersey, and the Niagara Mohawk Company were under his control. This group of utilities companies was organized as the United Corporation in 1929. On the surface, it appeared to be something of a throwback to the days of Pierpont Morgan: a capital-intensive industry organized to take advantage of the growing need for electricity and all of the investment banking fees that the holding company could generate.

The United Corporation was run out of Morgan's headquarters at 23 Wall Street. After 1927, banks were allowed to underwrite stock—something they were not permitted to do previously. Stock in the United Corporation became one of Morgan's few ventures in the equities market between 1927 and 1929. Equities underwriting was a new area for the bank, but it did not approach it in a traditional Wall Street manner. J. P. Morgan & Co. sold the stock in United not to the general public but in "preferred lists" to select customers, all of whom were friends and colleagues. The stock was sold at cost, and the bank apparently took no commission from these select customers. Often, the price was already higher in the market and some were able to sell immediately for a handsome gain. The bank made its profits by underwriting the issues in the first place, charging the companies it formed under the banner of the United Corporation its customary underwriting fee. The electric power industry in general was dominated by a few large companies able to raise enough capital to consolidate. The Federal Trade Commission reported that Insull's company, along with Morgan's and the Electric Bond and Share Co., controlled more than 50 percent of the nation's electrical production. If the Crash of 1929 had not occurred, the outcry against the power trust, as it was known, would have come even sooner than it did.

Morgan's involvement with the United Corporation was not the only major deal in which the bank engaged during the boom years. It consolidated several food companies into Standard Brands and helped create the Alleghany Corp., a railroad holding company that was the brainchild of the Van Sweringen brothers from Cleveland. The two eccentric brothers convinced the Morgan partners to help them finance the latter-day railroad empire, but it soon fell apart under the weight of heavy borrowing and the brothers' eventual deaths. The entire affair was a throwback to when Pierpont dominated American railroads, but by the 1920s the deals done for the brothers seemed anachronistic. Alleghany Corporation is usually singled out as the financing venture that earned Morgan the most opprobrium at the Pecora hearings, which would begin during the early years of the Depression. But it was the United Corporation that illustrated that the old empire-building ideas of Pierpont were not entirely dead even though the bank was now run by his son and a fresh generation of partners.

The utilities problems of the 1920s and early 1930s always played second fiddle to other news of the time, notably the stock market's rise and crash, Prohibition, and organized crime. But beneath the surface a quiet war was raging between financiers, regulators, and the utilities barons over the course of electric production in the country. Morgan's history was notable here as well. General Electric had remained loyal to Morgan since its early days, using the bank for financing whenever necessary. But Sam Insull gave the industry a bad name despite the fact that his utilities companies were both efficient and profitable. When his empire finally collapsed after the Crash, he could have been forgiven for thinking that he was dealing with Pierpont rather than Jack Morgan, because his empire collapsed as quickly as Henry Villard's dreams had decades before.

Fearing a takeover, Insull began to pyramid his holdings so that a holding company controlled by him owned the other utilities companies. To achieve control, he borrowed significant amounts of money from banks and essentially leveraged the holding company to the breaking point. After the Crash, the empire began to unwind. Insull decided to ask the banks for assistance and appeared to be on the road to saving his empire when the Continental Illinois Bank in Chicago decided to invite Morgan and other New York banks into the rescue loan package. They demanded the stock of his enterprises as collateral. Once that was achieved, Insull's days were numbered. The stock began to drop precipitously on the NYSE during the bad days of 1932, and the creditors moved in. Insull fled to Greece to avoid the accusations flying around, and he stayed abroad for some time. When he did return, he was ultimately absolved of any wrongdoing, but it was too late for his holdings. His empire was gone, in the hands of his lenders, and he had the distinction of being one of the most reviled men in America, although his sins appeared no greater than average for the 1920s.

J. P. Morgan & Co. appeared to be on the road back to its buccaneering days when the Crash came. Although other banks had developed strong securities departments during the 1920s, especially the National City Bank of New York, Morgan was still the undisputed leader in American finance. The bank's list of clients was a roll call of major American corporations, and its partners were well known in their own right as major figures on Wall Street. Jack Morgan appeared to be Pierpont's rightful successor after almost twenty years on the job, although his hold on the bank was not as autocratic as his father's. When the Crash occurred, there was little reason to assume that a Morgan-led rescue team could not put things right, as it had done in 1907.

When the market averages began to drop in the autumn of 1929, it seemed a natural consequence of the high prices that some stocks commanded. But when they continued to drop during the third week of October, panic began to set in. When Black Thursday (October 24) finally arrived, the market was already down almost 7 percent from the previous day. By noon of that day, bankers met in New York to see what could be done to stop the market slide. The group included Thomas Lamont of Morgan, Albert Wiggin of Chase, Charles Mitchell of National City, and George F. Baker Jr. of First National. Their response was traditional: they committed $130 million to stabilize the market. They would buy certain stocks to prevent them from dropping further, and that would stop the overall market from sliding. But they misinterpreted the extent of the market rout. It was proving to be a crash rather than just another market downturn.

Symbolically, the first order intended to stabilize the market was a buy order for U.S. Steel. The order was placed on the floor of the NYSE by its president, Richard Whitney, brother of Morgan partner

---

J. P. Morgan's decision to commit funds to help prop up the stock market in October 1929 was greeted with enthusiasm on the floor of the NYSE. It had become a tried-and-true method of attempting to calm the market after a disastrous drop. Vaudeville comedian Eddie Cantor, probably best known for his song "Making Whoopee," lost heavily in the market crash but was still able to take a light view of the whole affair. In a little book titled *Caught Short: A Saga of Wailing Wall Street*, published in 1929 immediately after the Crash, he recalled a "conversation" held with a friend as the market became unraveled:

"When I heard the news of the first rally I said to a famous songwriter: 'Well, Jack, we're all right now. Things are going to go up. The Rockefellers are buying, and the bankers are backing up the market.'

"'Good Lord!' he moaned. 'Yesterday I died, and today they are giving me oxygen.'"

The songwriter he was referring to was Irving Berlin, one of the first investors to trade stocks from a floating brokerage installed on a Cunard Line ship on the transatlantic route. Like many other celebrities, both men lost a substantial amount of money in the Crash.

George Whitney. Other buy orders were for Anaconda Copper, GE, AT&T, and the New York Central Railroad, all stocks with strong Morgan ties. At first, the action appeared successful: the market stabilized for a few days. But then it resumed its downward spiral, and the continued pressure forced many margin accounts to be liquidated, ruining thousands of investors in the process. The market lost 50 percent of its value in the later months of 1929, and the Depression came roaring in behind it. There would be no more bailouts by J. P. Morgan & Co. The economy was too large and there were too many investors involved for a bankers' coterie to save the market by adroit manipulation. There was a serious dent in Morgan's armor as a result, and even greater trouble was on the horizon.

Tell All

The events of 1933 proved to be a watershed for Jack Morgan. First came the Pecora hearings into the causes of the stock market crash. But the hearings were ephemeral compared to legislation—introduced and quickly passed during the first months of Franklin D. Roosevelt's administration—that would change the face of banking and Wall Street. Morgan was faced with making monumental business decisions that would change the nature of the partnership and could easily erode the Morgan image.

The twenty years following the Pujo hearings were prosperous ones for Morgan. The economy was strong and fear of antitrust had receded, allowing the consolidations to occur across a wide array of industries in corporate America. The investment banking business had more competition than ever before, although it dropped off significantly after 1930. The Crash caused a few traditional firms, like J. & W. Seligman & Co., to rethink their business strategy, but for the most part, the Wall Street banking community was intact. Still, a feeling was growing that the Crash was a product of rampant speculation and traditional Wall Street greed. In four short years, the mood of the country had changed significantly. Upon leaving office in 1928, Calvin Coolidge said that it was a good time to buy stocks. By 1932, the firm that tried to sell stock was considered crooked to the core even if it had a good reputation. That antipathy would result in radical legislation that would sever the banking and securities business so that the term "Wall Street banker" would become an oxymoron.

The Pecora hearings were conducted at the same time that the Roosevelt administration was packaging the Securities Act and Banking Act. The Banking Act—or Glass-Steagall Act, as it was better known—jolted Wall Street; no legislation even remotely resembling it had ever been implemented before. Passed during a time of national economic crisis, it proved more effective than any of the antitrust laws in breaking up the money trust.

Glass-Steagall was directed at the entire banking industry, but there was no doubt that Morgan's dominance of the banking system was the motivating force behind it. The role of private bankers was so severely diminished by it that many quickly had to reconsider their entire banking operations. Several provisions of the law made it the most controversial legislation ever passed affecting banking. Besides providing deposit insurance for bank customers, a provision detractors considered a socialist concept, the law effectively divorced commercial banking from investment banking. With the simple stroke of a pen, Glass-Steagall proclaimed that no commercial bank could engage in the corporate securities business. The arrow was aimed straight at private bankers, who often earned the better part of their revenues by underwriting securities and providing investment advice for corporate clients. If they still wanted to stay in the securities business, they would have a year to relinquish their commercial banking activities, and vice versa. Bankers could have it one way or the other, but not both.

The nature of Wall Street was about to change radically. Bankers were sure they saw the hand of Louis Brandeis in the legislation, which certainly did bear the imprint of his thesis, written twenty years before, claiming that bankers used other people's money to underwrite securities and invite themselves onto corporate boards. Although the new law was met with some skepticism, it soon became obvious that it would stand, and there was little that even the most powerful bankers could do to avoid it. Jack Morgan was understandably furious about it. Roosevelts were the bane of the Morgans; Jack Morgan was heard to exclaim on more than one occasion, "God damn all Roosevelts."[29] His father had fussed and fumed about the same things twenty years before, but then, as now, there was little that could be done to stem the tide of reform. Morgan had a year to decide how to react. Would his future course be investment or commercial banking? All of the other private bankers, except Brown Brothers Harriman, chose the securities business. The Seligmans decided on investment management as their best course, and the large money center banks—National City, First National, and Chase—chose commercial banking. They divested their securities affiliates, and these castoffs created the first generation of post–Glass-Steagall investment banks. The Morgan partners, somewhat unexpectedly, chose commercial banking. Apparently thinking that the Roosevelt reforms would prove ephemeral, they spun off the investment banking activities to the newly created Morgan Stanley & Co. For all practical purposes, the new investment bank could easily have been called J. P. Morgan & Co. once removed. Morgan partners owned its stock, and its capital was provided by J. P. Morgan & Co. Apparently, they were willing to wait until the Roosevelt phenomenon ran out of gas. This proved to be a dramatic misreading of the political climate and set the stage for a decline in the House of Morgan's fortunes.

Morgan Stanley was headed by Harold Stanley, a Morgan partner, and Henry S. Morgan, Jack's son. Three others also became partners of the new firm, all former Morgan employees. No one doubted for a moment that the new securities firm was anything more than the old bank legally skirting the Glass-Steagall Act. Morgan Stanley immediately assumed all of Morgan's old investment banking clients and was quickly in business in 1935 as if a roadblock had never occurred. The entire situation was reminiscent of the breakup of Standard Oil ordered by the Supreme Court twenty years before. When the smoke cleared, Standard Oil was still the dominant force in the oil industry and John D. Rockefeller was wealthier than before. No one doubted that the same thing had happened again, regardless of what the New Deal desired. Ironically, the day that Morgan Stanley was officially created, all of the partners assembled for a group photo with the exception of Jack Morgan and Henry S. Morgan, both of whom had gone grouse hunting. They apparently did not think the occasion momentous enough to interrupt their favorite pastime.[30]

Insult was added to injury once gain when the second bit of legislation was passed. On the surface, the Securities Act seemed quite tame. It required all companies that wished to sell new securities to register them first with a government agency, which at the time was the Federal Trade Commission. That simple requirement ran against the historical practice of the entire investment banking industry. Underwriters of stocks and bonds had for years used Pierpont Morgan's idea that personal relationships formed the bedrock of the investment banking business. Asking them to undergo the indignity of actually registering their new issues with a government agency was an incursion into their privacy. So, too, was the requirement that they use standard methods of accounting for their financial statements. In the past, simple accounting statements by companies had been good enough. If a banker took a corporate head at his word, why bother with such formalities?

The answer, provided almost as a continual sidebar by the Pecora hearings, was that the corporate heads and bankers could not be taken at their word. The hearings revealed too many examples of corporate heads and bankers who ignored simple due-diligence practices. In short, they failed to monitor their clients' financial positions carefully. Samuel Insull's leveraging of his utilities empire was one example. Another was Lee Higginson's ignorance of the financial situation of one of its biggest clients, Ivar Kreuger of Sweden, which led to the downfall of his empire and caused a fair amount of collateral damage to American as well as European investors. The Securities Act completely changed the nature of creditworthiness in the country. Corporate financial statements were now to be open to public (investor) scrutiny, and Wall Street would have to change with the times. In more contemporary language, some "transparency" had been cast over affairs that previously were known only to companies and their bankers.

The Pecora hearings were not kind to the House of Morgan, casting some much-needed light on the workings of the private bankers in the 1920s. Pecora interviewed Jack Morgan first among the private bankers, in deference to his position. Morgan's revelations, along with those of other bankers, showed that many of them were still living in a comfortably insulated world of their own making. Pecora examined the preferred-investor lists at some length, showing that clients received Alleghany and United stock at issue price when their prices were actually higher in the market. Loans to other notable New York bankers by

Morgan also were disclosed in an attempt to show that Morgan could control these other senior men by granting them loans for personal reasons. Most revealing was the fact that J. P. Morgan & Co. did not publish its financial statements and saw no reason to do so, maintaining Pierpont's original position that a man's word was good as long as it was not proved otherwise. In the same vein, it was disclosed that several of the Morgan partners had paid no income tax for the past several years.

Testifying before Pecora proved unsettling for the Morgan partners, and especially Jack Morgan. The ordeal ultimately convinced them that remaining a commercial banker without indulging in the securities business was a wise decision. They did not fully comprehend the implications of their actions in what was proving to be a very fast-paced period of history. Congress was still a year away from passing the Securities Exchange Act. That legislation would rankle Wall Street more than the two previous laws, because it put in place a series of regulations over the stock exchanges. While stock exchange regulations would not bother either J. P. Morgan & Co. or Morgan Stanley, the act also established the Securities and Exchange Commission, a very visible symbol of the Roosevelt administration's determination to control the markets. Now the primary and secondary markets had new regulations in place along with a potentially strong overseer. Making money on Wall Street during the Depression was proving to be more difficult than anyone could have possibly imagined only a few years before.

Carrying On the Tradition

The Morgan Stanley partnership picked up where J. P. Morgan left off and continued financing for all of the bank's traditional clients. The new group was a carbon copy of the old in more ways than one. Morgan Stanley did not provide research for its clients, nor did it sell securities to the public. In fact, the only selling it did was allocating blocks of new securities to others to be sold. The entire operation was a classic wholesale investment banking operation that was very short on personnel and long on business and social connections. And its original capital of $7 million was relatively small. It was the same amount that Morgan had had at the time of the gold operation forty years before. Pierpont Morgan was correct when he stated that personal connections were the chief ingredient in his form of banking. Twenty years later, Morgan Stanley would begin its life by continuing to be the very embodiment of the idea. No one could accuse the new bank of being capital intensive. In the 1930s, it was business as usual, despite the Depression.

Immediately after the Securities Act of 1933 was passed, many Wall Street underwriters went on a capital strike, refusing to underwrite new corporate securities according to the new guidelines. They helped their clients by issuing private placements instead, bonds that did not require registration because they were sold to customers pri-

---

Partners from J. P. Morgan & Co. were again on the witness stand in 1936. Owing to popular demand and a new book titled *Road to War*, many Democrats in Congress had pushed for a hearing on the roots of American involvement in World War I. According to the book, written by Walter Millis, the country was dragged into the conflict by the interests of the bankers. Morgan acted as purchasing agent for the British government in the United States, in charge of procuring war supplies. The huge loan to Britain and France in 1915 was supposedly made to help them pay for the goods purchased, adding to the bankers' profits. As Millis wrote: "The mighty stream of supplies flowed out and the corresponding stream of prosperity flowed in, and the U.S. was enmeshed more deeply than ever in the cause of Allied victory."

The committee probing the accusations was known as the Nye Committee, named after Senator Gerald P. Nye of North Dakota. At one point during the hearings, Jack Morgan was seated next to his partner Thomas Lamont, who was attempting to answer a question from the committee. Morgan appeared lackadaisical and somewhat disoriented until Lamont, attempting to quote the Bible, referred to money as the root of all evil. Morgan then interrupted him with the correct quote: "The Bible doesn't say 'money.' It says 'the *love* of money is the root of all evil.'"

The hearings never proved the allegations, and they concluded tamely.

---

vately. This act of defiance was not meaningful, because new issues were at low ebb during the Depression. It would earn them the wrath of the government, though the Justice Department would have to wait until after the Second World War to pursue its historic complaint against the investment banking community.

The World War II years witnessed a profound change at J. P. Morgan & Co. The bank finally went public in 1940, ending the partnership that had begun between Junius Morgan and George Peabody before the Civil War. The culprit behind the momentous change again was the need for capital. The three senior partners—Jack Morgan, Thomas Lamont, and Charles Steele—were advancing in years, and when they died the bank's existing capital would be depleted. In addition, its asset base had diminished from $119 to $39 million due to taxes, and the bank realized that it could no longer continue as a partnership and still remain a premier institution.[31] After years of complaining about the effects of the Glass-Steagall Act and the Securities Act, the partners agreed to do the unthinkable. The securities were registered with the SEC and sold to the public, lead-managed by Smith Barney & Co. Finally, after years of secrecy, the bank published its financial statements as required by law and entered the realm of publicly traded companies. Unlike Brown Brothers, it sold its seat on the NYSE and became a full-fledged commercial bank with no more lingering investment banking ties because of the partnership arrangement. The event was a milestone in American banking.

Three years later, in 1943, Jack Morgan suffered a stroke while vacationing in Florida and died at the age of seventy-five. The honors bestowed on him were similar to those bestowed on Pierpont. The stock exchange closed to honor him, as it had for his father. Although Jack had not been able to "save" the NYSE from the Crash of 1929, the closing gave testimony to his importance on Wall Street. The bank he left behind was materially different from the one he inherited from his father. In many ways, it was only a shadow of its former self.

After World War II, the Justice Department filed suit against seventeen Wall Street firms, charging them with colluding to exclude competition in the investment banking business by arranging cozy syndicates among themselves. The suit was filed as the *U.S. v. Henry S. Morgan et al.*, an indication of which firm the government believed was Wall Street's premier underwriter. Named in the suit with Morgan Stanley were familiar Wall Street firms—Kuhn Loeb, Smith Barney & Co., Lehman Brothers, Glore Forgan & Co., Kidder Peabody, Goldman Sachs, White Weld & Co., Eastman Dillon & Co., Drexel & Co., the First Boston Corp., Dillon Read, Blyth & Co., Harriman Ripley, Union Securities Corporation, Stone & Webster Securities Corp., and Harris Hall & Co. This was no longer the money trust; it was Wall Street's top underwriters, who allegedly had conspired since 1915 to dominate what the Street called the "league tables" of top underwriters. By tracing the suit back to the First World War, the Justice Department clearly demonstrated that it had Morgan in its sights.

The presiding judge in the case, Harold Medina, did not agree. After reviewing thousands of pages of testimony and documents, Medina ruled several years later that the government had not made its case. The suit against the Wall Street Seventeen was dismissed. Later events would support his decision, as many of the defendants quickly began to fade from the top brackets in the tombstone ads in the years ahead. Morgan Stanley clearly maintained its status as Wall Street's number-one underwriter of corporate securities and maintained its hold as the top investment banker for companies such as AT&T, U.S. Steel, General Motors, and International Harvester. In fact, it laid claim to more Fortune 100 companies as clients in the postwar years than did any other investment bank. It continued to do so by offering the same brand of wholesale investment banking that it had for years—underwriting, mergers and acquisitions services, and financial advice.

Superficially, the case correctly cited Morgan for its dominance of underwriting. Between 1938 and 1947, Morgan Stanley ranked first among Wall Street's underwriters of corporate securities, followed by First Boston, Dillon Read, and Kuhn Loeb. But what it could not detect was that by 1950, Morgan Stanley would be replaced by Halsey Stuart and Co. That firm's chairman, Harold Stuart, had been instrumental in advising Judge Medina on Wall Street practices during the trial of the Wall Street Seventeen and his firm temporarily captured the leading spot while the trial was still active. Morgan Stanley would regain the top spot during the 1950s and hold it for a considerable number of years before relinquishing it to other, upstart firms with more capital and a broader sales force. Competition was building for underwriting business by the late 1950s, but it would still take more than a decade for firms like Merrill Lynch and Salomon Brothers to make a serious impact in corporate securities underwriting.

Losing Prominence

The postwar years saw Morgan Stanley retain its position as Wall Street's most prominent investment bank. The bull market of the 1950s and 1960s created enormous demand for new financings, and many traditional Morgan Stanley clients brought new issues to market to keep pace with the booming economy. But in keeping with its traditional position atop Wall Street, it still insisted on being its clients' only investment banker, a trait that would lead to its decline in the 1960s and 1970s.

At the same time, transaction-oriented firms like Salomon Brothers, Goldman Sachs, and Merrill Lynch were making great inroads in the underwriting business. Traditionally, these firms had established their reputation as bond traders and retailers. As the world's markets became more closely integrated due to improved communications and computerization, demand for global services such as foreign exchange trading, eurobond trading, and trade financing gave them an edge on traditional firms like Morgan Stanley and Dillon Read. These upstarts were able to compete for underwriting business because of the other services they provided to companies. Corporate treasurers quickly realized the value of an investment banker who wore many hats. The hustlers on Wall Street made significant gains on the traditional firms in the 1950s and 1960s, and Morgan Stanley began to feel the pinch. The firm did not add investment management, equities research, or government bond trading to its activities until the 1970s. It continued to rely on underwriting and mergers and acquisitions to provide revenue.

Morgan Stanley's prowess in underwriting was underscored by a massive bond issue done for AT&T in 1969. AT&T needed money for expansion and talked about a massive billion-dollar-plus issue with its foremost underwriter. Regulators were watching the company closely at the time, so the issue needed to be coordinated properly and not appear to be too generous to investors—the phone company was still a government-tolerated monopoly. Morgan Stanley's response was innovative. It tied equity warrants to the bond issue, giving investors an opportunity to convert the warrants to common stock at a future date. The issue was managed by Robert Baldwin at Morgan Stanley, and when it was completed it totaled $1.6 billion for the bonds alone, the largest bond issue in American history, and dominated Wall Street for the better part of 1969. That year was especially critical for the Street because it was in the midst of its backroom crisis—the order backlog that plagued so many firms and caused many to finally close their doors. Morgan Stanley followed the deal with other huge issues for U.S. Steel and General Motors, both old Morgan allies.

Baldwin became CEO of Morgan Stanley shortly after the deal. A Princeton graduate, Baldwin was mainly responsible for bringing the firm into the mainstream of the 1970s. He served as an undersecretary of the Navy under Lyndon Johnson on sabbatical from the firm and returned with an ambition to run it. He established many of the departments that Morgan Stanley had been lacking and engineered the move from Wall Street to Rockefeller Center, taking the firm so long associated with Broad and Wall to a new midtown address. His style was markedly different from that of the older Morgan partners, several of whom remained active in the firm. Harry Morgan, a limited partner in the 1970s, still had the final say on many of the firm's decisions, but he was aging and his influence was beginning to wane. As Morgan Stanley was developing investment management services, it was approached by the Teamsters Union with an appealing offer. The union wanted the firm to manage its entire real estate portfolio, one of the largest in the country. The fees that it could have generated made it an enticing proposition. But Morgan would have none of it. He stated to the partners bluntly, "As long as I am alive, this firm is not going to do business with the Teamsters."[32] No more discussion was needed, and the union was rejected. His word was still law at Morgan Stanley, even though the firm had incorporated in 1970 and his role was limited. This preserved it to an extent from a capital outflow as the older partners began to retire. In their place, managing directors were created; the firm had about twenty during the early 1970s before it began to expand.

By the 1970s, the competition for underwriting was beginning to be seriously felt. One particularly prized Morgan Stanley client was IBM, which the firm considered one of its blue-chip clients. In 1979, as a huge bond issue for the company was being planned, IBM asked Morgan Stanley to include Salomon Brothers as a co-lead manager on the deal. If accepted by Morgan Stanley, Salomon's name would have appeared at the top of the tombstone ad that was published in all the major newspapers when the deal was completed. The top line of the ads was jealously guarded by investment bankers and was not easily relinquished to the competition. Morgan Stanley rejected IBM's offer on the grounds that only it could occupy the top line as lead manager of a deal. IBM refused to back down and awarded the deal to Salomon, which invited Merrill Lynch to be a comanager. Morgan Stanley was stunned that a long-standing client would contemplate using another lead underwriter, but the handwriting was on the wall. The new Wall Street powerhouses that had made their reputations by sales and trading were now openly pillaging the sacred preserve of the traditional underwriters. Defections of that nature would become more common for Morgan Stanley in the future, and the firm had to adjust in order to avoid the fate that had befallen Kuhn Loeb and Dillon Read.

For twenty years after the war, Morgan Stanley had managed to retain one distinct trait that had lingered ever since the days of J. P. Morgan: The firm had no sales facilities. Underwritings were distributed to other securities houses through syndication, allowing Morgan Stanley to avoid the costs associated with direct selling. In that sense, it remained a purely wholesale investment bank, similar to J. P. Morgan in commercial banking. But the situation began to change in the 1970s. First, the firm added institutional sales, and then later a small retail sales force. Negotiated commissions, introduced to NYSE member firms for the first time in 1975, forced many securities firms to reconsider their traditional game plans. With institutional investors demanding—and getting—better commissions on their trades, the new system forced Morgan Stanley to abandon its old method of securities distribution and enter the sales arena for the first time. Within ten years, it would face another startling change.

Despite its slow-paced moves to change the business, Morgan Stanley did embark on a deal in 1974 that was considered by many a watershed in investment banking. It engaged in the first hostile-takeover bid for a company with no forewarning. The firm advised International Nickel on its bid for ESB, a maker of batteries. By agreeing to help in the acquisition, the firm broke a long-standing tradition whereby investment bankers stayed out of the fray when one company made an unwanted bid for another. Morgan Stanley advised on a bid of $28 per share. ESB then called Goldman Sachs for help defending itself and the price was eventually raised to $41 per share, where the deal was consummated. The battle lines were also set for the next decade of merger activity. Morgan Stanley often found itself advising the bidders while Goldman advised the target companies.

The 1980s brought more wrenching changes. Although not as well publicized as the legislation of the 1930s, the events were almost as profound, since they altered the way the firm did its primary underwriting business. Ever since the turn of the century, underwriting new stocks and bonds had been a gradual process. Even the Securities Act built this gradualism into its procedures. When a company wanted to issue new securities, it would register with the SEC and then wait a mandatory three weeks before actually coming to market. During this time, the SEC would gather the information it needed before allowing the company's underwriters to proceed with a deal, and the lead underwriter of the deal would assemble a syndicate of other investment banks, which would subscribe to the issue. When the securities were officially designated for sale, the underwriters would open and close the books on the deal, since they had been actively lining up buyers during the interim. Usually, by the time the cooling-off period ended, the securities had already been sold.

The process benefited the investment banks, because they did not have to commit any money to the deal until it closed, at which point they owed the issuing company a check for the deal. Since most orders were lined up already, they simply took their customers' money and turned it over to the issuer, less their commission. Because of this process, which had not changed substantially in decades, firms with limited capital could still play in the big league of underwriters because their own money was not at risk for very long. The cooling-off period required firms to have little capital on the line, and that suited many, including Morgan Stanley, Kidder Peabody, and

Dillon Read. If the process changed, however, the firms would have to quickly change as well.

The process changed significantly when the SEC passed Rule 415 in 1982. This became known on Wall Street as the shelf registration rule, allowing companies to file preliminary papers with the SEC in anticipation of a new securities deal. If they did so, they could then bring a new issue to market when conditions were favorable by simply freshening up the documents already "on the shelf." The cooling-off period was waived and the company could get to market much more quickly. While touted as a significant step toward circumventing the old apparatus, Rule 415 also caused considerable consternation among the underwriters, who quickly discovered that the old way of doing business had just been bluntly circumvented.

Instead of waiting three weeks to provide the company with funds, underwriters discovered that they would now have to guarantee their clients the funds and then organize a syndicate. This left the lead manager on the hook for the value of the deal without firm commitments from other syndicate members. The assumption of underwriting risk changed mechanically—and substantially. Now the securities houses would need additional capital in order to play according to the new rules. They would, in effect, have to buy the deal and then sell it afterward. Many, including Morgan Stanley, needed fresh capital in a hurry. They were not in the same envious position as many of their larger rivals, like Merrill Lynch, which had gone public a decade earlier.

Rule 415 had a serious impact on Morgan Stanley. For a couple of years following its introduction, most of the new securities issues that appeared technically were issued without the aid of syndicates. They were "bought deals," securities that were purchased by a few managers and sold to investors. As *Institutional Investor* stated, "For companies [underwriters] with abundant capital and close ties with institutional investors, the post-syndicate world has become an underwriting bonanza." For the first time in decades, Morgan Stanley fell out of its top position as Wall Street's leading underwriter. The year after the rule was introduced, its place in the league tables of underwriters was taken by Salomon Brothers. Merrill Lynch followed in the second spot, while Morgan Stanley dropped to number six. Lehman Brothers Kuhn Loeb, infused with capital because of the merger, also rose in the standings, because it was able to combine successfully historic ties with companies and enough capital to buy deals.[33] Morgan Stanley's reputation was as great as ever, but it clearly recognized that it was being nudged out of the top spot on Wall Street by firms like Salomon and Merrill that were transaction-oriented. Bought deals were being done by firms that traded profitably on the Street, while traditional deals were done by those that relied on connections. The world was changing quickly, and Morgan Stanley would have to adapt to retain its blue-chip reputation or go the way of Dillon Read.

Finally, in 1986, the once unthinkable occurred. Morgan Stanley sold a 20 percent stake and went public. The need for additional capital had proved overwhelming, and the firm officially ended its history as a partnership. The firm raised about $292 million through the offering. At the time, it had 144 managing directors, many of whom did quite well by the offering. The firm's four top officers held stock valued at $55 million. Between them, the managing directors and others with a vested stake in the company held about $1.4 billion before the new offering. That raised capital to about $1.75 billion. Richard B. Fisher, president, noted that the new capital would be used "across the board" to allow the firm to provide new services and improve the old.[34] But in a traditional twist to an old problem, the firm made it difficult for an unwanted suitor to bid for the company in a hostile-takeover attempt. Employees of Morgan Stanley who purchased the stock agreed to vote their shares to an outside bidder according to the wishes of the majority of shareholders. If a majority did not agree, shares could not be offered. Many believed that an eventual link with J. P. Morgan & Co. would again be established after those years of separation, but Morgan Stanley continued on its independent way for another decade. Still, the shareholder agreement was put in place to ensure that the company was not swallowed by one of its larger competitors.

Morgan Stanley maintained its independence but did merge with Dean Witter in 1997. The result was a large, full-service Wall Street firm that used Dean Witter's large retail network to complement the traditional investment banking services for which Morgan Stanley was known. The merger, considered an unusual marriage by many, showed that the traditional investment banking firms no longer had the luxury of standing alone if they intended to maintain their grip on their traditional preserves. Even going public was not the final answer—at least not for Morgan Stanley. The marketplace valued franchise names as much as ever, but the economics of the situation dictated that the names be supported by an actual franchise. In many cases, that meant merging with a large retail-based operation, a prospect that would have rattled Pierpont and Jack to their bones in their heyday.

6

CORNER OF WALL AND MAIN: MERRILL LYNCH AND E. F. HUTTON

THE TWENTIETH CENTURY brought with it new challenges for Wall Street and a different way of doing business. The new partnerships that sprang up before and after the First World War were markedly different from the legendary banking houses of the nineteenth century. Gone were the days when a successful merchant business eventually moved into private banking and then worked its way into the securities-issuing business. The new securities house also was less likely to be a wholesale institution and more a retail or trading operation in which securities were bought and sold for the house account or sold directly to the public.

Over the course of the nineteenth century, Wall Street was fairly isolated from trends affecting the great majority of the population. Wall Street and Main Street remained poles apart. Until 1920, Wall Street catered primarily to corporations and wealthy individuals. The average citizen played almost no role in the process. And the reputation of the stock exchanges did not help the image, either. For most of the nineteenth and the early part of the twentieth centuries, the exchanges had a reputation for being the preserve of professional traders who frequently warred with each other on the trading floors. Main Street, on the other hand, placed most of its savings in small banks and had little contact with finance. Individuals with limited means knew little about the exchanges, and what they did know was not complimentary.

As the 1920s began, this image began to change. The years preceding the stock market boom that began in 1922 witnessed a new optimism. Consumers found a cornucopia of new products to purchase, ranging from new automobiles to radios and household appliances, and began to dabble in the markets. But the wise investor committed only disposable funds to the market. The floors of the exchanges were still predatory places, and inside information was rampant. For a price, an investor could pay a "tipster" for information on hot stocks. Often, these professional gossips steered those investors to companies that were being touted on the Street. It was possible to make money in this fashion, but it also was easy to lose it. Investor education was not something that Wall Street specialized in. The investor either knew what he was doing or he did not. "Let the buyer beware" was the acknowledged mantra of investing before the 1930s.

While the 1920s have been variably called the Jazz Age, the Prohibition Era, or the years of Coolidge Prosperity, Wall Street will best remember them as the decade of the salesman. Sales techniques began to become highly developed, and the same gimmicks could be applied to all sorts of selling. Jingles and slogans became popular, and products from cigarettes to mouthwashes had their own catchy one-liners to attract customers. But the underlying motive to spend was fueled by more practical matters than customers simply reacting to sales pitches. Frederick Lewis Allen identified two stimulants that ignited the purchasing binge—installment buying and stock market speculation. As he recalled, "If these were the principal causes of Coolidge Prosperity, the salesman and the advertising man were at least its agents and evangels."[1] The 1920s were the years of adman Bruce Barton and publicist Ivy Lee. And the stock market had its own evangels who preached the gospel of untold wealth for only a few dollars down.

The booming market began to attract individual investors despite all the pitfalls. Wall Street was still dotted with bucket shops, places where small investors could put down a few dollars in the hope of making a fast buck. But the larger banks and brokers began to make an earnest effort to bring the greater mainstream of investors into the market. They had good reason. During World War I, the Treasury financed the American war effort with enormous Liberty Loan bond drives that raised large amounts that began to be paid back in the

1920s. This left the population with cash during the greatest boom in American history. Brokers scrambled to bring the wealthier of these new investors into the mainstream. The brokerage subsidiary of the National City Bank of New York ran ads in major newspapers extolling the virtues of intelligent investing. The advertising helped National City, under its aggressive chairman Charles Mitchell, create the largest network of brokerage offices ever seen. The offices were linked to the home office and the exchanges by a series of private telecommunication lines called "wires," or telex. This gave birth to the term "wire house," meaning a brokerage with many branches linked by telex and the telephone.

Catering to the broader population was not a mainstream Wall Street idea. The traditional private investment banks still dominated the Street and securities distribution was mainly a wholesale affair, with the underwriter selling directly or indirectly to institutional investors. But this new phenomenon could not be dismissed easily. While the number of investors was potentially huge, individual buying power was still small, so any operation that intended to cash in on the 1920s boom would have to have a large sales organization to generate high turnover. The chief executives of these new retail-oriented operations needed to be good salesmen themselves in order to inspire their sales forces.

No boom could have occurred if the 1920s were not the decade of the salesman. Charles Mitchell of National City was one of the best, having held various sales jobs since leaving college. He adapted many of the "pitches" used in other industries to motivate and cajole his sales force. The securities would come from National City's own underwriting mill, which was busy turning out new issues of bonds and, after 1927, common stocks. Mitchell claimed that during the 1920s his bank was literally "manufacturing securities" because it produced new issues so quickly. This activity made the bank the number-one retail broker during the decade, but the path to success was clear. Most other established securities dealers did not want to cater to the small investor in a meaningful way, although a few dabbled by establishing their own small retail operations.

After the Crash, the whole idea of retail sales disappeared into obscurity as the Depression loomed. And after the Glass-Steagall Act, large banks like National City had to divest themselves of the operations that had made them infamous at the Pecora hearings. The hearings divulged that many of the bonds that National City underwrote were essentially worthless when the borrowers defaulted. Since there was little due diligence at the time, the general feeling was that the underwriters had defrauded the public by ignoring the creditworthiness of some questionable companies and foreign governments, many of which also issued bonds for sale in the United States. After J. P. Morgan testified that a man's character was of vital importance in granting credit in the markets, a host of other bankers and brokers gave testimony that proved just the opposite. Retail sales died with the Crash and the Pecora hearings provided the epitaph, which was not very complimentary.

But the idea certainly was not dead. The economy would begin to grow again after World War II, and the idea of retail sales would be translated as "people's capitalism." Despite the fact that the securities business was moribund for the Depression years and the war years that followed, reputations lingered. The average man in the street remembered the stories about the great bankers of the past and the wealth they had accumulated. The generation before the Second World War was quite accustomed to hearing jingles about J. P. Morgan's wealth and influence. When prosperity returned in the 1950s, investing again became a popular pastime, but it still had to vie for the average investor's dollar. In the 1950s, purchase of homes and automobiles again became priorities, and the only people who could actually afford investments in the markets were those in the higher income brackets. Within thirty years, however, the phenomenon would include over half the population, making the drive toward "people's capitalism" one of the most successful of its type.

The Rise of Charles Merrill

The revolution brought to Wall Street by the wire houses was fomented by Charles Merrill, whose brokerage house rose to become the world's largest securities dealer. The story behind the rise of Merrill Lynch runs counter to those of all of the prominent investment banks prior to World War II. The mold had finally been broken as the demographics of the United States outstripped the capacities of the older, private investment banks to respond to the increasing needs of a rapidly growing economy and society. Investment bankers no longer dealt with just the larger companies with established connections. Now they catered to all sorts of companies and sold their securities to all sorts of investors, not just their institutional friends at insurance companies, pension funds, and trusts. Charles Merrill was the first Wall Street legend whose origins were modest and whose business plans never included a major corporate financing or big deal like those characterizing the careers of Clarence Dillon and Philip Lehman.

The career of Merrill began in traditional fashion, however. Born in 1885 in Florida, Merrill was sent north to attend prep school and college. He spent two years at Amherst and one year at the University of Michigan before making his way to New York to find work on Wall Street. Amherst produced some of the better-known bankers of the 1920s. Besides Merrill, Charles Mitchell of National City Bank and Calvin Coolidge also attended the college. After Michigan, Merrill made his way to Wall Street, where he eventually landed a job at George H. Burr & Co., a financial firm that provided inventory financing to small companies. He was put in charge of a new venture for the company, the underwriting of low-quality corporate bonds for some of its small corporate customers. The venture was new, and Merrill employed sales techniques not common on Wall Street at the time. He advertised the offering through direct mail and wrote sales material touting investing in general for the small investor. He also hired a friend, Edmund "Eddie" Lynch, a former soda fountain equipment salesman, to be a salesman for the firm, beginning a relationship that would become known to millions of investors in later years. But bad luck plagued the issue, and within a short time, the issuing company had defaulted. Merrill wrote to many investors apologizing for the bad investment. He learned a lesson that would greatly benefit him in his later business life about the value of good, transparent financial information.

While at Burr, Merrill also helped organize a stock offering for S. S. Kresge, the Michigan-based retail store chain. He bought some of the offering for himself, beginning a long relationship with retailers that was to earn him a fortune. The first great retailing revolution came before the First World War; many retail chains, including Sears and Montgomery Ward, were expanding their operations nationally. Burr was not as large or prominent an underwriter as Lehman Brothers, but Merrill calculated correctly that expansion was the wave of the future. It would be interrupted only briefly by the war.

Before the war, Merrill left Burr to take a position at Eastman Dillon & Co., a leading retail broker. Looking for more money and responsibility, he believed that the new firm could help him improve his budding reputation. But the move did not work out successfully. Merrill decided to go into business for himself, and Charles E. Merrill & Co. was officially established in early 1914. The firm specialized in selling stocks to customers and participating in underwritings. The stocks for which he had the most affinity were the retailers. Soon, he had taken on Edward Lynch as a partner. The two men established a sales force and often bought part of the underwriting commitment for themselves or the firm's own account, capitalizing on the popularity of the retail sector. Their personal favorites were retail stocks, many of which did very well in the market. Merrill and Lynch began to accumulate their fortunes by investing in the same sorts of securities they sold their customers.

Participating in underwriting earned them fees and increased their prestige, but the heart of their business was selling the issues to customers hungry for new stocks. In 1916, Merrill sent a memo to his sales force outlining his philosophy of selling. He stated that "what we do particularly object to is to turn an investment issue into a semi-speculative issue without our approval . . . please bear this in mind and remember that in every sale you are either increasing or destroying a good-will which up to this time has been our most valuable asset."[2] Merrill approached investment banking in a manner opposite to the way traditional investment bankers had since the Civil War. Securities were simply items for sale; they did not represent a long relationship with the issuing company, although a successful issue could open doors for the underwriter in future deals. This was the basic philosophy that would dominate Wall Street fifty years later. But in 1916 it was a novel approach.

Merrill was certainly not the only retailer of stocks during the early years of the twentieth century. Before World War I, several brokers established retail sales operations that were better known and larger than Merrill's and would continue through the booming 1920s. N. W. Halsey & Co. and N. W. Harris & Co. both had extensive organizations for selling new issues to the retail public. While they were able to sell large amounts of new bonds and to a lesser extent stock issues on an annual basis, their average sale was relatively small, usually in the $2,000 to $3,000 range.[3] The retailing concept of the chain stores was certainly familiar to them as well. Their salesmen would make house calls if necessary, armed with sales literature describing securities for the benefit of customers. Halsey was acquired by the National City Bank and its sales organization became the cornerstone of the bank's push into the retail securities market in the 1920s.

During the First World War, Merrill underwrote several issues for retailers, including McCrory Stores, Kresge, and the Acme Tea Co. The latter years of the war interrupted his career briefly when he volunteered for service in the Army. He and Lynch both served but neither was sent abroad, and after their brief stints they returned to the firm. The timing was perfect, because the 1920s were about to begin and all of the money invested in Liberty Bonds was finding its way into the marketplace. Unlike past booms, the 1920s had both the cash necessary to fuel a stock market rally and the brokerage mechanisms in place to ensure that it would continue. It appeared that Merrill was on his way to stardom on Wall Street that would last for decades. But the Crash and his own reluctance to continue his career as a "customer's man" (broker) temporarily intervened.

Into the Abyss

Brokerage and underwriting provided the backbone of the Merrill Lynch partnership during the 1920s. Merrill started the decade as an unabashed bull, recognizing the millions of new customers flocking to the market. He added new chain stores to his stable, including J. C. Penney & Co., and issues for them became popular after the recession of 1920–21. The brokerage offices expanded, with new branches added in the Midwest and California. Twelve junior partners were added as commission revenues continued to mount. Luckily for the fortunes of the firm and Merrill and Lynch personally, outside interests also vied for their time and they did not have to rely entirely on brokerage and underwriting profits to make a living. Beginning in 1921, they both became involved with the New York operation of a French motion picture production company called Pathe Frères Cinema, one of the silent era's best-known movie producers. Within several years, Merrill and Lynch controlled the company and had become, in effect, movie tycoons. The movie industry was rapidly changing in the 1920s as many production houses set up their own chain of cinema theaters as a means of distributing their films. In 1927, the first "talkie" was released: *The Jazz Singer,* starring Al Jolson. The public clamored for more movies with sound, and the industry had to adopt expensive technology to provide it. The movie industry responded by attempting to control distribution of its films, thereby driving up prices in an attempt to recoup some of the costs. Merrill and Lynch understood the trend and the increased costs they would face if they stayed in the business. They finally decided to sell their interest in the company to a group headed by Joseph P. Kennedy and Cecil B. DeMille, who in turn used it to create RKO. Their investment netted them several million dollars in profit and helped cement their fortunes.

The firm added more retail investment banking clients during the 1920s, including Newberry, Walgreen Drugs, Western Auto, and Safeway Stores. Although less well known than Lehman Brothers as a financier of retailers, Merrill Lynch was on its way to becoming a solid Wall Street house. But Merrill was becoming uncomfortable with the course of the stock market, which was moving to historic highs. The generally speculative atmosphere of the 1920s did not appeal to him, and the market fever ran counter to his basic business philosophy. Underwriters were especially vulnerable to a downturn in the market because it had the potential to leave them with unsold inventories of securities that could easily slip below their issue prices, leaving the underwriters with losses on top of the unsold securities. Beginning in 1928, at Merrill's insistence, the firm began to sell its holdings in the market to reduce its exposure.

Merrill explained his methods to employees in a memo. "We try to run our business in a safe and high-grade manner," he wrote, "giving our customers the maximum of protection at all times." Customers were sent a letter urging them to lighten their exposures to speculative issues and trade less on margin. The result encouraged him. "The average [customer] margin comes nearer to being 40 percent than 25 percent," he told employees, an indication that he considered the warning successful.[4] Customers were less indebted to his firm, and its own inventory was lighter than before. The move proved prescient about a year later when the market came under severe pressure: Some firms had granted margin credit to customers for as much as 90 percent of a stock's value, forcing many margin calls that only added to the general panic in October and November 1929. Merrill's firm was safe because it had avoided the practice.

Merrill's fear of the market did not abate quickly, however. In the summer of 1928, he again ordered his principals to lighten up on the firm's holdings. The strategy worked well after some initial resistance. Along with Bernard Baruch, Joseph P. Kennedy, and some better-known Wall Street personalities, he had correctly anticipated the Crash. His clients and employees were grateful for his conservativeness, for the firm had a large cash position to bolster itself against the consequences. But Merrill's attitude toward the retail brokerage business had changed. He no longer saw it as a growth area, again correctly anticipating a future trend. Accordingly, in 1930 he and his partners transferred the brokerage business to E. A. Pierce & Co., a successful broker who had been in business for more than twenty years. They put up several million dollars in capital to support Pierce, although Merrill and Lynch did not take an active part in his firm.[5] For all practical purposes, Merrill and Lynch were retired from the securities business.

But Merrill was not retired from his investments. He retained a sizable interest in Safeway Stores, one of his favorite retailers, which he had acquired during the 1920s. By 1930, he held a controlling interest. Over the course of the 1930s, he devoted his energies to expanding the chain through merger. Within several years, Safeway had become the third-largest supermarket chain and one of the most profitable. It acquired other smaller chains and was able to survive during the Depression by selling at low prices while generating high volume. But trouble was brewing for chain stores in general throughout the country. Many small merchants were determined to fight the trend toward consolidation that was forcing many small mom-and-pop stores to close in favor of the larger stores that offered more variety. The movement was championed in Congress by Rep. Wright Patman of Texas, who adopted it in the 1920s. In 1936, he introduced the Robinson-Patman Act in the House, where it passed with few opposing votes before being passed in the Senate unanimously. The bill was an antimonopoly defense against the price-discrimination powers of the large chain stores. It also contained prohibitions against interstate selling by chains. If the bill were enacted, these provisions could have seriously hurt the chains financially by forcing them to adopt other legal forms of organization.

Merrill correctly saw the problems the "chain store" law would create, and he was convinced that it was time to find other avenues to pursue. For the second time in a decade, he had correctly anticipated negative government reaction to a business in which he had traded. The Glass-Steagall Act had proved his decision to leave investment banking and brokerage to be fortuitous, and now the Robinson-Patman Act did the same in retailing. This time, the act was passed before his exit from actively managing the business, but it would prove nettlesome to chain store operators of all sorts over the course of the next two decades.[6] Merrill was not actively seeking new challenges, but an old one resurfaced that he could not resist.

By the late 1930s, the firm in which Merrill maintained a silent interest was in poor financial shape. The bad investment climate of the 1930s had worn down E. A. Pierce & Co. to the point where it was not far from closing its doors. Retail investors were for the most part absent from the market and the major market indices were not gaining much ground during the decade. A recession in 1937 only delayed the recovery from the Depression, and the firm had not responded to the challenging conditions. The partnership agreement Merrill signed with Pierce in 1930 was due to expire at the end of 1939 and the firm needed both management expertise and financial support if it was to survive. The prospect was not that appealing to Merrill at first. He was fifty-four years old at the time and married to his third wife. And war clouds were brewing over Europe. Many would have remained in the grocery business and watched the securities business from the sidelines, since it had been fraught with trouble for ten years.

Despite those difficult conditions, Merrill negotiated a new agreement with Pierce and became the new managing director of Merrill Lynch & Pierce. The new partnership began in 1940 under rules radically different from those governing the rest of Wall Street. Merrill was to practice a new sort of operational philosophy within his own firm that made the Street uncomfortable. Brokers were now to be compensated on a fixed-salary basis rather than on commissions alone. The idea was to show that the firm's brokers had customers' interests at heart rather than their own and that their accounts would not be churned simply for the sake of generating commissions. A national advertising budget was also introduced, and a management study was made of the firm's accounts to determine what areas of brokerage actually made the most money through good times and bad.[7] By the time that Merrill was finished, the entire business of the firm had been turned upside down. The Pierce firm lost most of the investment that Merrill and Lynch made in it in 1930, and Merrill was determined not to see the same thing happen again. The only question that remained was if Merrill could make the brokerage business as efficient and profitable as Safeway had become.

Merrill also introduced several innovations that flew in the face of Wall Street convention. In 1940, he published the partnership's annual report, becoming one of the few firms to do so. Only public companies were required to publish their financial statements, following SEC rules. He also decided that the new firm would cater to all sorts of clients, from the small to the large. The challenge confronting stockbrokers in the 1940s was to convince people to invest part of their savings in the market. The firm's advertising emphasized the new version of "My Word Is My Bond," the slogan used by an earlier generation of bankers to ensure others that they were honest. Now "trust" became an operational slogan and philosophy at Merrill Lynch. Customers trusted their stockbrokers, who provided them with solid brokerage services and investment research. Research especially became a Merrill forte—helping to inform investors of investment opportunities that did not necessarily pander to the firm's own underwriting book. The firm advertised that it would research a potential client's portfolio free of charge to determine if it was meeting its objectives. Merrill became one of the first firms to preach asset allocation to retail customers.

During the 1940s, new underwritings on Wall Street were few and far between, so investment research meant exactly what it said. The research was not geared to sell off inventories of underwritings that happened to be on the firm's list of unsold securities. It was intended to point the investor toward suitable investments to make him feel more comfortable with the whole process. Basic business integrity was not something associated with Wall Street in the late 1920s and 1930s, so Merrill Lynch was performing a needed service as well as serving its own needs at the same time.

In 1941, Merrill merged with Fenner & Beane to form an even larger brokerage firm. Fenner & Beane was primarily a commodities broker that brought a different emphasis to the firm. Like many other brokers, it had lost substantial amounts of money during the 1930s, especially when commodities prices collapsed during the Depression. Commodities brokers also developed a nasty reputation during the early to mid 1930s when many of them openly sold short futures contracts, adding to the general commodities price collapse and the farm crisis that followed. The new firm was called Merrill Lynch Pierce Fenner & Beane. Now Merrill was beginning to take on the characteristics of a full-fledged brokerage firm, since it allowed investors to use its own facilities to invest in the major capital or derivatives markets in operation at the time. The commodities side of the business would be especially valuable when the war ended and speculation in commodities futures contracts again became respectable. The commodities trading business was capable of generating high-commission revenues because of the nature of the business. Traders tended to turn over contracts frequently, and that would help compensate for lack of stock trading.

After the rebirth of the firm and the merger, Charles Merrill took a less active interest in the partnership and his role began to diminish on a day-to-day basis, mainly because of poor health. While he was still the dominant partner, the firm was actually run by his longtime deputy, Winthrop (Win) Smith, Robert Magowan (Merrill's son-in-law), and Michael McCarthy. The firm owed its philosophy and basic structure to him, but the charge into the 1950s and beyond would be led by others as the firm expanded into all areas commonly associated with investment banking.

During the 1940s, the firm, under Charles Merrill's direction, made a concentrated effort to increase its investment banking activities. It hired investment bankers from established firms and began to enjoy success as an underwriter. By 1950, it ranked fourth on Wall Street's league tables of underwriting participations, ahead of Kidder Peabody, Lehman Brothers, and Dillon Read. But the high rank was a bit illusory. The firm managed to participate because of its prowess in selling securities, not because of its ability to originate them by its reputation as a relationship-based underwriter, like Kidder Peabody or Dillon Read. Within several years, however, it had climbed into the top ten list of lead managers, where it remains today. Nevertheless, even before the great bull market of the 1950s, Merrill Lynch was able to achieve a high-profile position on Wall Street and set a precedent for the future. In the postwar period, how many securities a firm could sell would become more important than how long it had known its corporate clients when determining which firms would win underwriting mandates in the new competitive environment. But the old methods of recognizing long-standing partners who were not contributing to the firm were falling quickly by the wayside.

The firm added the name Smith and dropped Beane in recognition of Win Smith's management of the firm. But it was not changed without some rancor. Smith decided in 1957 to appoint a second in command at the firm and personally chose Michael McCarthy, another longtime Merrill employee. Alpheus Beane, the son of the original Beane, objected to the appointment, arguing that he was better qualified for the job. After the board chose McCarthy, Beane decided to take his capital and name from the firm and Smith was officially added to the letterhead. Donald Regan, chairman in the 1970s, looked back on the experience, recalling that "this Beane-sized experience, while insignificant in itself, pointed up some of the absurdities of the partnership form of management."[8] Partners tended to think of themselves as privileged and often wanted to run a new division or operation simply because of their status. Merrill was run more like a corporation, seeking practical and efficient solutions. The new economics of the Street would soon be felt.

As the bull market of the 1950s began, the firm upgraded its sales force so that it was reflective of the new consumer society it was serving. Stockbrokers had achieved a new social status that had come a long way from the 1930s when their reputations were badly tarnished. They now ranked high on the prestige scale along with physicians and lawyers. Merrill's stockbrokers were renamed "account executives" and the firm initiated a formal training program, Wall Street's first, to train brokers with college degrees. Until that time, educational requirements had been low and the licensing exam that brokers took was not considered very challenging. This became the hallmark of Merrill Lynch and was a major contributor to its continued success in retail sales over the years.

One of the first trainees was Donald Regan, who joined the firm in 1946 after graduating from Harvard and serving in the military. He would eventually become the firm's CEO and a member of President Ronald Reagan's cabinet. The firm he joined was beginning to emerge as a major force in retail sales. As the bull market began, Merrill Lynch had more than 100 offices and 4,000 employees. It accounted for 12 percent of the trading volume on the NYSE and 15 percent of all margin loans outstanding.[9] When combined with its increased prowess in investment banking, the firm became a major player on Wall Street in the short span of fifteen years since its rebirth in 1940. All of these factors, directly attributable to retail sales, would contribute years later to the greatest revolution yet seen on Wall Street.

Charles Merrill died in 1956. In 1959, the firm ceased to be a partnership and switched to corporate status as the markets became larger and its own capital increased. The revolution that Merrill began continued to snowball, however, as more and more retail customers were drawn to the market. The bull market of the 1960s introduced many new companies specializing in revolutionary technologies, ranging from defense companies to pharmaceuticals and electronics. The new-issues market was more active than at any other time, and when combined with the increased demand for brokerage services, the investment banking industry was becoming more capital intensive than at any time in its history. In the 1950s, volume on the NYSE grew from about 2 million shares per day in 1950 to 2.5 million in 1955 and 3 million at decade's end. By 1960, annual volume was 1 billion shares (the same as the daily average in 2000). The number of investors involved in the market also increased, but on average, the investor remained a middle-class, white male over the age of forty. As dramatic as the numbers were at the time, the real revolution unleashed by Merrill and other retailers was yet to come.

Merrill also scored a major coup in the early 1960s when it joined with Salomon Brothers, Lehman Brothers, and Blyth & Co. to form the "fearsome foursome." This group banded together to challenge the established underwriters in bidding for new issues of utilities holding companies, which were required to have their potential underwriters submit sealed bids for new deals. Wall Street stalwarts such as Morgan Stanley and Dillon Read bristled when the upstarts began to win mandates by very aggressively bidding on the new securities, but they could not do much to counteract their bids since they did not have sales organizations that could distribute the new securities. Within a year, the league tables of underwriters began to change as Merrill and Salomon moved within the top ten underwriters. Sales and trading, or transaction-oriented investment banking, was beginning to make itself felt on the Street, and all the older investment banks could do was watch as their once coveted positions were usurped by the newcomers.

The Backroom Crisis

Before the computer age, settling stock exchange transactions had to be done by hand. The processing of buy and sell orders was done by clerks without the benefit of electronic data transfers of any sort. When Wall Street hit its first twenty-million-share day in 1968, it became obvious that many firms could not keep up with the avalanche of paperwork that it created. In 1929, much of the panic that developed in the market was due to a backroom crisis that was caused by the inability of the clearing staffs to handle a twelve-million-share day. Ironically, prosperity brought Wall Street's capital problems to a crisis that almost wrecked the entire financial district again forty years later.

In the late 1960s, all Wall Street firms were still partnerships or limited corporations. Merrill Lynch had the largest capital base, but many others were marginal at best. The SEC's Rule 325 stipulated that a securities dealer needed capital that represented 5 percent of its total indebtedness. Put another way, the ratio of total debt to capital

Many of the smaller brokerage houses also suffered from the Crash of 1929 for similar reasons. Large inventories of undigested securities proved to be almost fatal to them as demand died and the firms were left with expensive, unwanted securities on their books. A small brokerage and trading firm, Herzog & Co., founded in 1915 by an immigrant from Austria-Hungary, was one example. Robert Herzog's firm quickly expanded, and by 1926 was known as Herzog & Chadwick. Then the Crash occurred. Unsold securities weighed heavily on the firm's books, but a solid credit history with its bankers allowed it to survive, although the partners suffered heavy personal losses as a result. After rebounding slowly during the 1930s, the firm went on to become a major trader in over-the-counter securities (later Nasdaq stocks) beginning in the 1970s, when it was known as Herzog, Heine & Geduld. By 2000, it was the second-largest market-maker on the Nasdaq and was purchased by Merrill Lynch for 3.5 million common shares valued at more than $900 million.

was 20:1. In addition to the actual cash contributed by partners and other limited investors in the firm, the other types of capital that were acceptable under the SEC and NYSE guidelines were suspect.[10] For years, this situation remained in the background. Underwriting was still being performed along traditional guidelines, using the SEC's three-week cooling-off period before bringing new issues to market, and the secondary markets remained within reasonable bounds in terms of volume. The capital demands also remained within reason, but Wall Street firms finally got caught in the bind when volume began to soar and securities began to change hands in record numbers.

And the problems did not stop there. Suddenly, the backroom operations of the brokers began to take center stage. Soon it became clear that the clerks who handled the transactions shouldered much of the responsibility for the fiasco. Most were not treated particularly well by their employers and worked in cramped backroom facilities. They were badly paid and sometimes not well trained in handling securities transactions at all. There also were rumors of organized-crime influence in the back rooms where millions of dollars of securities often simply disappeared. Since many were in bearer form, the securities never reappeared and presumably were sold in other accounts in the United States and Europe. Over the years, the partnerships had traditionally overlooked their back rooms as necessary evils and paid their staffs low wages. Now they were paying the cost.

The capital shortages became so acute that more than a hundred firms ceased operations in the last years of the 1960s. The NYSE had a trust fund established to deal with such problems, but it began to be severely tested in 1969. Several small brokers failed and the trust fund picked up their bills only to be faced by more failures. As the crisis deepened, partners at some firms decided to begin withdrawing their funds before the bottom fell out, only adding more fuel to the fire. Bache, another large, retail-oriented operation, added to the problem when it reported an $8 million loss for 1969, the largest in brokerage history to date. The trust fund was running dangerously low on its $25 million reserve when the NYSE decided to create a special surveillance committee to deal with the problem. Members included Ralph DeNunzio of Kidder Peabody and Felix Rohatyn, a partner in Lazard Freres & Co., who served as its chairman. One of its first problems was to sort out the mess left by Hayden Stone & Co., a well-respected firm that had been on the Street for years. After considerable difficulty on more than one occasion, the firm was finally saved from liquidation.

Within a short time, the NYSE reprimanded many firms for losing customers' funds. Then, in 1970, another major NYSE member firm, Goodbody & Co., was on the verge of failure. Goodbody was founded in the late nineteenth century by Charles Dow, the father of the Dow Jones averages. If it were allowed to fail, Wall Street's name, history, and probably its future would have sunk with it. The firm was clearly below the capital requirements, and its back room was a mess with little hope of redemption without outside assistance. Donald Regan attributed Goodbody's failure to its "over-ambitious effort to automate . . . it was trapped in the midst of change: efforts to automate failed while manual procedure was deserted in anticipation of automation's success."[11] The surveillance committee approached Merrill Lynch to persuade it to absorb its operations and customers, saving it from failure and creating calm again on Wall Street. Regan complied by agreeing to help save the firm. Merrill Lynch contributed $15 million of its own money but got a bargain. It acquired all 200,000 of Goodbody's clients and its assets. Other member firms provided standby funds to cover its losses.

The bailout reflected the changing times on Wall Street more clearly than any other event. Sixty years before, the role of savior was assumed by J. P. Morgan, the most patrician and aloof of all the private investment bankers. It was Morgan who refused to bail out the Knickerbocker Trust in 1907, contributing to the general unrest in the markets at the time. But times had certainly changed. In the crunch of 1969–70, it was the largest retail broker that provided the support necessary to keep the Street from collapsing under the weight of its own success. Merrill Lynch was hardly patrician, but it nevertheless also gained from the Goodbody bailout by absorbing all of its brokerage accounts. But even its capital position was not strong enough for the challenges ahead. The backroom crisis made it clear that the days of the Wall Street partnerships were limited. As trading volume and the size of new issues grew, the amount of capital on the books would have to grow across the board if the Wall Street securities houses were to meet future challenges successfully. Partnerships were not capable of providing capital in those amounts.

And then there was the problem of succession in the firms themselves. Anytime a partner neared retirement age, there was the problem of capital being withdrawn, eroding the firm's balance sheet. The problem had already occurred at F. I. duPont & Co., which subsequently was bailed out by Ross Perot. Perot infused cash into the ailing firm assuming that he could sell other Wall Street firms data services provided by his company, EDS. In 1969, W. H. Donaldson, one of the founders of Donaldson Lufkin & Jenrette, the first Wall Street firm to go public, remarked that 90 percent of Wall Street's capital was held by men over the age of sixty.[12] Clearly, this put the Street in a peculiar and vulnerable position. The handwriting was on the wall. It was only a question of how long the traditional partnerships could hold out in the new demanding financial environment.

As the backroom crisis unfolded, many on Wall Street and in Congress realized that if something was not done to remedy the situation the whole process of raising new capital and trading securities could suffer seriously. The crisis occurred despite the presence of the SEC and an activist Congress, both of which bore some blame for the problems encountered by investors. In 1971, Congress passed the Securities Investors Protection Corporation (SIPC), which was intended to act as a sort of deposit insurance for securities accounts. Securities held in accounts at Wall Street firms would be protected against theft or loss. Investors could leave securities with their brokers without fear of a repeat of 1968–69. Regan wrote that the SIPC was necessary because "all the musty corners should be swept clean—in Wall Street, the SEC, and the Congress—and the regulators as well as the regulated should cross the threshold of change."[13]

Change was indeed coming. The partnership and limited-corporation forms could no longer adequately serve these increased needs. Regan recalled how unwieldy the partnership form had become. "I can recall myself the day when Merrill Lynch had 117 partners. That made for a huge and unwieldy kind of organization . . . each year new agreements were drawn up, pored over, and then signed by each of the 117 individuals . . . whenever there was a need for additional capital the managing partner would go around to each of the partners and ask for additional capital contributions in order to finance Merrill Lynch's growing business."[14] The biggest firm on the Street was suffering from partnership sclerosis. Finally, in 1971, Merrill Lynch followed the smaller Donaldson Lufkin by going public. The battle was not easy, especially for Donaldson Lufkin, which originally flaunted NYSE regulations by going public itself. When the NYSE objected to a member going public, Donaldson chairman Richard Jenrette said bluntly, "For nearly 200 years the New York Stock Exchange has been a cornerstone of the American free-enterprise system, yet the lack of access by exchange members to permanent public capital has begun to erode the exchange's historic role as the nation's central auction market."[15] Then quickly Merrill Lynch became the first NYSE member firm to be listed on the exchange itself. Its sale of shares ended perhaps the shortest partnership history on Wall Street and certainly one of the most successful. The pressures being brought on Wall Street by the investing public were clear. Between 1962 and 1970, the number of individual shareholders almost doubled, from 16.5 million to almost 31 million. Their average portfolio was less than $25,000 and they represented about 79 percent of NYSE turnover, falling to 65 percent as mutual funds became more popular in the 1970s.[16]

By the mid-1970s, Merrill Lynch had achieved the top spot on Wall Street, a position it never relinquished. Capital exceeded $500 million, several times that of second-place Salomon Brothers, and it stood atop the league tables of underwriting for both lead manager positions and participations. The firm had 250 offices, more than half a million accounts, and 20,000 employees, far more in all three categories than anyone else on the Street. As a testimony to the popularity and financial strength of retail brokers turned investment bankers, the other top capital positions were occupied by Bache & Co., E. F. Hutton, and Dean Witter.

The addition of Fenner & Beane years before helped Merrill Lynch become prominent in the new derivatives markets that appeared in the early and mid 1970s. Trading in listed options contracts was introduced after the oil crisis in 1973, and trading in commodities futures contracts also increased markedly. The firm's expertise in this sort of contract trading helped it substantially when stock market commissions began to decline with the poor market at the same time. And it also provided something of a buffer when the NYSE introduced negotiated commissions in 1975, putting further pressure on traditional commission revenues, which previously had been fixed.[17] Donald Regan eventually spoke out in favor of the new structure, recognizing the handwriting on the wall. The simple blueprint that Charles Merrill established years before was well suited for

---

For years, Merrill Lynch was familiar to investors and television viewers for two reasons. The first was the nickname "The Thundering Herd" and the second was the slogan "Merrill Lynch Is Bullish on America." The second showed stampeding bulls, an idea evoked by the nickname. The original nickname had nothing to do with bulls but was associated with the long name that the firm used after 1940, Merrill Lynch Pierce Fenner & Beane. Journalists gave the firm the nickname because the name was the longest on Wall Street at the time.

---

the expanding markets in the 1970s and beyond. And the basic maxim about customers having trust in their broker also lived on. In an SEC investigation of a broker in its San Francisco office suspected of defrauding customers in the early 1980s, staff members turned up an internal memo written by the manager of the Merrill Lynch office to his immediate supervisor. In it he described the broker's attitude toward his customers once his clients had been fleeced of their money. It read, "He is now saying—just get rid of the customer—he no longer is of any value to Merrill Lynch—he has no more money! Unconscionable behavior for a Merrill Lynch broker."[18] Clearly, Merrill's original business philosophy was still alive and well, if not being always adhered to.

Merrill Lynch achieved its status by avoiding the limelight that the traditional investment bankers sometimes found themselves in and carved a niche out of a neglected but quickly growing demand for brokerage services. A high-visibility brokerage office was added in Grand Central Station in New York City during the 1960s so that investors could check and trade their stocks on the way to work. Almost fittingly, it was also a Merrill product that provided the greatest challenge to banking regulators during the 1970s as the demand for market-related instruments produced some serious cracks in the banking structure. During the tenure of Donald Regan as Merrill Lynch CEO, the lines of distinction that separated banking from brokerage began to blur substantially. Traditionally, bankers offered simple banking services while brokers concentrated on stock market accounts. But when interest rates began to rise in the 1970s, brokers found that they could offer banking-related services that made regulators furious. The public flocked to the services, leaving the banks seriously weakened.

Merrill offered the cash management account (CMA) beginning in 1977. Investors left cash balances at their brokers that could be invested or left to accrue interest at money market rates that were substantially higher than the rates of interest that banks offered. The banks were limited by Federal Reserve regulations in the amount of interest they could pay. While individuals were able to beat the bank rate of interest, they could also write a limited number of checks against the CMA, getting the best of both worlds in a sense. The concept caught on

229

quickly at other brokers, many of whom scrambled to open similar accounts for fear of losing customers to Merrill Lynch. Merrill scored a major coup by introducing the account through its retail branch network. The problems that it created with regulators were serious, although Merrill was not a bank and could not be found in violation of banking laws. But the account provided another chisel that would gradually chip away at the somewhat privileged realm of commercial banking. Within several years time, brokers would be offering more banking services and banks would try to reciprocate by offering brokerage services. The CMA proved to be one of the early battles in the war between bankers and brokers in the later 1980s and 1990s.

Rise of E. F. Hutton

Merrill was not the only successful retail broker of his era to survive the Depression and rise to dominate retail brokerage. The traditional path to Wall Street glory of the nineteenth century was now almost impossible to plow, since the established investment banks were firmly entrenched by the turn of the century. But brokerage was a field that did not have any imposing barriers to entry, and it saw a wide array of entrants after the panics in the earlier part of the twentieth century. Many of these entrants were as successful as Merrill, although their motives and business philosophies were markedly different.

One such entrant was the firm E. F. Hutton & Co. Founded by Edward Hutton, a native New Yorker, in 1903, the firm opened for business on April 1, 1904. Despite the commotion caused by the short-lived Panic of 1903, Hutton went into business to capture small investors' accounts after having worked as a broker previously and being a onetime member of the Consolidated Stock Exchange, a small operation that specialized in trading odd-lot (smaller than 100) share orders. He opened for business on the West Coast almost immediately. The firm was still young when the 1906 San Francisco earthquake hit, decimating the city and making brokerage by wire impossible. Undaunted, the manager of the San Francisco office went across the bay to Oakland to transmit orders to New York so that his clients' trading would not be interrupted. Dedication to clients made Hutton a success very quickly.

Hutton rapidly built his business through a series of dynastic marriages. His first was to the daughter of a member of the NYSE. After she died, he married the daughter of the Post cereal empire. *Time* described him as an "aggressive, dapper hustler."[19] And hustle he did. His firm opened brokerage offices in all the fashionable watering holes of the day—Palm Beach, Miami, Saratoga, and several spots in California—to cater to wealthy clients using his own and his wife's family connections. Most of his successful offices were on the West Coast. As a result, E. F. Hutton was not a Wall Street brokerage operation. It was one that assiduously avoided the New York market except to maintain a presence on the Street to be near the NYSE and have access to clearing facilities for its trades. Unlike Merrill Lynch, Hutton reached for the stars and became a blue-chip stockbroker. For more than fifty years it eschewed investment banking and was content to operate a series of branch offices to serve wealthy clients. The Depression and war years did not seriously hurt Hutton, because its clientele was from the strata of society not bothered by the economic slowdown.

After the war, Wall Street went back to doing business as usual until the bull market brought about substantial change. The retail side of the business was well represented. Along with Merrill Lynch and E. F. Hutton, notable retailers of the period included Paine Webber Jackson & Curtis, Glore Forgan & Co., Dean Witter, Bear Stearns, Smith Barney, A. G. Becker, and later F. I. duPont & Co. All participated in underwriting to some extent, because the traditional investment banks still relied on retailers to sell part of an underwriting to the public when necessary. But none of them could seriously affect the business of Morgan Stanley, Kidder Peabody, First Boston, and Dillon Read until the bull market put demands on capital that the older firms found hard to endure. But Hutton remained almost aloof from underwriting during the entire war and postwar period. The niche it carved for itself in the upper end of retail brokerage served it well.

That was to change in the 1960s. Investment banking became the rage during the bull market when brokers discovered that they could earn underwriting fees in addition to their ordinary commissions on issues of new stocks. Most Wall Streeters were well aware of the fortune that Herbert Allen of Allen & Co. (no relation to the Allens of upstate New York mentioned in the first chapter) made by bringing Syntex to market. Syntex was a small Mexican-based company that manufactured the birth control pill, which Allen discovered and helped market in the United States. Hutton decided to enter the fray by hiring John Shad to head its new investment banking division.

Hutton did not make the mistake that many other entrants to underwriting did in the 1960s. Rather than try to compete against Morgan Stanley or Merrill Lynch on their own terms, Shad instead sought smaller companies to bring to market. The field was more open, with many companies seeking an initial public offering or attempting to upgrade their status. Shad, a graduate of the University of Southern California and the Harvard Business School, decided on a new strategy that would bring many companies with low credit ratings to the market. Among some of Hutton's investment banking clients during this period were Caesar's World, the old Jay Gould favorite Western Union, and Ramada Inns. None was a Fortune 500 company, and more senior investment bankers would have frowned at them, but they did help Hutton establish an investment banking presence in a very crowded market.

During the backroom crisis, Hutton fared comparatively well and received only a minor censure from the SEC for its backroom problems. But the crisis only helped underscore its need for more capital. As a result, the firm, under its new president Robert Fomon, sold stock to the public in 1972, ending almost three quarters of a century of partnership. Fomon was a longtime Hutton employee who joined the firm after graduating from the University of Southern California and being rejected as a broker trainee by both Merrill Lynch and Dean Witter. His subsequent reign at Hutton would last for the next fifteen stormy years and was mainly responsible for the firm's demise in 1987. At the time, Hutton was doing what all other Wall Street firms were doing: trying to clean up a mess and benefit from it at the same time. The onetime stockbroker to the wealthy had come a long way since the early days. After going public, the firm boasted 1,400 brokers in eighty-two offices and more than 300,000 customer accounts. The public offering netted it more than $30 million in new capital and it ranked as the eighth-largest NYSE member firm.[20] It stood second only to Merrill Lynch in terms of size and reputation among the

Street's premier retail-oriented houses. Then it had a stroke of good fortune that helped it challenge Merrill even more.

In 1974, the duPont firm bailed out by Ross Perot was again in trouble and needed outside assistance to survive. DuPont actually had more branch offices than Hutton, and Fomon recognized an opportunity to present a real challenge to Merrill. Remembering Merrill's stellar reputation as a result of the Goodbody takeover, Fomon offered to take some of duPont's branches from Perot. After the deal was completed, Hutton also was seen as a major power on Wall Street, capable of helping out a distressed firm in trouble and adding to its branches at the same time. Retail brokerage was still its forte and was continually being built up by George L. Ball. Ball's aggressive leadership led the firm into some questionable sales, such as promoting tax shelters for its wealthy clients. But for the most part, Hutton's prowess in sales was second only to Merrill Lynch, although both firms had to make serious adjustments because of negotiated commissions, introduced on May 1, 1975. The new structure caused some serious short-term distortions on Wall Street, forcing many brokers to lower commissions to their institutional clients by as much as 60 percent. Many of the dire predictions made about the new commissions never panned out, although they sounded serious at the time. The president of the Securities Industry Association claimed that the cuts were "a form of Russian roulette, forcing brokers to scramble for positions of leadership in a march to the precipice."[21] As commission margins eroded, a new product would be needed to shore up revenues.

Flying a Kite

The new commission package charged by NYSE member firms in 1975 gave rise to the discount broker and a more competitive environment among retail-oriented securities houses. Much of the pressure was brought by institutional investors, several of whom threatened to buy their own seats on the NYSE and trade for themselves if their brokers did not charge lower commissions. One of its indirect by-products also caused a fair amount of distress for Hutton and eventually led to its being absorbed rather than continue as an independent. Competition and high interest rates were to blame.

After 1975, the next several years witnessed a relatively strong stock market accompanied by slowly rising interest rates. Like many other mainly commission houses, Hutton needed a way to find revenues to replace the lower commission margins. One idea concocted at the time proved enduring but found only a limited positive response from customers. Hutton introduced a commission-free brokerage account that would forgo commissions in favor of a flat fee (3 percent at the time) leveled against accounts enrolled in the program. By 1980, it had about 2,000 accounts enrolled, totaling $100 million, but that represented only a small portion of its overall account base. Clearly, it needed other sources of revenues, especially if the stock market turned down.

Hutton's response, under Fomon's administration, was to begin a sophisticated number of cash transfers between its branches and their local banks. By effectively keeping funds on the move at all times, it found that it could also write itself checks for far more than the actual balances involved. Basically, it was writing itself interest-free loans at its banks' expense. But when it wrote the excessive checks, it was engaging in what is known as "kiting," or writing checks with insufficient funds to back them. By 1980, the firm was making more money kiting than it was in any other single line of business. Despite repeated warnings from the individual banks and auditors involved, the practice continued unabated. No one was going to stop the goose from laying the golden egg, especially when the entire practice seemed to be invisible to everyone except the banks that occasionally complained.

Hutton's problem was compounded by the fact that float management, which included kiting, was a hot topic among bankers and regulators. A major piece of banking regulation passed by Congress in 1980 attempted to shorten the amount of time it took to clear a check, so Hutton's practice was clearly going against the grain of accepted practice. Float management—the practice of trying to delay the cashing of a check in order to gain a few extra days of interest before it was cleared to the recipient's account—was considered an art by cash managers. When interest rates were high in the late 1970s and early 1980s, many firms used out-of-state banks to write checks, knowing that it would take extra days to clear them by customers and clients.

Merrill Lynch was fined for the practice. But kiting was frowned upon as being a sophisticated method of writing checks that could not be covered. Inadvertently, Hutton adopted a practice not unlike that practiced by Clark Dodge during the Mexican War, using Treasury funds that it held on behalf of the government. But Clark Dodge did not face the trouble that Hutton found itself in when the scheme was discovered.

Finally, in 1981, two small upstate New York banks blew the whistle after they discovered that Hutton branches had been kiting against them. Both state and federal regulators became involved. An examiner for the Federal Deposit Insurance Corporation wrote a memo in which he described Hutton as "playing the float . . . but further investigation revealed evidence of an apparent deliberate kiting operation almost 'textbook' in form."[22] When the facts became known, Hutton's fate was sealed. Regulators from almost every imaginable agency became involved with the case, and after considerable publicity, in 1985 Fomon pleaded Hutton guilty to more than two thousand charges of mail and wire fraud and agreed to pay a fine of $2 million.

The kiting case hurt Hutton's position on Wall Street. The 1984 rankings of the top brokers found Merrill Lynch in the top spot, followed by Shearson Lehman Brothers, Salomon Brothers, Dean Witter, and then Hutton.[23] The firm had given up ground to Shearson and Dean Witter but was still doing a considerable business despite being

---

For years, E. F. Hutton was best known to the public for its television slogan "When E. F. Hutton Talks, People Listen." Commercials showed people discussing investments while attending polo matches and sailing, the sorts of activities that Hutton liked to portray its clients pursuing. The commercial was developed by New York ad agency Benton & Bowles. In 1980, the agency was fired at the insistence of a young woman in her twenties who happened to be the girlfriend of Hutton's chief executive. She became the head of advertising, and one of the most successful ad campaigns for a single company ended abruptly. Later in the 1980s, when the firm was on the verge of failing, it briefly adopted the slogan "E. F. Hutton, We Listen," but it was too late to save the firm from its own vices.

---

tainted by the scandal. But the absence of a strong new product division was clearly hurting the firm's ability to market to customers. Investment banking was able to supply new issues to customers and also devise other new products on occasion. A breakdown of the firm's profits in 1984 showed just how important kiting for interest was. Investment banking accounted for 9 percent of its business, commissions 19.5 percent, and interest, by far the largest item, 33 percent.[24] Hutton was making more money by skinning the banks than it was in its traditional core business.

After the kiting revelations, Hutton was excluded from a syndicate selling New York City bonds at the city's request. Several other similar incidents occurred in rapid succession. But internecine warfare and the past were beginning to erode the firm's stature and position. John Shad already had departed to accept the chairmanship of the SEC in 1982. The departure was something of a public relations coup for Hutton, but the firm was not making significant strides in underwriting. In addition, the tax shelters sold in the late 1970s were coming back to haunt, since many proved worthless in the long run or were challenged by the Internal Revenue Service. Stories also abounded of the firm procuring prostitutes for special clients and charging the expense as a business write-off. While not uncommon on Wall Street, the practice leaked out to the press, causing further erosion of Hutton's image as a blue-chip retail firm. Pressure was building on Fomon, who still retained the top spot at the firm. In the aftermath of the kiting case, Fomon was still able to assert boldly, "We feel our record stands on its own." The press was less hospitable, especially about the paltry $42 million fine. William Safire of the *New York Times* described the small fine "like putting a parking ticket on the Brink's getaway car . . . no personal disgrace for the perpetrators; no jail terms; not a slap on one individual wrist."[25]

Fomon responded to the scandal by hiring former attorney general Griffin Bell to determine who was responsible for the kiting mess. Fomon always claimed that he did not have direct personal knowledge of it. But even more damaging, other defections followed. The most damaging loss to Hutton at the time was George Ball, who left to join Bache & Co., another giant retail broker. At the same time, Wall Street began to undergo its own version of merger mania, with many broker-age firms and investment banks joining forces. After the stock market began to recover from the bear market in 1982, a record-setting num-ber of mergers and acquisitions were recorded in corporate America that was interrupted only temporarily with the stock market collapse in 1987. At the forefront of the trend was the consolidation on Wall Street itself. Many of the mergers would not stand the test of time, but they were significant in the early and mid 1980s.

The trend began in 1981. American Express acquired Shearson Loeb Rhoades; Philipp Brothers, a commodities trading firm, bought Salomon Brothers; and Sears, the giant retailer, purchased Dean Wit-ter. None of the buyers was a traditional investment bank or securities firm, and it appeared that Wall Street was being absorbed by outside financial services companies. Hutton was still stumbling at the time, living off its past reputation rather than its current market status. Fomon even offered to purchase Dillon Read but was turned down by the traditional investment bank as far too pedestrian for a firm with Dillon Read's history and reputation. The only question was how long Hutton could afford to remain independent.

Considering the firm's problems, it remained independent longer than anyone expected. The vexing issues that plagued it—namely, the kiting issue that took three years to be aired—and problems with its trading portfolio and capital base kept potential buyers at arm's length for fear of buying a firm that had hidden liabilities. Complicat-ing matters was the fact that the Justice Department was taking a hard line with the kiting issue, threatening to make Hutton the tar-get of a new aggressive attitude toward white-collar crime. At the heart of Hutton's slow but steady decline, however, was its person-ality-oriented management structure that valued individuals over management expertise. In contrast to Merrill Lynch, which was oper-ated in a regimented, corporate manner, Hutton was the apotheo-sis of the freewheeling, loosely organized firm that was the norm on Wall Street a generation before. Management never caught up with the times or adopted new techniques to run the firm effec-tively. Despite having moved into the era of the publicly held secu-rities house, it was still operated much as the partnership it used to be, with lines of accountability often blurred by personality clashes. Whoever eventually bought it would have to take the firm without its top management, since they were no longer well regarded on the Street.

A suitor appeared in the form of Shearson American Express. The firm, headed by Peter Cohen, had previously purchased Lehman Brothers and was itself owned by the American Express Co. In the 1970s, it had been headed by Sanford Weill, who sold it to American Express after merging with Lehman Brothers. Hutton's branch system was the main target of its affections. Negotiations for the purchase were torturous. Originally, Hutton offered itself to Shearson for $50 per share, an offer that Cohen thought too rich. As the deal bogged down, several senior Hutton officials recognized that a change was needed at the top. Fomon was replaced as chairman by Robert Rittereiser, an ex–Merrill Lynch executive recruited in 1985. But it was too late for the firm to resurrect itself from years of bad management and self-indulgence.

A year later, in October 1987, the stock market suffered one of its worst performances in years as the Dow Jones Average dropped 20 percent. The poor performance tied up many deals currently in syndication and hit underwriters with serious losses. Proposed mergers also suffered. Hutton's stock price dropped to $15, a far cry from the previous asking price. Hutton realized that it had to act quickly to survive despite the depressed stock price. The credit-rating agencies in New York were on the verge of downgrading its debt. If they did, the firm would technically have collapsed, because it would no longer be able to raise funds necessary for day-to-day operations in the money market. Finding itself with its back to the wall, it again offered itself for sale and gave potential bidders only a week and a half to make an offer. Merrill Lynch and Dean Witter were involved in the bidding along with the Equitable Life Insurance Co., which eventually purchased Donaldson, Lufkin & Jenrette. Shearson again emerged, offering a buyout package worth slightly less than $1 billion, down about $500 million from the price originally bandied around by Hutton before the market collapse. The offer was accepted. Hutton had no choice.

The price that was agreed upon was based on a share value of $29. The deal was worth $821 million in cash and $140 million in bonds. Some argued that Hutton was no longer worth that much money, but

Shearson clearly was looking beyond the sagging market for better days. Cohen remarked that "our industry is more and more becoming an oligopoly, we're a very high fixed cost business."[26] His assessment was right on the mark. The trend was clearly toward larger, full-service firms that offered all sorts of investment banking and brokerage services. The new firm had a combined capital of $3.75 billion, more than 12,000 brokers, and 600 offices; only Merrill Lynch was larger. The consolidation trend would continue into the 1990s, as many firms tried to combine in order to add capacity while reducing back-office costs.

Looking back over its checkered history since the 1960s, Hutton appears to be a firm that never recovered from the backroom crisis of 1968–70. The forays into investment banking eventually proved disastrous for the firm, and its sales practices began to give Wall Street a bad name by the 1980s. At the end of the day, the only real value it had was its original core of branches that housed its account executives, still a sizable sales force despite being poorly managed. When Shearson stepped in with its offer to buy the firm, it emerged as the most recent securities house that helped save another. Without its purchase, Hutton would have failed, giving Wall Street a black eye at the time of the market collapse of 1987—something everyone desperately wanted to avoid. As Merrill Lynch and Hutton had done before it, Shearson assumed the position of white knight, ready to step in to save another. Wall Street appreciated the gesture but secretly wished that competent management at some of its better-known firms could have avoided the problem in the first place.

7

UNRAVELED BY GREED: SALOMON BROTHERS AND DREXEL BURNHAM

DEVELOPING A STRONG retail business was not the only way small firms were able to break into Wall Street in the early part of the twentieth century. Niches existed in places other than investment banking and retail brokerage, although the rewards of doing business were not great. Only those firms that succeeded in these gray areas had a chance of entering the Wall Street fraternity. Once they did, they quickly capitalized on their good fortune and became accepted members of the coveted group of investment bankers that would survive both world wars and help shape finance in the second half of the century.

Salomon Brothers was the best example of a tiny marginal firm that emerged from the shadows to vie with Merrill Lynch for the top underwriting spot in the 1970s and 1980s. At first glance, it appeared to have all the traditional characteristics of a turn-of-the-century firm in place, although it departed from the model very quickly. Another example was Drexel Burnham, the once proud firm that had been affiliated with J. P. Morgan for years prior to the Glass-Steagall Act. After years of decline, it too developed a specialty that vaulted it into the top leagues of Wall Street underwriters. But Drexel's second chance at success came much later, in the 1970s. Oddly, Drexel's specialty—junk bonds—was one of Wall Street's hottest financial products in years, although the new market bore an uncanny resemblance to the type of bonds that a 1920s banker would have easily recognized.

The success of both Salomon and Drexel proved that firms on the way up often employed well-known but little-used techniques to vault themselves to the top of the Wall Street league tables. Salomon began as a money broker, making the rounds of established banks and brokers in New York in much the same way that money brokers had done in London for over a century. Using the goodwill it established, it then entered the bond business where it eventually made its fortune. Drexel, on the other hand, was a well-respected house that had gone into decline after parting with J. P. Morgan in 1933 and resurfaced as a Wall Street force with the advent of junk bonds in the 1970s. Junk bonds, a new method of finance, were based on an underwriting fee structure that Morgan and his predecessors easily would have recognized because it was borrowed from earlier days when bonds were the most popular and lucrative form of financing on the Street.

Both firms suffered from serious cases of avarice in the late 1980s that drastically changed their respective futures. Salomon became embroiled in a scandal involving the rigging of Treasury bond auctions that would begin a period of transition, ending when the firm was purchased by Citigroup. Events surrounding Drexel were even more severe. The firm was shut down after Michael Milken pleaded guilty to charges stemming from an insider trading scandal. During the 1980s, both firms were known for their extravagances. Salomon senior executives were known for their well-publicized high living, while Milken held the famous "Predators Ball" each year in Beverly Hills where he wined, dined, and entertained investors and bond issuers alike. But those events came at the end of the firms' independent histories. Three quarters of a century before, each firm was cast in a different but classic mold of early Wall Street partnerships. Drexel was a Morgan firm that was widely respected on the Street for its long list of corporate connections. Salomon, on the other hand, was the Jewish newcomer. To survive it had to be opportunistic and, in its earliest days, be thankful for any crumbs that fell from a major bank's table.

The Jewish Jay Cooke

Ferdinand Salomon opened a money brokerage in New York in 1910. He learned the business from his father, who had been in a similar business in western Germany in the nineteenth century. He immigrated to the United States with his family as a boy and eventually set up shop not far from Wall Street. Unlike other Jewish-American Wall Streeters, Salomon did not deal in stocks or bonds but only in the money market. He was joined by three of his four sons—Arthur, Percy, and Herbert—when they came of age and settled down to a modest business. Within a year, a family rift had caused the sons to set out on their own and Salomon Brothers was officially born at 80 Broadway with $5,000 in capital. Their business was the same as Ferdinand's: They dealt only in the money market, acting as middlemen between banks and brokers, offering to provide short-term call money to brokers in need, taking a tiny commission for bringing borrower and lender together. As far as anyone on the Street was concerned, their business was of no consequence since they were only brokers and not very visible ones at that.

Money brokers at the time paid business calls on their clients in order to serve them on a daily basis. This was a quaint but effective tradition that enabled the brokers to meet their better-known clients, especially the private bankers upon whom much of their business depended. Paying calls on banking and brokerage clients had been a tradition in the City of London, Britain's financial district, for more than a century and was a hallmark of the U.K. money market. In London, the Bank of England, like many other European central banks, imposed a regulation that all money dealers be within a mile of itself and the London Stock Exchange so that their operations could be monitored. Ferdinand Salomon's sons picked up his European heritage and practiced similar methods in New York. Arthur Salomon headed the firm, and it was he who paid visits to the large banks, including Morgan, National City, and First National. His dour demeanor and natty, mustachioed appearance made him the ideal person to visit the captains of finance. The other brothers divided the rest of the work between themselves, while office operations were run by Ben Levy, a former employee of Ferdinand, who left to join the sons. But the work was not highly rewarding for the fledgling partnership. In their first month of operation, the Salomons arranged forty-one loans totaling slightly more than $7 million, earning gross commissions of $2,800.[1] For their business to be profitable, they had to do a large-volume business because their commission structure suggested that they were living off the crumbs from larger institutions' tables.

Money brokering was too limited, and they quickly recognized that they had to expand. The bond business was the next logical step, because most of the institutions with which they dealt were fiduciary bond investors. Brokering bonds was much the same as money brokerage. The firm simply purchased bonds for clients and delivered them without taking on the risk of being a principal in the transaction. The activity added another dimension to the firms' activities, however, and the brothers began to eye a seat on the NYSE. But an NYSE seat was expensive at the time, well out of their reach. Arthur decided to seek a new partner who already had a seat and put him in charge of trading on the exchange. His choice was Morton Hutzler, who owned a seat and operated as a "two-dollar broker." Similar to the Salomons, Hutzler executed orders for others on the NYSE floor for a flat $2 commission. When approached, he was receptive to joining them and signed a partnership agreement that changed the name of the young firm to Salomon Brothers & Hutzler. It was still 1910, and the firm was making great strides in expanding beyond its original, limited base of operations.

Despite the NYSE connection, Salomon Brothers still did an active business in the money market, discounting commercial paper for investors and borrowers and becoming an active part of the secondary money market. In recognition of the activity, they changed the name of the firm to the slightly grandiose The Discount House of Salomon & Hutzler. This put them firmly in the money market, and the NYSE seat became an adjunct of their money market activities rather than the primary focus of their attention. The bond business continued to develop rapidly, and the firm added Charles Bernheim as a partner in 1913 to look after the bond side of the business. But the bond business presented its own obstacles since it was the premier securities business in the country at the time. Salomon was an unknown to everyone except insiders on Wall Street, and it was unlikely that it would ever be involved in underwriting a corporate bond as long as the business was dominated by J. P. Morgan and Kuhn Loeb. Without joining that fraternity, it was destined to remain nothing more than a broker. Arthur Salomon realized his predicament and chose to circumvent the problem, much as Jay Cooke had done fifty years before.

The establishment of the Federal Reserve in 1913 and the outbreak of war changed the structure of the securities markets. Money market dealers now registered with the government in order to sell Treasury issues, and the war made those issues, the Liberty Loans, extremely popular among investors. When the first Liberty Loan was issued in 1917, Salomon saw his opportunity and signed on as a dealer in Treasury securities. This was a strategic move of great importance, because he had the field mostly to himself. The traditional, old-line investment banks were busy underwriting bonds for foreign governments while others were busy doing corporate deals. Wall Street assumed that the Liberty bond business was ephemeral and would end with the war. In the interim, however, Salomon Brothers made secondary markets in the bonds and learned a great deal about the bond trading business—more than it would have done during peacetime. In fact, Ben Levy made his reputation at Salomon successfully selling the war bonds and was rewarded with a partnership in 1918. Since 1913, he had followed in Arthur's footsteps by paying a daily courtesy call on the Federal Reserve Bank of New York. Salomon was quietly winning points with the New York establishment by acting like a classic London discount house, seeking to continually act as middleman between the central bank and the rest of the market.

Salomon's foresight and aggressive trading paid off once the war ended. Underwriting commitments from the major banks began being offered to the firm, although they were usually small. But Arthur Salomon never demurred; he always accepted an underwriting regardless of its size. He realized that joining the club was time-consuming and entailed a certain amount of groveling by his young firm—a price worth paying, he felt. He worked as hard as any J. P. Morgan partner, hardly taking any time off. Slowly, the firm began to depend on his leadership and vision for the future. He made many innovations that spelled success for the firm but were at odds with standard Wall Street practice. They never made the headlines, because they were mostly matters of internal operation. Unlike innovations at retail brokers, these innovations at institutional firms remained trade secrets.

Because they worked for an institutional firm, Salomon's salesmen and traders often had overlapping functions. Salesmen sold bonds while traders made prices on them and traded them for the firm's own account, effectively making a market. Often, an institutional client wanted to buy or sell, and the salesman sometimes knew better than the trader where another investor could be found. At Salomon, traders acted as salesmen and salesmen often acted as traders. In another words, salesmen had the authority to buy or sell a bond position without the express consent of the trader involved. This helped the company take firm positions in the market and service its clients quickly. The system helped facilitate quick turnover, which was needed since the margins were often thin. While traditional investment banks were interested only in underwriting bond issues for their clients, Salomon helped develop the much-needed secondary market where investors could buy and sell them after they were issued. The gambit soon paid off.

In 1924, the firm undertook what was the first bond swap. Familiar among institutional investors today, at the time the operation was somewhat breathtaking for its size. The firm bought from an institutional client $220 million in Liberty bonds and Treasury notes and exchanged them for a new issue of Treasury bonds.[2] Then it assumed the responsibility of selling what it had purchased to others. The successful operation improved the firm's reputation on the Street considerably, especially since its capital was still limited. But the deal showed that Salomon's client connections were deep. Without a good client base and an able sales force, it would have been forced to buy the bonds for its own books, putting its capital at risk. Swaps became a Salomon mainstay over the years and earned it many grateful clients who otherwise would have had great difficulty selling large positions of bonds in thin secondary markets.

The later 1920s were boom years for Salomon as well as the rest of the Street. Yet the firm never moved into the retail end of the business, nor did it participate in the equities boom in any meaningful way. Bonds were its main business, and it kept to that for the most part. However, Arthur Salomon, like many better-known financiers of the day, began to see the handwriting on the wall for the stock market as early as 1927. Joining the ranks of celebrity financiers Bernard Baruch and Charles Merrill, he moved to ensure that his firm was on safe ground, especially after banks were allowed to underwrite equities in 1927. He made certain that the firm extended no more margin money after 1927, fearful of what a precipitous fall in the market might do to investors' holdings. The situation in the market was brought about by both a fear of skyrocketing stock prices and the high rates charged for margin loans. Money could be borrowed in the money market at around 4 percent. Many borrowers themselves turned into lenders by reoffering the money to brokers at 12 percent. Since many speculators deposited only 10 percent of a stock's value when purchasing, the 12 percent rates on 90 percent of a stock's value were too enticing to ignore. When the Crash came and prices collapsed, many of the lenders as well as the speculators were wiped out. Arthur Salomon recognized the problem and withdrew from the market entirely before the Crash occurred. The decision saved the firm and gave it a reputation for being both aggressive on the trading desk and conservative in its management practices.

The firm's development was seriously affected when Arthur Salomon died prematurely in 1928 at the age of forty-eight, after complications from gallbladder surgery. The seven surviving partners, including Hutzler and Percy and Herbert Salomon, suddenly found themselves rudderless without the best-known and most visible member of the firm. In 1929, Hutzler sold the firm his seat on the NYSE and retired. His name remained on the letterhead until 1970, however.

Despite all of the inroads the firm made in the first twenty years of its existence, Salomon was still a small-time player on Wall Street in the 1930s. And that was not the decade when reputations would be made in any event. The lean times for securities firms were exacerbated by the capital strike on Wall Street after the Securities Act of 1933 was passed. Refusing to ask their clients to disclose their financial statements fully as the new law required, many traditional underwriters openly flouted the law and had their clients sell private placements instead of publicly issued bonds. Would Salomon be able to toe the traditional Wall Street line concerning the new securities and banking laws in general and the New Deal in particular, or would it set out on an independent path?

While the capital strike was in full force, Salomon was able to win its first lead management under Herbert's leadership for Swift & Co., the food processor. The issue landed the firm squarely in the middle of the Wall Street conflict. Many firms refused to comply with the new SEC regulations, but Salomon arranged for the Swift $43 million issue to be a public one. Following SEC guidelines closely, the new issue was sold in March 1935 and became the largest bond issue since the Crash. Clearly, Salomon did not yet have the capital to support an issue of that size, especially if other Wall Street firms boycotted it since it was violating the spirit of the strike. But true to form, the partnership avoided those sorts of problems by arranging to sell the issue on a "best-efforts" basis. Fees would be collected only for those bonds sold; if demand was weak, the company simply would not issue any more. Salomon did not act as a traditional underwriter for the issue but as a selling agent only. It had no responsibility for unsold bonds and therefore its capital was not at risk.[3] The issue proved to be a great success and Salomon began to build its reputation as an investment banker.

The Swift issue broke the ice and other corporate borrowers began to file for new issues. The capital strike came to a sudden close, and Salomon Brothers was seen as the strikebreaker. The firm won few friends on the Street for its action, but considering the general lull in the market because of the Depression there was little retaliation. Salomon showed itself as opportunistic at an appropriate moment in Wall Street's futile, brief battle with the new SEC. The audacity the firm showed would prove beneficial in the years to come if it wanted to continue its development and emerge as a major Wall Street power.

During the 1940s, Arthur Salomon's earlier decision to become a government bond dealer again proved itself invaluable. The massive drive organized by Treasury Secretary Henry Morgenthau to sell war bonds was a broad-based strategy aimed at the investor and the banks alike. Banks were encouraged to buy war bonds, and when they did, their reserve requirements were loosened considerably. As a result, Treasury bonds became the bank's greatest assets, ahead of loans. Investors were encouraged to buy as many bonds as possible, and marketing drives were aimed even at schoolchildren. Although the press poked fun at Morgenthau by suggesting that he was taking ice cream money from schoolchildren's pockets, the drives were successful in raising billions of dollars to support the war effort. Investment banks played much less of a role in financing the war than they had between 1915 and 1918. But all of those Treasury bonds in existence required market makers, and Salomon again quickly filled the role, maintaining prices in the best-known issues, standing ready to buy or sell from its institutional clients. Despite the strike-buster reputation it gained during the 1930s, Salomon emerged from World War II with a reputation as one of the Street's most astute and opportunistic bond traders.

On the Way Up

Herbert Salomon died in 1951. His role as the leader of the firm was assumed by Rudolf Smutny, a longtime employee. Herbert's reign was not as autocratic as Arthur's because he never developed the serious following necessary to rule as undisputed head of the firm. Many important decisions were made by a committee of senior partners as a result. Percy, the obvious choice to succeed him, had not been active in the firm for years because of outside interests and physical problems, so Smutny became the logical choice. The 1950s were crucial years for Salomon because professional investment managers, their major institutional clients, became interested in common stocks; bonds decidedly took second place. Smutny's reign was the most controversial the firm suffered through in its forty-year history. Violating the unwritten Salomon code, Smutny accepted a seat on several boards of directors, a practice that Salomon partners had assiduously avoided. Several of the ventures caused the firm to lose substantial amounts of money that Smutny had invested. In addition, Smutny also indulged himself in what was becoming the traditional Wall Street vice of an outlandish expense account and all the visible perks of his position as the managing partner. By 1957, the partners had decided to replace him and he resigned, taking his capital out of the firm. The next managing partner would be faced with the traditional Wall Street capital problem, plaguing Salomon as it did many other firms. The departure of a partner meant that his stake in the firm left with him.

Finally, the vacancy at the top was assumed in 1963 by William Salomon, Percy's son. Bill was forty-three at the time, and unlike the third generation of many Jewish Wall Streeters, he had not attended college. After joining the firm at the age of nineteen, he developed a reputation as being very amiable and something of a lightweight intellectually. After Smutny's departure, the partners were not yet willing to give him the top job. At a retail-oriented firm, he would have been an ideal choice because of his gregarious personality. But at an institutional firm, he had to earn his position so that Salomon's clients would hold him in high regard. Ironically, for someone not universally assumed to be up to the task, Bill earned his stripes by tackling the capital problem—something that had been plaguing Salomon for the previous decade.

Like many other partnerships, Salomon's capital was subject to the comings and goings of the partners. In the early 1950s, it was about $11 million but began to decline. When a partner retired, he usually took his capital out of the firm, reducing its equity base—in some cases substantially. After capital declined by about $4 million because of Smutny's departure, Bill convinced the senior partners that they should receive an annual salary in addition to interest on the capital they had invested in the firm, plus an allowance for each dependent, rather than allow them to dip into the capital. In most cases, that worked out to be about $100,000 each.[4] Some of the partners did not consider it enough to live well, but the new rule worked successfully. Salomon's capital stabilized, and the firm was better able to meet the challenges of the 1950s and 1960s than it had been. After a brief interlude of bad management and exorbitant expenses, the firm was on the road to stability in what was becoming the biggest bull market yet seen.

Before Bill assumed command as managing partner in 1963, the firm was run by an executive committee consisting of Ben Levy and Edward Holsten in addition to him. Holsten was one of the few college graduates to become a Salomon partner. He was fond of telling colleagues that he wrote his college thesis on Machiavelli's *The Prince* and that he used it as a constant guide when trading in the market. Unfortunately, the anecdote was lost on some of his other colleagues, many of whom had barely graduated from high school. One later confessed that when Holston told him the story, he thought "the prince" referred to Arthur Salomon.[5] Traders did not require higher education as much as they did a good short-term memory and fast reflexes.

In the late 1950s, Salomon was still very much a 1920s firm in terms of personnel and physical facilities. But that image would quickly begin to change in the 1960s.

The differences between Salomon and other, more established Wall Street firms were legendary. While most partners at the older firms enjoyed respectable office space, Salomon's partners all sat in the trading room, known simply as "The Room," where they and less senior employees spent long hours trading bonds and short-term paper in a frenetic atmosphere. And the facilities were not up to standard either, being dirty and disheveled. Only the partners' dining room equaled the facilities at some of the larger houses on the Street. Once Bill Salomon began to take charge of the firm, the office received a much-needed overhaul. New facilities were put in place and the firm's image was polished so that it became more recognizable outside Wall Street. A new generation of employees was added, many of whom would become major figures on the Street in the years following, including John Gutfreund and Henry Kaufman. The late-1950s face-lift changed Salmon Brothers and vaulted it into the limelight after decades of obscurity.

After years of accepting underwriting positions from anyone willing to extend a position to the firm, Salomon began to make serious inroads in the early 1960s in the rarefied air of the underwriters club. Teaming with Merrill Lynch, Blyth & Co., and Lehman Brothers, Salomon formed what became known as the "fearsome foursome," a group of firms willing to challenge the inside group for underwriting mandates. Lehman was included because it had fallen from Wall Street's top ranks and wanted to regain some of its former glory. The four began bidding on new issues for utilities companies. Those mandates were won by underwriters submitting competitive bids, a practice itself mandated by the SEC and prescribed by law.[6] The foursome proved equal to the task, winning many mandates for new issues and rankling the Wall Street establishment in the process. Their aggressiveness paid off. In 1960, Salomon ranked outside the top fifteen largest underwriters on the Street. By 1964, it had jumped up to sixth place, joining Merrill Lynch, another relative newcomer to the league tables. More important, the opportunistic move violated the unwritten rule that underwriters would not compete for one another's corporate clients. Although the competitive bidding law had been on the books for more than two decades, its aggressive application by the fearsome foursome changed etiquette on Wall Street. The newcomers to the underwriting ranks changed the way investment bankers did business, although few immediately recognized it for the revolution it was.

By the 1960s, it had become apparent that any Wall Street house that was going to survive needed to become involved with equities to satisfy either institutional or retail demand for stocks. In Salomon's case that meant institutional demand, but the house was a bond trader by nature and a switch to stocks would not be easy unless the strategy was well planned. True to its nature, the firm responded by introducing trading in large blocks of stocks for its clients, in much the same way it had done for bonds for the last forty years. This technique would become known as "block trading." While risky, it also allowed the firm entry into the world of equity investment managers—a place it could not have penetrated by being solely in the bond business.

Block trading involved trading large orders for shares directly between buyers and sellers, away from the floor of an exchange. Before the early 1970s, commissions were still fixed, so the larger an order for a trade the more commissions the dealer arranging them could earn for its trouble. Although highly lucrative, block trading also was risky and very capital intensive. The dealer was not merely crossing orders for a commission, but often buying from the seller with the intent of selling to another potential buyer. In the interim, it owned the position. But Bill Salomon saw it as an opportunity to make inroads in the equities market despite the firm's lack of expertise in the area. By the 1960s it had enough capital to forge ahead. In characteristic fashion, it drove straight into the business with no hesitation. John Gutfreund noted, "We didn't have the corporate finance capacity, we didn't have the research capacity, so how would you get into a market that was institutionalized? You muscled your way in by trading—block trading."[7] This was another example of a trading-oriented firm using its strengths to make an impression on corporate clients that would ensure it an even higher position on Wall Street within ten years.

But trading alone would not ensure Salomon's future. New hires were being added constantly, and the twenty partners were supported by five hundred other, less senior employees. The old-fashioned Salomon trader with only a high school diploma was quickly being replaced by a new generation of MBAs. Research was still bond-oriented, led by Henry Kaufman and Sidney Homer, but moves were afoot to add equity research and corporate finance capabilities as well. The plum of the business on Wall Street was still underwriting, and John Gutfreund made it a top priority. He was seen as the heir apparent to Bill Salomon, and in 1978 succeeded him as managing partner. Like E. F. Hutton, Salomon realized that without a serious underwriting presence it would never be considered a top-notch house. With that in mind, Daniel Sargent was hired from outside Wall Street to head the effort. The effort soon began to pay off. Like many other newcomers to underwriting, Salomon took an extremely aggressive attitude toward winning mandates from companies. Often it would negotiate terms that the other mainline underwriters would have considered impractical and then set about selling the issue successfully. In the beginning, the most success in underwriting came in bonds—and it paid off handsomely. By the late 1970s, the firm was a top-notch Wall Street underwriter. Nearly a hundred of the Fortune 500 had done business with Salomon by 1980 at a time when old relationships between issuers of securities and their once traditional investment bankers were wearing extremely thin. The firm's major coup undoubtedly was winning the mandate for the first IBM bond issue from Morgan Stanley in 1979.

The IBM $1 billion deal clearly was a signal of the changing times on Wall Street. In addition to being IBM's first venture into the bond market, it was one of the largest offerings to date. Morgan Stanley, apparently offended at not being awarded the top underwriting position, refused to be a comanager along with Salomon and Merrill Lynch, and the two upstart firms shared the top billing as a result. And the deal also enhanced Salomon's reputation in another way: It was announced the day before Paul Volcker, the new chairman of the Federal Reserve, orchestrated a monumental change in monetary policy that quickly forced interest rates higher. Salomon put together a syndicate of 225 investment banks to underwrite the IBM deal, and the issue was still in syndication when rates rose. The syndicate took a collective loss on the deal, but rumor had it that Salmon's portion was already sold, meaning that it did not incur any loss itself.[8] When coupled with the firm's legendary bond-trading abilities plus the presence of interest rate prognosticators like Henry Kaufman, word spread quickly that Salomon knew of the rate rise in advance. If that were the case, investors would have been extremely unhappy at Salomon's chicanery, but its reputation among potential bond issuers was only enhanced. The firm clearly had arrived on Wall Street, since only a major house could have commanded the sort of rumors that spread after the deal.

Top of the Street

The IBM deal provided a convenient reminder that Salomon had not only arrived but was at the very top of Wall Street's league tables by the late 1970s. Transaction-oriented deals had taken the place of the cozy arrangements that old-line investment banks had enjoyed with their corporate clients. Morgan Stanley had been nudged aside by Salomon and Merrill Lynch, and although it was still among the top ten underwriters it clearly felt the heat from the new generation of aggressive investment bankers. Muscle was not all that Salomon employed to fight its way to the top, however. Expertise in the bond market acquired since World War I helped the firm develop the largest-growing sector of the bond market yet seen in the twentieth century. The reputation and goodwill that it enjoyed as a result would be desperately needed when the firm suffered its greatest crisis in the early 1990s.

Despite climbing to the top of the league tables in underwriting corporate issues by 1980, Salomon's greatest contribution to Wall Street and American finance was accomplished in the early 1970s. Many of the firm's smaller clients, accumulated over the years, were institutions like savings-and-loan associations and savings banks. These relatively small, regional banks were the heart of the American residential mortgage market. In the 1950s and 1960s, the demand for mortgages burgeoned along with other sectors of the economy. But a market for them did not exist and the mortgages remained with the banks, which would grant them to homeowners and then hold them on their books until they were eventually paid off. A federal agency—the Federal National Mortgage Association, or Fannie Mae—would buy certain types from the lenders, but for the most part, no real market was in place if the banks wanted to sell the mortgages.

In the early 1970s, Salomon became involved in the market for the new federal mortgage agencies that were created during the latter part of the 1960s following the passing of the Housing and Urban Development Act of 1968. William Simon, the partner in charge of government bond trading, introduced trading in these new types of bonds, although it was Robert Dall, a partner, and Louis Ranieri who made Salomon the central dealer to the agencies' expanded operations. By the early 1970s, there were three mortgage assistance agencies operating with a direct or implicit government guarantee, all borrowing in order to purchase mortgages from bank lenders. Salomon's traders helped fashion these obligations so that they were not direct obligations of the U.S. Treasury but represented off-balance-sheet financing—better known as mortgage-backed securities. As Wall Street's premier bond house, Salomon was in a prime position to take most of this new business under its wing. The new instruments were complicated and required that potential investors be familiar with their unique features, but once the market was established, trading became one of the firm's substantial profit centers. As Henry Kaufman recalled, "Such complexities forced Salomon to staff up, but also moved the firm into a profitable new domain with relatively few competitors at the start."[9]

Salomon was the first to be able to use its traditional trading expertise to fashion these new securities, which would become known as securitized mortgage obligations.[10] Ranieri became the king of mortgage trading at Salomon, and the instruments represented a hybrid of trading expertise and corporate finance features. They transformed the bond market in the 1970s and led to the opening of the mortgage market for many more homeowners than would have been the case otherwise. Although Salomon clearly made money from the new operation, it accumulated a great deal of goodwill as well. On a more general level, the securitization process, a clever application of older money-market techniques, made heavy borrowing by the agencies possible without fear they would lose their high credit ratings. The market was quickly becoming vital to the mortgage industry, and Salomon was at the very top of it, with little competition.

Salomon also played a pivotal role in helping to bail out the finances of New York City in 1975. After the city crept perilously close to bankruptcy, Mayor Abraham Beame requested assistance from the state to help overcome its problems. A gubernatorial panel headed by Felix Rohatyn of Lazard Freres suggested that an institution be established to borrow money and hand it to the city. The Municipal Assistance Corporation (MAC) was established, and bonds were floated in its name. Syndicates had to be organized for the bond sale, which initially totaled $1 billion. Two were formed, one by Morgan Guaranty Trust and the other by Salomon Brothers. Between them, they successfully disposed of the bonds and the city began a slow, painful process back to financial health. As in the case of E. F. Hutton and Merrill Lynch, it became apparent that large securities houses like Salomon were still being asked to provide financial assistance to both the private and public sector. Ironically, the last time an institution (J. P. Morgan) provided assistance to New York was during the 1907 Panic, before Salomon Brothers was organized.

When combined with the inroads made in underwriting, Salomon had developed a reputation as the smartest and most aggressive house on the Street by 1980. By the beginning of the 1980s, it had slightly more than $300 million in capital, second only to Merrill Lynch. Despite its enviable position, additional capital was not an option but a necessity—and it was beginning to become more urgent. The same problems that caused higher interest rates and a poor stock market in the late 1970s and early 1980s also created a large cash hoard for commodities trading firms, whose business boomed during inflationary times. The most successful of them were actively seeking to expand into other financial services. Fortunately, a merger partner emerged in the nick of time.

In the 1980s, mergers between investment bankers and other types of financial service institutions were not common. An exception was the Phibro Corporation, a commodities-trading firm formerly known as Philipp Brothers. In 1980, Henry Kaufman, a senior partner at Salomon, was approached by Phibro executives David Tendler and

Hal Beretz, who were looking for a merger partner. The company desperately wanted to diversify its operations away from commodities trading. After a year-long unsuccessful search for a partner, it became clear that a Salomon-Phibro match would be advantageous for both parties. Capital was a main concern for Salomon at the time. William Voute, a managing director, recognized that the markets were becoming more capital intensive than ever when he stated that Salomon "saw the size of the market expanding and the U.S. Treasury needs expanding. We had only in the neighborhood of $300 million in capital, and it was felt that this wasn't enough to bring us into the next century."[11] And there was the problem of retiring partners. Kaufman noted that "the withdrawal (or potential withdrawal) of capital by recently retired partners under the terms of their limited partnership made it difficult to sustain a permanent and predictable capital base."[12] Capital was not a problem for Phibro, which had been making extraordinary trading profits during the inflationary years of the late 1970s.

The merger between the two firms was actually a buyout of Salomon by Phibro. Phibro paid $550 million for Salomon, allowing the existing partners to take their cash out of the firm. The new holding company became Phibro-Salomon, and the two operating divisions retained their own original names. It was now a publicly traded company, officially ending the seventy-one-year history of the Salomon partnership. Some of the older partners, functioning in a limited capacity, including Bill Salomon, were not informed until the deal was done, and they were very distressed by the announcement. The new company had two co-chairmen, Gutfreund and David Tendler of Phibro. Both firms were represented about equally in the new entity, which had capital of more than $1.7 billion.

Although both firms were trading companies by nature, the marriage was not one made in heaven. Tensions appeared within a short time, suggesting that the two cultures would not fuse as easily as originally thought. Yet Salomon was well served by the deal, which allowed it to take larger positions, especially in Treasury bonds, which were becoming more popular in the early 1980s. Then the bottom fell out of Phibro's commodities business as revenues began to decline and Salomon became the predator in the arrangement. When the smoke cleared, the Phibro name would disappear.

After a short union, the tables were reversed on Phibro as Gutfreund orchestrated a reverse buyout. Four years later, in 1985, a *Business Week* cover story crowned him the "King of Wall Street" for reversing the deal and effectively putting Phibro in mothballs. By that time, the combined company had more than $65 billion in assets and was the dominant trader in U.S. Treasury securities, in addition to its other businesses such as underwriting, mortgage-backed securities, derivatives trading, mergers and acquisitions, and block trading. Using its additional capital to expand, Salomon became highly leveraged, taking on even greater trading positions than in the past, willing to work for small spreads on very high turnover. The trend clearly bothered Henry Kaufman, who retired from the company in 1988. He wrote that "Salomon's thirst for capital seemed insatiable. As markets continued to securitize and globalize at a rapid clip, Salomon's need for capital continued to grow . . . that began to trouble me, and eventually contributed to my departure from the firm after 26 years."[13]

Salomon's history as a partnership ended with the Phibro buyout, but it was the goodwill accumulated during the partnership years that eventually saved it in the early 1990s. As it expanded its activities in the 1980s, the firm developed a reputation that was different from its historic role as an opportunistic trader willing to serve its clients on a transaction basis. Gutfreund ruled the firm with a tight and often unpredictable hand and developed a reputation as an extravagant party thrower and lavish spender. In a well-publicized incident, his wife had an enormous Christmas tree lifted into their New York apartment by using a neighbor's window without permission since the tree was too large to navigate the building's lobby. The 1989 publication of Michael Lewis's *Liar's Poker* also revealed some inside secrets. In the book, the former junior trader described the inner sanctum of Salomon as a bettor's paradise where trading took on a form of wild speculation and personal confrontations were common. Gutfreund and Ranieri were reputed to make sizable personal bets with other traders on the outcome of a deal, sometimes almost $1 million. While the book portrayed the firm as a typical Wall Street boys' club, it also left the lingering impression that the game itself was more important than those for whom it was being played. *Business Week*, in the same article that anointed Gutfreund king, also noted that "the instability resulting from Gutfreund's high-pressure mercurial personality needs to be defused."[14] A year later, that image was confirmed by Salomon's most serious crisis since its inception in 1910.

Slippery Slope

Ironically, Salomon's greatest crisis involved its actions in the Treasury market, which had been its greatest source of pride over the years. Salomon fell afoul of the SEC and the Fed in 1991 in what became known as the most serious Treasury market scandal of the twentieth century. Traders at the firm's government desk literally cornered an issue of Treasury notes put up for auction. The resulting fallout began a period of decline for Salomon from its once preeminent position at the top of the Treasury bond market. The standard practice was for the thirty-odd primary dealers (recognized by the Fed) at the time to submit bids for the notes, which would then be allocated on a best-bid basis. Being one of these dealers, Salomon naturally submitted a bid on behalf of itself and its customers. Regulations forbade it from subscribing for more than 35 percent of the notes on offer. In order to gain more, Salomon fraudulently oversubscribed, claiming that it was bidding for customers when in fact it falsified the bid sheets with bogus customer names so that the notes would be allocated to it at the auction. If the bids had been for valid customers, the process would have been legal. Once the bidding was finished, the firm had cornered almost the entire issue. Unsuccessful bidders, including many hedge funds that needed Treasury notes to protect their arbitrage positions, found themselves short of paper and were subsequently squeezed and lost money on their other market positions that required Treasury notes for hedging.

Over the years, financing Treasury issues had become a contentious issue. Jay Cooke experienced difficulties with the Treasury during the Civil War in a market environment much more simple than that of the 1980s and 1990s. Criticism of how new issues were brought to market had been heard since the War of 1812. When the Fed finally was created, the criticism did not disappear by any means. Congress passed the Government Securities Act of 1986, putting all dealers in Treasuries under the surveillance of the SEC. A primary dealer had two regulatory authorities with which to deal. After the Treasury note squeeze became apparent, hedge fund managers complained to the Fed, sparking an investigation of Salomon. At the same time, the firm was discovered to have falsified its list of potential customers for the notes, a Fed requirement that had to be disclosed at the time of bidding. The firm was in extremely difficult straits. If the authorities had decided to make an example of Salomon, the firm could have been forced to close its doors.

A white knight coming to the firm's rescue was its major outside shareholder, Warren Buffett, whose Berkshire Hathaway Co. held a sizable block of Salomon Inc. stock. The scandal put the stock under pressure, and he decided to travel to New York to protect his holdings from any more serious price erosion. Raiders like Ronald Perelman also were beginning to show interest in the firm. After meetings with company officials, structural changes were immediately implemented. John Gutfreund was released as CEO, and the trader responsible for filing the actual bid was dismissed, among others. In defense of the company, the trader claimed that bids submitted by the firm often were materially correct and that the entire bidding process was loose and not well regulated. Salomon's defense against misconduct was that the trader acted alone and that senior management was not aware of any conspiracy to rig auction prices in the firm's favor. Ironically, this was the same defense that Paine Webber would use when it was discovered that one of its government bond traders lost several hundred million dollars a few years later. But the SEC was not impressed. Salomon was fined $290 million and sanctions were imposed, designed to last several years. But the Federal Reserve did not act as harshly. The firm never lost its primary dealer status, although it did receive a minor slap on the wrist and was limited when bidding at future auctions. The Bank of England took a dimmer view, however, and refused to allow Salomon into the syndicate being formed to sell shares in British Telecom, which was being privatized through a new stock offering. Salomon Brothers survived, although its reputation was tarnished at a time when investor skepticism was on the rise, especially in the wake of the closing of Drexel Burnham and the insider trading scandals of the late 1980s. Part

Salomon was able to remain independent for several more years in the 1990s after the Treasury auction scandal before it again became a target for a larger financial services company. In 1997, The Travelers Group, which already owned Smith Barney, bought Salomon for more than $9 billion and merged it with the broker, and the firm became known as Salomon Smith Barney. A year later, when Travelers, headed by Sanford Weill, merged with Citibank to become Citigroup, the investment bank / broker became part of the new banking environment that was finally sanctioned by the Financial Modernization Act of 1999. Lost in the merger was the fact that the twentieth century's best-known government bond trader had merged with that of the nineteenth. Smith Barney was the successor firm to the original Jay Cooke & Co. Charles Barney, Jay Cooke's son-in-law, maintained the firm under his name when Cooke was forced out as a result of his unsuccessful venture in railroads. Throughout the years and its own mergers, Smith Barney remained true to Cooke's original business plan. In the last years of the 1990s, it still retained a large retail sales force.

of the previous goodwill it had accumulated in the Treasury and mortgage-backed securities markets saved it from the same fate that befell Drexel.

Salomon's misfortune in the 1980s was that it became too good at making money and forgot about internal controls designed to protect the firm against isolated actions that seriously damaged its reputation. When individuals were discovered to have violated securities regulations or Fed rules, the defense was that they were just the actions of rogue traders acting on their own. The argument did not hold much water, even though it was well-known that management practices on Wall Street often left something to be desired. Once a firm's integrity was challenged, capital again became a serious issue. Lawsuits or penalties could quickly erode its capital and threaten its existence. Salomon emerged from the crisis chastened and proceeded with business on a more conservative path. But the capital problem remained. The firm was still very aggressive in the bond markets and needed a healthy dose of capital so that it could keep abreast of Merrill Lynch and other market leaders. The crisis put its stock under a cloud, so issuing new stock immediately was not a viable option. Eventually, it became a merger target. Once the regulatory environment permitted the merger of an investment bank with a commercial bank, it was purchased by The Travelers Group in 1997 and merged with Smith Barney, already a subsidiary of the insurance and financial services company.

The Second Coming of Drexel

While Salomon was able to capitalize on Wall Street's problems in the 1930s, most other securities firms found themselves with diminished business in a hostile new regulatory environment. The breakup of the private banking business by the Glass-Steagall Act in 1933 was especially destructive for Drexel & Co. in Philadelphia. The original Drexels were no longer active in the firm, and the firm slipped into decline after being severed from its Morgan connection. Without strong family leadership or powerful friends on Wall Street, the firm was no longer in the upper echelons of finance. As late as 1929, the firm, along with J. P. Morgan & Co. and Bonbright & Co., helped organize a massive utilities combine, the United Corporation. After the mandated divorce from Morgan, the firm settled into a quiet existence in Philadelphia and remained a regional firm, working mostly there and in New York, devoted to whatever business it could attract based on its previous reputation as a Morgan house.

The highlight of the 1940s for Drexel came when it was named in the antitrust suit filed against the Wall Street Seventeen by the Justice Department. While the period since 1933–34 was not known for its issuing activity in new securities, the firm's inclusion came as something of a surprise since it had accounted for only a minuscule amount of the new issues listed in the government's suit. According to papers filed by the Antitrust Division in support of its case, the top manager on Wall Street between 1938 and 1947 was Morgan Stanley, with more than $3.3 billion in lead managements. First Boston was second, with almost $2.6 billion. Drexel, on the other hand, was the smallest fish in the pond of seventeen, with only $90 million in lead positions managed. Certainly, other firms, including Merrill Lynch and Salomon Brothers, beat that figure, but they were not included. Drexel was being charged for its past association with Morgan more than for its own prowess in the market, which had become almost negligible. Harriman Ripley, the firm with which it would merge in 1966, had more than $600 million in lead managements and was certainly included because of its ties to what the Justice Department considered the money trust of the previous generation.[15]

Similar to Clark Dodge, Drexel & Co. managed to limp through the 1950s and 1960s, maintaining some of its old clients and watching its position on the Street slowly slip. But it also developed a money management business over the years and had almost $1 billion in funds under management by the late 1960s. A merger partner was necessary to help the firm maintain any hopes of reentering the underwriting league tables. On offer was its lucrative funds management division. In 1966, it thought it had found the perfect marriage partner in Harriman Ripley & Co., the investment bank that was spun off from Brown Brothers Harriman in 1938. Harriman maintained a

---

Rarely did the Wall Street dynasties produce a saint, but the case of Katherine Drexel certainly was an exception. Born in 1858 to Frank Drexel, brother of Anthony Drexel, partner of J. P. Morgan at Drexel Morgan & Co., Katherine went to live with her uncle after her mother died while she was still an infant. Interested in charitable causes at an early age, she became a missionary at the suggestion of Pope Leo XIII, with whom she had a private audience. Using a well-endowed trust fund established by her father valued at $20 million, she began studying needy causes at an early age, trying to decide which of them she could help. She became a nun in 1889 and two years later founded her own order, the Sisters of the Blessed Sacrament. She established a school in Santa Fe for the Pueblo Indians and then established a dizzying array of charities and schools for both Indians and African-Americans. Xavier University in New Orleans is probably the best known of the sixty institutions she helped found during her lifetime. She died in 1955 at the age of ninety-seven and was canonized in 2000.

prestigious client list and, on paper, complemented Drexel perfectly. The new Drexel, Harriman Ripley & Co. seemed to be a match made in heaven, because it joined two blue-blooded firms at a time when the rest of the Street was under attack by what old-line investment bankers considered the proletariat of retail brokerage and trading. But the marriage did not accomplish its desired objective. Low capital again was the problem.

Within four years of the merger, partners were retiring, taking capital out of the firm in what was quickly becoming a serious capital flight following the backroom crisis of the time. The old guard was retreating from the Street, proving that partners' capital was transient. Drexel found a new source of capital in an unlikely source—the Firestone Tire & Rubber Co., a client. Firestone bought into the firm for a capital infusion of $6 million, and its name was changed to Drexel Firestone. The day was saved, but not for long. The investment bank soon began losing its senior corporate finance specialists at an alarming rate and again was under threat of losing both capital and influence. Another merger partner was needed.

At the same time, another firm was looking for a partner. At first glance, it appeared that the two had little in common. Burnham & Co. was founded by I. W. (Tubby) Burnham II in 1935 with $100,000 borrowed from his grandfather, a successful businessman who founded the distillery that made I. W. Harper Bourbon. Tubby Burnham's securities firm was mainly Jewish and was very similar to Salomon Brothers at the time, only smaller and less developed. It made its living by brokerage and trading but certainly was not part of the New York elite or the Philadelphia mainline, as was Drexel. The capital crisis brought about by the backroom problems in the late 1960s and early 1970s brought pressure to bear, and although the two firms had dissimilar backgrounds, they could not afford to ignore each other. They decided to merge in 1971 when Burnham bought Drexel Firestone. The new firm, Drexel Burnham, began its new life with $40 million in capital and about $1 billion in funds under management. The kindest remark that could be made about the odd couple was that it was a mixed marriage at best. Besides the usual tension between traders and investment bankers, there was the cultural tension between the Drexel bankers, mostly from traditional banking backgrounds, and the Burnham traders, who were Jewish, less educated, and coarse by Drexel standards.

The new firm made sure that the name Drexel was used first on its new letterhead. Using Burnham first would have relegated the firm to second-tier status almost immediately, since it had no Wall Street cachet and would be immediately relegated to the bottom of any tombstone ads listing a deal's underwriters in which it may have appeared. The new name suggested that investment banking came first, followed by trading and sales. After the merger, Tubby Burnham sought to discover how many Jews actually worked for his newly acquired investment banking partner. That was perhaps the most cogent yet innocent question ever asked about Drexel. He was told that there were only several among 250 Drexel employees. The president of Drexel, Archibald Albright, told him, "They're all bright, and one of them is brilliant. But I think he's fed up with Drexel, and he may go back to Wharton to teach. If you want to keep him, talk to him."[16] Burnham called the young trader to have a personal chat with him. His name was Michael Milken. After spending a few years at Drexel Firestone, he was frustrated at the firm's lack of aggressiveness. He asked Burnham for some capital so that he could trade his specialty, high-yield bonds, later dubbed "junk bonds." Burnham immediately agreed, and retained Milken.

Milken joined Drexel upon leaving the Wharton School in Philadelphia in 1970. A graduate of the University of California at Berkeley, he was a native Californian who almost immediately kept Wall Street at a distance, both physically and intellectually. Drexel Firestone offered him a job when he was finishing his MBA at Wharton, and he moved across the Delaware River. But he did not move to New York City, instead settling in Cherry Hill, New Jersey, a suburb of Philadelphia. Traveling to and from Wall Street by bus, he spent four hours a day commuting. Early-morning passengers became accustomed to seeing him on the bus wearing a miner's hat with a light affixed to the top so that he could read before the sun came up. As soon as his operations became successful, he moved the entire junk bond operation to Los Angeles, to be closer to his family. From the very beginning, he remained a Wall Street outsider, someone who became known by name and reputation only, somewhat aloof to the Street itself.

Milken was not the only young investment banker whom Burnham helped launch a successful career. In 1958, he helped a struggling young broker named Sanford Weill by giving him a job at his firm. Weill began to prosper almost immediately, and within a short time he and some friends had founded their own trading firm, Carter, Berlind, Potoma & Weill. Initially, they rented space from Burnham to house their operations. Generosity of that sort was characteristic of Tubby Burnham. Over the years, he had become one of the most respected names on Wall Street. His reputation came from his generous personality rather than from his firm, which was distinctly second tier in the early 1970s. The acquisition of Drexel Firestone was not earth shattering at the time, but it would become significant because he also acquired Milken in the deal and had the foresight to keep him. Milken's specialty, high-yield bonds, were something of an esoteric specialty on Wall Street and not highly regarded. Within fifteen years, however, the second-tier firm would leap into the top ten of underwriters because of that specialty and Milken would assume Jay Gould's old mantle of most hated man in America. He also was the king of Wall Street before Gutfreund at Salomon was anointed, although officially he was only the king of junk because of his intellectual and emotional distance from Broad and Wall. But in the early 1970s, he was just another ambitious young trader on Wall Street, trying to convince his firm that this new niche in the market had potential.

Unfortunately, the marriage between Drexel and Burnham did not work well. The two firms failed to assimilate, remaining as separate cultures. One Drexel investment banker described the firm as essentially two, with "the Drexel people sitting at one end of the hall, waiting for Ford Motor Company to call us up. And you had the guys from Burnham and Company running around Seventh Avenue trying to underwrite every schmate factory they could find."[17] To rectify the situation, Drexel hired Fred Joseph to head its corporate finance decision. Joseph was no stranger to investment banking intrigue, although he was only six years out of the Harvard Business School when he was hired in 1974. His first job on Wall Street was at E. F. Hutton as John Shad's first lieutenant. He made partner in four years, but when Shad lost his bid for chairman to Robert Fomon, Joseph resigned and went to work at Shearson. He quickly rose to become chief operating officer when Shearson merged with Hayden Stone. Joseph then left for a smaller firm that was in need of his talents and he found Drexel Burnham to his liking. After restructuring the corporate finance department to make it more aggressive, Joseph became familiar with Milken, whose distressed bond group was one of the most profitable parts of the firm.

High-yield bonds had been traded on Wall Street since the end of World War II. Before the 1970s, they were referred to as "fallen angels." Traditionally, in the bond market only companies with investment-grade ratings were allowed to borrow. Those without them were considered too risky and had to rely on bank financing to satisfy their capital investment needs. Fallen angels were investment-grade bonds that had fallen on hard times and whose ratings had sunk. Investing in them was speculative at best but could be highly rewarding if the companies regained their investment-quality ratings. Their prices would then jump from the deep discount at which many traded in the market. Milken studied this odd niche of the bond market while he was an MBA student at Wharton and became a devoted follower of the market, realizing that while some fallen angels sank into default, many others regained their health. Those that survived provided a gain that offset the loss on those that went bankrupt. Investors who recognized this phenomenon could do well by investing in a broad array of these bonds. The problem was that a broad array of fallen angels was not always available. But if a new market could be designed to produce new issues of fallen angels, then the same effect could be achieved. Milken needed to develop both a primary and a secondary market for these new bonds in order to develop a broad investor appeal. But the capital problem again was brewing, and Drexel needed another merger partner.

Drexel Burnham merged again in 1976, buying William D. Witter & Co., a small research-oriented firm. It was the second marriage in less than a year for Witter, which had merged months before with Banque Bruxelles Lambert of Belgium. Drexel now became Drexel Burnham Lambert and boasted capital of almost $70 million. The Belgian bank owned 35 percent of the operation. Now the firm had the capital necessary to finance its new forays into the high-yield market that Milken was actively pursuing. From the mid-1970s, the entire operation centered around Milken and his new business unit. And yet Milken's relationship with the firm would always be that of a kingdom within a principality. In the first years of the junk bond market, he never indicated any interest in owning stock of his parent, preferring to work for an oversized split of the investment banking fees that was established from the very outset of his junk bond operations. Eventually, he was convinced to own the firm's stock and became the largest single shareholder by the end of the 1980s, when the firm eventually ran afoul of regulators.

Peddling Junk

The odd marriage of Drexel and Burnham proved to be the crucible for the junk bond market. A more established, old-line firm would not have accepted Milken or his different ideas as readily as the firm did in the 1970s. The firm needed brains and money, and the new market appeared profitable although unproven. Milken started his trading of distressed issues by making money in real estate investment trusts, or REITs, and proved that there was a large untapped market for trading in high-yield issues. Then, in 1977, Lehman Brothers brought four high-yield issues to market for well-known but troubled companies. The junk bond market was born, but Lehman proved to be only a midwife. The firm never pursued any more issues, leaving the field open to Milken, who quickly jumped into the breach.

The first Drexel-led junk bond issue was for Texas International, a small oil and gas company in need of fresh financing. Since the company was not familiar to investors, Milken designed issue interest payments that would quickly attract their attention. The bonds bore a coupon of 11.50 percent and the original issue amount was for $30 million, which was soon increased to $50 million because of a warm reception.[18] The issue was syndicated to sixty other firms, with Drexel retaining $7.5 million for its own distribution. The firm earned $900,000 in underwriting fees for the deal, and according to his agreement with the firm, Milken's group would keep 35 percent of that for itself. Drexel did six more deals in 1977 with underwriting fees between 3 and 4 percent of the amount issued. It grossed almost $4 million in fees in that year alone—not bad for a firm struggling to find its footing. Most unusually, there was little competition from other firms on the Street and none of the old-line investment bankers participated after Lehman withdrew. Junk bond underwriting was a niche business and the older firms and the new powerhouses had more important things to do than bring what were admittedly "schlock" companies to market. Drexel had no such qualms. Income was desperately needed, and Milken proved that he was able to generate it without much trouble. In fact, business was so good that future issues would not even be syndicated. Drexel found demand so strong for them that it could afford to bring them to market alone, keeping its distribution system and all of the associated underwriting and selling group fees for itself.

Demand for junk bonds, stronger than anyone could have imagined in the late 1970s, continued well into the 1980s. Milken helped develop the market by introducing a mutual fund based primarily on high-yield bonds that helped defuse investor risk by being diversified while offering yields far in excess of what could be achieved on investment-grade obligations. The same concept was then sold to fund managers, who quickly realized the potential for gain while employing diversification principles themselves. Milken was able to corner the market by originating, selling, trading, and creating funds in junk bonds, reaping enormous profits for Drexel and his unit.

Drexel was one of the few firms able to attain lofty status as a major underwriter in the 1980s while remaining private. The firm created a stock company, but the shareholders remained its partners and employees. Milken created his own partnership within a partnership by allowing his core employees to share in the profits of his own high-yield group, which remained at arm's length from the rest of the firm. Almost from the beginning, his group's profits accounted for almost all of Drexel's profits, so working within the group was a plum for any employee he invited to join. They were able to enjoy a direct share of 35 percent of the company's overall profits without seeing a larger proportion of the revenues go to other divisions within the firm. And Milken was not finished with the profits. He insisted on investing his group's share in the same sorts of instruments that he was underwriting and trading. Since he had the knack of trading and underwriting companies with low rates of default considering their lowly credit ratings, this only added to the considerable profits he was accumulating. The high-yield group became the cash cow for Drexel and the model for Wall Street.

Drexel added a new panorama of investment banking clients through high-yield bonds, many of whom were overlooked by traditional investment bankers. Critics maintained that Milken picked up clients wherever he could, while supporters claimed that he saw opportunities that others overlooked. In any event, companies that once had no chance of hiring an investment banker and doing a new issue were now becoming prized Drexel clients. E. F. Hutton was doing the same with less spectacular results. Fred Joseph claimed that Drexel was doing nothing more than going back to the glory days of its alliance with Morgan and financing the robber barons. This time, the cast of characters was certainly different, but the point was well taken. These clients, if successful, would remain loyal Drexel clients for years, helping the firm attain a sound footing on Wall Street again. Leon Black, one of Milken's close associates, put it more bluntly when he said that Drexel's avowed goal was to search out and finance the robber barons of tomorrow. The trick would be to remain at arm's length if any of them fell by the wayside, casting shadows over Drexel in the process. Unfortunately, Drexel failed in this latter respect.

By the early 1980s, the fortunes of Drexel were firmly tied to Milken's California unit. His list of clients included many well-known names, but not the sort that other investment banks wanted to be associated with. Rather than Fortune 500 companies, Drexel listed gambling casinos, oil and gas companies, and other cyclical companies as its prime clients. Throughout the late 1970s and early 1980s, Drexel had a common trait with Salomon Brothers that was to be its legacy in the markets for years to follow. Like Salomon's success with mortgage-backed securities, the junk bond trend helped ignite what is known as the "debt revolution." New issues of bonds became the preferred way of financing companies, especially with the equities market in the doldrums. As the merger and acquisitions boom developed after the stock market's rebound in 1983, junk bond financing became the centerpiece of the trend, especially for doing heavily leveraged deals on behalf of the corporate raiders whose antics became the basis for the 1980s' nickname: the Decade of Greed.

Bad Company

Almost from the beginning of his career at Drexel, Milken developed a coterie of followers who invested in high-yield bonds and learned to appreciate his fascination with them. The group included some well-known names in industry who did not have ties to a major investment bank but who operated on the fringes of Wall Street. This became his constituency, the industrialists and entrepreneurs who would benefit most from the market for new junk bonds. The same group also would leave an indelible mark on Milken and Drexel, because by the end of the 1980s, guilt by association was becoming more important on Wall Street and in the Justice Department than long-standing investment banking ties.

The junk explosion became the hottest market that Wall Street had experienced in years. In 1983, the market for new junk issues jumped almost 50 percent over the entire existing number of issues outstanding and totaled an estimated $40 billion in par value. Two large deals came to market: one for MGM/UA Entertainment and the other for MCI Communications, which was in the last stages of its battle with AT&T for the right to offer long-distance telephone services. Drexel underwrote both issues successfully, adding to its reputation as a new Wall Street powerhouse. Billion-dollar deals were a new phenomenon, and the ones that were completed successfully had all been done for highly rated companies by established investment banks such as Morgan Stanley and Salomon. Drexel's ratings in the league tables reflected its new ability to underwrite and apparently place the paper. In 1983 it was ranked as the Street's sixth-highest underwriter, with profits of $150 million. Four years earlier it had earned only $6 million. Its sudden rise to fame was one of the most spectacular Wall Street had ever witnessed.

Both the economic and the political climates made a contribution to Drexel's success. New corporate bond issuance was falling as interest rates rose after 1979 and many companies decided to forgo new bond issues until rates again dropped. Many companies decided to borrow short-term instead, causing dismay among many on Wall Street who argued that long-term capital investment would be stymied and America's competitive position in the world market would suffer as a result. Those concerns did not bother junk bond issuers, who knew a good thing when they saw one and plunged into the market with Drexel. Junk issues as a percentage of all new corporate bond issues rose, and Drexel's standing naturally rose with them.

In 1982, Congress passed a new law, which gave Drexel and Milken their biggest boost. Without it, it is doubtful the market for junk would have developed to the next stage in the mid-1980s. The Depository Institutions Act, or Garn–St. Germain Act, allowed savings institutions (thrifts) to purchase corporate bonds to enhance their return on assets, which at the time was very small. Since the Glass-Steagall Act was passed in 1933, no banking institution had been allowed to purchase corporate securities at all. This new legislation was something of a milestone in banking history. At the time, most observers concluded that it would help the thrift industry regain its feet after several years of losses that almost sank it in 1981. President Reagan announced the signing of the new law with Treasury Secretary Don Regan at his side, proclaiming it a significant piece of deregulatory legislation that would change the industry. He was correct on that count: Within five years, it almost destroyed the industry it was designed to save.

The Garn–St. Germain Act became the single most important factor in the growth of the junk bond market other than Milken himself. Now thrift institutions were able to allocate some of their assets to corporate bonds, and Milken's salesmen quickly moved in to acquaint them with the virtues of high-yield securities. While the yield on investment-grade bonds was high, the yield on junk was too tempting because it exceeded quality bonds and even the return on home mortgages—the thrifts' usual asset. Thrift treasurers began to gorge themselves on the new securities. Not immediately apparent was that these bonds were akin to common stock in one important respect. Due to their fragile credit ratings, any slowdown in economic activity would hit them hard and very quickly, making them the first potential victims of a recession. But no economic slowdown was in sight, and the market for both bonds and stocks continued to rise in the mid-1980s.

One of Milken's first and biggest thrift customers was the Columbia Savings & Loan of California, headed by Thomas Spiegel. Spiegel began buying junk bonds as soon as the new law allowed and was able to completely overhaul the institution within a few short years. He offered the usual thrift products to his customers and placed their deposits in the junk bond market, where the yields were substantially higher than the interest he paid them. In the process, he also was creating a "moral hazard." The deposits he was investing in junk were insured, but the bonds certainly were not and were high-risk investments. If the bonds defaulted then the government would have to bail out the depositors. Spiegel was placing his customers' funds at risk with an implicit government guarantee behind them. And it was apparent that he was not doing his homework concerning the bonds he bought. He simply followed Milken's guidance. A former employee said, "Tom was a newcomer to this market. It was all Mike—there was no research staff at Columbia, no documentation, everything was in two file cabinets."[19] Columbia fell into a pattern that would bring down the thrift industry later in the decade: buying bonds from Milken simply because of their terms rather than doing any independent investigation of them. The thrifts also assumed that Drexel would continually make a secondary market for the junk bonds, an assumption that would lead to serious problems in the latter 1980s.

Milken also created a Drexel high-yield mutual fund in 1983 that could be sold to investors. Called HITS, it was created to be primarily a home for some of the bonds he underwrote but could not sell easily. Mutual funds based on junk were growing in popularity and were a good way for investors to mitigate the risk of buying any single issue. To date, his track record was very good, so worry over defaults was not a major concern. And, like the thrifts, the funds' investors assumed that Drexel would stand ready to redeem them at any time if they wanted to sell.

The mergers and acquisitions trend that was exploding in the 1980s brought about a major change for Drexel and its fortunes. It also created a phenomenon not seen on Wall Street since the days of J. P. Morgan Jr. and Clarence Dillon. Many of Milken's clients needed money to participate in the boom. Normally, investment bankers provided the capital to finance mergers, and his clients were certainly acquisitions minded. But one small problem presented itself: Drexel did not have access to the sort of capital necessary to finance a corporate raider of the 1980s. But that did not bother Milken, Joseph, and the rest of Drexel's senior executives. They lacked a blue-chip roster of corporate clients and a pool of capital with which to play the merger game, but they made a conscious effort to play nevertheless. In short, they were going to finance mergers with promises rather than with the actual cash initially required. A shortage of wealthy clients was not going to stop them.

Drexel decided to play poker with no chips. To cash in on the merger trend, it simply announced that it had $1 billion to commit to the merger game. But the side of the merger business it would enter with its clients was the rough side, through the hostile-takeover bid. Although introduced when International Nickel attempted an unwanted takeover of ESB in 1974, hostile takeovers were still not that common on Wall Street. In the 1980s, the game changed dramatically when takeovers were dominated by flamboyant individuals rather than conservative corporate types. Rather than announcing a target company and then displaying enough cash to buy it fully or partially, the new takeover game involved announcing interest in the company first and then attempting to find the necessary cash to finance it after the announcement. Often, the potential buyer had a stake in the company to begin with and the announcement would force up the price of the stock. Often, the potential bidder did not actually want the company but only wanted to sell his holding back to it at a higher price, a process called greenmail. In other words, he wanted to be paid to go away. Ivan Boesky described it somewhat blandly when he said, "Occasionally, management will buy out a hostile shareholder group even if there is no other bidder. When done at a premium, this is known as greenmail."[20]

Many of Milken's clients entered the arena because of Drexel's commitment to financing their needs, even if it was originally playing with less than a full deck. Most of the famous, or infamous, corporate raiders of the decade were represented by Drexel, including Carl Icahn, T. Boone Pickens, Sir James Goldsmith, Saul Steinberg, Ronald Perelman, and Victor Posner. In the beginning, Drexel's audacity was nothing short of startling. The nonexistent pool of money that the firm claimed it had raised to handle mergers was nicknamed the "Air Fund." At first, its assets were nothing but hot air. One Drexel executive recalled, "We would announce to the world that we had raised one billion dollars for hostile takeovers. There would be no money in this fund—it was just a threat. The Air Fund stood for our not having a client with deep pockets who could be in a takeover. It was a substitute for that client we didn't have."[21] At first, it was audacious. Later it seemed like a stroke of genius.

Through the Air Fund, Drexel began playing at mergers and acquisitions in the classical investment banking mold of the nineteenth century. It was inviting itself into deals and then staying and taking a piece of the deal for itself. Since most of the financing was for takeovers, the bonds were rated as junk and the underwriting fees reflected it. For underwriting fees of around $3\frac{1}{2}$ percent, deals of $500 million could bring around $15–$20 million to Milken's unit alone, not to mention the lawyers' fees and other costs attached that had to be paid by the bond borrower. Sometimes, Milken would also create equity warrants for himself that could be exercised at a later date. He also insisted on representation on the company's new board of directors, usually for one of his lieutenants or an ally. Much like Pierpont Morgan and Clarence Dillon, he simply invited himself to the party, raising the money necessary for the deal after the fact. As the deals grew larger, the cast of supporting characters also got larger and came to include corporate finance specialists and arbitrageurs from other firms, including Dennis Levine and Ivan Boesky.

During the 1980s, Drexel began an annual tradition that brought together financiers and fund managers from around the country and the world for a few days of festivities in Los Angeles. Officially it was a high-yield conference where investment bankers, money managers, corporate heads, and politicians would meet to discuss financing and the economy. Informally, the meetings became known as the "Predators' Ball," so named because the junk bond business had turned to financing corporate raiders and other leveraged-buyout specialists. The balls became legendary for their scope, list of participants, and sheer economic power represented, not to mention the good times. Corporate heads, investors, and politicians were treated to a king's feast enlivened by a small army of professional models as escorts. Milken was clearly the "king," if not of Wall Street then certainly of junk. The annual event became the symbol of the Decade of Greed—the outing where everyone who ever performed a leveraged buyout, hostile takeover, or takeover defense wanted to be seen. Journalists were fond of making comparisons with the economy: The participants represented more investment power than the total of the U.S. economy and that of the entire Third World, which gathered at the annual World Bank/IMF conference. But by 1986, the ball had run its course and reality had set in. The conferences lost their luster when the gilt came off the junk bond market in 1987 and Milken ran afoul of the SEC.

By the mid to late 1980s, previous predictions about the growing power of the new robber barons fondly spoken of by Milken and Leon Black were becoming reality. Drexel arranged financings for some of the best-known deals of the decade. Included were Kohlberg Kravis Roberts' bid for Beatrice Foods, GAF's bid for Union Carbide, and deals done for notorious raiders Carl Icahn and Boone Pickens and the financing of Rupert Murdoch's media empire. The sheer size of the deals and the profits Milken and Drexel were able to reap pushed the firm into the top echelon of investment banks on Wall Street. Within the space of nine short years, Drexel had vaulted from a distinctly second-tier investment bank with a past brighter than its prospects to the most profitable securities house on the Street.

The annual Predators' Ball was held in Los Angeles every year from 1980 to 1986. Technically, it was a bond conference sponsored by Drexel Burnham Lambert and hosted by Michael Milken, but it was also a gigantic party. Mixed with the technical speeches about everything from bond ratings to economic policy was a phalanx of celebrities. The usual corporate raiders and deal makers like Boone Pickens and Carl Icahn mixed with television stars and "deal makers" like Larry Hagman of *Dallas* and Joan Collins of *Dynasty*. Many of the stars were either investors in junk bonds or represented companies that had been financed by Drexel. But the celebration had a single purpose to educate investors and fund managers on the virtues of less-than-investment-grade bonds. To make the point, a film clip was shown at one ball in which Madonna appeared singing her hit song "Material Girl." The words had been changed slightly so that it became, "We're living in a high-yield world and I'm a double-B girl."

Although technically a limited corporation, Drexel's stock was still owned by its employees. Many were rapidly becoming rich as the 1980s wore on. The firm's dramatic rise in the Wall Street league tables brought unimagined wealth to Drexel and its employee owners. By the end of 1984, Drexel occupied the second spot among corporate securities underwriters, the fastest rise ever recorded. Ironically, within a year, it was displaced from the spot and slipped to fifth as First Boston moved into second spot, fueled in part by winning mandates for junk bonds and providing some competition for Milken. Drexel's hold on the junk market loosened slightly, dropping from 68 percent of all new issues to 56 percent. But even that percentage still represented more than $8 billion of new issues, reaping more than $300 million in fees alone. More important, in early 1986, Drexel's capital exceeded the $1 billion mark for the first time. A year earlier, it had only $560 million. Almost all of the increase came from retained earnings. In addition to junk bonds, mergers and acquisitions and mortgage-backed securities contributed most heavily to the bottom line. Merrill Lynch led the Street with $2.6 billion in capital at the same time.

Despite its good fortune, Drexel did not plan to join other Wall Street firms in going public, as Morgan Stanley would do shortly. Robert Linton, chairman of Drexel, noted that "going public is a great one-time gratification but I don't think it would suit us."[22] The business was too strong to allow others to share in the wealth. And Drexel did not display any long-term strategy at the time. The business was still centered on Milken and the junk bond unit. Planning did not extend beyond the simple strategy of trying to make as much money as possible.

Running Out of Air

Clouds started to appear on the horizon when one of Drexel's corporate finance specialists was arrested for insider trading. Dennis Levine, a thirty-three-year-old investment banker who had joined the firm after working for Smith Barney and Lehman Brothers, was a $1-million-per-year employee who had worked his way up the investment banking ladder after graduating from Baruch College at the

City University of New York. In 1986, he was indicted on charges of insider trading leveled by John Shad's SEC. It was disclosed that he had maintained a Bahamian bank account for some years through which he passed the profits of illegal inside trading. He would trade and pass on to others information he garnered by working in mergers and acquisitions departments at his various employers. During the 1980s, he reputedly salted away more than $12 million. In his negotiations with the SEC, he agreed to provide information on a well-known Wall Street arbitrageur named Ivan Boesky with whom he had been doing business. Like Levine, Boesky was enormously successful in the bull market of the 1980s although he did not come from the Wall Street social or business school elite. When Levine "rolled over" on Boesky, the chain of events that would destroy Drexel was set in motion.

Arbitrageurs bought and sold stocks of takeover and potential takeover companies in hopes of profiting in the price differentials between them. They were among Wall Street's most anonymous and well-paid individuals when deals worked out in their favor. Boesky was certainly making money at his own firm, but he was hardly anonymous. He authored a book on the trend called *Merger Mania,* tried to be seen at all of the important places and events in New York, and drove a pink Rolls Royce on occasion. But his timing on some merger deals appeared to be too timely. Rumors spread on Wall Street that he was in trouble with the regulatory authorities when scandal erupted again. Another Drexel employee, Martin Siegel, pleaded guilty to insider trading charges as well. A former Kidder Peabody employee who had been lured to Drexel to work in mergers and acquisitions, Siegel agreed to a fine of $9 million in restitution and in turn rolled over on Boesky. Over a period of years beginning in 1982, he had been providing the arbitrageur with inside information that made him millions. The information he provided to the SEC led to Boesky's indictment shortly afterward.

The stock market's dramatic fall in October 1987 brought severe pressure on the economy and the junk bond market. The growing problems at Drexel and the hardships of many of the junk companies that followed dried up the secondary market for junk at a time when many thrift institutions desperately wanted to sell their holdings. By late 1988, the thrift crisis was emerging as a crisis of the first magnitude: Thrifts were failing, putting pressure on the deposit insurance fund to guarantee the customers' funds. As the crisis deepened, many began to blame Milken and Drexel, noting that they had developed the market years before. The rash of public sentiment against Milken would not help his prospects in the years ahead.

Once the daisy chain had been put in motion, it would only be a matter of time before charges were filed against Milken. Boesky admitted his guilt and agreed to pay a $100 million fine and serve a prison sentence. Many argued that the fine was too light since Boesky could well afford it. George Ball, formerly of E. F. Hutton and now chief executive officer at Prudential Bache Securities, echoed a familiar refrain on Wall Street when he said, "It's quite possible others will be implicated or the SEC wouldn't have let Mr. Boesky off as comparatively lightly as it did."[23] That proved correct. Wall Street was still reeling under all the scandals when the SEC dropped the biggest bombshell of all. While Levine, Siegel, and Boesky were admittedly transgressors worthy of prosecuting, the ultimate target in the investigations was Milken. The king of junk had moved from being simply a whiz kid who had developed a new market providing capital for hundreds of small, cash-starved companies to being persona non grata among regulators for his close ties with the raiders of the period and their unbridled greed. The massive two-hundred-page indictment against him was filed in September 1988, charging insider trading and fraud. Charges also were brought against Lowell Milken, his brother and a close confidant at Drexel, and Victor Posner, among others. The SEC claimed that Boesky's firm served as a front for Milken's illegal stock market activities and that the arbitrageur was acting for Milken as well as himself when he bought stocks in anticipation of a takeover bid in order to benefit from their price appreciation.

At first, Milken refused to settle the charges, claiming he would be vindicated in the end. But the case was too comprehensive, and both he and Drexel suffered as a result. Besides being charged with securities violations, he was also threatened with charges under the RICO laws—that is, treating a Wall Street firm in the same way that organized crime was for influencing organizations engaged in interstate commerce with racketeering. Separate indictments also were brought against Drexel itself. The firm settled with the SEC and Justice Department by agreeing to a $650 million fine, the largest ever paid, to settle the charges rather than face RICO prosecution. Unfortunately, the money came from the firm's capital, and since it had never gone public, the bill had to be paid by the employees. Drexel was quick to settle so that the firm could continue to do business. Rudolph Giuliani, the U.S. Attorney for the Southern District of New York and the one who had brought the charges, noted that the six charges to which Drexel had agreed to settle were not yet specified. The firm thought it in its best interests to get the matter finished as soon as possible. Milken resisted the charges initially brought against him, but to no avail.

Finally, Milken was charged with more than a hundred counts of violating the RICO laws and was sentenced to ten years in prison and fines amounting to almost $1 billion. Part of the settlement was based on the money he had earned at Drexel in the 1980s. Between 1983 and 1987, he reportedly earned $1.1 billion from Drexel, and of that amount, $550 million was for 1987 alone. Those amounts made him the highest-paid executive ever. They also left him little room for sympathy from the press. Milken served three years of his sentence. After all of the publicity concerning the charges and the eventual sentencing, Milken was punished for his role in the junk bond market as much as he was for the actual conspiracy and fraud charges. After the market collapse of 1987, he had much to answer for in the view of the public.

Fears abounded at the time that there would be an anti-Semitic backlash against Milken and many of his colleagues and clients. Since he had begun working at Drexel, the overwhelming majority of his clients had been Jewish, and his co-conspirators in the insider trading scandal were Jewish as well. One article in the *Boston Globe* put it bluntly when it said, "Neither is there any doubt that their targets were usually companies run or owned by WASPs." There was a suspicion on Wall Street and in corporate America that Milken's aims were messianic in scope and that he wanted to upset the traditional Wall Street applecart by peddling Jewish influence. But this was not uncharacteristic of Wall Street where ethnic and religious differences often were bandied about without much discretion. The article went on to say, "When Warren Buffett rescued Salomon Brothers from the clutches of raider Ronald Perelman, some traders griped that an Omaha Episcopalian had rescued a Jew with a Christmas tree."[24] Regardless of the interpretation, Milken was extremely generous to Jewish causes both at home and in Israel, and his fate irritated both Jews and gentiles for different reasons. Some feared, incorrectly, that the entire savings-and-loan debacle that was developing would be attributed to a Jewish conspiracy in much the same way that conspiracy theorists had suspected the original Our Crowd generation of all sorts of cabals and financial skulduggery. But the entire affair was finally laid at Wall Street's door, where it was easier to absorb the blows. And a little humor managed to shine on the topic. Not everyone thought of Milken as an evil genius. An article in the African-American *Amsterdam News* in New York supported him, outlining his support of black issues. The article ran under the headline "In Defense of 'Homeboy' Michael Milken."

Adding insult to injury, Columbia Savings & Loan of California, one of Drexel's first customers for junk bonds in the early 1980s, sued Drexel and Milken for $6 billion, claiming that they used deceptive and manipulative sales practices to coerce Columbia into buying junk bonds. At the heart of the matter was the liquidity problem caused by the slackening of activity after the market collapse. Also, Columbia officials claimed that they were led to believe that they were entitled to a stake in Drexel's leveraged-buyout deals. The money paid in those deals went to employees in the firm instead. The suit cited Milken and his brother along with Fred Joseph, the former chief executive, and Drexel's head trader. A Milken spokesman responded to the suit by saying, "Michael Milken has been blamed for every problem facing the U.S. economy except the Iraqi invasion of Kuwait. Columbia's 'let's blame Milken' approach is a transparent attempt to ignore the facts and rewrite history."[25]

Some Wall Streeters came to his defense after the fact. While not mentioning Milken by name, Ted Forstmann of Forstmann Little & Co. argued that junk bonds were not to blame for the recession that developed after the thrift crisis began. The U.S. tax code was the real culprit. No stranger to the takeover battlefield, Forstmann was involved in some of the biggest and most bitter takeover attempts of the Decade of Greed. He argued that the tax code, especially after it was revised by Congress in 1986, treated interest payments more favorably than dividends, and while the situation lasted, equity financing would take a backseat to bond financing. "The U.S. tax structure has made it virtually impossible for corporations to sell equity, and made it attractive for them to borrow money," he argued somewhat ingenuously.[26] Within two years, the new-issues market for stocks would begin a long boom, making the argument sound a bit lame. But Forstmann's message was clear: Milken was not the direct cause of the thrift crisis.

Drexel did not survive the crisis. After paying its fine, the firm's capital was severely depleted. The crisis in the junk bond market also strained its capital to the breaking point. Finally, in February 1990, the firm filed for liquidation. The sizable retail division was sold to Smith Barney and the rest of the firm was liquidated. Many employee retirement plans were worthless since the LBO partnerships the firm invested its money in were now worthless. And regulators did not come to the firm's aid. Drexel became the largest securities firm to fail, while regulators simply watched its demise. No attempt was made to recapitalize it or find another potential owner. Tubby Burnham's company, the odd amalgam of the old Morgan firm and the brash firm of traders that held center stage on Wall Street for more than a decade, faded out of existence.

The *New York Times* summed up the Decade of Greed by noting the ambivalence surrounding Milken, describing him as a convicted felon but also as "a financial genius who transformed high risk bonds—junk bonds—into a lifeline of credit for hundreds of emerging companies." It also issued a warning that if "overzealous Government regulators overact by indiscriminately dismantling his junk bond legacy, they will wind up crushing the most dynamic part of the economy."[27] The economy eventually recovered from the aftermath of the market collapse in 1987 and the S & L crisis, but Drexel was gone, the most notable casualty of the Decade of Greed.

8

THE LAST HOLDOUTS: GOLDMAN SACHS AND LAZARD FRERES

T HE ENORMOUS PRESSURE brought by the need for additional capital caught up with most Wall Street firms by the early 1990s. Yet two were steadfast holdouts, preferring to remain private. Tradition ruled at the two firms, which were determined to preserve their cultures until the very end. Goldman Sachs finally went public in 1999, succumbing to the ineluctable pressure for more capital, ending over 130 years of its partnership. The last remaining holdout is Lazard Freres, the New York- and Paris-based investment bank that was founded by a group of Jewish traders before the Civil War.

The origins of both Goldman Sachs and Lazard Freres were similar to those of Lehman Brothers, J. & W. Seligman, and Kuhn Loeb. All were Our Crowd firms that followed remarkably similar business practices and experienced great longevity as a result. The Seligmans were the first to enjoy success and became the model and envy of the others. Kuhn Loeb followed, eclipsing the Seligmans by the turn of the twentieth century and becoming a member of the "money trust," that group of money center banks assumed to hold the reins of credit in their hands. Kuhn Loeb, under Jacob Schiff, was the only Jewish-American firm to be so "honored," and it remained the dominant Our Crowd house until World War II. Goldman Sachs and Lazard Freres represented the generation of the Jewish partnerships that rose to prominence after World War I, but their success was no less spectacular.

Despite the fact that Lehman Brothers, Goldman Sachs, and Lazard Freres were all founded about the same time as J. & W. Seligman and Kuhn Loeb, their success was much slower and their impact on Wall Street was not as immediate. In this respect, they were similar to Salomon Brothers, whose start also came later. But several differences between the firms stand out. Goldman Sachs developed a specialty that it never relinquished, eventually using it to propel it to the top of Wall Street's investment banking community. Goldman developed its commercial paper business early and never lost sight of what made it successful. Lazard, probably the least known of the investment banking partnerships, established a transatlantic business that enabled it to become one of the first truly international investment banking operations on a small scale and later combined it with a significant mergers and acquisitions capacity.

The Goldman Sachs partnership in particular illustrates how a simple commitment to conservatively managing a core business led to great success on Wall Street. But the Jewish bankers after World War I did not find success as rapidly as the generation preceding them. Due to increased competition on Wall Street, several of them entered into strategic alliances that would enable them to establish reputations on the name-conscious Street. They also recognized that they would have to develop transaction-oriented businesses if they were to climb to the top of the league tables, nudging aside the traditional firms like Morgan Stanley and Dillon Read. But the battle was worth joining because, as Marcus Goldman discovered, selling financial assets from Wall Street was much better than peddling his wares behind a horse-drawn wagon.

Marcus Goldman arrived in the United States in 1848 from Bavaria. To make a living, he became a peddler, selling his wares as an itinerant merchant before settling in Philadelphia. Marriage proved to be as important to many Jewish merchants as business itself, and he married shortly after establishing himself in Philadelphia. After the Civil War, he moved with his family to New York and opened an office on Pine Street in lower Manhattan. Goldman was a stone's throw from Wall Street, and his business was simple: He would make the daily rounds of merchants in the area and offer to buy promissory notes from them at a discount. He would then sell the notes to banks in the area, taking a commission for his trouble. In order to succeed, he would have to do business in quantity, because his only profit was a commission, normally a rediscount from the original price of the note.

Although the business was very mundane, Goldman helped establish a European tradition in the United States that would quickly help merchants raise short-term working capital for their businesses. Originally called trade bills in Europe, this type of short-term liquid note later became known as commercial paper in the United States. Goldman became expert at it, and the firm he founded, Marcus Goldman & Co., never relinquished its lead in the market. But as Arthur Salomon of Salomon Brothers discovered years later in the money-brokering business, although turnover was good, it was not particularly exciting unless it could be parlayed into other, more lucrative areas. Goldman needed to expand—and he needed partners as well. The commissions associated with commercial paper were respectable but were not as high as those associated with stocks and bonds.

In 1882, Goldman took in a son-in-law as a partner. Sam Sachs was married to Marcus's youngest daughter, and Marcus needed help in running his successful business. Sachs did not bring new capital to the firm, which at the time exceeded $100,000. In fact, Goldman had to loan him the money to buy his partnership, but he was successful at keeping the young firm under family control. Subsequently, Marcus's son Henry joined as a partner, and he took in all three of Sam's sons and Henry's son-in-law as well and changed the name of the firm to Goldman Sachs & Co. in 1885.[1] The firm had the management structure it needed to ensure stability. And it also had an abundance of capital. Prior to the Panic of 1907, Goldman Sachs held almost $5 million in capital.

A new generation entered the firm in 1904 when Samuel's sons Arthur and Paul arrived fresh out of college. Marcus Goldman died the same year. The firm had become ambitious and was searching for something other than commercial paper in which it could trade. The logical, if not best, choice was corporate bonds—railroad bonds in particular. Schiff made a reputation in them at Kuhn Loeb, but Goldman Sachs was not in the same category and there was no way that the firm could penetrate the ranks of underwriters. Goldman's strategy, not unlike that of many other ambitious firms, was to enter the ranks of Wall Street's major houses by assuming a large position in railroad bonds in order to show them that it had the capital necessary to become a major force in the market in its own right. Unfortunately, its first brush brought it directly into conflict with the establishment. James Speyer of Speyer & Co., one of the Morgan–Kuhn Loeb underwriting syndicate's lesser members, told Henry Goldman that his interest in railroad bonds was not appreciated and that newcomers to the ranks were unwelcome.[2] He offered to buy Goldman's holdings, but Henry refused and retreated to consider his options. After lengthy deliberations, Goldman Sachs decided to strike out on a new path that would prove to be much more profitable to the firm and substantially raise its visibility on Wall Street.

Goldman Sachs entered into an agreement with Philip Lehman of Lehman Brothers that allowed the two firms to share underwritings on new, emerging companies. The senior partners entered into an oral agreement that would last for almost twenty years. Goldman had already brought a new issue to market for the United Cigar Co., and now Sears, Roebuck also wanted to do a new public issue. The presidents of both companies were personal friends of the Goldmans, and Goldman Sachs already had underwritten commercial paper for Sears. But the firm could not accomplish it without help, and it sought the aid of Lehman Brothers. While the market for large, well-known companies was dominated by Morgan and Kuhn Loeb, smaller companies often were overlooked by the bankers, who frowned upon them. Stepping into the breach was natural for both Goldman and Lehman, and they embarked on a long relationship that would earn them healthy underwriting fees and establish long-term relationships that would continue for years.

Retailing became a specialty of Goldman Sachs as it did for Lehman Brothers. Family-run retailing stores, small and large, were expanding operations nationally and constantly were in need of money. Banks like Morgan and Kuhn Loeb looked disparagingly at the "five-and-dime" retailers, hardly considering them worth their time. But Philip Lehman and Henry Goldman recognized the need as an opportunity to become full-fledged investment bankers and happily undertook the job of underwriting. The period from 1920 to 1927 was free of antitrust actions, and the lax regulatory environment helped create a boom that witnessed an expansion of all sorts of retailers, from department stores and grocery chains to cigar stores and mail-order houses. The second generation of American entrepreneurs and their investment bankers were not necessarily industrialists or well-connected, but they made their fortunes from the nationwide selling and distributing of all sorts of goods and services.

The Sears issue bore a resemblance to earlier issues of railroads and industrial companies floated by Morgan and Kuhn Loeb in one striking respect: much of the stock was sold by Goldman Sachs in Europe. Since the end of the nineteenth century, the firm had an established connection with Kleinwort Benson, the English merchant bank. As a result, Henry Goldman was able to place a large portion of his underwriting in the hands of British investors through Kleinwort. Until the outbreak of World War I, the British were still avid investors in American stocks, and the connection between the two investment banks became stronger and stronger. Other notable underwritings followed on the heels of the Sears success, and many more were placed in Britain. Lehman and Goldman underwrote issues for B. F. Goodrich, F. W. Woolworth & Co., Studebaker, and the United Typewriters Corporation, among others. Between them, they brought more than a hundred issues to market in their twenty-year history of collaboration. But the First World War caused internal dissension at Goldman, producing a rift that would never fully heal.

When war broke out, Henry Goldman supported the Germans while Samuel Sachs supported the British and the French. As a result, at Goldman's insistence the firm rejected an underwriting in the $500 million Anglo-French war loan arranged by J. P. Morgan. The support for the Germans was so embarrassing for the firm that Samuel and Harry Sachs personally informed Morgan that they would subscribe for over $100,000 to make amends. But the gesture did not help the firm's reputation in London with Kleinwort Benson and the British government. The British intercepted transatlantic cables suggesting that Goldman Sachs was doing foreign exchange business with the Germans. As a result, it forced Kleinwort to cut its ties with the firm.

Goldman's links with London went into abeyance until after the war.[3] The affair was a sorry one, because it also caused irreparable damage to the relationship between the Goldman and Sachs families, who refused to speak to each other for years after World War I had passed.

Henry Goldman left the firm in 1917, retiring a wealthy man. As it turned out, he was the last Goldman to work at the firm. His absence caused a void that needed to be filled so that the partnership could regain its place in the underwriting side of the business as quickly as possible. The partners went outside the firm and brought in a Harvard-educated southerner named Waddill Catchings, a lawyer who had once worked at J. P. Morgan & Co. Catchings possessed a loquacious charm that many of the other partners lacked. He was also an author, having written several books on business and economic affairs. The main premise in his writings was that increased consumption was the key to economic success. While that reflected the spirit of the decade, it was certainly at odds with the traditional Goldman Sachs philosophy of conservativeness. But the partners never spotted the tension, perhaps because they never bothered to read his books. Good intentions went awry within ten years, however, as Catchings helped Goldman embark on some of the poorest choices the firm ever made. The years of effort devoted to building the business would be undone as Goldman embarked on the packaging and selling of investment pools, designed to help investors participate in the roaring bull market of the 1920s. Less clear at the time was the fact that Henry Goldman's departure also would spell the end of the firm's association with Lehman Brothers.

Shooting for the Moon

One of the major sources of demand for stocks in the 1920s was the unit trust. Aside from purchasing individual stocks in the 1920s, investors were able to buy units of these forerunners of mutual funds. These were pools of stocks similar to mutual funds that were sold on a unit basis. Many were not issued until the late stage of the bull market in 1928 and 1929. By that time, their original offering prices had quickly soared as investors clamored for the new products. Somewhat uncharacteristically, Goldman joined the fray behind Catchings's leadership and issued several different unit trusts. They all proved enormously successful among investors. But good intentions quickly went awry.

Following in Dillon Read's footsteps, Goldman Sachs created its first unit trust with the Goldman Sachs Trading Corporation (GSTC). It issued a million shares in the trust in 1928 at a selling price of $100 per share. Keeping 10 percent of the issue for itself, the firm sold the other 900,000 shares at $104, a premium. Investors did the rest. The shares rose to almost $225 within two months. And the immediate success did not stop there. More trusts were organized and quickly sold. The trading company made investments in other Goldman Sachs trusts—Shenandoah Corporation, Pan American Associates, Frosted Foods, and Central States Electric. The trusts suddenly were being formed into a large pyramid. The GSTC then organized and invested in the Blue Ridge Corporation, which itself was invested in Central States Electric. Every time shares were sold, the public repeatedly clamored for them and usually more were issued. However, critics of this type of pyramiding claimed that the trusts served "absolutely no useful purpose in industry, in finance, in society."[4] The pyramiding could last only as long as the market remained strong. Then the potential for collapse was imminent.

When the stock market crashed in October 1929, the collapse of the unit trusts was swift. The GSTC's stock fell to $1.75 from a high of over $300 per share. To make matters worse, some investors had traded in their common stocks for shares in GSTC. They were enticed by Goldman Sachs to trade in their individual equity holdings for the unit trusts that were totally worthless. Many felt that they had been swindled. Eddie Cantor, the vaudeville comedian who was an investor in the scheme, lost his sense of humor and sued the firm for $100 million in damages. Other investors followed. None of the suits was successful, although Goldman did settle with some of them privately. But the Goldman name clearly had been tarnished. Its name ranked high on the list of pyramid schemes that failed in the late 1920s and early 1930s, along with Samuel Insull's utilities empire in the Midwest and the trusts organized by Dillon Read. Fortunately, the firm was not as heavily dependent on retail investors as Merrill Lynch or E. F. Hutton were, or it quickly could have seen an end to its business.

The firm acted quickly to sort out the mess. Catchings did not survive the cleanup and left the firm to become a radio producer in California. The incident was unfortunate, because it demonstrated to the partners that going outside its closely knit group for expertise produced poor results. But it did not change the fact that Goldman went along with the Catchings plan because the opportunity potentially was too profitable to ignore. The amount of money it made on the initial offering of GSTC stock added significantly to its capital base and bottom line. The damage to its reputation lasted decades.

Cleaning up the mess was administered by a longtime Goldman employee who was the opposite of Catchings in terms of background and disposition. While the southern lawyer had excellent educational and work experience on his résumé to match his aggressive marketing-oriented nature, Sidney Weinberg was the opposite. He was born poor and his education was minimal. Born in Brooklyn in 1891, Weinberg left school after the eighth grade and learned about Wall Street and life the hard way. During the Panic of 1907, when investors were lining up outside the Trust Company of America to withdraw their funds, Weinberg would charge $5 for customers to keep their place in line if they decided to take a break. Shortly thereafter, he landed a job as the janitor's assistant at Goldman Sachs and eventually worked his way up to the mailroom. For a number of years, the diminutive Weinberg was nothing more than another menial employee until Paul Sachs, the son of Samuel, noticed him and encouraged him to further his education at night. From that point, Weinberg's career took a different turn. He became a commercial paper salesman after World War I and then entered the corporate finance department. Catchings made him his assistant and he learned the intricacies of bringing new deals to market. In 1927, he was made a partner, becoming another real-life Horatio Alger story. From that point, he advanced to the pinnacle of power and was rightly considered one of the most influential people on the Street from the late 1930s through the 1960s.

Weinberg carried on the Goldman tradition as if he were a family member. His accession to power came at exactly the right moment, because the firm could easily have retrenched after the GSTC affair. Weinberg was instrumental in ending the association with Lehman Brothers, feeling that the link no longer benefited the firm. The two firms drew up a formal memorandum severing their connection and split their investment banking clients. Of the sixty clients served by the arrangement, Goldman took forty-one and Lehman nineteen. They agreed not to poach on each other's turf and went their separate ways. At the time of the split, Goldman had overtaken Lehman as the more influential of the two firms. Philip Lehman was left on his own to hunt for new clients, while Weinberg was certain that Goldman could make it alone, having been the more accomplished of the two firms in recent years. But the underwriting business quickly would be in the doldrums in the 1930s and it would be years before economic conditions improved enough to make it a profitable business again. In the interim, investment bankers could only bide their time.

Despite his own lack of formal education and his early objections to hiring MBAs, Weinberg became a Wall Street legend. He was fully in charge after Sam Sachs died in 1934. His sardonic wit and ability to save the day with a quip became legendary. During the slow days of the late 1930s, he received a phone call from the chairman of the National Dairy Co. asking him to come to his office immediately. Weinberg served on the board of the company, and it was a good client of Goldman Sachs. The chairman, Thomas McInnerney, informed him that Henry S. Morgan of Morgan Stanley was in his office and that Goldman was in danger of losing the National Dairy account. Morgan brought his father, Jack Morgan, along to prove that the still relatively new Morgan Stanley was in fact the heir to the Morgan underwriting tradition. Upon entering the office, Weinberg remarked, "I'm sorry, gentlemen. My father is dead. But I have an uncle in Brooklyn who is a tailor and looks like him, and if that would mean anything to you, I'd be glad to bring him over."[5] The remark broke the tension in the room and Goldman kept the company as a client.

Politically, Weinberg did not follow the traditional Wall Street line that the New Deal was a socialist wolf in disguise. In fact, he was an ardent supporter of Roosevelt and his policies. When the Investment Bankers Conference was created in late 1935, Weinberg was one of its board members. The group was formed as the securities industry's response to the New Deal's call for professional groups to unite in order to fight the Depression. The SEC designated securities dealers as a profession, and as such, they were able to unite and form a professional group that would look after their own interests and voice opinions on public policy without fear of the antitrust laws. In addition to Weinberg, the original board members representing New York securities firms and private banks included George Whitney of J. P. Morgan, Joseph Swan of Edward B. Smith, and George Bovenizer of Kuhn Loeb. Many firms from outside New York also were represented, although many dyed-in-the-wool Wall Streeters were still refusing to cooperate with the SEC. The Investment Bankers Association (the predecessor of the Securities Industry Association), the designated professional group of the securities industry since the First World War, chose to remain independent and aloof and would not deal directly with the SEC.[6]

Goldman Sachs received an offhanded compliment during the trial of the Wall Street Seventeen during the Truman administration after World War II. Goldman was listed as one of the defendants in the case, the *United States v. Henry S. Morgan*. While the Justice Department's suit was clearly concerned with Morgan and its various allies, Goldman, Kuhn Loeb, and Lehman were the three Our Crowd firms included. Of the three, Goldman was clearly trailing the others in influence in underwriting. Nevertheless, the trial helped highlight the firm's achievements, providing valuable if indirect advertising for its investment banking prowess. Between 1938 and 1947, Goldman managed $288 million of new securities, placing it twelfth among the seventeen. Morgan Stanley, the clear leader, managed $2.78 billion during the same period. At the time, not everyone was pleased to be included. Goldman's legal bill amounted to several hundred thousand dollars and took a serious bite out of its capital. But once the trial concluded and the Eisenhower bull market gained momentum, earning the money back would be easy.

Like most other successful Wall Street firms, Goldman did little business in the 1940s. Some of the internal operations of the firm were expanded. A retail sales operation was added to service wealthy clients, and a new trader, Gustave "Gus" Levy, was hired to help develop an arbitrage department. Along with the rest of the Street, Goldman waited for better days. Then its prospects brightened considerably during the 1950s. One of Weinberg's greatest coups in the 1950s was the restructuring of the Ford Motor Co. In a deal analogous to Clarence Dillon's monumental deal with Chrysler and Dodge,

Sidney Weinberg's coup in underwriting Ford's first stock issue was remarkable in more ways than one. Henry Ford was virulently anti-Semitic and often berated Jews in his Michigan newspaper, the *Dearborn Independent,* in the 1920s. The common complaint was that Jews were planning with bankers to overthrow the international power structure. And the one banker whom he would have dealt with in the early days, Jack Morgan, had no particular use for Ford or his cars. Although Morgan partner Thomas Lamont suggested on more than one occasion that Ford should sell shares in his company, the idea was never seriously adopted. Ford's distrust of Jews and bankers played a large part in keeping the company private until his death in 1947. But Henry Ford II's friendship with Weinberg proved to be more than just that of a client with his investment banker. After the initial public offering, Weinberg sat on Ford's board of directors. When he died in 1969, Ford cut short a vacation to attend his funeral.

Weinberg secretly worked on the restructuring deal that brought Ford public in 1956. Henry Ford II had been working to revamp Ford and had brought in a team of management whiz kids in the early 1950s to help with the effort. Included in the group were Charles "Tex" Thornton, the future architect of Litton Industries, and Robert McNamara, a former Harvard instructor who would go on to become Secretary of Defense in the Johnson administration during the Vietnam War. Ford wanted to sell to the public a large portion of the company's stock that was in the family's hands. Weinberg worked on the deal for several years before the public offering of the stock was finally announced. It proved to be one of the more memorable deals in Wall Street history. The syndicate for the issue, totaling $650 million, included more than 700 underwriters in one of the largest deals ever for an equities offering. The following year, Ford used part of the proceeds to launch an expensive new model named the Edsel. The deal helped underscore Goldman's reputation as an underwriter in addition to its considerable success in the commercial paper market. Weinberg helped Goldman emerge not by using family connections or school ties but through hard work and ingenuity. Unlike Lehman, which joined the "fearsome foursome" in the 1960s along with Merrill in order to win underwriting mandates, Goldman no longer needed alliances. It had arrived on its own.

Sidney Weinberg provided the continuity Goldman needed to achieve greater status and respect on Wall Street. But as in all firms run by a strong central figure, the continuity problem would resurface once he no longer ruled the roost. By the late 1960s, Wall Street had begun to change. Competition for clients was slowly becoming the norm as transaction-oriented firms offered corporate customers a full array of investment banking services. Under Weinberg, Goldman was still very much a traditional investment banking firm that slowly developed other services to complement underwriting. But it needed to become more fully integrated with other sides of the industry if it was to survive in the new environment that was becoming dominated by firms such as Merrill Lynch and Salomon Brothers.

After Weinberg died in 1969, leadership of the firm was assumed by Levy, Goldman's head trader. In many ways, they were exact opposites. Weinberg came from the traditional investment banking environment, while Levy was used to the trading room and speculative profits. Levy, born in 1910, joined a small securities firm after college, but the firm failed and he sought work at Goldman. He originally was hired as a trader in 1933. He became known for his volatile temper and short-term views as well as his keen mind. After World War II, he was made a partner and was responsible for developing the firm's bond-trading capabilities, as well as its risk arbitrage and block-trading departments. The top job was given to him because he was the second most profitable partner at Goldman after Weinberg.[7] The choice proved a correct one, because Levy became the most visible symbol of the new Wall Street. Investment bankers now had to make room for traders. New securities were of limited use unless a strong market for them could be developed and a firm was willing to stand by its underwritings if a customer wanted to trade them later. The role of the trader was no longer questioned on Wall Street. The only real question was whether a trader could successfully run a firm. At the time, the jury was still out on Levy.

Unfortunately for Levy, Wall Street was undergoing wrenching changes when he assumed command at Goldman. The backroom crisis was in full bloom and the stock market was beginning to feel the effects. Then the firm made a strategic blunder that nearly cost it its hard-earned reputation in the commercial paper market. In 1970, the Penn Central railroad reported poor earnings and its commercial paper ratings came under review. The firm maintained that the railroad was only having temporary problems and that all would be well in the long run. Levy personally sold much of Penn Central's commercial paper to investors. When the railroad declared bankruptcy, many of Goldman's customers cried foul since the firm had never bothered to apprise them of Penn Central's problems.

The problems for investors ran much deeper, however. It was discovered that Goldman knew about the railroad's problems but never bothered to inform customers. In fact, on the same day that the firm learned of the Penn Central's losses, it called the company and got its assurances that it would repurchase $10 million of paper from Goldman's own inventory. And further commercial paper from the railroad would only be sold on a "tap" basis. Goldman would sell only what it could place with investors; it would not purchase more from the company, putting itself at risk.[8] This "best-efforts" basis of selling bonds and commercial paper was prevalent at the time. When investors combined this with the fact that Goldman owned no outstanding Penn Central paper when the railroad announced its financial problems, they became enraged, feeling that they had been "stuffed" with worthless paper by an unscrupulous dealer.

The firm eventually found itself in court charged with fraud. The value of the paper sold to customers that was in dispute exceeded the firm's capital, and an adverse judgment and harsh penalty could have destroyed the firm. Goldman was forced to reimburse its customers, but it avoided disaster by being able to sell paper it was forced to buy back at a profit when the railroad's fortunes changed. A trader's problems were solved by a stroke of a trader's good luck. The firm suffered from the incident, but it learned that keeping abreast of market conditions was essential for maintaining customer confidence.

The early to mid 1970s were not the best times for customer confidence in Wall Street. The stock market dropped during the Watergate crisis, and Wall Street underwent some wrenching changes in the aftermath of the backroom crisis and the change to negotiated commissions in 1975. Goldman Sachs suffered a serious blow when Levy died in 1976, putting it under another cloud. The firm, which had been ruled by a single, authoritarian managing partner, now clearly needed leadership in order to survive. The two candidates for the top job, John Whitehead and John Weinberg, could either vie for the job in typical Wall Street fashion until the stronger of the two emerged, or they could reach an accommodation. Fortunately for Goldman, they chose the latter route. While Goldman would ease into this transition successfully, another old-line firm was in the throes of change as well.

Resurgence at Lazard Freres

The merger trend of the 1960s helped many new and established investment banks to leave an indelible mark upon Wall Street and corporate America. While Goldman Sachs found itself on the side of the takeover targets, another old established bank resurrected its name on Wall Street by adeptly assisting takeovers on the buyers' side. Prior to that time, the firm's name was known on the Street, but it was certainly not the fixture that many other Our Crowd firms had become. In fact, it did not belong to any crowd at all but remained something of an outsider despite its long-established origins.

Lazard Freres was established in 1848 in New Orleans. Three brothers, Alexandre, Lazare, and Simon Lazard, emigrated from France to New Orleans in 1848 and established a dry goods business with $3,000 each. The following year they were forced to close shop when a devastating fire engulfed the city. They moved the company to San Francisco to set up a similar business and were fortunate enough to arrive just as the gold rush began. They soon began trading in gold rather than dry goods, and within the short span of only four years since their arrival in the United States had opened a Paris operation called Lazard Freres et Cie. As the American Civil War was ending, they became full-fledged bankers who specialized in gold trading. In 1877, the brothers opened a London house called Lazard Brothers, which quickly became an accepting house recognized by the Bank of England, meaning that it was authorized to clear payments and deal in trade bills (commercial paper in the United States). A relative who was hired to be an accountant in the San Francisco operation,

Alexandre Weill, opened a Wall Street office in 1880 known as Lazard Freres & Co. In the breathtaking period of only forty years, Lazard had become the largest dealer in gold between the United States and Europe and a respected bank recognized by both the Banque de France and the Bank of England.

Despite its unique success and wide international connections, Lazard Freres remained a minor house on Wall Street. A presence in New York was necessary, because the firm had access to a wide array of foreign investors upon whom the markets depended in the nineteenth century for their buying power. Of all the private banks on Wall Street, Lazard was the most private in the years leading to World War II. Its name was known on the Street but virtually nowhere else in the country, although it was much better known in Paris and London. Its role as a financial adviser was respected, although its activities in underwriting were much less publicized. In the 1930s, Lazard managed about $190 million in new issues, ranking it about the same as Salomon Brothers & Hutzler and Drexel.[9] By the early 1940s, changes had occurred at Lazard in New York that would pull the firm into the limelight after years of a demure private banking presence.

The firm's far-flung organization made it one of the first investment banking houses to become truly international. Yet it was not the international characteristics that made it a presence on Wall Street in the 1950s and 1960s but anti-Semitism in Europe. During the Second World War, one of its investment bankers from Paris immigrated to New York. Andre Meyer's arrival at Lazard Freres in New York marked a distinct turn in the fortunes of the very private organization that would equate its name with the mergers and acquisitions trend that would begin in the 1950s and continue until the early 1970s. After Meyer landed in New York, Lazard would become the prime investment banker in one of the most ambitious strategies of empire building during the conglomerate era.

Meyer became one of the most famous bankers of the postwar generation on Wall Street. His reputation derived from his ability to put together deals on a scale not seen since the days of J. P. Morgan and, later, Clarence Dillon. At the same time, he acquired a reputation for being the most loathed man on the Street by his employees and competitors. In short, he was a man who inspired strong feelings among friends and enemies alike. Meyer was born in 1898 in Paris, the son of a French printing salesman. An apathetic student, he took a job at a small French bank while still a teenager. While France was in the midst of the First World War, Meyer was able to learn a vast amount about French banking since so many of the bank's employees were serving in the military. Trading quickly became his preoccupation at the bank, and he acquired a reputation for possessing a quick mind for the intricacies of commercial IOUs and foreign exchange. In a country where bankers usually passed their profession to their sons, Meyer soon became an exception. In 1925, at the age of twenty-seven, he was offered a position at Lazard Freres by David David-Weill, the son of Alexandre, one of the founders. He accepted and was made a partner within a year. His penchant for trading won him wide notice in the Paris market, and he was already established despite a formal education and no family bloodlines to his credit.

But Meyer's reputation was not fully established yet. Ironically, his first deal of note would be for an ambitious French company with an American twist. Lazard was a major shareholder in the French automobile manufacturer Citroën, founded by Andre Citroën. The company was in the midst of taking the French market by storm, producing cars on a large scale and selling them on credit—two innovations borrowed from American car companies. The finance arm of Citroën was Societé pour la Vente a Credit d'Automobiles, or SOVAC. Citroën needed more money for his ambitious expansion plans, and Meyer recognized an opportunity. He proposed that Lazard buy the finance company and expand it into other areas of consumer financing as well, while still agreeing to finance Citroën. In short, he was helping create one of the first consumer credit companies. Citroën agreed. Other partners in the venture included two American companies, Commercial Investment Trust and J. P. Morgan & Co. Through his insatiable appetite for new ventures in finance and his equally voracious appetite for financial information, Meyer helped bring the American idea of consumer finance to France, although at the age of thirty he had never set foot in the United States. That was soon to change.

During the 1930s, Meyer again came to Citroën's aid by arranging a merger to bail the company out. Andre Citroën had extended his company's finances in the 1930s, misjudging the extent of the Depression in France and the effect it had on demand for his automobiles. Meyer arranged for the Michelin tire company to purchase a controlling interest in the company, taking pressure off the French government in the process. The government was so impressed by his ingenuity that it subsequently awarded him the Legion of Honor. But the political situation in Europe was deteriorating quickly. In 1939, he decided to move his wife and children to Spain to avoid the Nazis, who invaded France shortly thereafter. From there, his next stop would be Lazard Freres in New York. The French bank effectively would be closed during the Occupation.

By the time Meyer arrived in New York, he was already a legend in the bank and quickly assumed control of the American operation. Lazard had been a family-run operation since being founded, and the New York office was run by Frank Altschul when Meyer arrived. During the late 1930s and early 1940s, Lazard's independent New York office was something of a sleepy backwater, not unlike many houses waiting for better times. It had a small retail operation and several offices around the country, but it did not have a specialty, nor were there any prospects of developing one. Meyer was determined to change it permanently. Another partner arrived in New York shortly after him, complicating the matter of seniority at the office. With the arrival of Pierre David-Weill the firm was looking somewhat top heavy. Quickly, Meyer and Weill displaced Altschul at the top and forced him into semiretirement. The way was then clear for them to run the firm as they pleased. But Meyer's dominant personality soon came to the fore and he gained primacy at the firm in a very short time. Lazard Freres was now set to adopt the path he chose.

One of Meyer's first tasks was to close the retail operation and return Lazard to the business for which it was best known in Paris—a private investment banking operation that did not disclose much about itself or its clients. This aura of mystery served Meyer well in the next ten years, because Lazard was at best a marginal firm that needed a complete overhaul. By invoking the French firm's good name, he set about to establish Lazard as an underwriter in the United States, a business still dominated by the top-tier firms. In order to do so, he would have to establish good relations with senior bankers at the top firms—a difficult if not impossible task. The easiest way to do that was through the Our Crowd firms with whom he had some social connections.

In the 1940s and early 1950s, Meyer established good working relations with Bobbie Lehman at Lehman Brothers and also a useful link with Perry Hall at Morgan Stanley. Using his personal relationship with them to his full benefit, Meyer was able to cut himself into deals that Lazard had no business being included in because of its lack of financial prowess and small size. His personality dominated Lehman, who was obviously in awe of Meyer and gave him too much underwriting business as a result. He gave Lazard a 50 percent portion of Lehman deals for reasons that are not totally clear. Meyer was able to gain a valuable foothold with some prestigious Lehman clients, among them RCA and the Chase Manhattan Bank. One of Lehman's junior partners admitted, "It was considered a terrible blow when Lazard got half the RCA business."[10] Lehman had been RCA's primary investment banker since the 1920s. Meyer was able to cut himself into established American investment banking business without proving that he could actually sell the deals to investors or by extending the firm's capital.

Meyer also made some strategic personnel moves in the late 1940s and early 1950s that enhanced the firm's reputation. Felix Rohatyn joined the firm in 1948 after graduating from Middlebury College. Like Meyer, he was something of a peripatetic, having come to the United States with his parents in 1942. Born in Vienna, he received part of his secondary school education in France before emigrating about the same time that the Meyers fled France. He was admitted as a Lazard partner in 1961 and would gain his reputation by working with Harold Geneen at International Telephone & Telegraph (ITT) on its acquisitions in the 1960s. Later, in the 1970s, he sat on the committee that helped sort out the mess left by the backroom crisis on Wall Street and then chaired the Municipal Assistance Corporation, which bailed New York City out of its financial difficulties. And in 1997, he left the firm to become ambassador to France during the Clinton administration. But in 1951, Rohatyn was not the best-known new hire of Meyer. That distinction belonged to David Lilienthal, the head of the Tennessee Valley Authority under Franklin Roosevelt. One of the New Deal's most visible figures, Lilienthal joined Lazard after an invitation by Meyer. It was following a pattern of hiring well-known public figures even though they had little if any investment banking experience. In a name-conscious business, hiring individuals with reputations made in the public realm was a good way to ensure notice for the firm and its deals.

In the 1950s, Lazard Freres began to take on the personality of Meyer and develop into its own distinctive form of investment banking. Rather than attempt to be a large-scale underwriter or trader, Lazard became a deal maker. In classic merchant-banking style, it also invested heavily in the deals rather than simply bring them to market to be bought by others. At a time when the balance of power on Wall Street was beginning to shift toward transaction-oriented deals by large wire houses like Merrill Lynch or traders like Goldman Sachs and Salomon Brothers, Lazard was content to follow the blueprint established by the Morgans and Clarence Dillon earlier in the century. As if to underscore the point, Meyer formed a link with a former Dillon Read deal maker who had worked on some of Clarence Dillon's best-known deals.

More than twenty-five years after the Dodge and Chrysler deals, Ferdinand Eberstadt teamed with Meyer to do some notable deals. Eberstadt's firm regularly began to appear in Lazard deals, and the two were instrumental in constructing some new companies through a series of mergers that went on to become major corporations. Avis and Warner Lambert were two firms they helped restructure and bring to market, collecting both investment banking fees and sizable capital gains on their shareholdings. At one point, Lazard held almost half the outstanding shares in Avis before selling it to Harold Geneen of ITT in 1965.

Despite Lazard's prowess in cobbling together companies through merger and then selling them, the economics of Wall Street in the 1960s worked against the firm. In the mid-1960s, the firm had slightly less than $20 million in capital, a pittance when compared with Goldman Sachs and Salomon Brothers. Extending the firm's capital through venture capital deals was no longer feasible, since these were becoming larger all the time. Lazard departed from its postwar strategy and began to help others arrange mergers rather than be a principal in the deals. Merger advice was based on fees, so the more mergers that were consummated the more fees that were collected. Fortunately for Lazard, Meyer read the trend correctly; the 1960s became the decade of the conglomerate, and the aggressive individuals who commanded them, the conglomerateurs.

The Avis sale was the one of the first transactions that Lazard completed for Harold Geneen's ITT. Geneen, already known as one of the country's most aggressive and acquisitions-minded CEOs, was determined to diversify the company's activities and make them more domestic. He had run the company since 1959. To date, most of ITT's activities were found outside the United States. Since he could not expand telephone services in the country because of the AT&T monopoly, he adopted the conglomerate strategy and began acquiring

---

At the height of the conglomerate craze in the late 1960s, congressional hearings about the phenomenon were held. Felix Rohatyn of Lazard Freres was called to testify, since he was the chief architect of ITT's acquisitions strategy. He testified that of sixty-eight mergers arranged by Lazard, twenty-seven of the companies had at least one partner of the firm on its board. Testimony of that type recalled the testimony of the Morgan partners, at both the Pujo hearings in 1912 and the Pecora hearings in 1933, that revealed the numerous board seats they occupied on companies with which they had an investment banking relationship.

Also revealed at congressional hearings was an ITT practice called *reciprocity*. This required the employees of one ITT company to deal exclusively with the employees of another. In other words, an ITT employee at one division might be required to purchase insurance from another. To do otherwise would be considered disloyal. But the practice of avid selling was not new to the company or its affiliates. Even in its early days, Avis executives would place sales literature on the seats of securities analysts when they made presentations to them. If they were not allowed to do so, they would not give the presentation. As one Avis executive put it, "Every security analyst had to take a charge card application or we wouldn't talk. I mean, we never stopped peddling, OK?"

---

a wide array of companies, often with no apparent relation to one another. Conglomerates purchased a bevy of disparate companies and assembled them under one roof. In theory, the diversity would make them immune to changes in the economic cycle. One company's slump in earnings could be matched by another's surge. In reality, Geneen was anxious to accumulate as many companies as possible and incorporate them under the ITT umbrella. Acquiring profitable companies and absorbing their earnings into those of ITT caused the company's stock to soar. Once the stock price was favored by Wall Street, it could proceed with even more acquisitions, since many of the purchases were made with shares, not cash. In theory, as long as the acquisitions program was successful, the stock would continue to climb.

Rohatyn became the linchpin in ITT's acquisitions strategy. Although Meyer was clearly the senior partner at Lazard, Rohatyn was responsible for bringing in most of the firm's revenues in the 1960s. Between 1966 and 1969, Lazard and Rohatyn put together dozens of deals for ITT. The conglomerate absorbed the Nancy Taylor Secretarial Schools; Continental Baking; Williams Levitt & Sons (the builders of Levittown, New York); and Sheraton Hotels, to name but a few. They could immediately add to ITT's bottom line, and favorable accounting standards allowed the conglomerate to absorb their earnings immediately without any significant write-offs for goodwill. Lazard profited handsomely from the arrangement, and Rohatyn took a seat on ITT's board. However, while he was in charge of the ITT account, it was clear that Meyer still was fully in charge of the firm and its fortunes.

Lazard did other merger business as well. Acquisitions were done for RCA, Transamerica, R. J. Reynolds, Atlantic Richfield, and Loews Theaters. Lazard clearly had the corner on the takeover market, assisting on the acquirer's side. From 1964 to 1968, Lazard's total income increased 256 percent but its merger income grew by 584 percent.[11] The firm was also involved in risk arbitrage at the time and was rumored to have arbitraged on many of the deals it was arranging. The activity was dropped in later years. Although profits were good and Lazard's reputation increased substantially, not everyone took a kind view of the merger phenomenon. In 1968, Congress reacted by passing the Williams Act, requiring any company buying 5 percent or more of another's stock to register the purchase with the

SEC. Congress could not protect against the hostile takeover, but it could move against lightning strikes that often caught target companies totally unaware.

While the rest of Wall Street positioned itself for new markets and displayed a voracious appetite for capital, Lazard remained a traditional old-line firm during Meyer's lifetime. As in the past, he actively courted the rich and powerful as friends and clients, including David Sarnoff, Senator Jacob Javits of New York, Senator Charles Percy of Illinois, Charles Englehard, Harold Geneen, and Jacqueline Kennedy Onassis. But the 1970s did not prove kind to Meyer's or Lazard's reputation. The firm's close alliance with ITT caused it to come under congressional scrutiny. After President Salvador Allende of Chile was assassinated in 1973, ITT was implicated in the affair and long shadows were cast over Lazard as well. ITT became enmeshed in many controversies during the early 1970s, from the Allende murder to a controversy surrounding the Republican National Convention in 1972, where it was suspected of using its influence to have the event held in San Diego, where Sheraton just happened to be the largest hotelier. It was also suspected of illegal antitrust practices within the conglomerate itself.[12] With all of the negative press, Lazard was beginning to drift by the mid-1970s as Meyer became ill and spent less time directing its fortunes. Finally, it was clear that a new successor needed to be named before the firm disappeared from view entirely.

Pierre David-Weill died in 1975 and was succeeded at the Paris office by his son, Michel. Despite the fame of Meyer in New York and the growing reputation of Rohatyn, Lazard still was a family firm and one of the Weills naturally would be expected to assume the chairmanship. He quickly began to consolidate the offices by giving Paris stronger links with London. Finally, in 1977, he assumed the role of chairman in New York as well, with Meyer's agreement. He quickly reorganized the office, putting several partners out to pasture by making them limited partners, and added some new senior personnel. The changes came none too soon for Lazard. The torch had been passed fully, and Lazard was attempting a comeback on Wall Street after being directionless for most of the 1970s.

Andre Meyer died in 1979. The autocratic period of Lazard's history was now behind it, although Meyer was hailed as a great financier by many in the Wall Street community and in New York society. At his death, his personal fortune was reputed to be over $200 million. The firm that he left behind was distinctly small and a boutique, sorely out of step with the rest of Wall Street. But that was Meyer's plan over the years, and he never diverted from it. Before his death, his biographer asked him why he never built Lazard into a larger firm like Goldman Sachs or Morgan Stanley. His answer was characteristic of someone who hated large organizations: "I thought we were more financial engineers," he replied. "I was always very much afraid of big organizations. I was always afraid of large overhead expense . . . You know that when I started in New York we had 240 employees; now I believe we have only 250 or 260."[13] He was able to maintain his vision, but the firm almost disappeared in the 1970s as a result. Ironically, the reappearance of a family member was needed to resurrect its fortunes, demonstrating that the time-proven formula for partnerships still worked in an age where the small firm dominated by one or a few partners was rapidly becoming extinct.

Onward and Upward

While Lazard adopted a strategy based on advisory and venture capital services, Goldman Sachs was poised to rise to the very top of Wall Street. Unlike many managing partners who shared leadership, Whitehead and Weinberg at Goldman complemented each other well. They also recognized the need for more solid management practices than the informal ones that had characterized the partnership in the past. After they were officially designated as co–managing partners, they set about putting new procedures in place designed to make the firm less reliant on a single person's opinion about its future direction. Much of that could be attributed to the fact that they both had graduated from the same business school. Whitehead joined the firm in 1947 after graduating from Haverford College and Harvard Business School. Weinberg, the son of Sidney, joined three years later after graduating from Princeton and then Harvard. Of the two, it was John Weinberg who knew more about the firm, having grown up in his father's shadow. But the arrangement was a power-sharing one from the beginning. The two had worked together for two decades and recognized the pitfalls of the investment banking business in the 1970s. Andre Meyer's strategy would have been anathema to them.

The cast of characters at Goldman began to change. In addition to Weinberg and Whitehead, the next generation of partners included Robert Rubin and Stephen Friedman, both of whom joined the firm in 1966. Rubin joined after graduating from Yale Law School and briefly practicing law. He was made a partner within five years after learning to trade from Gus Levy, who was his exact opposite in terms of personality and attention span. Rubin's work was instrumental in helping Goldman become more transaction oriented so that it could compete with Salomon and overtake Morgan Stanley in the annual race for top positions in underwriting and revenues. In 1982, *Institutional Investor* named him, along with Peter Cohen of Shearson American Express, as one of Wall Street's power elite who would dominate the industry by the year 2000. Friedman, a graduate of the Columbia Law School, also joined after a brief stint practicing law; he worked within mergers and acquisitions, that enormously profitable area that came into its own in the 1970s.

In the late 1970s, Goldman began an ascent to the very top of the Wall Street league underwriting tables. In 1977, it ranked fourth in total deals underwritten, behind Morgan Stanley, Merrill Lynch, and Salomon Brothers. In 1981, the firm was rated Wall Street's best in block trading, with Salomon in second place. Goldman also rated second in equity research as rated by pension fund managers, another position that was attained by originally offering transaction services like block trading and arbitrage. By 1983, it was the top private investment bank and vied with Merrill for the top spot in underwriting. It had more than $700 million in capital and had earned $400 million (before tax) on revenues of almost $1.5 billion. At the time, it had ninety-eight partners, seventy-five of whom were full partners and the rest limited partners.[14] It slipped a year later as Drexel made its surge with junk bonds. As a result, the firm realized that it needed to revamp its bond operations, which for a long time had taken second place to equities.

Similar to Salomon Brothers, Goldman expanded into commodities trading in the early 1980s. After discussing a buyout of commodities trader J. Aron & Co. for almost two years, Goldman finally purchased the firm in 1981. Aron had declined an earlier offer to be purchased by Englehard Minerals, which had once been a part of Philipp Brothers, later Phibro. As in the Salomon-Phibro deal, the transaction began when Aron asked Goldman to find it a suitable partner. Quickly, the firm realized that it would be the best match for the commodities trader and moved to purchase it for many of the same reasons that Salomon and Phibro merged. Inflation was high at the time, and the commodities profits could help offset losses on Goldman's bond and stock trading book. Aron's profitability also meant that if Goldman did not acquire it, someone else soon would. Its precious-metal trading earned it $60 million in 1981 on capital of $100 million. In contrast, Goldman, one of the Street's most profitable firms, earned $150 million on partner's capital of $275 million. While the return on capital was similar, Aron's business was countercyclical and could be assumed to be an excellent hedge for Goldman's operations. Goldman paid $120 million for the firm, equal to two years' earnings, and gave Aron's senior partners six board seats in

---

For those who do not think Wall Street is a small place, consider the deal done by Andre Meyer at Lazard Freres that had a great impact on the fortunes of Salomon Brothers some years later. Meyer and Ferdinand Eberstadt of F. Eberstadt & Co., a firm created after he left Dillon Read in the 1920s, helped bring the commodities-trading firm Philipp Brothers public by merging it with the Minerals & Chemicals Co., another creation of theirs, formed several years before. A sizable stake in the new company, M & C Philipp, then was sold to Charles Englehard, the CEO of Englehard Industries, a precious-metals trading firm run by its larger-than-life founder. The new company became Englehard Minerals & Chemicals. Finally, in 1981, Philipp Brothers split from the company to reestablish itself on its own and sought another partner, eventually leading it to Salomon's door. After all of the wheeling and dealing, Meyer and Eberstadt made a total of about $50 million on the deals, up to the point where Englehard bought into M & C Philipp. The best part was that they originally started the series of acquisitions with a bank loan worth about $4 million.

return.[15] For the first time, Goldman had a rough-and-tumble operation in its midst to contend with, but the additional revenues helped keep it one of Wall Street's most profitable firms.

Like the Salomon-Phibro marriage, the acquisition of J. Aron did not work out as well as expected and Goldman eventually fired a large portion of its staff. But the part that survived finally brought Goldman into the volatile world of trading that it had only flirted with before under Levy. Bond arbitrage was added to the firm's activities, bringing it closer to Salomon in terms of trading activities, although Salomon was clearly Wall Street's leader in fixed-income trading and underwriting. Then a major change in the firm's management structure occurred when John Whitehead resigned in 1984. John Weinberg was left at the top of the firm after sharing power with Whitehead, and he moved quickly to institute changes that would bring Goldman full circle in terms of investment banking activities.

Whitehead went on to establish a distinguished record in public service after leaving Goldman. He served as an undersecretary to Secretary of State George Shultz, headed numerous charities, and more recently served as president of the Federal Reserve Bank of New York. After his departure, the fixed-income area was overhauled and expanded. New hires were brought in to make the firm more competitive with Salomon, which along with Morgan Stanley was Goldman's chief competitor in the marketplace. Extensive resources were allocated to fixed-income banking and trading so that the specialty would begin to measure up to Goldman's substantial expertise in equities. The firm also began adding new staff with expertise in quantitative methods who would work closely with arbitrageurs to create new products and perfect risk-management techniques. This again was following in Salomon's footsteps, since the bond-trading house had been hiring mathematicians and other scientifically trained college graduates for years in an attempt to provide its clients with better-quality research and its traders with more sophisticated methods of assessing risk.

Goldman was able to achieve expansion without worrying about the additional capital necessary to expand because of its enormous profitability. In 1986, it recorded $750 million in profits. Like many Wall Street firms, it was a money machine, especially after the markets began to recover in 1982, and its profits helped to sustain its capital. But the firm did not assume its role at the top of the Wall Street establishment without some embarrassing moments along the way. One of its investment bankers, Robert Freeman, was indicted and convicted on charges of insider trading in the same scandal that led to the downfall of Dennis Levine, Martin Siegel, and Ivan Boesky. And the firm did investment banking business with Robert Maxwell, the British publisher and deal maker who drowned under suspicious circumstances off the Canary Islands in 1991. In his later years, Maxwell's once solid reputation began to come apart under a torrent of charges of malfeasance in companies he had acquired. The most damaging was that he looted a pension fund of its assets and bankrupted it in the process, leaving scores of British pensioners without any means of support.

The Maxwell affair cost Goldman almost $300 million in settlements with the various parties that sued it, claiming it conspired with Maxwell to defraud them. The firm settled rather than risk the partners' capital in a suit that could also have cost the firm its independence. But in the heady days prior to 1994, it was a price worth paying because the firm's profits were high and it was sitting atop the Wall Street totem pole. The newly revamped bond-trading department substantially added to its profitability and all of its divisions were reporting record profits. New partners were being added at a higher rate each time a new group was admitted by the existing partners, and the firm clearly was firing on all cylinders. Several outside investors also contributed capital to the firm on a limited basis. Sumitomo Trust, the Japanese bank, made a cash infusion in 1986, and the Kamehameha Schools/Bishop Estate of Hawaii also bought a minority share. Between them they shared slightly less than 25 percent of the firm's profits. The new co-chairmen of the management committee, Rubin and Friedman, named in 1990, had remolded the firm's image into that of an aggressive international bank that was able to serve its customers in many markets and products. John Weinberg stepped down as chairman after forty years with the firm. And Rubin's tenure was to prove limited.

The new firm was more of a trader and less of an investment banker than the old. In 1989, investment banking accounted for 35 percent of its profits, but by 1993 it had slipped to 16 percent. Mergers and acquisitions fees also slipped, while trading, especially proprietary trading (for the firm's own account) picked up the slack. Compensation reflected the enormous profitability: Rubin and Friedman each earned $25 million in 1992 alone on their 2.25 percent partnership stakes.[16] Compensation for the other partners was calculated on their percentage holdings and contribution to the firm overall. To keep abreast of changing markets and partners' contributions, Goldman's partnership agreement was rewritten every two years. By 1993, it had 150 partners, twice the number of twenty years before. But in the years preceding 1994, no one thought of withdrawing early or going to work elsewhere. The partnership was simply too valuable. The limited partners usually left their capital with the firm, and while they did not split the profits with the active partners they did receive interest on their stakes. While things were going well for the firm, transient capital was not a problem. But when times got tough, the partnership itself would have to rethink its very existence.

Robert Rubin left the firm in 1992 to join the Clinton administration as an economic adviser, and the firm happily went its way under Friedman's tutelage, becoming more of an interest-rate-sensitive trader than ever before. Bad times began to appear for Goldman in 1994. The Fed abruptly began raising interest rates in the late winter of 1994, and the rises continued into the spring. The moves came as something of a surprise to Wall Street, which had become accustomed to lower interest rates. Hardest hit were the bond and currency traders, both of which were interest-rate sensitive. Goldman had substantial positions in both areas and began to record losses as its large proprietary positions sank in price. The same interest-rate hike also spelled doom for Orange County, California, which lost heavily on a derivatives portfolio, causing a national sensation at the time. A cloud descended over Wall Street, hedge funds, and many derivatives traders, who were caught unawares by the rise.

The trading losses weighed heavily on Goldman's bottom line. A new management team, put in place by Friedman after Robert Rubin's departure, inherited the problem. Jon Corzine, co-head of fixed-income trading, and Hank Paulson, co-head of investment banking, became the newest team in the spirit of Weinberg and Whitehead to run the firm. Both joined Goldman in the mid-1970s. They instituted new management controls and streamlined procedures so that the firm would return to profitability as quickly as possible. But the problem of partners withdrawing their capital definitely had deleterious effects. The profits for 1994 were the smallest in years, and an exodus of partners began. By late 1994, more than 30 percent of them had resigned. They were replaced by fifty new partners, all of whom were still eager to join the legendary money machine. Friedman also left the firm at that time, hastening the departures of other established partners who thought it best to get out while their funds were still intact. Their departures made it clear that Goldman was suffering the problem of all partnerships: No matter how well the firm tried to keep partners' funds in-house, it would only be a matter of time before the capital departed. Going public was the only alternative if the bank was to maintain its lofty position on Wall Street. Goldman was considered the best investment bank on Wall Street, but it was faced with a difficult problem. Expansion had clearly hurt it, but it still needed to extend its activities so that it could continue to capture new opportunities in the increasingly global marketplace. But it would be difficult to impress that fact on a group of employees who knew only the partnership form of organization. There was a strong case at Goldman for leaving things as they were.

To Go or Not to Go

Corzine actively advocated an initial public offering for Goldman in 1996, but the partners could not be convinced. The capital problem was temporarily solved when the firm made it more difficult for partners to withdraw their funds. At retirement, partners put their funds into a capital account, which paid out retirees over a three-year period.[17] Although all partners' capital was transient, this measure at least ensured some stability while the funds were being withdrawn. The accommodation worked well in 1998, when Goldman earned over a billion dollars and defections were few. But the handwriting still was on the wall. Archrival Morgan Stanley, although a public corporation for ten years, merged with Dean Witter in a clear move to remain atop Wall Street's league tables and infuse itself with additional capital. And although extremely wealthy by any standard, Goldman was still considered a takeover target on Wall Street, not by another investment bank but potentially by a commercial bank with deep pockets. The Glass-Steagall Act was in the process of being relaxed by the Fed and officially would be replaced by the Financial Modernization Act in late 1999. Before it was replaced, the Fed allowed commercial banks to purchase investment banks, but the interim formula employed by the Fed made Goldman too rich for a commercial bank to purchase. By late 1999, that was destined to change. A move to go public needed to be implemented before that date to ensure Goldman's independence and infuse it with more capital. Otherwise, it would become a prime target for a wealthy commercial bank as the millennium drew to a close.

Finally, Corzine convinced the partnership that it was time for a public sale of stock. But Goldman's road to an IPO was much rockier than anticipated. The registration statement was filed with the SEC in August 1998, but the market suddenly collapsed during the Asian economic crisis at the same time. The crisis affected both stock and bond markets and caused a financial crisis in the United States when hedge fund Long-Term Capital Management was on the verge of failure and the Fed stepped in to prevent the problem from worsening. Corzine, who was closely involved with the bailout orchestrated by the Fed, offered $300 million of the firm's money in addition to that being offered by other banks and investment banks. The amount pledged to bail out the hedge fund caused major rumblings at the firm; many of the senior partners did not believe that Goldman should offer as much as it did. In addition, the firm also lost heavily during the market downturn. In September 1998, its trading book recorded losses of more than $500 million. Fingers started to be pointed at the trading side of the firm again, as they had several years earlier, for exposing the firm to too much risk at a time when it needed to portray itself as a solid investment bank whose earnings were not subject to wild swings.

The IPO was postponed until conditions were more favorable. In what was clearly a palace coup, Corzine was demoted from his position by the other five men on the executive committee. Henry "Hank" Paulson became the sole CEO. The old Wall Street tensions between investment bankers and traders surfaced again, as it had so many times in the past both at Goldman and other firms. Goldman registered pretax profits of $3 billion in 1998, but it would have been even higher if the losses had not occurred. Many of those at the top of the firm attributed the problem to the fact that Corzine was a trader and that it would be better off with an investment banker at its head before the IPO was sold. Unlike many other coups at Goldman, the prospect of an IPO made this one very public. "I've always been in awe of Goldman's ability to keep their dirty laundry private," remarked a rival investment banker, "so the story is, some laundry is getting washed in public."[18]

Finally, in May 1999 the issue was launched when favorable conditions returned. Despite the public airing of the internal troubles, it proved to be an enormous success. Goldman sold shares at $53 each, valuing the firm at $29 billion. At the time, it was the second-largest IPO ever (behind Conoco) and was oversubscribed by ten times, illustrating investor faith in the company's prospects. Corzine departed, and Paulson remained as the sole CEO. Goldman achieved the capital it needed, ending its reign as Wall Street's most effective and profitable partnership. The valuation ensured that it would remain independent since the offering price was on the high side of expectations, giving the firm a capitalization that many potential merger partners could not afford. But its much smaller counterpart did not follow suit.

Lazard Freres chose a different road and decided to remain a partnership. The boutique firm never grew at the rate of its competitors, and selling a public stake in itself did not appeal to its partners as an attractive option. By choosing to remain a partnership, the firm tacitly acknowledged that it would have to accept boutique status, specializing in mergers and acquisitions and financial advice since trading and large-scale underwriting would not be feasible with a small capital base. In 1989, Michel David-Weill became the first CEO of the three previously separate offices and the firm added asset-management services to its product mix in the 1990s. By the time that Goldman Sachs had gone public, Lazard's business was much the same as it was in the 1960s and 1970s. Its asset-management business had grown substantially, and the firm had approximately $60 billion under management. But the firm was still dependent on the mergers and acquisitions business for the bulk of its revenues. The historic merger trend that began in the mid-1980s continued unabated well into the 1990s, and the firm consistently ranked within the top ten merger advisers.

Finally, in 2000, Lazard Freres consolidated its assets as a single, global firm, recognizing that having three separate operating units even under one chief executive was not feasible in the era of the giant international financial services company. Yet it remains the last hold-out of the partnerships. How long it can survive in that form depends on its ability to generate fee income in markets that have become increasingly transaction-oriented, dominated by firms with billions in public equity capital. But as long as the merger trend continues, its revenues will continue to bolster its reputation.

CONCLUSION

O<small>VER THE LAST</small> two centuries, the Wall Street investment banking partnerships have been both catalysts of change and reactionaries. They helped corporate America raise billions of dollars for expansion while at the same time often resisting the same growth mentality. They helped restructure industry and municipal governments hungry for equity and debt capital, often with precious little of their own. Incredibly, one hundred years elapsed between the development of the modern corporation and the first sale of stock by the Wall Street partnerships. In a world increasingly characterized by rapid change, the partnerships often were the last bastions of conservativeness.

Despite incongruities, the partnerships have helped shape American finance and industry in a unique fashion. They also produced some of the legendary figures in American history, have been the subjects of much public adoration, and helped win wars. On the other side of the coin, they have been accused of stealing from the public purse, endangering the public interest, and starting those wars for their own profit. Regardless of the sympathy or enmity they inspire, it is clear that they were formidable institutions on the national stage ever since Alexander Brown founded his trading firm in Baltimore at the beginning of the nineteenth century.

At the heart of the partnerships' strengths and weaknesses was the problem of capital. Without adequate equity capital on their books, the investment banks could not underwrite enough deals or make their influence felt on Wall Street, where their reputation and status would be immediately questioned. Even when the firms had surplus capital, their futures were still not certain because, as their partners retired, they withdrew their capital, shrinking the firms' financial bases. Leaving their funds behind was not an option that all partners exercised. Some did for the sake of their firms, while others could not resist the temptation to cash out entirely. Many senior partners accumulated fortunes that became part of their legend. Despite his vast influence, J. P. Morgan Sr.'s $68 million estate prompted Andrew Carnegie to remark that the banker was not a very rich man when he died. Andre Meyer's $200 million earned at Lazard Freres almost seventy years later was small by comparison when adjusted for inflation, but the amount was still closely guarded in order to ward off the usual criticisms of overpaid investment bankers. When Michael Milken was paid $550 million by Drexel Burnham Lambert in 1987, admiration quickly turned to invective as the public wondered whether any one person was worth that much. Traditionally, even such large sums would be withdrawn from their firms within a short time. That would often impair the firms' ability to do future business on the same scale unless fresh sources of capital could be found quickly. The transience of partners' capital became the reason why many of the firms sought mergers with others. Eventually, the partners' capital problem became too thorny and the firms had to seek a public listing for their stock.

When the securities firms went public, they often gave up a colorful part of their histories. No publicly traded company could have produced J. P. Morgan, Otto Kahn, or Clarence Dillon. They were among the legion of investment bankers who etched their names on Wall Street and American history. Their strong personalities could produce mixed results at their firms, however. In the nineteenth century, most of the long-standing partnerships were led by these strong, paternalistic figures, setting the agenda for their firms. They would decide how much risk their firms would take on a deal and what activities their firms would participate in. Often, their vision spelled success for their firms but the succeeding generation did not measure up. The problem became compounded in the capital-intensive world of the late twentieth and early twenty-first centuries, when underwriting, mergers, and block-trading deals alone could be larger than all of the U.S. Treasury's reserves in the nineteenth century.

In contrast, decisions involving billions of dollars are no longer in the hands of one person in modern securities firms, although cases of misappropriation and scheming still arise. But modern Wall Street management makes the good old days of robber baron finances and laissez-faire economics seem all the more intriguing. The now quaint idea of not poaching another investment bank's clients was a real code of conduct on Wall Street until the Second World War. Companies had their bankers, and no one overtly crossed the line by suggesting that they could do a better job. Competitive pressures tore ideas of that sort asunder, although the myth lives on.

In some cases, the past occasionally still meets the present, as in the case of Drexel Burnham Lambert and Michael Milken. Drexel made a late rush to the top of the Wall Street league tables, only to fall quickly. Ironically, the results were the same as in the past: The firm died because of too much exposure to one individual. It was not a coincidence that Drexel was not a publicly traded company when it closed its doors in 1990. Its rise and fall were a testimony to the fact that partnerships and closely held firms all seem to display similar characteristics, regardless of whether they were prominent in the nineteenth or twentieth century.

The greatest testimony to the power of the Wall Street partnerships is that many of the securities firms are still remembered for their partners even today. No one doubts that J. P. Morgan's shadow is still seen at the banks that bear his name today, or that the spirit of Sidney Weinberg still imbues Goldman Sachs in some remote way. The partners symbolized an America that was led by larger-than-life men whose personal tastes and actions decided the direction of their firms. This is part of the present nostalgia. The anecdotes, myths, and war stories are part of their rich history. While that personality centered interpretation of history has faded, the myth of the partnerships lives on symbolically in a Wall Street now dominated by publicly traded securities houses whose capital exceeds the dreams of even the most flamboyant robber barons of the past. The extinct partnerships hark back to a simpler time when securities firms made money the old-fashioned way—they closed their eyes, cajoled the competition into submission, and hoped for the best.

NOTES

1: The Yankee Banking Houses: Clark Dodge and Jay Cooke

1. Quoted in Bray Hammond, *Banks and Politics in America: From the Revolution to the Civil War* (Princeton: Princeton University Press, 1957), p. 701.
2. Quoted in Ellis Paxton Oberholtzer, *Jay Cooke: Financier of the Civil War*, Volume 1 (Philadelphia: George W. Jacobs & Co., 1907), p. 61.
3. Ibid., p. 81.
4. See Niall Ferguson, *The House of Rothschild: Money's Prophets 1798–1848* (New York: Viking Press, 1998), p. 370.
5. Oberholtzer, *Jay Cooke*, p. 83.
6. Fahnestock became a member of the New York Stock Exchange after Jay Cooke & Co. failed, with H. C. Fahnestock as a special partner and William Fahnestock and Joseph Brown as regular partners. The firm was reorganized several times and still exists under the same name.
7. Oberholtzer, *Jay Cooke*, p. 9.
8. Cooke's family presence on Wall Street was maintained by his brother Henry, whose firm H. D. Cooke & Co. was established with Henry D. Cooke, Allen Campbell, and Grant Schley as the original partners.
9. Oberholtzer, *Jay Cooke*, p. 104.
10. Jean Strouse, *Morgan: American Financier* (New York: Random House, 1999), p. 148.
11. Oberholtzer, *Jay Cooke*, p. 207.
12. May 20, 1863.
13. Oberholtzer, *Jay Cooke*, p. 449.
14. On the general subject of railroad costs per mile and the problem of stock watering in the nineteenth century, see Charles R. Geisst, *Monopolies in America: Empire Builders and Their Enemies from Jay Gould to Bill Gates* (New York: Oxford University Press, 2000), Chapter 2.
15. Oberholtzer, *Jay Cooke*, Vol. 2., p. 275.
16. Ibid., p. 426.

2: *"Our Crowd": The Seligmans, Lehman Brothers, and Kuhn Loeb*

1. Quoted in Ross Muir and Carl J. White, *Over the Long Term: The Story of J. & W. Seligman & Co.* (New York: privately published, 1964), p. 27.
2. Ibid., p. 68.
3. Ibid., p. 74.
4. Quoted in Niall Ferguson, *The House of Rothschild: The World's Banker 1849–1999* (New York: Viking, 1999), p. 347.
5. Quoted in Vincent Carosso, *The Morgans: Private International Bankers, 1854–1913* (Cambridge, MA: Harvard University Press, 1987), p. 185.
6. Quoted in Maury Klein, *The Life and Legend of Jay Gould* (Baltimore: Johns Hopkins University Press, 1986), p. 111.
7. Muir and White, *Over the Long Term*, p. 98.
8. Ken Auletta, *Greed and Glory on Wall Street: The Fall of the House of Lehman* (New York: Random House, 1986), p. 28.
9. *Lehman Brothers: A Centennial 1850–1950.* (New York: privately published, 1950), p. 11.
10. Quoted in Vincent Carosso, *Investment Banking in America: A History* (Cambridge, MA: Harvard University Press, 1970), p. 145.
11. See Niall Ferguson, *Rothschild: Money's Prophets*, p. 43.
12. Kuhn Loeb & Co. *Investment Banking Through Four Generations* (New York: privately published, 1955), pp. 7–11.
13. Charles R. Geisst, *Wall Street: A History* (New York: Oxford University Press, 1997), p. 132.
14. Ron Chernow, *The Warburgs: The Twentieth Century Odyssey of a Remarkable Jewish Family* (New York: Vintage Books, 1993), pp. 168–169.
15. Muir and White, *Over the Long Term*, p. 127.
16. Ibid., p. 137.
17. Chernow, *The Warburgs*, p. 238.
18. *Investment Banking Through Four Generations*, p. 23.
19. Quoted in Mary Jane Matz, *The Many Lives of Otto Kahn* (New York: Macmillan, 1963), p. 255.
20. Warren Sloat, *1929: America Before the Crash* (New York: Macmillan Publishing Co., 1979), p. 174.
21. Ferdinand Pecora, *Wall Street Under Oath: The Story of Our Modern Moneychangers* (New York: Simon & Schuster, 1939), p. 52.
22. U.S. Senate Subcommittee on Banking & Currency, *Stock Exchange Practices*, 1934, p. 958 ff.
23. Muir and White, *Over the Long Term*, p. 144.
24. Stephen Birmingham, *"Our Crowd": The Great Jewish Families of New York* (New York: Harper & Row, 1967), p. 379.
25. Auletta, *Greed and Glory*, p. 35.
26. Ibid., p. 40.
27. Quoted in Connie Bruck, *The Predators' Ball: The Inside Story of Drexel Burnham and the Rise of the Junk Bond Raiders* (New York: Penguin Books, 1989), p. 48.

3: White Shoes and Racehorses:
Brown Brothers Harriman and August Belmont

1. Alex. Brown & Co. remained independent until the 1990s, when it merged with Deutsche Bank of Germany as part of the consolidation phase of investment and commercial banks in the era of bank deregulation.

2. Frank Kent and Louis Azrael, *The Story of Alex. Brown & Sons, 1800–1975* (Baltimore: privately published, 1975), p. 94.

3. John A. Kouwenhoven, *Partners in Banking: An Historical Portrait of a Great Private Bank, Brown Brothers Harriman & Co.* (New York: Doubleday & Co.), 1968), p. 57.

4. *The Revolution*, January 8, 1868, p. 366.

5. Gustavus Myers, *History of the Great American Fortunes* (New York: Modern Library, 1936), p. 436.

6. William Worthington Fowler, *Ten Years in Wall Street* (Hartford: Worthington, Dustin & Co., 1870), p. 524.

7. Kouwenhoven, *Partners in Banking*, p. 138.

8. Ron Chernow, *The House of Morgan: An American Banking Dynasty and the Rise of Modern Finance* (New York: Simon & Schuster, 1990), p. 57.

9. *New York Times*, May 10, 1901.

10. Kouwenhoven, *Partners in Banking*, p. 195.

11. Geisst, *Monopolies in America*, Chapter 4.

12. Ferguson, *Rothschild: Money's Prophets*, p. 371.

13. Irving Katz, *August Belmont: A Political Biography* (New York: Columbia University Press, 1968), p. 7.

14. Ferguson, *Rothschild: Money's Prophets*, p. 467.

15. Katz, *August Belmont*, p. 100.

16. David Black, *The King of Fifth Avenue: The Fortunes of August Belmont* (New York: Dial Press, 1981), p. 207.

17. Katz, *August Belmont*, p. 19.

18. Ibid., p. 494.

19. Ibid., p. 654.

20. Black, *The King of Fifth Avenue*, p. 724.

21. Cited in the *New York Times*, August 13, 1877.

22. *New York Times*, August 6, 1893.

23. Geisst, *Wall Street*, p. 112.

24. The source of the deposit with Belmont remains unclear. Apparently, it did not come from the Rothschilds, for there is no record in the Rothschild archives in London of it. I am grateful to Victor Gray of the Rothschild Archive Trust in London for establishing the seeming independence of Belmont from the Rothschilds on this matter.

25. *United States v. Belmont*, 301 U.S. 324 (1937). See the *New York Times*, December 22, 1936.

4: Crashed and Absorbed:
Kidder Peabody and Dillon Read

1. Philip Ziegler, *The Sixth Great Power* (New York: Knopf, 1988), p. 222.
2. Vincent Carosso, *More Than a Century of Investment Banking: The Kidder Peabody & Co. Story* (New York: McGraw-Hill, 1979), p. 28.
3. V. I. Lenin, "Imperialism, the Highest Stage of Capitalism," in *Selected Works* (Moscow: Progress Publishers, 1970), p. 709.
4. Carosso, *More Than a Century of Investment Banking*, p. 33.
5. Quoted in John Moody, *The Masters of Capital* (New Haven: Yale University Press, 1920), p. 182.
6. Ralph Hidy, *The House of Baring in American Trade and Finance* (Cambridge, MA: Harvard University Press, 1949), p. 611.
7. Bliss Perry, *Life & Letters of Henry Lee Higginson* (Boston: Atlantic Monthly Press, 1921), p. 271.
8. Ibid., p. 218.
9. Chernow, *House of Morgan*, p. 104.
10. Carosso, *More Than a Century of Investment Banking*, p. 40.
11. Ibid., p. 54.
12. Ibid., p. 68.
13. Ibid., p. 98.
14. Ian Kerr, "The Fall of the House of Kidder," *Euromoney*, January 1995, p. 32.
15. Robert Sobel, *The Life & Times of Dillon Read* (New York: Truman Talley Books/Dutton, 1991), p. 14.
16. Robert C. Perez & Edward F. Willett, *Clarence Dillon: Wall Street Enigma* (Lanham, MD: Madison Books, 1995), p. 24.
17. Ibid., p. 5.
18. Anonymous, *The Mirrors of Wall Street* (New York: G. P. Putnam's Sons, 1933), p. 187. The book was written by Clinton Glibert, a well-known Philadelphia journalist who also wrote anonymous books about other aspects of American life.
19. Perez and Willett, *Clarence Dillon*, p. 49.
20. Sobel, *Life and Times of Dillon Read,* p. 90.
21. Perez and Willett, *Clarence Dillon*, p. 86.
22. Ibid., p. 145.
23. Sobel, *Life & Times of Dillon Read*, p. 281.
24. Technically, the Presidential Task Force on Market Mechanisms.
25. Quoted in Sobel, p. 315.
26. *The Daily Telegraph*, May 15, 1997.

5: Corner of Broad and Wall:
J. P. Morgan and Morgan Stanley

1. Vincent Carosso, *The Morgans: Private International Bankers, 1854–1913* (Cambridge, MA: Harvard University Press, 1987), pp. 23–24.
2. H. R. Fox-Bourne, *Famous London Merchants* (London: James Hogg & Son, 1869), p. 78.

3. Carosso, *The Morgans*, p. 67.
4. Gustavus Myers, *The History of the Great American Fortunes*, vol. 3 (Chicago: Charles H. Kerr & Co., 1910), pp. 150–51.
5. Ibid.
6. Jean Strouse, *Morgan*, p. 111.
7. George Wheeler, *Pierpont Morgan & Friends: The Anatomy of a Myth* (Englewood Cliffs, NJ: Prentice-Hall, 1973), p. 78.
8. Strouse, *Morgan*, p. 117.
9. Carosso, *The Morgans*, p. 105.
10. Ibid., p. 177.
11. Strouse, *Morgan*, p. 198.
12. Carosso, *The Morgans*, p. 276.
13. John Moody, *The Masters of Capital* (New Haven: Yale University Press, 1920), p. 32.
14. Carosso, *The Morgans*, p. 169.
15. Strouse, *Morgan*, pp. 345–46.
16. Geisst, *Wall Street*, p. 112.
17. Alastair Burnet, *America 1843–1993: One Hundred Fifty Years of Reporting the American Connection* (London: The Economist, 1993), p. 70.
18. Theodore Roosevelt, *An Autobiography* (New York: Charles Scribner's Sons, 1926), vol. 15, p. 428.
19. *New York Times*, March 15, 1904.
20. Ibid., October 23, 1907.
21. Chernow, *House of Morgan*, p. 128.
22. William S. Stevens, ed. *Industrial Combinations and Trusts* (New York: Macmillan, 1913), p. 285.
23. *New York Times*, December 20, 1912.
24. Ibid.
25. Chernow, *House of Morgan*, p. 158.
26. Edward M. Lamont, *The Ambassador from Wall Street* (Lanham, MD: Madison Books, 1994), p. 56.
27. Louis Brandeis, *Other People's Money and How the Bankers Use It* (New York: Fredereick D. Stokes, 1914), p. 33.
28. Alpheus T. Mason, *Brandeis: A Free Man's Life* (New York: Viking Press, 1946), p. 546.
29. Chernow, *House of Morgan*, p. 380.
30. Ibid., p. 387.
31. Ibid., p. 467.
32. Ibid., p. 588.
33. *Institutional Investor*, March 1984.
34. *Wall Street Journal*, March 24, 1986.

6: Corner of Wall and Main: Merrill Lynch and E. F. Hutton

1. Frederick Lewis Allen, *Only Yesterday: An Informal History of the 1920s* (New York: Harper & Row, 1931), p. 128.

2. Edwin J. Perkins, *Wall Street to Main Street: Charles Merrill and Middle Class Investors* (New York: Cambridge University Press, 1999), p. 72.

3. Carosso, *Investment Banking*, p. 102.

4. Perkins, *Wall Street to Main Street*, p. 103.

5. Ibid., p. 107.

6. As an antimonopoly law, the Robinson-Patman Act actually ran counter to the intent of the second phase of the New Deal. Rather than try to stimulate economic activity by encouraging consolidations that would end in lower prices for consumers, the law called for protecting the small merchant, potentially resulting in higher prices that the consumer necessarily would have to pay as a result. For that reason, it has never been considered a broad, effective antitrust tool.

7. Perkins, *Wall Street to Main Street*, p. 148 ff.

8. Donald Regan, *View from the Street* (New York: New American Library, 1972), p. 128.

9. Perkins, *Wall Street to Main Street*, p. 211.

10. See John Brooks, *The Go-Go Years* (New York: Weybright & Talley, 1973), p. 310 ff. The other types of capital included securities owned by investors but held by brokers, accounts receivable, securities as collateral deposited by investors, regardless of their intrinsic value, and subordinated loans made by customers to the brokerage house.

11. Regan, *View from the Street*, p. 105.

12. Brooks, *The Go-Go Years*, p. 316.

13. Regan, *View from the Street*, p. 158.

14. Ibid, p. 124.

15. *New York Times*, May 23, 1969.

16. New York Stock Exchange, *Fact Book*, 1984.

17. The introduction of negotiated commissions also gave rise to the discount broker, a bare-bones brokerage operation providing order execution but no research.

18. David A. Vise & Steve Coll, *Eagle on the Street* (New York: Charles Scribner's Sons, 1991), p. 233.

19. James Sterngold, *Burning Down the House* (New York: Summit Books, 1990), p. 32.

20. Ibid., p. 59.

21. *New York Times*, May 30, 1975.

22. Sterngold, *Burning Down the House*, p. 87.

23. *Institutional Investor*, April 1985.

24. *San Francisco Chronicle*, May 25, 1985.

25. Sterngold, *Burning Down the House*, p. 134.

26. *Los Angeles Times*, December 4, 1987.

7: Unraveled by Greed: Salomon Brothers and Drexel Burnham

1. Robert Sobel, *Salomon Brothers 1910–1985: Advancing to Leadership* (New York: privately published, 1986), p. 8.

2. Ibid., p. 28.
3. Ibid., p. 49.
4. Ibid., p. 76.
5. Martin Mayer, *Nightmare on Wall Street: Salomon Brothers and the Corruption of the Marketplace* (New York: Simon & Schuster, 1993), p. 35.
6. Namely, the Public Utility Holding Company Act of 1935 that required competitive bids to be submitted to utility holding company issuers of new securities. The older form of negotiated bid, the traditional way Wall Street did business, was not permitted in these cases.
7. Sobel, *Salomon Brothers*, p. 103.
8. Geisst, *Wall Street*, pp. 319–20.
9. Henry Kaufman, *On Markets and Money: A Wall Street Memoir* (New York: McGraw-Hill, 2000), p. 92.
10. Securitized meant that the bonds were collateralized by a pool of residential mortgages that the agency purchased from the original lending banks.
11. Sobel, *Salomon Brothers*, p. 174.
12. Sobel, *Salomon Brothers*, p. 174, and Kaufman, *On Money*, p. 100.
13. Kaufman, *On Money*, p. 105.
14. *Business Week*, December 9, 1985.
15. *United States v. Henry S. Morgan et al.*, Civil No. 43-757. United States District Court for the Southern District of New York. Copy of Complaint, p. 49.
16. Bruck, *Predators' Ball*, p. 31.
17. Ibid., p. 42.
18. Texas International's issue defaulted ten years later when the company declared bankruptcy and the bonds sank to 20 percent of their original issue price. They picked up in price after a corporate reorganization.
19. Bruck, *Predators' Ball*, p. 92.
20. Ivan F. Boesky, *Merger Mania* (New York: Holt, Rinehart & Winston, 1985), p. 90.
21. Bruck, *Predators' Ball*, p. 102.
22. *Wall Street Journal*, March 19, 1986.
23. Ibid., December 3, 1986.
24. *Boston Globe*, February 18, 1990.
25. Ibid., December 13, 1990. The suit, brought by Thomas Spiegel of Columbia, quietly faded after Drexel's demise. But Spiegel's own problems continued. Columbia was one of hundreds of distressed thrifts whose affairs were being carefully monitored by the Resolution Trust Corp., the agency charged with cleaning up the crisis. In 1991, the agency began selling artworks that Spiegel accumulated while at the helm of the thrift during the 1980s. In 1994, he was acquitted of misappropriating the bank's funds and a year later made restitution in a civil suit brought by regulators when he returned $275,000 of the $40,000,000 the government originally sought.
26. *Wall Street Journal*, December 13, 1990.
27. *New York Times*, May 1, 1990.

8: *The Last Holdouts:*
Goldman Sachs and Lazard Freres

1. Lisa Endlich, *Goldman Sachs: The Culture of Success* (New York: Alfred A. Knopf, 1999), p. 34.
2. Ibid., p. 36.
3. Ibid., p. 42.
4. Carosso, *Investment Banking*, p. 290.
5. Judith Ramsey Ehrlich and Barry J. Rehfeld, *The New Crowd: The Changing of the Jewish Guard on Wall Street* (New York: HarperPerennial, 1989), p. 23.
6. Carosso, *Investment Banking*, p. 389.
7. Endlich, *Goldman Sachs*, p. 63.
8. Michael C. Jensen, *The Financiers: The World of the Great Wall Street Investment Banking Houses* (New York: Weybright & Talley, 1976), p. 201.
9. Carosso, *Investment Banking*, p. 480.
10. Cary Reich, *Financier: The Biography of Andre Meyer* (New York: William Morrow & Co., 1983), p. 53.
11. Ibid., p. 242.
12. Geisst, *Monopolies in America*, p. 225 ff.
13. Reich, *Financier*, p. 351.
14. *Fortune*, July 9, 1984.
15. Endlich, *Goldman Sachs*, pp. 93–94.
16. Ibid., p. 133.
17. Ibid., p. 238.
18. *Business Week*, January 25, 1999.

BIBLIOGRAPHY

Adams, Charles Francis and Henry Adams. *Chapters of Erie and Other Essays.* Boston: James R. Osgood & Co., 1871.

Allen, Frederick Lewis. *Only Yesterday: An Informal History of the 1920s.* New York: Harper & Row, 1931.

Auletta, Ken. *Greed and Glory on Wall Street: The Fall of the House of Lehman.* New York: Random House, 1986.

Beschloss, Michael. *Kennedy & Roosevelt: The Uneasy Alliance.* New York: Norton, 1980.

Birmingham, Stephen. *"Our Crowd": The Great Jewish Families of New York.* New York: Harper & Row, 1967.

Black, David. *The King of Fifth Avenue: The Fortunes of August Belmont.* New York: Dial Press, 1981.

Boesky, Ivan F. *Merger Mania.* New York: Holt Rinehart & Winston, 1985.

Brandeis, Louis. *Other People's Money and How the Bankers Use It.* New York: Frederick B. Stokes, 1914.

Brooks, John. *The Takeover Game.* New York: Dutton, 1987.

———. *The Go-Go Years.* New York: Weybright & Talley, 1973.

Brown, John Crosby. *One Hundred Years of Merchant Banking.* New York: privately published, 1909.

Bruck, Connie. *The Predators' Ball: The Inside Story of Drexel Burnham and the Rise of the Junk Bond Raiders.* New York: Penguin Books, 1989.

Burnet, Alastair. *America 1843–1993: One Hundred Fifty Years of Reporting the American Connection.* London: The Economist Books, 1994.

Carosso, Vincent. *The Morgans: Private International Bankers 1854–1913.* Cambridge, MA: Harvard University Press, 1987.

———. *More Than a Century of Investment Banking: The Kidder, Peabody Story.* New York: McGraw-Hill, 1979.

———. *Investment Banking in America.* Cambridge, MA: Harvard University Press, 1970.

Chernow, Ron. *The Warburgs: The Twentieth-Century Odyssey of a Remarkable Jewish Family.* New York: Vintage Books, 1993.

———. *The House of Morgan: An American Banking Dynasty and the Origins of Modern Finance.* New York: Simon & Schuster, 1990.

Clark, Dodge & Co. *Clark, Dodge & Co., 1845–1945.* New York: privately published, 1945.

Cleveland, Harold van B. and Thomas Huertas. *Citibank, 1812–1970*. Cambridge, MA: Harvard University Press, 1985.

Clews, Henry. *Fifty Years in Wall Street*. New York: Irving Publishing Co., 1908.

Cohen, Naomi Wiener. *Jacob Schiff: A Study in American Jewish Leadership*. Hanover, NH: University Press of New England, 1999.

Curcio, Vincent. *Chrysler: The Life and Times of an Automotive Genius*. New York: Oxford University Press, 2000.

Endlich, Lisa. *Goldman Sachs: The Culture of Success*. New York: Knopf, 1999.

Ehrlich, Judith Ramsey and Barry J. Rehfeld. *The New Crowd: The Changing of the Jewish Guard on Wall Street*. New York: HarperPerennial, 1989.

Ferguson, Niall. *The House of Rothschild: The World's Banker*. New York: Viking Press, 1999.

———. *The House of Rothschild: Money's Prophets*. New York: Viking Press, 1998.

Fowler, William Worthington. *Ten Years in Wall Street*. Hartford, CT: Worthington, Dustin & Co., 1870.

Fox-Bourne, H. R. *Famous London Merchants*. London: James Hogg & So, 1869.

Geisst, Charles R. *Monopolies in America: Empire Builders and Their Enemies from Jay Gould to Bill Gates*. New York: Oxford University Press, 2000.

———. *100 Years of Wall Street*. New York: McGraw-Hill, 2000.

———. *Wall Street: A History*. New York: Oxford University Press, 1997.

Grayson, Theodore. *Leaders and Periods of American Finance*. New York: John Wiley & Sons, 1932.

Greider, William. *Secrets of the Temple: How the Federal Reserve Runs the Country*. New York: Simon & Schuster, 1987.

Hammond, Bray. *Banks and Politics in America*. Princeton: Princeton University Press, 1985.

Henriques, Diana B. *The White Sharks of Wall Street: Thomas Mellon Evans and the Original Corporate Raiders*. New York: Scribner, 2000.

Hidy, Ralph W. *The House of Baring in American Trade and Finance*. Cambridge, MA: Harvard University Press, 1949.

Johnston, Moira. *Takeover: The New Wall Street Warriors*. New York: Arbor House, 1986.

Katz, Irving. *August Belmont: A Political Biography*. New York: Columbia University Press, 1968.

Kaufman, Henry. *On Money and Markets: A Wall Street Memoir*. New York: McGraw-Hill, 2000.

Kent, Frank R. and Louis Azrael. *The Story of Alex. Brown & Sons 1800–1975*. Baltimore: privately published, 1975.

Kerr, Ian. "The Fall of the House of Kidder," *Euromoney*, January 1995.

Klein, Maury. *The Life and Legend of E.H. Harriman*. Chapel Hill: University of North Carolina Press, 2000.

———. *The Life and Legend of Jay Gould*. Baltimore: Johns Hopkins University Press, 1986.

Kouwenhoven, John A. *Partners in Banking: An Historical Portrait of a Great Private Bank, Brown Brothers Harriman 1818–1968*. New York: Doubleday & Co., 1968.

Kuhn, Loeb & Co. *Investment Banking Through Four Generations*. New York: privately published, 1955.

Bibliography

Lacey, Robert. *Ford: The Men and the Machine.* Boston: Little Brown, 1986.

Larson, Henrietta. *Jay Cooke: Financier.* Cambridge, MA: Harvard University Press, 1936.

Lefevre, Edwin. *Wall Street Stories.* New York: McClure, Philips & Co., 1901.

Lehman Brothers. *A Centennial: Lehman Brothers 1850–1950.* New York: privately published, 1950.

Lind, Michael, ed. *Hamilton's Republic.* New York: Free Press, 1997.

Matz, Mary Jane. *The Many Lives of Otto Kahn.* New York: Macmillan, 1963.

Mayer, Martin. *Nightmare on Wall Street: Salomon Brothers and the Corruption of the Marketplace.* New York: Simon & Schuster, 1993.

———. *Stealing the Market: How the Giant Brokerage Firms, With Help from the SEC, Stole the Market from Investors.* New York: Basic Books, 1992.

Meehan, Thomas. *Thomas Meehan Papers,* Georgetown University Special Collections, Washington, D.C.

Moody, John. *The Masters of Capital.* New Haven: Yale University Press, 1920.

Muir, Ross and Carl J. White. *Over the Long-Term: The Story of J. & W. Seligman & Co.* New York: privately published, 1964.

Myers, Gustavus. *The History of the Great American Fortunes.* 3 vols. Chicago: Charles H. Kerr & Co., 1910.

New York Stock Exchange. *Fact Book,* various issues.

———. *List of Member Firms, 1875–1935.*

Oberholtzer, Ellis Paxson. *Jay Cooke: Financier of the Civil War.* Philadelphia: George W. Jacobs & Co., 1907.

Pecora, Ferdinand. *Wall Street Under Oath: The Story of Our Modern Moneychangers.* New York: Simon & Schuster, 1939.

Perez, Robert C. and Edward F. Willett. *Clarence Dillon: Wall Street Enigma.* Lanham, MD: Madison Books, 1995.

Perkins, Edwin J. *Wall Street to Main Street: Charles Merrill and Middle-Class Investors.* Cambridge: Cambridge University Press, 1999.

Perry, Bliss. *The Life and Letters of Henry Lee Higginson.* Boston: Atlantic Monthly Press, 1921.

Regan, Donald T. *A View from the Street.* New York: New American Library, 1972.

Reich, Cary. *Financier: The Biography of Andre Meyer.* New York: William Morrow & Co., 1983.

Roosevelt, Theodore. *An Autobiography.* New York: Charles Scribner's Sons, 1921.

Securities Industry Association. *Securities Industry Fact Book.* Various issues.

Seligman, Joel. *The Transformation of Wall Street: A History of the Securities & Exchange Commission and Modern Corporate Finance.* Boston: Houghton Mifflin, 1982.

Sobel, Robert. *Salomon Brothers 1910–1985: Advancing to Leadership.* New York: Salomon Brothers, 1986.

Sterngold, James. *Burning Down the House: How Greed, Deceit, and Bitter Revenge Destroyed E.F. Hutton.* New York: Summit Books, 1990.

Stevens, William S., ed. *Industrial Combinations and Trusts.* New York: Macmillan, 1913.

Stewart, James B. *Den of Thieves.* New York: Simon & Schuster, 1991.

Stone, Dan. *April Fools: An Insider's Account of the Rise and Collapse of Drexel Burnham.* New York: Donald I. Fine, Inc., 1990.

Bibliography

Strouse, Jean. *Morgan: American Financier*. New York: Random House, 1999.

Weeks, Edward. *Men, Money and Responsibility: A History of Lee Higginson Corporation*. Boston: privately published, 1962.

Ziegler, Philip. *The Sixth Great Power: A History of One of the Greatest of All Banking Families, the House of Barings, 1762–1929*. New York: Knopf, 1988.

INDEX